The Orientalist

The Orientalist

Solving the Mystery of a Strange
and Dangerous Life

TOM REISS

RANDOM HOUSE
NEW YORK

For Lolek,
who showed me how to travel,
and Julie,
who keeps me from going too far.
I wish they had met.

CONTENTS

PART 3

On the Trail of Kurban Said

O N A COLD NOVEMBER MORNING IN VIENNA, I walked a maze of narrow streets on the way to see a man who promised to solve the mystery of Kurban Said. I was with Peter Mayer, the president of the Overlook Press, a large, rumpled figure in a black corduroy suit who wanted to publish Said's small romantic novel *Ali and Nino*. Mayer tended to burst into enthusiastic monologues about the book: "You know how when you look at a Vermeer, and it's an interior, and it's quite quiet, yet somehow, what he does with perspective, with light, it feels much bigger—that's this novel!" A love story set in the Caucasus on the eve of the Russian Revolution, *Ali and Nino* had been originally published in German in 1937 and was revived in translation in the seventies as a minor classic. But the question of the author's identity had never been resolved. All anyone agreed on was that Kurban Said was the pen name of a writer who had probably come from Baku, an oil city in the Caucasus, and that he was either a nationalist poet who was killed in the Gulags, or the dilettante son of an oil millionaire, or a Viennese café-society writer who died in Italy after stabbing himself in the foot. In the jacket photograph of a book called *Twelve Secrets of the Caucasus,* the mysterious author is dressed up as a mountain warrior—wearing a fur cap, a long, flowing coat with a sewn-in bandolier, and a straight dagger at his waist.

Mayer and I were on our way to a meeting with a lawyer named Heinz Barazon, who was challenging Overlook over proper author credit on the novel. Barazon claimed to know the true identity of Kurban Said, and as the lawyer for the author's heirs, he was insisting that it be acknowledged in the new edition of *Ali and Nino* or he would block publication. At the lawyer's address, next to a shop where some old women were bent over tables with needle and thread, we were buzzed into a lobby that could have had the grime of the Anschluss on its fixtures. Mayer squeezed my arm with excitement and said, "It's *The Third Man!*" Barazon's appearance didn't do anything to dispel the atmosphere of a Cold War thriller. He was a small man with a gravelly voice, a stooped back, and a clubfoot that made a tremendous racket as he led us down his book-lined hallway. "You have both come a long way to discover the identity of Kurban Said," he said. "It will all soon become clear to you." He ushered us into a room where a gaunt and beautiful blond woman with enormous glassy eyes was lying motionless on a couch. "Pardon me, this is Leela," said Barazon.

"I hope you'll forgive me," Leela said in a fragile, precise voice. "I must remain lying down because I'm ill. I can't sit for long."

Barazon came directly to the point: the novel *Ali and Nino* was written by the Baroness Elfriede Ehrenfels von Bodmershof, the second wife of Leela's father, Baron Omar-Rolf von Ehrenfels, and when Baroness Elfriede died, in the early 1980s, having outlived her husband, all rights to the work had passed down to Leela.

Barazon produced a thick file of documents that backed up this story: publishing contracts, legal papers, and author lists from the late thirties, stamped with Nazi eagles and swastikas. Under the entry for "Said, Kurban" in the author's section of the 1935–39 *Deutscher Gesamtkatalog*—the Third Reich's equivalent of *Books in Print*—it said, in no uncertain terms, "pseudonym for Ehrenfels, v. Bodmershof, Elfriede, Baroness."

The Nazi documents seemed to tell a clear story—that Baroness Elfriede had been Kurban Said—but it was one that I believed to be untrue.

I had become interested in the identity of Kurban Said in the spring of 1998, when I went to Baku to write about the city's new oil boom—virtually the first signs of life since the Russian Revolution made time stop there in 1917. Baku is the capital of Azerbaijan, a tiny country that prides itself on being the easternmost point in Europe, though most Europeans wouldn't know it. Its proximity to Iran and the fact that the majority of its citizens are Shiite Muslims can dominate your vision of Azerbaijan until you realize that the most impressive public building in Baku is not a mosque but a copy of the grand casino at Monte Carlo. Baku is the sort of city that has been beyond rigid ideologies and religions for a thousand years. Its name is said to derive from a Persian expression, *baadiye-kubiden,* or "blow of the winds." Being situated at the head of a desert peninsula jutting into the sea, the city is in fact one of the windiest places on earth—one dapper ninety-seven-year-old man told me how, as a young man, he and his family had worn specially made goggles with their evening clothes to stroll along the boulevards without being blinded by the sands.

Just before I left for Baku, an Iranian friend had recommended Kurban Said's novel *Ali and Nino* as a kind of introduction to the city and the Caucasus in general, saying that it would be more useful than any tourist guide. I had never heard of it, and when I tracked down a 1972 Pocket Books edition, I was a little surprised by the cover. It featured two airbrushed lovers and an endorsement from *Life:* "If Kurban Said can't push Erich Segal off the bestseller list, nobody can!" But there turned out to be something of the eighteenth century about the book, as if *Candide* had been written with realistic characters and the intention of sweeping readers off their feet. Each scene continued only long enough to spring some miniature gear that moved the mechanism forward. The reviewer in *The New York Times* had written, "One feels as if one has dug up buried treasure."

The novel revolves around the love between a Muslim boy and a Christian girl and the progress of their relationship as they grow up; in the culturally tolerant world of old Azerbaijan, their courtship seems blessed, though they are constantly bickering: " 'Ali Khan, you are stupid. Thank God we are in Europe. If we were in Asia they would have made me wear the veil ages ago, and you couldn't see me.' I gave in. Baku's undecided geographical situation allowed me to go on looking into the most beautiful eyes in the world."

Over the course of its history, Azerbaijan had been conquered by Alexander the Great, the Mongols, the Ottomans, and the Persians. Finally, its "undecided geographical situation" was resolved when the Russians captured it in 1825. During the period of czarist expansion in the Caucasus, so vividly recounted by Lermontov, Tolstoy, and Pushkin, Europe discovered Baku and Baku discovered Europe. And everyone discovered oil. Lots of it. In Baku you did not need to drill for the stuff—it sat on the surface of the earth, in black ponds, sometimes enormous lakes—and the flow could be so strong that crude occasionally swallowed whole houses along the Caspian shore. The walled caravan outpost soon became the center of the burgeoning global oil industry—supplying more than half the world's crude—and the result was a fabulous nineteenth-century city built on the profits: extravagant mansions, mosques, casinos, and theaters from the period when the city was home to the Rothschilds, the Nobels, and dozens of local Muslim "oil barons," as they were called. There was Mir Babayev, a popular singer who, after discovering oil on his land, spent the rest of his days searching out his record albums and destroying them because he preferred to be remembered as an oil magnate. And there was Haji Zeynalabdin Taghiyev, who made his fortune when an earthquake struck his land, flooding it with oil; he built the first school for girls in the Muslim world. Building wars sprang up. Moorish palaces still sit next to Gothic manses, and Byzantine cupolas next to bejeweled rococo pavilions. The locals styled themselves cultured Europeans and "modern Muslims," right up to the point when the Bolsheviks decided they were decadent bourgeois and swooped in to crush them.

But Baku oil fueled Stalin's Five Year Plans, and during the Second World War, Hitler wanted Baku's oil so badly that he redirected the entire Russian campaign to get it. In September 1942, his general staff presented him with a giant cake in the shape of the Caucasus. A newsreel of the occasion shows the führer cutting himself the piece with BAKU spelled out in frosting. "Unless we get the Baku oil, the war is lost," Hitler shouted at a top commander, and he sacrificed the entire German Sixth Army at Stalingrad rather than redirect a single division out of the Caucasus to come to its aid. If they had succeeded in grabbing Baku, the combined Nazi armies would have controlled one of the greatest strategic energy reserves in the world—not to mention one of the most strategic pieces of territory, the land bridge between Europe and Asia—and, with the Soviet Union deprived of its oil, the Nazis would have for all purposes won the war. Instead of victory, the push for Baku brought utter defeat on the Russian front, and less than three years later, Soviet armored divisions, tanked up with Baku oil, were at the gates of Berlin.

After 1945, rather than being rewarded for having fueled the Russian victory, Azerbaijan saw many of its citizens deported to Siberia and its oil industry allowed to languish. The fin de siècle oil-boom city was deliberately ignored, forgotten, taking on a deserted, vaguely eerie quality, so that even today it is possible to imagine that one has wandered into some unusually sooty Right Bank neighborhood in Paris, mysteriously abandoned by its inhabitants.

My guide to Baku was Fuad Akhundov, a muscular young fellow who worked as an agent of Interpol, the international police agency, but seemed to spend most of his time sleuthing his city's hidden past. Growing up in the Soviet era, Fuad had always wondered about the lost culture that had built the decaying mansions all around him, so he began investigating the city's history, mansion to mansion, house to house. Fuad seemed to know the decaying mansions of Baku like members of his own family. "I entered these edifices, asking if anyone knew the descendants of the owner," he told me as we drove around the city in his battered Russian car. "As a policeman, I knew that often people who think they know nothing can provide vital information, so I used the crafts of interrogation, getting people to recall things their dead grandparents or parents mentioned to them over the course of the years." Fuad spoke fluent English that made him sound a bit like a nineteenth-century novel. When he needed to go somewhere, he would say things like "Now your humble servant must beg to take his leave, as he must attend to some pressing police matters."

As we explored Baku's medieval ramparts, nineteenth-century mansions, Zoroastrian temples, and palace gardens straight out of *The Arabian Nights,* Fuad rarely stopped talking. "From here I could see my world, the massive wall of the town's fortress and the ruins of the palace, Arab inscriptions at the gate," he rhapsodized. "Through the labyrinth of streets camels were walking, their ankles so delicate that I wanted to caress them. In front of me rose the squat Maiden's Tower, surrounded by legends and tourist guides. And behind the tower the sea began, the utterly faceless, leaden, unfathomable Caspian Sea, and beyond, the desert—jagged rocks and scrub: still, mute, unconquerable, the most beautiful landscape in the world."

It took me a while to realize that he was quoting, and that the passage was from *Ali and Nino.*

The mere smell of the air in a certain part of town would cause Fuad to launch into a quotation from the novel, and often we would stop in front of some Viennese imperial-style edifice—with holes where stone portraits of famous Communists had once been added to the design—and he would say, as though describing an event from history: "That is the girls' school where Ali first saw Nino with his cousin Ayeshe. We can be sure because of this doorway, which is approximately four hundred paces from the original door of the old Baku Russian Boys Gymnasium, which was destroyed during the fighting in 1918 . . ."

It could have been like one of those morbid literary tours of places mentioned in Chekhov or Pushkin, but Fuad's love of *Ali and Nino* seemed of an entirely different order. "This novel made me discover my country, it made me discover the whole world that lay beneath my feet, buried by the Soviet system," he told me one night as we sat in the empty Interpol headquarters at three in the morning. "Only this one book—this Romeo and Juliet story at the height of the oil boom, between a Christian girl and a Muslim boy, it tears away the fabric which has covered me growing up here in Soviet Baku like a shroud, like a funeral veil dropped by the bloodiest version of the West, the inhuman Bolshevik Revolution, upon this fantastic world of the highest cultural and human aspirations— the hope of the total merger of East and West into something new and modern—which existed for but a moment in time. Can you imagine it?" Fuad said. "Kurban Said is like my lifeline. Without him, I would be trapped here in my own city and not really be able to feel or understand the beauty and yet tragic forces that are beneath my very nose."

Fuad's obsession with *Ali and Nino* was shared by many people in Baku. Educated Azeris I met seemed to consider it their national novel, telling me that they could show me the street, square, or schoolhouse where almost every scene had taken place. There was a resurgence of interest in the late 1990s in this small romantic novel from the late 1930s, though nobody seemed exactly sure why. I paid a call on an Iranian film producer who occupied a lavishly refurbished suite in a collapsing old mansion, and who explained to me his plans to make a movie of the book. (When the money didn't come through, he instead produced the Baku location scenes for a James Bond movie.) Another day I visited the National Literary Society, a Stalin-era building, where the chairman filled me in on the simmering dispute in Azeri academic and government circles over the novel's authorship. Kurban Said's identity had long been a subject of speculation, he explained, but fortunately, the issue had now been resolved: Kurban Said was the pseudonym for Josef Vezir, an Azeri author whose sons, the Veziroffs, had been very active in making sure his memory was preserved, and that he receive credit for Azerbaijan's national novel.

But when I got a copy of some short stories and novellas by Vezir, I was surprised that anyone could give this theory credence. Vezir was clearly an ardent Azeri nationalist whose novellas openly stated that ethnic and cultural mixing was a bad idea and a betrayal of the motherland. In *Ali and Nino,* Kurban Said offers nothing less than a passionate endorsement of ethnic, cultural, and religious mixing. The warmest passages in the novel describe the cosmopolitan Caucasus on the eve of the revolution—when a hundred races and all the major religious groups fought together only in battles of poetry in the marketplace—and the message seems to be that the separation of peoples is hideous and genocidal.

A few nights later, while I was supposed to be in a disco hanging out with young oil boomers from London and Moscow, I convinced Fuad to let me use the Interpol offices to interview one of the Veziroff brothers. The brother had gone so far as to appear before the Azeri Parliament to insist that his father had written *Ali and Nino* and that the scenes about interethnic love had been slipped in by a malicious translator. I had the vague hope that the atmosphere of the interrogation room might help get at the truth; however, my meeting with the bald, serious fellow in a sagging gray Soviet-style suit produced only an endless stream of documentation that proved nothing but that most everyone in Baku wanted to claim the novel for his or her own reasons.

The introduction to the English copy of the novel I had wasn't much help, either: " 'Kurban Said' is a pen-name and no one seems to know for certain the real name of the man who chose it. . . . He was by nationality a Tartar [who died] . . . where, and under what circumstances, I do not know and I do not think anyone knows."

Wherever I went, Kurban Said seemed to pursue me. The single book for sale in English in the gift shop of Baku's Hyatt Regency Hotel, where I was staying, was a smudgy-looking paperback called *Blood and Oil in the Orient.* On its cover, printed just above a sepia photo of a Caspian gusher and a bunch of oilmen in fur hats, the text stated that it was by "the author of *Ali & Nino,*" whose name was given as "Essad-Bey" and beneath that, in parentheses, as "Lev Naussimbaum." What happened to Kurban Said? A foreword by an Azeri scholar attempted to clarify matters:

Essad-Bey, the narrator of the tales in this book, eventually converted to Judaism and chose the name Lev Naussimbaum. . . . He then moves on to Berlin where he joins a circle of German intellectuals. In the early thirties, he travels to Vienna. Eventually, he publishes his beautiful novel, "Ali and Nino," under the pseudonym of Kurban Said. . . . In 1938 he tried to escape the German onslaught. Soon he was arrested and moved to Italy. There, in 1942, he stabbed himself in the foot and died of this self-inflicted wound.

I doubted that anyone would convert to Judaism just before moving to Germany in the late 1920s. But why would this Essad Bey change his name to "Lev Naussimbaum" and then Kurban Said? Could the national novel of Azerbaijan have been written by someone named Naussimbaum? And what did either of these people have to do with Kurban Said? *Blood and Oil in the Orient* carried the subtitle "Petroleum Industry and Trade in Azerbaijan"—it was hard to imagine that this was the same author who had written *Ali and Nino*.

But then I noticed odd similarities between the novel and the oil book—of village duels between fighting poets, in which beggars and aristocrats, Christians and Muslims, would meet on an appointed day and recite insulting doggerel at each other, all the while sweating and cursing, until one was declared the victor. (In the novel, the winner spits when asked how it feels to have prevailed: "There is no victory, sir. In former times there were victories. In those days art was held in high esteem.") Though the narrative style of the novel was more assured, the almost Oz-like quality of prerevolutionary Azerbaijan was vivid in both. Their poignancy was amplified by the fact that the villages of the fighting poets were in Nagorno Karabakh—a place virtually destroyed in the 1990s by a vicious Muslim-Christian border war, where the weapons were anything but similes and metaphors.

One day, when we were touring the decayed grand mansion of Teymur Bey Ashurbekov, with its peeling stairwell frescoes of cavorting maidens, Fuad asked me if I would like to meet the daughters of its original owner—the two surviving members of the Ashurbekov family, Sara and Miriam (now Ashurbeyly, since the post-Soviet Azeri government was Turkicizing everyone's names). Aged ninety-two and ninety-four, they were among the only surviving children of the oil millionaires still alive in Baku, I thought we would find them here, in some dank corner of the mansion, but instead we got back in the little white car and drove to a depressing late-Soviet-era building, where we climbed the back stairs and were ushered into a tiny flat by the younger of the ancient sisters, Miriam. Her sister, Sara, sat waiting for us next to a pot of tea and a very dusty-looking box of chocolates. The sisters' extensive library was crushed into a tiny living space along with their laundry, pantry, dining table, and twelve cats. Despite the opposition of the state, they had carved out distinguished careers for themselves: Miriam was a geologist, and Sara was Azerbaijan's leading medieval historian.

Speaking to me in the German and French they had learned as children, the sisters recalled their lives before the revolution. They told me how their father had invited people of all nationalities and stations of life to their mansion, preferring to acknowledge an elite based on intelligence and education rather than social status, even though he had been born into privilege and come upon great wealth (the family had financed two of Baku's four mosques).

They showed me stacks of dusty photographs—men in fezzes and evening dress on the way to the opera, camels walking alongside Rolls-Royces—and they described the wide circle of friends their parents entertained at home, when Christians, Muslims, and Jews, all the children of the capitalist set, mixed at banquets, games, and lavish parties. Most of all, Ashurbekov had valued European culture. His daughters remembered their Baku as a place where Islam and the Orient were filtered through a multicultural European lens polished by frequent trips to the West.

"My father often had to work," said Sara, "but he always said to my mother: 'Take the children to Europe!' " She showed me a photo of herself surrounded by little blond children in Germanic costume.

"This is me in Baden-Baden in 1913. I had just won the beauty contest," said Sara. "My sister, Miriam, started crying, and she said to our mother, 'But you always said I was the most beautiful one, how come Sara won?' 'Because you are too small,' replied our mother. 'When we come back next year, you will win.' But next year was the First World War, and then the Bolsheviks came, and none of us ever went back to Europe again."

The Ashurbekovs brought out a final picture, a group photo of their last Christmas party, on the eve of the Great War. Sara's bony finger pointed to the faces as the sisters recalled the names, nationalities, and religions of every child in the room, children of the oil barons, drillers, and servants alike—Azeri, Armenian, Muslim, Jewish, German, French, Russian—and what happened to each of them after the invasion of the Red Army in 1920: the pretty pink-cheeked girl in a gypsy headdress in the second row, the gangly boy with Indian features dressed like a Cossack in the back next to the tree, a little blond boy in a tightly buttoned suit who was probably one of the Nobel brood, though they couldn't quite see his face. Then, seated in the middle, in the third row, was a little boy with big ears and a rather arrogant but bold and open expression, staring directly into the camera, his arms crossed defiantly, a velvet jacket buttoned over a floppy Lord Fauntleroy collar.

"That was little Liova Nussimbaum," Sara said. Her sister nodded and smiled, remembering. "He was a Jewish boy about two years our junior."

Really? I asked, remembering the name on the jacket of *Blood and Oil.* Are you sure the name was Liova—the Russian diminutive for Lev—Nussimbaum? Exactly that name?

"Yes, Liova, Liova, little Liova Nussimbaum. He was the smartest of all the children, a very smart little Jewish boy whose father was a rich businessman in town. He never had a mother, and the family tried to compensate for this. He was a very nice and a very well-mannered boy, and since his earliest childhood, he was fluent in German. His governess was a German lady, I believe."

"Probably a Baltic German," Fuad put in. "It was very common to have a Baltic German governess here then—also French." I noticed a pair of stout fräuleins flanking the children, slightly rough-looking women incongruously dressed in sequined evening gowns for the occasion.

"He left Baku," said the ancient lady, "and we heard he later died in Italy."

I would discover that, in his wanderings after leaving Baku, Lev Nussimbaum, aka Essad Bey, aka Kurban Said, had become a famous man in Europe and the United States, the author of bestselling biographies of the czar and Stalin, and even a figure of tabloid scandal in New York and Los Angeles. When he arrived by ship in New York in 1935, the *Times* ran a story about it, under the headline "Czar's Biographer Here: Essad Bey Declares Ruler Was Not Understood." He lived in Berlin in the 1920s, travel-ing in the brilliant circle of exiles that included the Pasternaks and the Nabokovs, and he was a fixture in Vienna, New York, and Hollywood in the 1930s. But even during his lifetime, no one, on either side of the At-lantic, quite knew who he was or what to make of him. As Trotsky wrote to his son from exile in 1931: "Who is this Essad Bey?"

Through recovered letters and manuscripts, fascist police archives in Rome, a fourteenth-century castle in Austria, and an Art Deco mansion in the Hollywood Hills—where "everything in a foreign language" had just been thrown out by the cheerful new inhabitants—I entered the curious labyrinth of his life, a forgotten world at the darkest moment of the last century. I soon abandoned the question of who Kurban Said or Essad Bey was for a more problematic one—who was Lev Nussimbaum? This was his real name, the one he was born with, and as I discovered, for this writer who would be accused of turning history into fairy tales, his chief ongo-ing invention was himself. He was a Weimar media star, a professional "Orientalist" who courted Mussolini and told all of Berlin, including his heiress fiancée, that he was a Muslim prince, when all the time he was a Jew who had spent an isolated, protected childhood alone with his Kipling on the floor in his father's mansion in Baku.

In one sense, Lev Nussimbaum was an extreme example of a type once familiar in the nineteenth and twentieth centuries but now forgotten: the Jewish Orientalist. The phenomenon was first notable in Victorian En-gland, when young men from highly assimilated and influential families like William Gifford Palgrave and Benjamin Disraeli set off to find their "Oriental roots" in the desert. In Palgrave's case, the quest for Oriental au-thenticity led him to a wild life of role-playing: in the 1850s, posing as a Muslim doctor while secretly working for the Jesuits (oddly enough, he insisted on having the Jesuits call him "Father Cohen," resurrecting the name his family had jettisoned in the eighteenth century), he traveled to Arabia to carry out a plot funded by Napoleon III to stir an Arab Bedouin revolt—fifty years before T. E. Lawrence arrived in the Middle East. Pal-grave, aka Father Cohen, also tried to convert the Wahhabis to Christian-ity. His memoir was the bestselling English book about Arabia until Lawrence's memoir superseded it.

The Jewish Orientalist saw the East as a place not to discover the exotic

Other but to find his own roots, and for him the Arabs were nothing less than blood brothers—Jews on horseback, as Disraeli put it. But Disraeli himself defies the stereotypes of current postcolonial thought, for while whispering to Queen Victoria that she must become empress of India, he did not have in mind a straightforward domination of the East by the West. Rather, he idolized the East, and therefore dreamed of an empire that merged the best of both worlds—a British pan-Oriental empire. It must be British, so that it could be organized by the practical good sense of the English, but it must be "Oriental," guided by the wisdom and profundity of the East—interpreted for the West by its resident Orientals, the Jews.

The anti-Semitic slur, of course, was that the Jews were an alien, Oriental race in Europe—but Jewish Orientalists turned the slur on its head, embracing their ancient desert nobility. Jews drew themselves closer to their lost "brothers" in the East and attempted to explain Semitic culture, including Islam, in the West. Jewish Orientalists, in the narrowest sense of the term, were specialists in the field of Eastern religions, languages, and anthropology, yet even using this definition, the crucial Jewish presence in Oriental studies is surprisingly overlooked.*

Beyond the scholars, there were Jews who literally seemed to lose themselves in the reverie of "Eastern identity," as Lev Nussimbaum did. When they disguised themselves as Bedouins or dervishes to make long field journeys, the Jewish Orientalists seemed to feel a psychic transformation that was different from the experience of the gentile in Arab mufti. They would have a fascinating relationship to Zionism, most of them opting in favor of a Jewish state in Palestine but often as part of a "pan-Semitic," pro-Muslim worldview.

After the Second World War, the idea of Jewish Orientalism fell through the cracks of history, as the conflict between Jews and Muslims, reaching tragic proportions in the Middle East, buried their deeply in-

---

* In his influential book *Orientalism,* the late Edward Said tended to ignore the Jewish contribution to Islamic studies in the nineteenth and twentieth centuries, presumably because it would have complicated his arguments about Zionism and imperialism: as a rule, the early Jewish Orientalists took either a scholarly, neutral tone or a downright admiring one toward Islam, regarding it as a great religion and the Muslim world as a noble example, rather than an inferior heresy, which was the attitude taken by so many Christian scholars.

terconnected past. The reasons Muslims and Jews do not get along today seem obvious and inevitable. The reasons they once got along so well lie in the distance, on the other side of a historical chasm.

Pursuing the mystery of Lev Nussimbaum also brought me into the shadowy world of refugees and stateless people created by the Russian Revolution and the First World War—and the events in Germany that laid the groundwork for Nazism and the Second World War. Essentially, Lev was caught between one revolution, in Russia, and another, in Germany, which called itself by a different name. Entire empires would disappear without a trace in the space of a few years, and many people wouldn't survive them or, like Lev, would never really stop running for their lives.

When I first saw pictures of him, he immediately reminded me of my great-uncle Lolek, who escaped the crumbling Austro-Hungarian Empire and the Third Reich and came to New York in the 1930s: they would have been almost exact contemporaries. A hero of my childhood, Lolek and his remaining circle of friends—who had once filled an address book that seemed to be the size of a small-city directory—brought a world of wit and sophistication to their own corner of Manhattan's Washington Heights. My fondest childhood memories are of listening to his stories of growing up in the late Hapsburg Empire; the idea that he'd "had an emperor" always fascinated me as a kid, and that this emperor had been a good king, and that darkness had fallen over the world after he died. I came to regard Lev's Islamic conversion and love for the czar a bit like my great-uncle's socialism and simultaneous love for Kaiser Franz Josef.

And then there were Lolek's adventures in the wide-open future of the 1920s, when everyone had ideas for remaking the world and anything seemed to be about to happen—until anything *did* happen and all his friends and my relatives were suddenly trapped. My great-uncle Lolek told the first half of the twentieth century to me as a series of humorous adventure stories involving him and his friends and his big brother, Janek, whom everyone called the Bull because he was so strong. Then he would tell me about how he tried to convince Janek, my grandfather, to walk across the frontier with him into Switzerland to get out of France before it was too late. "Your grandfather had a family," said Lolek. "He never really thought of leaving them behind. He could have walked out with me and sent for them afterward."

My great-uncle's sense of humor—a particular kind of Viennese humor—could turn even a harrowing account of escaping the Nazis into something bordering on a Marx Brothers routine. I always wanted to hear the story of his girlfriend who hid on the balcony when the Gestapo came to her apartment, and who went into one room while they were searching the other and then did the reverse and somehow wasn't caught. "But you have to understand," said my great-uncle, chuckling himself at it, "it's not a funny story at all—if they caught her, they would have killed her."

When Lolek died in the summer of 1995, for me the unique culture of Austrian Galicia, where he was born, and fin de siècle Vienna seemed to die all over again. It was pure happenstance that he had survived it at all. He had gotten an Austrian passport when the Hapsburg Empire fell, in 1919; Janek received a Polish passport, even though they were brothers from the same town. That is part of the reason my grandfather Janek was deported to Auschwitz in 1942, from France, while my great-uncle Lolek survived and made it to New York.

I grew up, like many Jewish kids (and non-Jews, for that matter), with fantasies of going back in time and outwitting the Nazis. Lev Nussimbaum had the temperament to live out such a fantasy. When the Bolsheviks overran Baku, he and his father escaped by camel caravan across Persia and the deserts of Turkestan; Lev would later evade the Bolsheviks by posing as one of them, make his way across Europe, and convert to Islam at the Ottoman embassy in Berlin in 1923, in the final days of the Ottoman Empire's existence. All this happened before he was eighteen, but it was only the beginning of his adventures.

More significant to me than his early escapes and identity changes was the way he refused, throughout his life, to be forced into the role that the ideologies of the twentieth century wanted to impose on him. While most Jews in Germany after the First World War tried as hard as they could to assimilate, Lev did everything he could to make himself stand out as an ethnic outsider, sporting flowing robes and a turban in the cafés of Berlin and Vienna. But his identity as a desert warrior eventually fooled even himself. He chose to stay in Europe, missing opportunity after opportunity to save himself by going to live with his millionaire in-laws in New York. When he escaped Nazi-occupied Vienna for North Africa, he wasted no time in making his way back into the heart of fascist Europe, as though some strange attraction kept him in the orbit of the forces that would destroy him.

Lev managed to publish sixteen books, most of them international bestsellers and one an enduring masterpiece, all by the age of thirty. But his real genius was in creating his own protean identity: until his death in 1942, Lev kept much of the fascist establishment guessing, with bolder and bolder ruses, dancing his way close to the heart of power, like a thief at a masked ball.

Faced with both Communist and Nazi oppression, Lev survived by countering brute force with the power of imagination. He was simultaneously a Jew, an Oriental, and a German, but he never inhabited any one of these identities to the exclusion of the others—all were products of a defiant mind that refused to be branded or categorized from the outside. He was a rogue and a seducer, but never a con artist, as he was accused of being. He was an ideological Houdini, becoming a racial and religious cross-dresser in a decade when race and religion were as fixed as a death sentence.

The dogged miracle of old papers—remnants of time and memory shoved into cardboard boxes, clothes closets, and dresser drawers—was driven home to me again and again in my search for Lev. Over four years, I was lucky in tracking down more than three hundred private letters that had gone overlooked, though scholars had tried to find them; a number of unpublished book manuscripts (a Caucasian fantasia, a history of fascism, and the first part of a roman à clef set at the Waldorf-Astoria and his father-in-law's apartment on Park Avenue); a memoir manuscript by a classmate from Berlin, who knew him when he first came to Germany as a teenager; and, most extraordinary, six hidden deathbed notebooks, Lev's final account of himself—a wild, rambling epic in microscopic handwriting that nevertheless gives the clearest version of his life that exists.

The letters came to light in a villa outside Milan, where they had not been seen in more than five decades, and recorded an exchange over three years between Lev and a Mussolini-era salon hostess called Pima Andreae. The letters are strange, sometimes off-putting, and ultimately deeply moving. Having heard that a writer she admired, Essad Bey, was trapped in Italy without food or medicine for a worsening blood disease, Pima impulsively wrote to him. She had liked his books for their idiosyncratic views on monarchism and his loathing of Stalin's Russia, and she recommended Kurban Said's books to him without realizing they were also his. Now he was penniless and very sick, trapped by wartime and house arrest by the Italian secret police. She sent him money.

Pima helped keep Lev alive between 1939 and 1942. Most important, she engaged him in a correspondence that turned into an "intellectual love affair," a last friendship and link with the outside world, which otherwise was lost to him. Yet she is almost as troubling a figure as Lev himself, and while he would tell her everything, he could never begin to tell her who he really was. An influential woman from a half-German, half-Italian family, Pima hosted a circle that included a number of leading Fascist and Nazi intellectuals, including Americans like Ezra Pound and also members of Mussolini's family, who sometimes stayed in her villa in Rapallo.

Pima wrote to Mussolini on Lev's behalf, and to the man Lev called "Mr. Ezra," who promised to do what he could to help a fellow writer. In one of the oddest letters in the correspondence, on June 22, 1942, Lev wrote Pima with excitement:

> And the state has suddenly remembered me. In three weeks, three weeks only I'll get money again—if I'm still alive. For, in spite of everything, I still want to live. We'll certainly win the war soon and then I'll definitely visit you before I travel anywhere else—I can't imagine doing otherwise. Oh, the victory will be such a thrilling experience!

In this letter, "we" was Nazi Germany.

As riveting as these documents were to me, the people I met in the course of pursuing this story seemed equally fantastic. There was the Baroness Ehrenfels, whom I went to see in Castle Lichtenau—not, confusingly, the baroness who was supposed to be Kurban Said; that was her husband's first wife. The current, third baroness told me her story at 4 A.M. one winter's morning (she had been too busy to talk earlier, as she rose every day at midnight to begin work on her rock opera, to be produced by a German-Israeli company), then led me down to a frigid room in one of the castle's turrets, a cellar full to the ceiling with family papers and photographs.

In the United States, I spent a fascinating afternoon with Peter Viereck, whose father, George Sylvester Viereck, had been Lev's "New York" friend, occasional writing partner—they made visits to Kaiser Wilhelm's house in Holland together—and, as the leading interviewer for the Hearst papers syndicate, probably the first American ever to interview Hitler. A fanatic Germanophile, he would ultimately wage an absurd campaign to prove that one could be both a Nazi and a philosemite—that he could keep up relations both with Hitler and with friends like Sigmund Freud—and would be imprisoned as a Nazi agent. Flamboyant, contradictory characters like Viereck, to me, represented the confusion of the era, symbolized by the fact that one leading American magazine featured, as contributing writers for the year 1931, Lev Nussimbaum, Leonard Woolf, Joseph Goebbels, and Thomas Mann.

There is one other person to introduce here, because she placed in my hands the mysterious deathbed notebooks of "Kurban Said" and was herself a kind of mystery. I had just come from Positano, Italy, where I visited Lev's grave (a white slab with a marble turban on top, like a thin man wearing a hat), and was making one more trip to Vienna. I was looking, somewhat hopelessly, for Lev's last editor and publisher, Therese Kirschner. She had been an "Aryan" assistant at Lev's Austrian publishers in the 1930s, and when her Jewish employers were forced to flee, she purchased the company at one-thirtieth its value.

An expert on German Islamism whom I had talked to in Berlin had mentioned that she was still living in Vienna, but it was his impression that Kirschner, who now went under her late husband's name, Mögle, was too guarded about her past to talk to anyone.

Frau Mögle wasn't listed in the phone directory, but I walked to the address where the publishing house had been, and there at the top of the list of names was "Mögle" and beneath it the logo of the publishing house to which she had given her own name in 1940: "Therese Kirschner Verlag." I decided against ringing and went back and wrote a careful letter on my hotel stationery, emphasizing that all I was interested in was an author named Essad Bey and any recollections she might have of him or his works. I sent it by messenger. Twenty minutes later, I was drinking a coffee in the hotel lobby when the concierge called me over. A Frau Therese Mögle wanted me on the telephone. In my most formal German, I invited her to dinner.

Frau Mögle had a face like that of a small, defiant eagle. She was ninety-six but seemed much younger, and she talked about her writers like a schoolteacher remembering pupils from a class long ago. Most of them had been Jewish and had fled Vienna within weeks of the Anschluss, though the firm continued to record profits from their books up to two years later. Frau Mögle talked of their departure with a strange sort of indignation, referring to one author who "left without saying a word, just took off leaving me to look after his affairs."

Once she got started, Frau Mögle's memory was a strange, whirling thing, full of precisely recalled faces, manuscripts, sums of money, and accusations. The only intrusions from after 1945 were descriptions of the donations she had made to various children's societies in Africa. One refrain constantly surfaced: "I was not a bad person, you see, I was not bad, I saved people, I saved so many people, I had to look after everything for them, I could not stand to see suffering." It was the weighty task of looking after everything left behind by her fleeing Jewish authors that brought us back to Essad.

By this time, we had walked down the street to Frau Mögle's apartment, the former publishing office. We talked about *Ali and Nino*—"magical, really one of his best things"—and then she asked me if I had read "the other novel that he wrote as Kurban Said. Have you read *The Man Who Knew Nothing About Love?*" I said I'd never heard of it.

She looked at me slyly, then got up and shuffled into another room. I thought she might be going to get another sea-lion fur coat to model for me—she had shown me a number of them already, in a variety of styles—but she returned instead with a stack of six small leather notebooks, tied together with a ribbon. She put them down in front of me and untied the ribbon. "I have been keeping these in my closet for more than fifty years. I could have made a fortune with them, but I am not a greedy person, I am not a bad person, am I?"

I picked up the first notebook, which had a heavily embossed brown leather cover. On the first yellowing brittle page, in a childlike script, were the words "Kurban Said." Beneath the name, it said, *Der Mann, der nichts von der Liebe verstand*—"The Man Who Knew Nothing About Love." Beneath that was written, "Novel. Book One." I read aloud in German the first line, written in an awkward inky scrawl:

Pain is stronger than life, stronger than death, love, loyalty, duty.

A little below that, as I followed the crooked lines of ink, was a statement of intent: "This book is not supposed to be literature. I want to cast a retrospective glance over my life now, in the face of death. . . . My intention is to write down, as truthfully as possible, the strange life that has become my fate."

Frau Mögle said that Essad Bey had given her these six notebooks, his final work, when she went down to see him in Positano. "He wanted me to publish them, and I could have made a fortune, but I never did. I could not read them, it is too terrible to feel his pain, so I kept them and I never did anything with them. You can take them and read them, if you want."

I walked out of the ancient apartment building. It was the night of Vienna's Opera Ball, and people were trudging through new snow in full tails and ball gowns. I clutched the notebooks to my chest to keep them dry. Why had Lev given Frau Mögle these notebooks? Why had she given them to me? Back in my room, I threw myself onto the bed and opened the first notebook.

The tiny blue script told a sprawling, improbable tale.

PART 1

Baku, 1912

CHAPTER 1

Revolution

L EV NUSSIMBAUM WAS BORN IN OCTOBER 1905, the moment when the tolerant, *haute capitaliste* culture of Baku began to fall apart. On October 17, Czar Nicholas II promised his people a constitution, a false promise designed to short-circuit a growing call for revolution, and across the country rioting, looting, and murder were the order of the day. In Baku, the Cossacks rode through the streets attacking citizens, ostensibly to restore order, while Azeris and Armenians turned their cosmopolitan city into a medieval war zone. Elegant villas were besieged if their occupants were of an ethnic or religious group that inflamed a particular mob.

Like many writers born in the last years of a dying empire, Lev would idealize the world that finally collapsed just after his fifteenth birthday, its inhabitants running for their lives, leaving dinner on the table. Lev looked back on Baku as a place whose benevolence stemmed from the antiquity and relative weakness of the authority that ruled it. He would spend his life opposing the revolutionaries who swept away the complex web of the old religions and empires and replaced it with their new, totalizing creeds. For Lev, the forces of revolutionary political change would always be remembered as "a raging madness into which the city fell,"

the grimaces the people suddenly wore instead of faces. Everything infernal, everything animal, everything dull-witted that human nature is capable of stood written in these grimaces. It was as though the movable features of the face, once forcibly subdued, had now likewise attained their true freedom and now were clothed only by dull-witted, animal, "free" expressions. . . . Bolshevism began with the transformation of the human face into a grimace.

The city of Baku has no record of the birth of Lev Nussimbaum in its files. Nor, for that matter, do the cities of Tiflis, Kiev, Odessa, or Zurich. Lev suggested in one of the many accounts he published of his early life, this one in a Berlin newspaper in 1931, that he was actually born noplace:

Born in . . . ? Already here the problematic nature of my existence begins. Most people can name a house or at least a place where they were born. To this place, or to this house, one makes pilgrimages in one's later years in order to indulge in sentimental reminiscences. In order to indulge in such reminiscences I would have to make a pilgrimage to the carriage of an express train. I was born during the first Russian railroad strike in the middle of the Russian steppes between Europe and Asia, when my mother was returning from Zurich, the seat of the Russian revolutionaries, to Baku, the seat of our family. On the day of my birth, the czar proclaimed his manifesto in which he granted the Russians a political constitution. On the day of my arrival in Baku the city was engulfed in the flames of Revolution, and the slaughtering of the mob. I myself had to be brought to my father in a water trough, whereupon my father wanted to throw me out together with my nursemaid. So began my existence. Father: an industrial magnate in the oil industry; mother: a radical revolutionary.

In this version of his birth story, Lev is in every way smack in the middle of the historic upheaval that formed his life, and in his many accounts of his family and origins, he would never deviate from these basic facts.*

* The significance of the events on his birthday would haunt Lev his entire life, but he couldn't be sure what day that was. Sometimes he gave the date as October 20, but he also said late October, or even early November; his father told him October but also seemed unsure of the day. Adding to the confusion is the fact that Russia's traditional, pre-1917 Julian calendar differed from the modern Gregorian calendar by eleven days. Thus, Lev

And as absurd as it sounds, the story may actually be true. Some of it is echoed by other independent sources, including Lev's German governess, Alice Schulte. Frau Schulte composed her memories of Lev in a neat, careful hand in the 1940s, in the convent in northern Italy where she went to live after watching the boy she had followed around her entire life become a hunted man. She seemed to feel an obligation to put the facts of his confusing life in some order, but the document is frustratingly brief, and as Frau Schulte was buried in a pauper's grave near the convent in 1958, she cannot elaborate on it.

Lev's first book, *Blood and Oil in the Orient,* lays out the founding myths he would return to—the personal history linking him to the history of the Caucasus. Lev introduces his father, Abraham, promenading in front of the local prison, "an oriental sheepskin cap on his head and in his hand a rosary of amber, without which no one can get along in Baku." His father's sun-darkened features, which Lev elsewhere attributed to an evenly mixed racial heritage of Turkic and Persian aristocracy, betrayed "the facial expression, imperturbable, weary, and yet eager for activity, of an Oriental who has transferred the old traditions of command to the social life of the young oil-city." In this account, his father buys his mother ("a very young girl with dark eyes . . . a member of the Bolshevist party of Russia") out of the imperial prison, where she is awaiting deportation as a political agitator, then promptly marries her and brings her into his harem. Lev's mother, in turn, takes over the house and dispatches the harem.

The idea that Abraham Nussimbaum was a Muslim aristocrat of Persian and Turkic heritage—or anything other than a Jew of European background—was a deliberate part of Lev's self-creation. The elder Nussimbaum was, in fact, born in Tiflis, now Tbilisi, the official capital of the Russian-administered Caucasus, on August 24, 1875. (*His* birth certificate does exist.) He was an Ashkenazic Jew whose parents had come to the Caucasus from Kiev or Odessa, the great Jewish centers within the Pale of Settlement, outside of which Russia's Jews were not allowed to travel or work (although many bribed their way out to other parts of the empire). The Pale consisted of areas that had fallen under the waning Polish

---

could, in a sense, have been born in October *and* November. No wonder he once said that he celebrated his birthday in New York for an entire week.

Commonwealth—primarily Belorussia, Lithuania, and western Ukraine—until they were forcibly annexed by Catherine the Great in 1772, 1793, and 1795.* Along with millions of Orthodox and Catholic Slavs, nearly half a million Jews now became subjects of the expanded Russian Empire. Until the absorption of the Polish territories, the Russian Empire had had practically no Jews, and it was uniquely ill-equipped to handle this new addition to its ethnic and religious mix. The official Russian solution to the Jewish question became to restrict all Jews to the same Polish provinces where Catherine the Great had acquired them—the so-called Pale. Effectively, this created the largest ghetto in history, a vast geographic prison for the new "Russian" Jews. The territories that comprised the Pale were provincial, anti-Semitic, and prone to food shortages and other economic crises.

Russia was already a land of such wild religious fervor that even its Orthodox rulers were considered heretics by a large percentage of its people: the "Old Believers"—the millions of apocalyptic fundamentalists who objected to the minor changes in Russian church ritual made in the seventeenth century to bring it closer in line with standard Greek Orthodox practice. The Old Believers were so upset that the changes could complicate their eternal salvation that they staged vast rebellions against the czar's "legions of the Antichrist" and burned themselves alive by the thousands in protest (though there were still an estimated 13 million of them when Lev was born).

Still others became "Judaizers," Christians who decided to renounce Christ, follow only the Old Testament, and keep the Sabbath on Saturday, along with sundry other Jewish customs, while not considering themselves Jews. Aided by the more mainstream Trans-Volga Hermits, the Judaizers brought Russian Orthodoxy as close as it ever came to a reformation—and caused a reaction that barred real Jews from Russia for the next three

---

* What began as a limited landgrab by the monarchs of Russia, Prussia, and Austria became a full-scale dismemberment in the 1790s, after the Poles, inspired by the winds from France, abolished their monarchy and drafted a constitution. Czarina Catherine led the charge for eliminating Poland's "contagion of democratic ideas." From the perspective of the post-1939 era, Catherine's solution—the armed dismemberment of Poland, with German armies smashing in from the west, Russians from the east—seems like a kind of eighteenth-century dry run for the Hitler-Stalin pact.

hundred years. When Czar Ivan III took a liking to the Judaizers, they were invited to Moscow, where they managed to convert so much of the court nobility in the last decades of the fifteenth century that traditionalists felt the need to counter the trend through selective burnings at the stake. The Orthodox clergy also prevailed upon the czars to ban the Jews, who were thought to have started the whole "Judaizing" heresy; the ban took effect in the mid-1500s, which is why the empire had such a peculiar absence of Jews when it acquired the Pale in the late 1700s. Like Freemasonry—with which it was closely associated, especially after Russian Masons adopted the Kabbalah and began electing "Cohens" to their temples—Judaism was simply considered too explosive and contagious a faith to be allowed inside Russia.

Russia's ongoing religious crises added urgency to the official desire to convert its vast new Jewish population. In 1817, Czar Alexander I personally founded the Society of Israelite Christians but had less luck defeating Judaism than he'd had defeating Napoleon; gentile serfs and merchants in areas bordering the Pale even showed disturbing new signs of "Judaizing." Religion was still so anarchic and volatile a force in Russia that when Czar Alexander died in 1825, while visiting the Black Sea, many Russians insisted that he had not really died but had secretly become a wandering "fool-in-Christ" traveling the country under the name Fedor Kuzmich. The nineteenth century was filled with schemes, hatched by both the czar and his revolutionary opponents, for dealing with the "alien" element, the Jews. The schemes grew more violent during the course of the century. In the 1820s, Count Pestel, a freethinking noble, suggested giving the Jews an independent state in Asia Minor and deporting them there en masse. But by the end of the century, Constantine Pobedonostsev, chief adviser of the last two czars, was suggesting that Russia's "Jewish problem" should be solved by thirds: a third should emigrate, a third should embrace Christianity, and a third should die of starvation. The Okhrana, the czarist police, forged a document that became known as *The Protocols of the Elders of Zion,* a supposed plan for the Jewish takeover of everything through the promotion of global revolution. During the aborted revolution of 1905, pogroms swept Russia that shocked the world.

In this vast anti-Semitic empire, the Caucasus was a rare oasis. Here, the Jews were merely a minority among minorities, and an ancient and rather admired one at that. Jews had fled here from the destruction of the Second Temple, in A.D. 70, and Azerbaijan had absorbed remnants of the Babylonian exile, who fled to the highlands north of Baku during the Islamic conquest of Persia. Even the Judaizers, Russia's non-Jewish Jews, found sanctuary here and settled the jungle lands on the Iranian-Azeri border. In the eyes of the Muslim khans who ruled much of the Caucasus, the Jews' position as People of the Book raised them a notch above the Zoroastrians and the various pagan sects.

Ashkenazic Jews from the Pale clandestinely left for the Caucasus—a few days' journey across the Black Sea—throughout the nineteenth century. The pace picked up once the oil boom got started in earnest after 1870. It is likely that Lev's grandfather migrated from the Pale to Tiflis in the 1850s or '60s, and that his father left Tiflis for Baku in the early 1890s. Lev never revealed anything about this part of his past, but Abraham Nussimbaum may have regarded Baku much as did his contemporary Ossip Benenson, another Ashkenazic Jew who got rich there on oil. Benenson's daughter Flora recalled that shortly after his marriage in the 1880s, her father broke away from his family in the Pale because "he had his sights on faraway Caucasus, a realm which in the nineteenth century formed part of every young Russian's romantic dreams . . . [but he] was no romantic; it was the gambler in his strain that sent him so remote from his roots."

Flora Benenson grew up in the same social milieu as Lev. As fellow millionaires in a city with a small Jewish population, the Benensons and the Nussimbaums probably knew each other. Abraham Nussimbaum grew rich as the so-called oil commissioner of Baku, a kind of legal middleman who also owned wells, but Baku oil made the Benensons one of the richest families in Russia. In 1912 it allowed them to buy a mansion in St. Petersburg within sight of the czar's palace. Flora's recollections of her family's first Passover celebration in St. Petersburg, however, contrast starkly with the interethnic Christmas party young Lev would attend later that year. She recalled that on the evening of their seder, "just as all was ready, our butler led a delegation of servants to Mother's boudoir. They had done all their work, he said, and were now leaving the house. 'We cannot serve a meal while you consume the blood of a Christian child,' the butler informed Mother. 'We shall return tomorrow.' " This was the difference between the other cities of the Russian Empire and Baku. Pale or no Pale, with enough money, a Jew could live wherever he chose in the czar's empire. Only in the Caucasus could he forget the stigma of being a Jew, and the most cosmopolitan and tolerant place in the Caucasus was Azerbaijan's capital, Baku.

The Persian word for fire is *azer,* and since ancient times Azerbaijan's abundance of oil and natural gas, which led whole hillsides to naturally explode into flame, made it the center of Zoroastrianism, Persia's ancient pre-Muslim religion. Every religion known to man has found haven in the region. While Rome was still killing Christians, two kingdoms on Azerbaijan's borders, Armenia and Georgia, became among the first countries to officially convert to Christianity. When the Muslim armies swept out of Arabia in the eighth century, some of the fiercely independent Christians, Zoroastrians, and pagans of Azerbaijan adopted Muhammad's faith, but many did not. Islam merely joined the babel of religions in the area. When the crusader knights were driven out of Palestine three centuries later, they found a new home in the hills of Azerbaijan, where they established kingdoms that still existed and shocked anthropologists in the early twentieth century. Eventually, as its culture developed alongside that of Persia, Azerbaijan became the only Muslim country besides Iran to be officially Shiite—revering a line of saintly martyrs stretching back to Ali, the Prophet's nephew and son-in-law. The Azeri khans frequently seized the throne of Persia itself; from the sixteenth century on, the great Persian dynasties were ruled by ethnic Azeris.

Russian influence swept into the region in the early nineteenth century, as the czar's armies conquered the Caucasus, and the Azeris broke with conservative Shiites of Iran and became "Europeans." Umm-El-Banu Asadullayeva, who left Baku in 1922 and wrote her memoirs in Paris under the name Banine, recalled that in her own "fanatic Muslim family," the women cared mainly for clothes and jewelry, furniture from Paris and Moscow, and gambling (her father, a farmer, became a millionaire when oil was found under his fields). Her aunts, "fat, bearded brunettes," smoked, gossiped all day long, and "played poker with a passion that was unequaled." She dryly summed up the atmosphere in the turn-of-the-century Baku of her childhood:

Gambling is forbidden in the Koran—all of Baku played cards and huge sums of money changed hands. Strong alcoholic drinks, such as Vodka and Cognac, replaced wine, which was condemned by the Prophet, under the pretense that these beverages were not technically forbidden. The reproduction of the human face was likewise prohibited—photographers were nevertheless swamped by customers. Muslims allowed themselves to be photographed in profile, or from the front, standing before a painting of a park, or a draped curtain.

The oil boom in the United States began with the first gusher in Pennsylvania in the 1850s, but in Baku it had been on for two thousand years. Baku oil had lit the temples of Zarathustra, and Marco Polo described it as a mainstay of silk route traders. But for nearly two millennia, the perpetual flood of black gold had excited the passions of no one but the Zoroastrians, who made Baku the center of their cult. Stoic bands of emaciated, fire-worshipping monks traveled from as far as India to sit out their lives in fire fortresses, starving so that they might receive the pure nourishment of the eternal flames. For the rest of the population, crude oil was a perpetual muddy sludge in which the city's few thousand residents made their living; it poisoned the soil, sending the locals out to colonize the steppes and mountains and jungles of Azerbaijan—no other country has more climate zones in as small an area—in search of ground uncontaminated by crude.

The waters of the Caspian itself often caught fire when the sludge on it became too thick. "I have memories of the flaming waves," wrote one emigrant recalling her childhood in Baku, "lighting up the night as the vapours exploded into a thousand fires." Until the nineteenth century, oil had been used mainly in patent medicines, and almost everyone continued to believe that it had health-giving properties. Some Caucasian tribes worshipped oil as a divine element in itself. The vapors, it was thought, had spared Baku from the Black Plague.

On his tour of the Caucasus in the 1850s, Alexandre Dumas marveled at the anachronistic citizens of Azerbaijan, who had the free spirit and bravery of his legendary musketeers; he wrote in his diary that "entering Baku is like penetrating one of the strongest fortresses of the Middle Ages." That was all soon to change. In the mid-nineteenth century, when kerosene made from petroleum began to replace expensive whale oil, the

Age of Illumination began. Kerosene was suddenly the world's most valuable commodity, and the forces that made Rockefeller and Standard Oil were unleashed in Baku.

The Baku gushers, called "fountains," were of a size and power that had never been seen before. With nicknames like Wet Nurse and Golden Bazaar, they raged out of control, small wild volcanoes of oil. They turned the beaches of Baku black, and the shore of the Caspian was soon so thick with wooden and alabaster derricks in certain places that one could not see ships approaching. The first Baku fountain, struck in June 1873, shot oil into the air uncontrollably for over four months before its owners managed to tame it, and a few dozen million barrels of oil ran into the sand. For a few months, this single fountain caused the price of oil to plummet, and two years later, it was still powerful enough to send a nine-foot-thick column forty feet into the air.

By 1901, Baku was supplying half the world's oil. It became an international city overnight, and the local Azeris were soon outnumbered by Russians, Georgians, Ossetians, and others from the four corners of the earth. Between 1856 and 1910, Baku's population grew at a faster rate than that of London, Paris, or New York. The Nobel brothers, who dominated the industry in the first decades, invented the concept of the tanker to handle the demand for Baku oil in the Far East, appropriately naming their first tanker *Zoroaster*. They made the bulk of the family's fortune in Azeri oil, though brother Alfred's invention of dynamite is more famous.

The oilmen came in all stripes—Swedes and Jews and Poles and Armenians—but the dominance of big foreign groups like the Nobels and Rothschilds didn't last long. By the turn of the century, half of the tanker business and much of the production was in local hands. So-called oil barons arose from both the peasantry and the feudal aristocracy—anyone who dug a hole in the ground and got lucky. (The Nobels tried whenever possible to buy out these new oil barons, along with smaller producers. According to documents in the Baku archives, Abraham Nussimbaum sold the Nobels most of his wells in 1913, on the eve of the Great War, a highly opportune business decision.)

The new oil millionaires became great philanthropists, determined to turn their city from a provincial backwater into the finest Islamic city in the world—a showcase of the possibilities of the positive merger of East and West. As the representative local group, the Muslim oil barons felt the most obliged to make showy public statements with their new wealth. They took grand tours of Europe and hired architects to build copies of the mansions, museums, and opera houses they had seen, all in an attempt to anchor their city in the Occidental future rather than its Oriental past. While some Azeri Muslims were outraged by the education of women or their appearance onstage or in an office building, Baku benefited from having been so long at the crossroads of East and West that people were used to new fashions and change.

Equal parts Dodge City, medieval Baghdad, industrial Pittsburgh, and nineteenth-century Paris, fin de siècle Baku was the last great city built before the First World War spoiled the dream that the West could keep expanding forever in a grand civilizing pageant. It was a place of fantastic extremes of wealth and poverty, where gas lights and telephones made a stark contrast to camel caravans and emaciated Zoroastrian monks. The city's wild and clashing history came to a head at the turn of the century, when it was the "Wild East" frontier of Europe, the world's greatest oil-boom town. A British visitor at the time wrote, "One might almost fancy oneself in an American city out west. There is the same air of newness about everything, the same sanguine atmosphere. Everyone is hopeful."

Yet by 1905, the entire Russian frontier was bathed in blood, as the empire entered the first of its revolutions. The unrest reached from the coast of Korea to St. Petersburg's Nevsky Prospekt, and Baku was not spared. The revolution came, as many do, on the heels of a disastrous war, one of the bloodiest in history. The czar's advisers had dreamed up the 1904–5 Russo-Japanese War in part as a means of diffusing revolutionary tension, by acquiring, via quick victory, an injection of patriotism as well as some much-needed timber concessions on the Korean coast. Instead, the Russians experienced total defeat. The catastrophe in the Far East—against a people the czar called "little, short-tailed monkeys"—made the Russian Empire look fragile and moribund. As the war's losses sank in—in addition to the hundreds of thousands of dead soldiers, practically the entire Russian Navy was sunk by the Japanese fleet—years of left-wing terrorism and czarist oppression collided in a year of uprisings, ethnic cleansing, and generalized breakdown.

The semi-destroyed Russian military was in no position to quash the unrest. The only part of the vast czarist navy that had not been sunk by the Japanese was the famous Black Sea Fleet, and on its main battleship, the state-of-the-art *Potemkin,* the sailors rioted in the spring of 1905 and shot their officers. All around the Black Sea and the Caspian, public order broke down. While the staggering numbers of Russian dead, machine-gunned on the icy hills of Manchuria and the Korean peninsula, showed the new lethality of war, the revolutionary terrorism and pogroms that arrived inside Russia that year showed the new brutality of politics—and both foreshadowed what horror might be born through the mediums of modern mass violence.*

In the year that followed Lev's birth, approximately thirty-six hundred government officials were killed or wounded by terrorists—and this all *after* the revolutionary crisis had been subdued by the czar's promise of constitutional reform. Acts of terrorism became so common during Lev's childhood that many Russian newspapers introduced special sections devoted solely to printing daily lists of political assassinations and bombings throughout the empire. The political violence of revolution mixed with religious and racial violence. While most historians no longer believe that the czar's government planned and directed the pogroms, it is clear from his letters that Nicholas and his advisers applauded them, since he believed that the revolution was a Jewish plot and that the pogroms helped fight it, as well as encouraging "traditional values" in the population. But the two types of violence and upheaval merely fed off each other. Nearly seven hundred pogroms occurred in the two weeks following the czar's October 17 announcement promising a constitution.

Every manner of thug, bigot, bandit, and terrorist descended on Baku because the city was the great juggernaut, the capitalist frontier. Bolshevik gangs attacked from the left, raiding banks and treasuries to finance their new movement. The czar's Cossacks attacked from the right, to put down the uprisings.

Thirty-five years later, as he lay dying, Lev would reflect again and

---

* The Russo-Japanese War showed how machine guns could kill thousands in a matter of hours, forcing soldiers to dig into trenches and charge over them, in waves, to their deaths. Millions died at Verdun and Ypres as their officers relearned the lessons already drawn from the Battle of Mukden, which had shocked journalists and generals alike at the time. But even by 1914, the lessons of the Russo-Japanese War had been relegated to a footnote.

again on how "blood flowed the day of my birth over the European-style paving stones of the streets. . . . Houses went up in flames and Cossacks on little, long-maned horses flew through the city." In the rest of the Russian Empire, Jewish blood was flowing in the streets, but in Baku, the blood Lev "remembers" at his birth was mostly Armenian. The Armenians had lived in relative peace and prosperity in the ethnic mix of Azerbaijan for hundreds of years, fulfilling the role Jews played elsewhere as traders and moneylenders; some of the richest oil barons were Armenian. But as the old balance collapsed, this industrious minority bore the full brunt of the emerging chaos. Some of the most vivid recollections of these events came from a young Armenian woman, Armen Ohanian, who survived the riots as a girl and wrote about her experiences for *Asia,* "the American Magazine on the Orient."* She describes how the Cossacks were called in to restore order after days of rioting, causing the carnage in Baku's streets that formed the specter of Lev's birth year (and was the reason his pregnant mother would have been sent to Switzerland only to be stranded in a train carriage outside Baku on her return). She recalls:

Thousands of dead lay in the streets and covered the Christian and Mussulman cemeteries. The odor of the corpses stifled us. Everywhere women with mad eyes were seeking their children, and husbands were moving the heaps of rotting flesh.

In the hallway we were met by a manservant. "The Czar has given them a constitution!" he said. His stiff lips fascinated me. "Everyone is free to do as he likes. That is why—that is why—the Cossacks are burning the quarter." . . . The whole city was in flames and even the waves of the Caspian Sea, covered with oil from the burning wells, spit fire like a dragon.

Thus the Cossacks celebrated the constitution the czar gave Russia after his defeat.

---

* One of the great magazines of the 1920s and '30s, *Asia* fed the public appetite for news of "the Orient" that was such a force in those decades. *Asia* published the top writers of the day—John Dos Passos covered the Palestine question in the wake of the Balfour Declaration—but it featured mainly the voices of people like this Armenian girl, as well as British ambassadors and Indian revolutionaries, Ottoman butlers and Siberian industrialists. Even as it catered to the romantic fascination with "the East," *Asia* belied notions of

The revolution was eventually contained, and for a brief time it seemed that the autocratic, unwieldy empire of the czars might actually be able to reform itself. But the massacres and chaos of 1905 were to find their fatal amplification in the catastrophe of the First World War. Eventually, the czarist regime would fall to an even greater tyranny, and among its unsung losses was the unpredictable, interethnic capitalist dynamo on the Caspian, where "everyone is hopeful."

I initially assumed that Lev's lifelong portrayal of his mother as a revolutionary was intended for effect, symbolically containing the tragedy of his life, the collapse of his world, within his own family: by taking his mother out of a czarist prison, Lev's father had sown the seed of his own destruction. Yet while the idea of his father as a Muslim aristocrat was a pure fabrication, I discovered that the idea of his mother as a revolutionary had a basis in fact. Indeed, the antagonism between these two dissonant poles in the same household—the oil baron and the Communist—may have been responsible for her death in 1911 or 1912, when she was in her twenties and Lev was six or seven years old.

While Lev's published accounts of his family always painted his father as a masterful Muslim lord of mixed Asiatic bloodlines, he rarely mentioned his mother's looks, character, or family background, as though a revolutionary did not really need such baggage. He offered the provocative—and self-aggrandizing—fact that his mother was from a noble Russian family. This turned Berta Slutzki—the name that would somehow become listed in fascist police files in the 1930s—into a fallen woman who had been sucked into the Red whirlwind until his father plucked her out of prison that fateful day: a young woman of revolutionary habits but impeccable aristocratic pedigree. After Lev's death, his most detailed obituary would recite this grand maternal heritage: "The Sluzki lineage is part of Russian nobility, whose head was Boyar Sluzky, a functionary in the court of Wesley (Vasil) the Dark. A member of the Sluzky house was beheaded during the reign of Ivan IV. The Sluzky line appears in the Third Book of Russian Heraldry."

_____

Orientalism as some patronizing or hostile exercise, providing armchair Orientalists with carefully reasoned articles about the sins of Western imperialism and what to do about it.

Lev himself never described his mother in such detail (at least not until forced by circumstances to provide "airtight documentation of Aryan ancestry three generations back" on both sides of his family tree). In fact, there was a studied vagueness in his published accounts of her. During his career as a writer and "professional man from the East," he always maintained elaborate fairy tales about his father's background and built freely on them. His close friends understood this was nonsense, for when they met Lev's father, who for years shared a flat with him in Berlin and Vienna, they could see he was no feudal lord from the steppe. Over time, I tracked down surviving acquaintances and heard their accounts of a dapper, elderly Mr. Nussimbaum, who apparently made a striking, if decidedly non-Muslim, impression.

But I began to despair of getting an account anywhere of Lev's mother. Nobody remembered anything about her or Lev even mentioning her. Most surprising, the six leather notebooks, the sprawling deathbed memoirs, lavishing thousands of words on everyone who ever meant anything to him, spare only one frigid thought for her: "My mother brought me into the world—that's the only thing she did for me." The notebooks do not leave out other people who have caused him pain—they are treated in tidal waves of angry, descriptive, detailed prose. But about his mother, in the entire memoir, there is merely a ghostly echo.

I felt sure that I would never get to the bottom of the matter until one day I learned that a man in Israel was trying to reach me. He had called *The New Yorker* years after my article on Lev appeared there, but the message never got passed on; he then tried the Israeli publisher of *Ali and Nino*, until the publisher referred him to my literary agency and again he called New York. This time my agent's assistant promptly called to say that Lev Nussimbaum's cousin would like to be in touch.

Lev Nussimbaum has a cousin? I waited, wondering if this would be the breakthrough it promised to be or some sort of crank. Finally, a rather sober-sounding e-mail arrived saying that the writer was interested in "the tragic story of Lev Nussimbaum (Assad Bey, Kutban Said) [*sic*]" because, as he had been investigating his family's history for the past decade, he had found out that Lev, or "Liova," as the family had called him, had been a cousin of his grandmother. He was contacting me, he said, because, as I had read Lev's unpublished memoir, the six leather notebooks, he hoped I could "unveil mysteries" regarding his family. Specifically, he wanted any information "about Lev's mother's suicide that she committed while he was eight years old, or his married life to a German lady for four years."

I quickly responded and had a long phone conversation with the man in Israel shortly thereafter.

At first I withheld any information about Lev that had not been in the *New Yorker* article, to see if indeed it was likely that he was thinking of the right Lev Nussimbaum. For instance, I had never mentioned in print the mother's name I had seen in documents about Lev in the Fascist archives: "Berta Slutski" (Lev never uses her name in any of his writing, published or unpublished). When, unprompted, he started giving me the history of the entire Slutz*kin* family, including his great-aunts Tamara and Sophie, who had left Belorussia for Baku at the end of the nineteenth century, led by their fearless older sister Berta, who somehow married a Baku millionaire named Nussimbaum—I knew I was speaking to the right person. And I learned that Lev's mother was Jewish. Like his father, she was an Ashkenazic Jew from the Pale, hardly Russian nobility.

Suddenly, the picture got much clearer. His mother's Jewishness was a fact Lev would deny his whole life in the most outrageous terms, even to intimate friends. Whereas his friends would know that his paternal Muslim lineage was a fiction, his mother's status as a Christian turned communist Russian noblewoman was preserved by her absence. But according to the cousin in Israel, a retired scientist who had mapped his family with the precision of a periodic table, Lev's mother arrived in Baku from a dirt-poor village in Belorussia called Petrovichi. The family name, Slutzkin, referred to Berta's father's ancestry in the town of Slutsk, fifty kilometers away. Berta's mother was Jewish on both sides of her family. (Her mother's maiden name had been Ratner, and after Mr. Slutzkin, she had remarried a Mr. Katz.)

Most of the time, Lev danced around issues of race by presenting the Jewish problem, even to high-ranking Fascists, as something that did not apply to the Caucasus, where racial and tribal allegiances were complex and protean. ("All Caucasian peoples without exception have taken over some legacy from the Jews," Lev wrote, "here an Old Testament word used by them in their prayers, there some custom, such as levirate marriage. In any case, the Jewish facial type is remarkably widespread among the populations of the Caucasus.") But to have a Jewish mother from the Pale was an irrefutable fact and one to be avoided. His father could be a Muslim lord publicly, a Jewish businessman to his friends, and somehow Lev could talk and write his way around this. Coming from Slutzk, Lev's mother had, at all costs, to be a gentile Russian. His efforts to establish a non-Jewish lineage for Berta heated up during his last years, when he was literally dying to offer his supposed Aryan credentials to anyone who would listen. As he wrote to Pima Andreae in 1942:

> Yes, there is a reason why people believe that my mother was a Jewess. Her clan originated in Slutzk, a Slutzk that no longer exists. The rulers of Slutzk are called Slutzki in Russian. The land belonged to them even during the time of Vassily the Dark. They were princes from Moscow, but the people who lived on their land were their subjects. The poor people had no last names for a long time, i.e. the subjects of Slutzk did not have family names, only a given name, like Ivan, serf of the Slutzki order, or in Russian, Ivan Slutzkin. There is only one Slutzki family. There are, however, many Slutkins, and among them, many Lithuanians and Jews. I know a number myself.

Of course, I may have learned more from Lev's Israeli cousin about Berta's family and origins than Lev ever knew, since, as he complains in letter after letter, his father and her closest relatives all but refused to speak about her. ("Believe me—it's better for you not to know anything," Berta's younger sister Sofia had once told him when he badgered her to tell him something, anything, about his mother.) And Lev's cousin soon put me in touch with another relative who became a truly invaluable guide to the murky waters of Lev's childhood: Noam Hermont, an elegant eighty-year-old man who had been born in Berlin in 1923 but had lived in Paris—except for a brief period of escaping the Nazis by moving to Italy—his entire life. Berta, though Noam never knew her, had been his aunt. His mother, Tamara, Berta's sister, had been close to Lev. Noam had even met Lev in Paris once, when he was about ten years old; he remembered only that Lev "never smiled." From him I was able to piece together the essential parts of Berta's story.

In our initial conversation, Monsieur Hermont told me that Berta and her sisters had left Belorussia for Baku because their father had died; their mother had remarried but couldn't support them, so they were essentially orphans. He also confirmed that Berta had committed suicide. No one knew why, exactly; all his mother, who was living with the family at the time, told him was that Berta "had very revolutionary feelings," and that there was a fight of some kind in the household. (Lev told Pima that when he got older, he found two letters of his mother's in the house in Baku, "very revolutionary letters.") Later, when we met in Paris, Noam said his mother had told him that Berta had killed herself by drinking acid.

Around Lev, family members referred only to the "terrible accident," "the tragedy." That was the way people who had known Berta talked, if they talked at all: cryptic, darkly hinting, even accusatory. "She was right back then. There was no other option for her. Time showed it to be an error. More I cannot tell you"—that was all Sofia would say to Lev. Another time, in Paris, Tamara told him in tears, "In truth only two people are to blame—you and your father!" No wonder it all practically drove Lev mad. What could it mean? In his letters to Pima, he was still in anguish over it, especially the suggestion that he—at six or seven years old—had been somehow to blame.

Could Berta have been active in the revolutionary movement in Baku, and could it have been divided loyalties that tore her apart? It's not implausible. The Pale was a fertile breeding ground for revolutionaries, men and women, in the nineteenth century, and there had been a cell in Baku for several years by the time she arrived, around 1900. The army of oil workers—a ready proletariat, and almost a quarter of the city's population—had attracted vying Menshevik and Bolshevik factions eager to convert them to their cause. One connection Lev focuses on in the letters to Pima is particularly startling. Several letters in 1940 and 1941 rail against the *Pockennarbige*—"Pockmarked One"—or "the Seminarist," as Lev invariably calls Joseph Stalin. Stalin, then Joseph Djugashvili, but more often known by his early nom de guerre, Koba, was based in Baku starting in 1907, when he was twenty-seven (and had indeed been severely pockmarked since a childhood attack of smallpox).* He lived there off and on until 1912, sometimes in prison, but mostly underground.

* Stalin suppressed many of the records of his early life. (According to several sources, this may be because he began his career as a spy for the Okhrana, the czarist secret police.) But it's well known that he took the nickname Koba from a character in his favorite novel, *The*

Expelled from the Theological Seminary of Tiflis in 1899, a year away from qualifying for the priesthood, he had joined the revolutionary movement in Georgia, where he became known for organizing violent "expropriations"—robberies of banks and treasuries to finance the growing Bolshevik movement (a tactic that had Lenin's stamp of approval). The only other major source of funds for the party at this point was donations from wealthy patrons.

Lev would recount that his mother had helped "the Seminarist," and indeed, he wrote in a 1940 letter that Stalin himself had told him that she "had helped him often in the past." Bizarrely, Lev writes in the same letter, "Only when the *Pockennarbige* lived with us did he tell me many things about my mother." This was supposedly about 1920, in Baku, shortly before Lev and his father fled the city for good and Stalin briefly returned with the triumphant Bolsheviks. Could Lev be embroidering his role as witness to the revolution? It's impossible to know. But he clearly expects Pima to be familiar with the circumstances. At different times, Lev implies that Stalin was somehow involved in his parents' meeting, and in whatever came between them. It's suggestive that Berta and Stalin, not yet a significant figure in the movement, would have been close in age when he came to Baku. And that he had every reason to seek out a sympathizer who had married into money.

It remains hard to picture any member of the cultured, pampered Nussimbaum household as an associate of Koba Djugashvili's. At this stage, he was somewhere between a thuggish mafioso and a dogmatic student radical, with a beard and sideburns and a passion for Esperanto, which he was convinced would be the language of the future. But I discovered at least one possible connection. In a short article, Lev once referred to his mother and Stalin in much the same terms he would use writing to Pima twenty

---

Patricide, by Alexander Kazbegi, a story of love and vengeance set in the Caucasus during the 1840s. The fictional Koba is a kind of ruthless Robin Hood who fights the Russian occupiers. The novel is suffused with the romantic traditions of Georgian chivalry and the code of the mystical Caucasian Mountains, much the same themes that Lev invoked in his flight from the Bolsheviks. Though they could not have turned out more differently, "Essad Bey" and Stalin were both deeply influenced by the dreamy romanticism that saw the region as a mountain redoubt of rebels and knights holding out against a hostile world.

years later: "My mother, along with Krasin, who at the time directed the electricity plants in Baku, financed Stalin's illicit communist press with her diamonds." I had read this sentence half a dozen times before it occurred to me that I should find out more about this Krasin—who I assumed had nothing to do with Leonid Krasin, a central figure in the Russian Revolution and both a close friend and rival of Lenin's. Yet it turned out to be the same person. Along with Stalin, Krasin had been a Bolshevik plotter in Baku before 1917. As Alan Moorehead writes in his book *The Russian Revolution*, Krasin was

> a perfect specimen of the double life. So far as the authorities were aware, he was a well-to-do engineer; secretly he was a Bolshevik agitator who operated in a very large way. He ran an illegal press, collected money from sympathetic liberals, passed agents to and fro across the Russian border, and as a sideline manufactured bombs for the terrorists.

So Krasin and Stalin were doing much the same thing in Baku. Stalin, however, would have had no entrée with the oil commissioner of Baku, whereas Krasin—"immaculately groomed, erudite, and culturally sophisticated with impeccable manners and immense charm"—easily could have sat at Abraham Nussimbaum's dinner table, all the while planning to destroy him. A double life indeed. I could begin to see how, once Berta was exposed—as she clearly was, leading to the fights in the household that her younger sister Tamara remembered from growing up—she might have seen no way out. She would have been revealed as a saboteur under her own roof, working for the downfall of her own husband. It's hard to imagine the level of anguish that would cause someone to deliberately drink acid ("She suffered horribly," Noam said), but I thought I was beginning to get some idea.

And Lev clearly had an idea, because in his correspondence, he refers to his mother's "crime . . . for that is how I experienced it and that is what I still think." She "poisoned my father's life and to a lesser extent, my own." His bitterness toward his mother is often displaced, in the letters anyway, onto Stalin: "He took my homeland away from me, the house, everything." In 1931, Lev published one of the first biographies of Stalin, and it became a bestseller; it carried the subtitle "The Career of a Fanatic."

While it is always unusual to have your mother belong to an underground revolutionary movement, it would have been far less unusual in the Russian Empire in the early 1900s than in most other times and places. By the turn of the century, women made up almost one-third of the Social Revolutionary's Combat Organization, the terrorist wing of Russia's most popular revolutionary party. Young women built and threw bombs, plotted and carried out assassinations, and showed they were the equal of men in fanaticism, selflessness, and ruthlessness.

Their paragon was Vera Zasulich, who visited the St. Petersburg police chief in 1878 to protest his harsh treatment of a student revolutionary. She waited her turn in the line of petitioners, and when she reached the head of the line, she pulled a small-caliber pistol from her muff and began firing point-blank, severely wounding him. At her trial, the jury ignored the evidence and found her not guilty, based on the high-minded "compassion" that had motivated her attack: Miss Zasulich had shot the police chief because he had ordered the flogging of the student. She became a heroine of salon liberals, who began to think it fashionable to target members of the government in order to effect change.

The problem was that Miss Zasulich and her comrades had chosen to terrorize the most liberal government in Russian history—in fact, the only reason she got a jury trial at all was that Czar Alexander II had liberalized the Russian judicial system. The "struggle," which found voice in a broad range of radical leftist groups advocating the overthrow of autocracy through terror, succeeded in defeating liberal reform every bit as effectively as it opposed autocracy. The one czar the terrorists ever succeeded in killing was Alexander II, a progressive monarch widely known as the "Liberator Czar." He had received the nickname for his most momentous reform, which he had carried out twenty years before his assassination.

On March 3, 1861, two years before Abraham Lincoln announced the emancipation of the slaves, Alexander II signed the manifesto that freed Russia's serfs. While the analogy between the American republican and the Russian autocrat shouldn't be pushed far, the Liberator Czar had ended a notorious quasi-slave system in order to save his country, a vast frontier society threatened by violently opposed factions. The Russian abolitionist movement had been building to almost a fever pitch throughout the

1850s. Turgenev's *A Sportsman's Sketches,* which showed serfs as complete human beings, was the *Uncle Tom's Cabin* of Russia (if arousing less fervor). What the serfs themselves thought was an entirely different question, one that well-meaning nobles rarely seemed to understand. Young Count Leo Tolstoy found this out when he tried to free his own serfs and sell them the land they worked. His serfs not only turned down his emancipation offer but reacted bitterly to the idea. "[Their] obstinacy put me into such a rage that I could hardly control myself," wrote the future champion of Russia's common man. The novelist subsequently sent a nearly hysterical letter to Czar Alexander predicting that the serf situation was so dangerous that "we are in for a holocaust . . . only one criminal hand is needed to fan the flames of rebellion, and we shall all be consumed in the blaze."

What Tolstoy's peasants were objecting to was the idea that they might have to purchase their land, which they considered a sort of collective birthright. Unlike slaves, serfs were liable to taxation and military service, and serfs could own land, though by the mid-nineteenth century, they owned very little. Russia had no European-style tradition of hereditary landed estates owned by titled nobility; there had been no gradual development of feudal rights and responsibilities, as in the West, with peasants owing their allegiance to lords who in turn owed theirs to higher lords with eventually one lord chosen as king. In the Empire of the Russias, ever since Ivan built it, only one person had really owned anything: the czar. Everyone else, whether noble, priest, or serf, had been essentially a piece of imperial property who could be thrown to the dogs, or whipped like one, at a whim. Many were.

In the early 1790s, while the king of France was having his head cut off, Empress Catherine had applied her own novel interpretation of human emancipation to keep revolution at bay: she had granted rights exclusively to the nobility. Since Russia had started with a system where no one possessed rights except the czar, or czarina, this had been deemed great progress and the beginning of enlightened civil society in Russia. Russian nobles now basked in their new freedom from whipping and poll taxes and arbitrary arrest; no noble could be deprived of life, property, or title without trial by a jury of his peers. But with their new inalienable rights, the nobles began to treat the serfs more and more like slaves. Under Catherine, Russian nobles bought, sold, and traded serfs—using them to settle gambling debts or equip brothels—both privately and at open markets, which visiting Europeans and Russian abolitionists took to comparing to the slave markets in the Americas (though Russian nobles like Pushkin violently objected to the comparison).

By the 1830s, a Russian noble's status was measured in the number of "souls" he possessed. But as Russian nobles came to feel more and more like the elite in the rest of Europe in terms of their own status, they developed a sense of embarrassment and guilt over the outmoded system under which they held human beings in bondage to their land. Abolitionist proposals almost always included plans to sell the emancipated serfs small parcels of land, or to let them sharecrop, after they were freed. But the serfs did not acknowledge that the nobles had the right to sell them anything. A kind of organic socialism already existed among many serfs under which land was held by a rural commune, the mir, that distributed the right to work it according to a household's size and needs. (Some reformers, like Prince Kropotkin, the famous anarchist, formed their ideas of socialism by idealizing the communal relations of the serfs their family owned.) The serfs believed that when the czar gave them their freedom, the Little Father must naturally also recognize their right to the land as well—for what was freedom without land? It was a potentially devastating clash of interpretations.

Coming to the throne in the 1850s, Czar Alexander II had resolved to modernize his country from the ground up, and he not only set about freeing the serfs but also reformed a host of other institutions: the press laws (eliminating most censorship), the universities (ending most government control over professorships and academic speech), the military (dropping the twenty-five-year draft that had made Russia's armies a kind of martial serfdom), and the judiciary (replacing secret government courts with public trial by jury). The Liberator Czar also vastly improved conditions for Russia's Jews. In her *Memoirs of a Grandmother,* Pauline Wengeroff, who was born in the Pale in 1833, describes the hope she and her family felt after Alexander II "liberated sixty million peasants from bondage and the Jews from their chains." She described how the czar opened the gates of Russia's cities, welcoming a generation of Jewish youth "to quench their thirst for European education in the universities. In this brilliant period of intellectual flowering, the Jews took part in the ferment in the whole country, the rise of the fine arts, the development of the sciences."

It is important to resurrect the forgotten optimism of those days—when the original term *glasnost*, "openness," was coined—in order to understand the true horror of what followed.

During Alexander's reign, the disaffected children of the elite exploited the new freedom at the universities to join countercultural organizations that grew consistently more violent. Always the author to write the headlines, Turgenev, in his novel *Fathers and Sons*, gave the sixties generation its most popular new word—"nihilist." The turning point was the "mad summer" of 1874, when Russian students ditched school en masse, in a movement they called To the People. The students dressed like peasants, or at least their romantic impression of peasants—overalls, red shirts, and unkempt long hair for the men; loose white blouses, black skirts, and short hair for the women—and walked or hitched rides out of the cities into the countryside, carrying sacks of tools they barely knew how to use. Like the hippies a hundred years later, they planned to work the land, shoeing horses or planting crops. The students were shocked when "the People" regarded their strange appearance suspiciously, often turning them in to the local police. Stung by the peasants' rejection, the student radicals returned to the cities determined to shock the system by other means. ("The ideal of the French Revolution, draped in the barbaric vestment of Russian nihilism, inspired the upper classes of St. Petersburg's youth," as Lev would later write.) They formed the People's Will, a self-proclaimed terrorist organization.

By altering his mother's background to make her a fallen aristocrat, Lev gave her almost exactly the background of Sofya Perovskaya, the most famous People's Will terrorist. Like Berta Slutzkin, Sofya was a young woman with a great destructive rage, and the People's Will was the precursor organization to the Social Revolutionaries, to which Lev claimed his mother belonged. While Lev's mother fit the mold of women who joined the movement after 1900, however—often Jewish and poor—Sofya Perovskaya was a classic mid-nineteenth-century Russian revolutionary: a disaffected child of the ruling class, a rich kid with a grudge.

Like the fathers of so many leading revolutionaries, including Lenin himself, Sofya's father was a prominent member of society from an old and distinguished family.* In fact, he had been the governor general of St. Petersburg—the equivalent of mayor of New York City—at the time of an 1866 assassination attempt on the czar (by a member of a student radical group called Hell), which, occurring on his watch, had ended his career. Like a Bader Meinhof or Red Brigade terrorist of a hundred years later, Sofya hated the whole ruling establishment into which she'd been born, hated her father, hated the military, and even hated the talk-talk-talk style of her fellow male terrorists. She wanted to see royal blood spilled and the revolution happen as a result of her divine act of violence. The revolutionaries worried that the liberal czar's gradual reforms might leave Russians contented with the status quo. Instead, they wanted the society to coil like an overtightened spring so that when it popped, it would break.

In 1881, Sofya led a group of five terrorists who staked out the czar's carriage route when he left the Winter Palace to visit other parts of the city. They would tunnel under a street the czar was likely to cross and mine the tunnel with dynamite. When the czar's carriage passed over, they would blow up the whole street—that they would kill dozens if not hundreds of bystanders would be a benefit, since it was more likely to spark a spontaneous nihilist revolution. The terrorists rented a basement on the street, to begin digging their tunnel, and opened a cheese shop in the front room as a cover. On the appointed day, Sofya ordered her operatives into place and prepared to blow up the street.

At the last minute, the czar changed his carriage route, making months of tunneling irrelevant. Sofya coolly switched to plan B. The People's Will bomb-maker, Nikolai, had invented a new kind of hand grenade as a backup—a metal globe filled with two glass vials of nitroglycerin—and Sofya gave the signal to her accomplices to overtake the czar's carriage and

* Lenin's background was faked by Soviet historians to make it seem as though he descended only from serfs. In fact, Vladimir Ilyich Ulianov registered himself as a member of the landed nobility when he was arrested in 1900, and, as Lev would note in his 1938 biography of Lenin, there was "a slight hissing characteristic in his speech, the classical manner of speaking among Russian aristocrats." Lenin's mother's father was a baptized Jewish doctor, who also owned serfs. (After his death, Lenin's sister wrote to Stalin, describing their family's Jewish ancestry and urging Stalin to publicize it to combat anti-Semitism; instead, it was covered up until after the fall of communism.) Lenin's paternal great-grandfather had been a serf.

attack with the volatile bombs. The first accomplice got cold feet, and the second, a boy of nineteen, missed his toss, causing an explosion that disabled the back of the czar's carriage, wounded two Cossacks, and killed a baker's boy in the crowd. This might have been the end of it, but Alexander, ignoring pleas to drive on in another carriage, trudged back through the bloody snow, apparently wanting to confront his attacker and to comfort the wounded. A third assassin pushed through the crowd and tossed a bomb from so close that he could not miss; he was also killed by the blast. Alexander managed to tell his guards that he did not want to die in the street and was carried back to the Winter Palace.

On the day the People's Will struck him down, Alexander had just signed a series of legal and legislative reforms that put Russia on the road to limited constitutional government, which could have changed the course of history. Instead, within hours of signing them, he was dead. His murder hardened the new czar, Alexander III, into a fierce reactionary who reversed every one of his father's reforms within days. The People's Will issued an open letter proposing a "truce" with the government if it would only transform society promptly, according to a laundry list of demands. Instead, Alexander III hunted down its members—Sofya Perovskaya was hanged in front of a crowd of eighty thousand—and spent the rest of his days suppressing terrorists and liberals with equal zeal. In place of the reforms his father signed on the day of his murder, Alexander III signed a series of laws that gave theoretically unlimited new powers to the police and a new domestic spying agency. Russia now became a true police state.

The assassination of Alexander II killed all hope of real political reform in Russia. Terrorism and revolution thrived on the repression of Alexander III and exploded under the obtuse leadership of his son Nicholas II, the ill-fated last czar. Sofya Perovskaya's bombs succeeded in carrying out the mandate of the People's Will charter—"to bring about a political upheaval"—to a far greater extent than she would ever know, and in a sense, her cold persistence, and a few ingeniously encased vials of nitroglycerin, indirectly caused the deaths of tens of millions who would perish in the famines and gulags of the next century.

At least Lev thought so, and he would develop a lifelong obsession with this "revolt that was as demonical as it was intangible." His bestselling 1935 biography of Nicholas, the last czar, begins with the day Nicholas's grandfather was assassinated. After the murder, Lev describes the czar's family retreating into a dark, paranoid routine, where "the frail boy . . . with beautifully shaped eyes, slender limbs, and delicate, small hands—His Imperial Highness, the Grand-Duke Czarevitch Nicholai Alexandrovitch, heir to the throne of All the Russias" grows up "cut off from the entire world, living more like a prisoner than a czar." Lev shows how, even in the years before Sofya's plot finally succeeded, as they had narrowly escaped one murderous assault after another by groups such as Hell, Death, and the People's Will, "the imperial family had come to suspect a herald of death in every stranger, every guest, and every lackey. A single step outside the palace might mean catastrophe." The most revealing passages in the book, otherwise a sober biography of the ineffectual Nicholas, are when Lev examines the psychological effects on the young czarevitch of his grandfather's murder and of these years of perpetual terrorist threats to the life of his family:

> Because of the staggering event the youthful mind of Nicholas had formed the belief that the world outside the palace was full of bombs, conspiracies, and death itself. The long series of plots against his grandfather's life, through which he himself had lived half-consciously, had not passed without leaving telltale traces in the soul and mind of the child.

It is revealing because the child in question is not only young Nicholas II but also young Lev Nussimbaum. Lev would publish a biography of the last czar, in nine languages to much international acclaim, that was actually a thinly veiled self-portrait. And even as he would transform himself from a Jewish refugee into a dashing Muslim author and adventurer, he would develop his deep identification with Nicholas. As he would write to Pima in 1940, "The Czar and I, we have the same character. . . . I would always have done the same thing as he."

Though he would become famous as a sophisticated analyst of political revolutions, on some level Lev would always interpret the revolution in terms of his parents' fatal conflict—"father: an industrial magnate in the oil industry; mother: a radical revolutionary"—and its horrifying consequences. Born at a moment when years of terrorism and reaction had made his society ripe for collapse, Lev mirrored that historical collapse in his own fractured personality. The social forces that came together at the time of his birth caused him to feel at once overprotected and fearfully exposed. They left him longing for the past almost from the moment he could conceive of it.

CHAPTER 2

Wild Jews

HE OLDEST PICTURE I HAVE OF LEV is a staged portrait in full Caucasian Mountain gear: he wears a splendid white coat with a bandolier and a white fur hat twice as big as his head, cocked at an angle; one hand rests on his hip and the other casually grips a riding crop. To all appearances it was taken a year or two before the Christmas party of 1913, and in place of the supercilious expression on the Fauntleroy in the flouncy-collared suit, the lad in the mountain warrior's getup has a jaunty, almost rakish air. He cannot be more than seven years old.

Though he was dressed as a mountain warrior, Lev was never allowed to leave the house by himself. In Baku between the revolutions of 1905 and 1917, the threat of kidnapping and extortion shadowed wealthy families. To compound the fear sown by the Bolsheviks and the Socialist Revolutionaries, innumerable small terror organizations sprang up. They often claimed anarchism or some obscure variant of socialism as their principle, but their names suggested that terror itself had become the ideal: Death for Death, League of the Red Fuse, Terrorist-Individualists, Black Falcon Anarchists-Blackmailers. In the Caucasus, "expropriations" and other forms of political terror blended with local traditions of highway robbery.*

---

* Lev's biography of Stalin would show how, as a young revolutionary in the Caucasus, the future Soviet leader specialized not only in extortion but in particular subspecialties, such as blackmailing potential victims of ethnic violence: he would send a subordinate to the Armenians, say, in an area where anti-Armenian riots had broken out, and offer a family protection for the right fee. His functionaries would of course also solicit regular "dona-

(In one small city, terrorists from various organizations assassinated fifty local businessmen in April 1907 alone.) The Bolsheviks dominated the field, but sometimes radical groups broke away, such as the Social Democratic splinter group called Terror of the City of Tiflis and Its Surrounding Districts.

In his deathbed notebooks, Lev recalled the atmosphere in Baku:

> My father was a millionaire at the time, and our city, not unlike the American wild west, was teeming with bandits and robbers, who would very much have liked to avail themselves of a portion of these millions. Kidnapping of children was a routine matter at the time, for everyone except for the parents of the children affected. This state of affairs gave rise to a peculiar manner of watching over and rearing children that is unknown in Europe, even among the children of princes.

The Asadullayevs, friends of the Nussimbaums, had been targeted by kidnappers. Banine Asadullayeva recalled that her grandfather was seized twice in Baku and released each time following the payment of an enormous ransom. In Lev's case, the "peculiar manner of watching over and rearing children" meant that he was not allowed to go outside unless surrounded by an almost comic retinue of heavily armed guards and nurses:

> I see them again, the three servants who ran behind me when I was learning to ride, and the fourth servant, mounted and armed, with a melancholy, martial face, who rode behind me. Passersby would stop and smile. I thought they did so because they liked me and I smiled back. But theirs were smiles of contempt. Later I found out that people in town had told each other that my nanny, the dignified German woman Alice, ran along behind the horse and held it by the tail. . . . I see the pale boy in the magnificent Circassian coat and I, too, feel contempt for this hothouse plant sprouted from oil millions. . . .
>
> It was actually more tragic than ridiculous—a child as the prisoner of

---

tions" to the cause of world revolution, and if a merchant did not respond with the requisite cash . . . well, nobody wanted to tangle with Koba Djugashvili. In her memoir, Alice Schulte noted that Lev's father paid protection money like everyone else.

doctors and bodyguards. I was not even allowed to climb the staircase in our house, but would be lovingly carried up by a eunuch servant.

"Surrounded by teachers, servants, playthings . . . no acquaintances," Lev found himself even more isolated after a misdiagnosis of a heart condition, which made his father even more nervous about letting him out-of-doors. After his mother's death, his father hired Frau Schulte, the German governess, and she became like a foster mother to him, a role she would play with devotion, in many countries and through fantastic ups and downs, until the end. Her name was Alice, and Lev called her "Ali." Frau Schulte recalled that Lev was not allowed to attend school until he was eight, even though most of the other children in his set began going at four. Instead, he was taught by a series of tutors.

Lev's education proceeded with the help of a vast home library, left behind by his mother. "Not a single person touched the books until I learned to read," he would recall. "From then on I had the keys and read whatever I wanted. No one was allowed to disturb me. My father said that it was my inheritance and that I could do with it as I pleased." Lev remembered the world of "books, books, books," which was all he had left of his mother. "For days and days I sat motionless in my armchair and read books about Arab bards, Persian wise men, and Turkish knights and horsemen."

When Lev *was* allowed to go out, "his favorite walks took him to the Asian quarter of the town," Frau Schulte recalled, "with its mosques, its minarets, its narrow streets and low houses." He spent hours walking in the old Muslim walled city, where the narrow streets twisted and turned through courtyards with antique wells and huge doors with medieval Arabic inscriptions. All these streets led him to the rambling, half-ruined palace of the khans, which became an oasis of calm in a city that was increasingly menacing. "My love for the old, dilapidated palace grew gradually into a love for the people who were born in the palace," Lev wrote. "Around the palace of the old Khans, around the city, stretched the desert. At the age of eight I sat, immobile and lazy, on the roof of our house and wrote verses about both the desert and the palace. Both became for me the epitome of peaceful, ancient, silent grandeur." In *Ali and Nino,* Lev bases the young Muslim prince Ali on himself, making him a poetic dreamer who spends much of his time lying on the roof of his parents' house and looking out over the palace rambling along the Caspian. Like Lev, Ali is fearful of the modern city. But Lev gives his protagonist an enormous extended Muslim family, with even a large branch in Persia, where Ali and Nino retreat in the middle of the novel. For Lev the only retreat was into his own imagination:

> Things I had read, heard, and thought mixed themselves into these dreams. I saw the broad expanse of the sandy Arabian desert, I saw the horsemen, their snow-white burnooses billowing in the wind, I saw the flocks of prophets praying toward Mecca and I wanted to be one with this wall, one with this desert, one with this incomprehensible, intricate script, one with the entire Islamic Orient, which in our Baku had been so ceremoniously carried to the grave, to the victorious drumbeats of European culture.

His identification with Islam and the Orient began here, when he was not yet ten years old. "To this day I still do not know whence this feeling came, nor how to explain it. Perhaps it, too, was inherited from an unknown ancestor? I do know that throughout my entire childhood, I dreamed of the Arabic edifices every night. [And] I do know that it was the most powerful, most formative feeling of my life."

"Liova was fascinated by these things, and you see, for a Jewish boy to assume a Muslim name and convert here in Baku would not have been anything so horrendous as it seems today." The ancient lady leaned forward on her chair, spitting sour cherry pits and catching glimpses of herself on local Azeri TV. Her cigarette-scraped voice boomed like a sports announcer's in heavily accented but perfect English. Her name was Zuleika Asadullayeva, and she was Banine's cousin. Since Sara Ashurbekov, the older of the two ancient sisters with cats, had died in 1999, Zuleika was now one of the last living sources on pre-Soviet Baku's oil-boom days. She said she had vivid memories of "Liova" Nussimbaum as a boy.

"Liova was the greatest friend with my older brother," Zuleika barked, "and I can tell you why he chose the name Essad! It was the name of my older brother, whom Liova just adored. They were inseparable for a time, for Liova did not have many friends. His father did not let him go out, you see."

We sat together in a vast, Stalinist-style dignitary suite in a hotel next to the presidential palace, the view from the cement balcony sweeping past a line of rusty tankers and fishing boats out over the Caspian. Zuleika's father had once been the richest Muslim oilman in the world. ("The Ashurbekovs were not really rich!" she'd say, recalling a pecking order now more than eighty years out of date. "They were *well off*.") I had seen her family's crest on buildings all over Baku and its outskirts; her father, Shamsi Asadullayev, had been a great philanthropist. Like so many others, the Asadullayevs had fled in 1920 to escape the revolution, and Zuleika had lived in obscurity outside of Azerbaijan for almost eighty years—first in Turkey, then in the suburbs of Washington, D.C. Now, suddenly, in her nineties, the country that had driven out her family was inviting her back to be a local celebrity. She was always in town for the annual Baku "oil show," when lobbyists and representatives of the world's oil companies descended on the city. Perhaps Zuleika was a kind of good-luck charm for the modern oil prospectors, a reminder that this city had once upon a time made a lot of people very, very rich. "Let me tell you about my life, Tom, you wouldn't believe it! You'd say I was lying," she'd begin, and often interrupt herself to point to the television, where we could see her chatting with the Azeri president and various representatives of Exxon, Chevron, and Royal Dutch/Shell.

Zuleika didn't find it strange that Lev would have converted to Islam or changed his life story to adopt one closer to that of her brother. "To be a Muslim like my family were Muslims was to have a universal religion, a respect for tradition but never dogma." She told me that her father never let her or her sisters wear the veil except at funerals. "He saw it as a sign of backwardness, and there was nothing backwards about our kind of Islam. It is not like today, with these horrid fundamentalists who are as bad as the Nazis or the Bolsheviks. . . . No, no, there was never anything rigid about this identity, quite the opposite. It was Bolshevism, the anti-religion of our time, that was rigid. We were simply open to the currents of culture into which we were born."

Zuleika promised to look for her brother Asad's correspondence with Lev, and I brought it up again when I visited her at her retirement community outside Washington the next year. But she seemed so much older then, though she promised to "pull strings with the president" for me on her next trip to Baku; the promise got her blood going and she looked younger again. Then she, too, died, later that summer, after doing one last oil show. Now, to my knowledge, no children are left of the original Baku oil barons anywhere in the world, at least none who are old enough to have memories of the time and coherent enough to recall them.

Though Lev would later glorify the world of the oil millionaires, when he was growing up, he hated it and escaped whenever he could into the city of the old Orient. Walking along the massive ramparts of the khan's palace, he pretended to be a prince—a prince with no heart condition who could defend himself with his dagger, not a half-dozen bodyguards and a nursemaid. "The wall," he remembered,

> over the great arched portal ran the secret arabesque symbols of a van-ished past. Mighty, incomprehensible letters and delicate ornaments. I looked at them for hours, during which I would fall into a sort of dreamy, trancelike meditation. It was a state of true bliss that lasted for hours and hours. After I had returned home I changed back into my lazy, sickly, good-for-nothing self.

Lev became fascinated by all the small tribes of Azerbaijan. When his father permitted it, his bodyguards and Frau Schulte trucked him off into the countryside to meet these traditional "Caucasian types." Azerbaijan is a compact country, and a few hours' ride by horse in any direction from Baku could take one on a journey spanning cultures and centuries. Of course, in *Blood and Oil* and in his later book *Twelve Secrets of the Cauca-sus*, it's often hard to tell where Lev's experiences leave off and his fervid imagination begins. He would write about his encounters with the "Jassai-ans," for example, a quasi-Amazonian tribe whose men were not allowed to work and whose women carried weapons, chose their mates, and wore pants. Then there were the Khevsurs, blue-eyed, red-haired people who claimed as ancestors "the great knights from the Land of the Crescent" (that is, the Crusaders), who wore coats of chain mail and carried straight swords and small round shields with crosses painted on them. In describ-ing these encounters, Lev almost certainly embroidered actual events with things he'd read or heard. The areas within a day's journey of Baku or Tiflis were exotic, atavistic landscapes to the city dwellers, and the ways of the mountain folk gave rise to infinite speculation, gossip, and rumor.

Traveling south of Baku, Lev found the Aisors, the last descendants of the Assyrians, who seemed to him to have faces like ancient temple carvings. And traveling north, to the mountainous small kingdom of Kuba, he had his first encounter with the people who were to have a unique impact on the Jewish boy who wanted to become a Muslim warrior: the so-called Kipta, or Bani Israel—the mountain Jews of Azerbaijan.

These tribal Jews wore daggers, boots, and fur hats fairly indistinguishable from their Muslim neighbors. They were "always armed," Lev noted with approval, "and like the other clans of the country, are shepherds, nomads, warriors, at times even robbers, who plunder the caravans of the merchants on the Persian border." Indeed, it's possible the picture of little Lev as a Caucasian warrior was inspired by the Kipta.

Most Ashkenazim who migrated to Baku from the Pale found the appearance of these local Jews to be one of the most remarkable things about their new home. Flora Benenson marveled that the Azeri Jews "in their Oriental dress were barely regarded as Jews; more Cossack than the Cossacks, the men carried the sharp-edged *kingal* dagger and their women, swathed from head to foot in coarse garments decorated in filigree, were rarely seen."

Lev threw himself into studying the many theories about the origin of the mountain Jews. They were objects of fascination for historians and ethnologists down to the Nazi period, when the SS was thrown into doctrinal controversy over their fate. Some theories held that they were the lost tribe, or remnants of the Babylonian expulsion, who had spent countless centuries in Persia before migrating north to Azerbaijan; the language spoken by many mountain Jews is a medieval dialect of Persia, suggesting at least some validity to that theory. When I interviewed the Jewish headmen in Kuba, they kept pointing me toward the south when I asked the origins of their group. "Persia?" I asked excitedly through Fuad, who accompanied me. "Your ancestors journeyed here from the south?"

"Yes, yes," one headman replied, adjusting his yarmulke, which had the look of a Persian carpet.

Upon further cross-examination, Fuad explained to me that the man was saying that, many centuries ago, his ancestors had journeyed here from the south—from ten miles to the south of the spot where we were standing. "In other words," said my Interpol historian helpfully, "he has no idea where his people originally come from. These Jews have been in these hills for at least a thousand years."

At first Lev attached himself to the theory that the mountain Jews were descendants of the Babylonian exile. This would mean that they were in Azerbaijan centuries before even the majority population had migrated there from the deserts of Turkestan and Mongolia, and that they were thus among the oldest inhabitants of the country. Another theory he investigated was that the Kipta were the lost tribe that had established various kingdoms before finally migrating to Azerbaijan. Here they became independent vassals of the shah of Persia, "proud families of princes who . . . several centuries ago . . . founded a mighty kingdom, in which however only the fighting caste, the nobles and the king were Jewish. Judaism was at that time the religion of the privileged classes."

All these notions led him finally to the most interesting theory of all, a theory that would later tantalize the Nazis with the thought that perhaps these Jews were Aryan allies rather than Semitic enemies: this was the speculation that the Jews of Azerbaijan were descendants of the Khazar tribes, a confederation of Turkic-speaking warriors who underwent the only mass conversion to Judaism in postbiblical history, in the eighth and ninth centuries. Lev became enthralled with the idea that "a Jewish emperor once ruled from the steppes beyond the Volga to the shores of the Caspian Sea, and bore the title of Kagan. For two hundred years the Kagan was the most powerful man of the East; everything was subject to him, and even the Christian kings were forced to pay him tribute." Lev noticed that the Azeri Muslims regarded the native Jews as former Muslims who had become Jews "through some error; the name Kipta means: those who err."

But the Kagan's "error" had been more fundamental than that. The earliest historical record of the Khazars dates from the sixth century A.D.; by the late 700s, this Finno-Ugric tribe—related by blood to both Turks and Huns—overran the areas from the Black Sea to the Caspian and dominated all the nations of Caucasia. This gave the Khazars the distinction of being the prevailing power in the region when it faced the advance of the Islamic armies, sweeping up through Anatolia and Persia in the century after the Prophet's death. The Khazar kagan successfully repulsed the

Muslim forces, and Khazaria became the crucial buffer state between the Islamic and Christian worlds. Were it not for the Arab-Khazar wars of the seventh and eighth centuries, the Russian Slavs likely would have been converted to Islam.

The Khazars were pagans and shamanists, practicing human sacrifice, when they decided to convert en masse to Judaism. Legend has it that when the Kagan Bulan, who reigned in the 730s and '40s, studied the two great revealed religions—Islam and Christianity—he noticed that they were both derived from Judaism, which he found more sensible than either. Most historians now believe that more practical considerations prevailed: the kagan was loath to ally himself with either of two profoundly antagonistic religions when he could choose the one that seemed to be the source of both, and which he presumed the others would respect. The kagan's decision has been immortalized in Jewish literature as a noble act—but also as a butt of Jewish jokes, because of his logic in assuming that choosing Judaism would make one more respected among Christians and Muslims, when in fact it would make one equally despised by all.

Whatever the reason, in the mid-eighth century, most of the Khazar nobility and much of the common people converted to Judaism, and in the next centuries, under Bulan and his successors, synagogues and rabbinical schools were built throughout the Caucasus. During the early Middle Ages, as Jews were persecuted throughout Christian Europe, Byzantium, and in Muslim Persia, Khazaria provided sanctuary to those who made the journey to the Caucasus. But Jewish Khazaria was also tolerant and welcoming toward all outsiders, allowing Greek Christians, Muslim Iranians, and pagan Slavs to live there without converting to Judaism. The Khazars established a supreme court composed of seven members, representing every religion, and a contemporary Arab chronicler records that while the Khazars were judged according to the Torah, the other tribes were judged according to the laws of their faiths.

The hunt for "wild Jews" in the Caucasus turns up still more recent and unlikely groups of converts, such as the descendants of Russian serfs who decided to reject the divinity of Jesus Christ and worship like Jews. This group, the Subbotniks, knew nothing of rabbinical law, converted apparently spontaneously and without contact with other Jews, and worked from the Old Testament directly—becoming, among other things, expert bakers of unleavened bread, which some chose to eat all year round, just to be on the safe side. The Subbotniks were circumcised and preached that all men could become rabbis. Instead of following Jesus, these post-Enlightenment peasants believed in an occult philosopher who would soon come to earth to unlock the secrets of the universe. In 1817 the Sub-botniks petitioned the czar to accept their reverse conversion; at just this moment the czar was trying to convert all the Jews of the Pale to Christianity, and he was furious at these serfs who were converting to Judaism. According to the great historian of the Jews in Russia, Simon Dubnow,

> Entire settlements were laid waste, thousands of sectarians were banished to Siberia and the Caucasus. Many of them, unable to endure the persecution, returned to the Orthodox faith, but in many cases they did so outwardly, continuing in secret to cling to their sectarian tenets.

Of those banished, many ended up in the Caucasus, the world of noncon-formists, apostates, and people with hybrid creeds. In Azerbaijan, these colonies of "new Jews" were especially common along the southern border with Iran, but strangest of all were those Cossacks who turned Subbotnik in the nineteenth century, secretly keeping the Sabbath rules as strictly as the most Orthodox of Jews. Contemporary observers during the 1905 rev-olution describe "Jewish" Cossacks riding into the areas of the pogroms in the Ukraine and attempting to prevent them, while most Cossacks were taking part viciously.*

Lev grew increasingly fascinated with the native Jews of the Caucasus, no matter their origin. He found they were hostile to "foreign Jews," con-sidering them corrupt and inferior, and because, as Lev saw it, "the free nomad does not want to recognize the Czar's Jew, without any rights, as his brother in faith." Lev even claimed to have discovered that these Jews exchanged weapons and made secret blood oaths with their Muslim neighbors. The blood brotherhood of Caucasian Jews and Caucasian Muslims fueled Lev's emerging vision of himself as an untraceable hybrid

---

* The Subbotnik legacy would take many bizarre twists and turns over the next century and a half. In the legal arcana of Vichy France, one finds cases of Subbotnik White Rus-sian émigrés desperately fighting to prove their unique heritage to the French racial bu-reaucracy, which persisted against all argument in classifying them as Jews, confiscating their property, and preparing to deport them to Auschwitz.

from a place where "savage, brutal warriors, knights and brigands, would be indistinguishable from Galician rabbis or workers if they were dressed in the correct clothes." While never admitting publicly that he had any Jewish blood, Lev reminded his public: "Many Caucasian races confess their Jewish origin with pride and are considered honorably distinguished by it."*

Lev would come to see the Muslim and the Jew united in their struggle against the West and its mass violence. It is no coincidence that when he began to write of his adventures escaping the Bolsheviks, one of the first incidents he described was that of the insurrection of the Kipta during the Red takeover of Azerbaijan. Lev claimed that his father, expressing concern for the fate of the mountain Jews, was offered the position of governor-general of Kuba, the region where most of them lived. Of course, Lev told the story in the context of his tales of his father as the fierce Muslim aristocrat who was universally feared by the authorities and the bandits of Baku—rather than a mild-mannered businessman in no position to command a tribe of rebellious, sword-wielding mountain Jews.

"As incomprehensible as my love for the Khan's palace was my hate for that Revolution," Lev recalled.

But even with revolution bubbling beneath the surface of everyday events, whether through Koba's extortions or Krasin's more genteel fund-raising, the decade leading up to 1914 was arguably the pinnacle of the czarist Russian Empire. The violence and anarchy that had been unleashed in 1905 had finally dissipated, and despite the assassination of half his family by terrorists, the czar's maverick prime minister, Peter Stolypin, had, through pacification and reform, returned order, stability, and economic growth to Russia.† A period of decadent prosperity peaked in 1912,

---

* Lev's Caucasian fantasia of wild Jews is backed up by more sober accounts, and not only on the subject of the Khazars. In his book titled *The Exiled and the Redeemed*, Itzhak Ben-Zvi, then president of Israel, writes: "The conversion of the Khazars was by no means an isolated or even unusual incident, for Judaism was then dominant among several other Caucasian tribes, particularly the Georgians and Armenians. The entire tribe of the Komeks traces its descent to Jews to this day, and their Tattic language proves their kinship with the mountain Jews."

† Stolypin himself would be a victim of his own success, assassinated in 1911 by nihilistic terrorists out to prove that bourgeois reform of Russia was impossible.

a year when the Russian newspapers devoted vastly more space to professional wrestling than to revolutionary unrest. The cabarets of St. Petersburg hosted futurist poetry nights. Russia was booming, and Baku remained Russia's industrial powerhouse. The government of France sent the economist Edmond Terry to Russia in 1914 to assess the state of things (France being Russia's largest creditor), and M. Terry had returned a glowing verdict: "By mid-century Russia will dominate Europe." The economic gains were accompanied by an artistic flowering that produced Rachmaninoff, Diaghilev, Stravinsky, Malevich, and Mayakovski. But the apotheosis was short-lived.

In August 1914, the czarist state mobilized its vast army—the largest in the world—and swept westward, gloriously defeating Austrian forces in some of the first great battles of the First World War. But by the end of Lev's first year at the Imperial Russian Gymnasium, the Germans had turned Russia's spectacular advances into a rout reminiscent of the debacle against Japan nine years earlier. And much as in 1904–5, the stunning failure of the czar's military machine in the field led to revolts across the vast empire, from St. Petersburg to Vladivostok. Baku, much as it was always the center of prosperity, was also a center of revolutionary unrest. Frau Schulte remembered frequently withdrawing Lev from school, as his father became afraid of the deteriorating situation.

By the spring of 1918, a civil war raged not only between Whites and Reds but between Bolsheviks and every other political party. The Bolsheviks could not win a single election and, in fact, they could not gain even a simple majority. The solution, to Lenin, was clear: the Bolsheviks harnessed the mob justice, looting, and persecution of the nobles and bourgeois that had spontaneously erupted from the lowest orders of society. While the democratic coalition government of the liberals in 1917 had sought to prevent looting and terror, the Bolsheviks devised a policy of encouraging popular terror as a first step toward institutionalizing it. The Bolshevik replacement for the czar's secret police, the Cheka, recruited many of the same policemen but gave them a new license to deal with the state's enemies: whereas the czar's policemen had been restrained by some conventions of decency and morality—however often they individually violated them—the Cheka was constrained by no code except class warfare.

Obsessed with "hardness," Lenin developed a newfound respect for

Koba Djugashvili, whose *nom de revolution* had, by 1913, evolved into the more industrial Stalin, or "man of steel." Lenin brought the great robber and extortionist of the Caucasus north to serve as the Bolsheviks' point man on minority affairs. In November 1917, as the new Commissar for Nationalities, the Man of Steel drafted a sweeping "Declaration of the Rights of the Peoples of Russia"—especially addressed to the "Turks and Tartars of Transcaucasia" and the "Caucasian Mountaineers"—in order to bring the minority nationalities into the revolutionary fold. In what has to be one of the most cynically betrayed set of promises ever made, Comrade Stalin asserted the right of all the minority nationalities of the now vanished Russian Empire to "free self-determination, even to the point of separation and the formation of an independent state."

The citizens of Baku knew better than to trust their adopted black sheep, who had terrorized their city for more than a decade. That spring, the streets of Baku sprouted barricades manned by factions both for and against the Bolsheviks.

For three days, while the shooting went on in the street, Lev, his father, Frau Schulte, and others took to the cellar of their mansion, living there on canned rations, peanut bread, and caviar. Day and night, Lev heard the rattling of the machine guns from their basement hideout. It was impossible to know what was going on out in the street, who was killing whom, but Abraham Nussimbaum thought it prudent to refrain from leaving the cellar. The grown-ups sat in one corner, discussing what they would do next, where they could go with their Russian passports, and what they would take with them. Lev sat in the other corner, watching and listening to the sounds from the street. There was a window on the upper right on the cellar wall, but no one dared go near it while the machine-gun rattling was near.

To the twelve-year-old daydreamer of Turkish warriors and Persian princesses, the days hiding in the cellar seemed a game. Lev later recalled being of two minds—one frightened and depressed, the other abstracted and dispassionately observant. On the third day, the guns stopped, and he pressed his face against the window. From here he could survey the entire street. Their block of elegant mansions was in ruins: broken coaches, collapsed lampposts, scattered clothes, and dead camels.

Lev made out human corpses lying on the road, but they did not affect him much at first, because they looked so much like rag dolls or piles of straw. Then, suddenly, the window yielded an image that would stay with him throughout his life:

> Local carts were squeaking through the empty streets. One, two, three, an entire caravan loaded with corpses. People. Corpses with severed limbs, dripping with blood, mangled by the savage hate of the enemies. The hands and feet of some of them hung over the sides of the carts. The movements of the carts made the limbs jiggle. It seemed as though they were still alive, with noses and eyes gouged out. A mountain of corpses, men, women, children. One cart after another. Even the faces of the cart drivers gazed out like those of corpses. . . . Then the caravan had passed. The rattling of the machine guns increased again. I went back into the cellar.

Whenever I consider Lev and his father hiding in the basement of the mansion, I think of the fate of another oil baron who did not go into his cellar. On our tour of Baku's grand houses, Fuad had shown me a building nicknamed the Wedding Palace. Its owner was one of the few oil millionaires who did not flee, and the story of his mansion seemed to capture perfectly the violent end of capitalist Baku once the 1917 revolution spread south.

The Wedding Palace was built by a Muslim oil baron named Mukhtarov, of humble peasant origins. After he got rich, in the early 1900s, he took to building mosques all over southern Russia. He also became a traveler and a lover of foreign languages. On one of his mosque-building expeditions, on the Terek River, he met and fell in love with a mountain girl of noble birth. The girl's family would not have him, because he was not aristocratic enough, but when he built a magnificent mosque in honor of their daughter, they were impressed by his sincerity and relented.

The couple went on a wedding tour of Europe, speaking newly learned French and English with each other, and while in France, the bride saw the house she wanted to live in: it was a Gothic cathedral. Mukhtarov promptly commissioned a Polish architect (in prewar Europe, many of the best architects were Polish), and, arriving in Baku a few weeks later, the architect proceeded to build a replica of the cathedral that Mukhtarov's new wife had seen in France. The structure was erected in 1911–12 and became the most magnificent of the many flamboyant mansions in Baku. But just as construction was being completed, one of the builders fell to his death while installing a life-size statue of an Arthurian knight on the roof. The builder's wife committed suicide from grief, which caused the young bride for whom the Wedding Palace was built to decide that it was too depressing to live there. With yet more funds from her husband, she turned her just-completed home into a boarding school for orphaned girls. So it was that, in a miniature Gothic cathedral built on a whim, a generation of orphaned Muslim girls received a Western education, many of them going on to study in St. Petersburg and Moscow.

In 1920, as the Red Army entered Baku, the school was abandoned. But Mukhtarov, the proud man who had journeyed from peasant farmer to philanthropist, refused to leave. He waited in the lobby, pistol in his waistcoat, for the coming of the Bolshevik "boors." When a pair of Red Army soldiers crashed into the front hall on horseback, breaking the marble stairs, smashing statues, and calling on him to evacuate the premises in the name of the People, Mukhtarov took aim and shot both of them dead. He then turned the pistol on himself and blew a hole in his chest.

Abraham Nussimbaum, by contrast, was bribing commissars, making final deals, and preparing to flee the country by boat, east across the Caspian, with only his sheltered son in tow and his cash, jewels, and oil deeds sewn into the pant legs of his fashionable European suit.

CHAPTER 3

The Way East

L EV'S ORIENT HAD NEVER BEEN ONLY A THING of the imagination. He had grown up around descendants of the medieval Crusader knights and the mountain Jews with their jewel-encrusted daggers, and he had an ear for stories. The 1917 revolution at first drove away his thoughts of exotic customs and glorious adventures, but it was now about to drive him further into the world of the Wild East than he had ever imagined—to the red sands of Turkestan and the mud fortresses of Persia. The books Lev later wrote based on these travels would put him on the literary map, though they would betray a bias for colorful anecdote over hard fact.

In tracking Lev's much-obscured—often deliberately obscured—path, I started with skepticism about his nonfiction, which he wrote as Essad Bey and which often carries the air of the larger-than-life history writing that was popular in the era. "Truth can only be obtained in a police blotter," he wrote at the beginning of his deathbed memoir. But years of collecting every shred of evidence I could of his existence revealed that the most unlikely elements of his life and his stories often turned out to be true—if not taken straight from his own amazing experiences, then borrowed from the experiences of family members or friends or cribbed from the pages of some Turkish journal or German anthropological text. Lev's simplest statements about himself—name, race, nationality—are the ones that can least be trusted. As I found when going through fascist police sur-

veillance files of the 1930s, the very *last* place the truth about Lev Nussimbaum could be found would be in a police blotter.

For the next phase of his life—the whirlwind journey with his father
from occupied Baku across Turkestan, south to Persia, then back across
Azerbaijan into Georgia—virtually no outside sources exist. I have heard
so much nonsense from so many people in contemporary Azerbaijan, all
duly recorded, cross-referenced, translated, and discarded, that I concluded that searching for Lev in this part of the world, at this date, was
likely to produce far more myth than could be found in his own works.
Too many prerevolutionary records have been either lost or destroyed, and
the people of the Caucasus excel in too many things above record-keeping.
Lev grew up in a tradition of hoary eyewitness accounts and miraculous
sightings—he was from the land, after all, where the ground burst spontaneously into flame.

The story of his escape across Central Asia, Persia, and the Caucasus,
which is told in *Blood and Oil,* almost certainly contains Zelig-like ma-
neuverings of space and time to place him at the scene of some of the most
dramatic confrontations of the Russian Civil War, like the siege of the
Georgian city of Ganja—where thirteen-year-old Lev supposedly manned
a machine gun and was captured by the Cheka. By contrast, the account
of that week, recorded by the faithful Alice, implies that Lev was nowhere
near Ganja at the time and was harassed by the Cheka because they mistook his school uniform for some sort of military garb.

The very fact that Lev, in *Blood and Oil,* casts himself in the role of
young Essad Bey, traveling with his father the Muslim aristocrat, alerts us
already to its fantastic elements. At heart, the journey functioned as a
myth, even if most of the details were true: it was Lev's original Orientalist myth of himself—the courtly Muslim prince, confronting the revolutionary destroyers of all tradition with a bravery and sophistication that
are, to say the least, impressive for a twelve- or thirteen-year-old boy. And
in the end, I concluded that Lev probably did witness most of the events
he describes, including some of the most unlikely-sounding (if not the last
stand at Ganja with the machine gun). Lev's autobiographies, along with
his letters and deathbed notebooks, form the only extensive surviving
record of these months, but I compared them with press reports, other
memoirs from the period, and historians' accounts, and the story I present
of the journey is what struck me as the truest part of what he later wrote.

As Lev tells it, a cousin had joined the new Baku Soviet, and one night he came with big news. Moscow felt the Baku commissars were losing their grip on power, and Lenin had suggested a public liquidation of capitalist bloodsuckers to help build support. Abraham was on a list of "ten former bloodsuckers" to be arrested and shot. It was time to leave Baku.

Lev and his father decided to sail east across the Caspian to Turkestan, or Muslim Central Asia, a vast stretch of Russian-controlled territory where a handful of potentates and tribes were holding out against the Communist forces. Most Turkmen were still horse-riding nomads, though ancient cities like Kizel-Su, on the Caspian, and Samarkand and Bukhara in the interior, were connected by railway, and settlements had grown up as Russia expanded in the region in the previous century. Abraham told his son that they had relatives in Turkestan who might be welcoming, should they manage to find them, and he also owned some properties in Kizel-Su, where they were headed—properties cared for by someone he had never met, but at least they would have a place to stay.*

In the middle of the night, Lev and his father went down to the docks to hire a boat and, as luck would have it, found one piloted by a seaman who had worked on one of Abraham's oil tankers. He agreed to help them escape.

But into what? Though the Germans were about to lose the First World War, huge sections of the crumbling Russian Empire were still under the occupation of nearly a million of the kaiser's troops: the Bolsheviks had given them away as part of their peace at any cost with the Central Powers. Withdrawal from the Great War had freed up Russians to fight against one another, and a civil war raged among every conceivable faction, broadly divided into Reds against Whites. The Reds stood for radical revolution and were led by the Bolsheviks. The difficulty of explaining just what the Whites stood for accounts in large part for their failure as a movement. They stood for everyone else—from moderate socialists to liberal democrats to conservative monarchists to renegade Muslim khans.

---

* In *Blood and Oil,* Lev makes much of his father's supposedly elaborate family connections in Turkestan and Persia, even claiming that the family's "seat" was in Samarkand— clearly a lie, since Abraham Nussimbaum actually came from Tiflis. This was part of Lev's lifelong strategy of planting his roots farther and farther east, deeper in the world of Islam and the desert. Of course, it's also possible that Abraham *did* have such cousins: Russian Jews who had, like him, managed to move outside the Pale and establish themselves.

In Turkestan, Russia's southeastern desert frontier, the forces of the Reds and the Whites were joined by the great armies of Germany, Britain, and the Ottoman Empire, converging on the region from every direction for nearly every sort of reason: the Germans were coming to get cotton for artillery shells, the Turks were coming to realize their quasi-mystical dream of a pan-Turkic empire stretching from the Bosporus to Bukhara, and the British were coming to protect India from the Turks and the Germans. This barren territory represented the farthest extent of the czar's Muslim conquests—the heartland of the Russian Islamic world—and Russia had imposed its rule there far less than in the Caucasus or the Crimea. European influences in its wastes, indeed modern influences of any kind, were rare. Turkestan consisted of 1.5 million arid square miles—roughly half the size of the continental United States. Its deserts and bare mountainsides stretched east to the Himalayas and Afghanistan. The Russians began colonizing the region during the nineteenth century, when the czarist armies were absorbing territory at a rate of fifty square miles a day. Nikolai Danilevski, a contemporary of Dostoyevsky's and the founder of "scientific Slavophilism," the theory of the sacred Russian role in history, emphasized the importance of Turkestan above all other objects of czarist conquest: "What *role* on the universal stage does Europe assign us, her adopted children? To be the bearers and propagators of her civilization in the East—that is the lofty mission allotted to us. . . . Eastward-ho!"

But the distances in Turkestan were judged too enormous and the people too wild for effective colonial control. Instead, the Russians had settled on a series of expedient deals and treaties with the local khans, whose kingdoms dated back to the days of Genghis Khan and the Golden Horde. The khans were only too happy to bargain away the absolute sovereignty of their "nations" in exchange for Russian money, industrial machinery, and weapons. In addition to the material payoff, they were appointed generals and field marshals in the Russian Army, presumably to make them more enthusiastic about their new role as cotton masters of Central Asia. With their mountainous wool hats, Turkmen warriors became fixtures of czarist military parades, riding alongside the Cossacks.*

---

* The last gasps of the Great Game between Russia and Britain for control of Central Asia and the trade routes to the Far East happened in Turkestan. As they were completing their

Many of the natives of Turkestan resented their recent Russian "conquerors," and after the revolution, some tribes rebelled wherever they could. But the ethnic Russian colonists were more sympathetic to the Bolsheviks, and in 1917 they set up their own soviet in Samarkand, declaring the people of Turkestan officially liberated. The Turkmen did not want to be liberated by Russian radicals, and they fought the Bolsheviks as furiously as they fought any other infidel outsiders. The leading Communist newspaper, *Izvestia*, complained that while throughout the Russian Empire "the sun of liberty has risen . . . only Turkestan remains aloof from all these changes." It would be a formidable challenge for the Bolshevik government in Moscow to assert control over Turkestan, and one that they were not yet up to by the time Lev and his father arrived at the port of Kizel-Su, in the late summer of 1918.*

At the entrance of the once great desert empire of Tamurlane, whose minarets were said to have been built of human skeletons, Kizel-Su was known as "the city of the red water," for the river of the same name that runs near it—a river so dirty that only camel drivers were said to bathe in it. Surrounded by high sunbaked stones on three sides, the city looked like a medieval fort to Lev, and its streets were so bare and unshaded that they would burn anyone who went barefoot. An American journalist who stopped there wrote in 1918 that Kizel-Su "had the distinction of being the worst hole I know of to be detained in."

The first officials Lev and Abraham met were less than friendly, not recognizing the refugees from Baku as anyone worthy of notice. In the clamor of the revolution, the city and surrounding desert had proclaimed itself the Socialist Republic of the Red Water; though it was not linked to the Bolsheviks, a certain disdain for authority was already apparent in the new order, and everyone in town seemed to be appointed some sort of minister or other. But when Abraham inquired after his properties, he and Lev were suddenly treated with an about-face in local manners. It turned

---

pacification of the Caucasus in the 1850s and '60s, the Russians turned their sights across the Caspian to the conquest of the Muslim khanates of Kokand, Bukhara, and Khiva. These feudal kingdoms were sandwiched exactly between British-controlled India, Afghanistan, and Persia, hence strategically perfect playing pieces in the Game.

* Kizel-Su is now Turkmenbashi, in the post-Soviet state of Turkmenistan.

out that their property manager held, "as a secondary occupation," the position of minister of Foreign Affairs of the Republic, and hence was not an unimportant man in local political circles. The ad hoc citizens' committee of Kizel-Su promptly arranged a heroes' welcome for Lev and his father. In *Blood and Oil*, Lev drew a comic scene of the "parade" of dignitaries that escorted them through the town. The minister of Foreign Affairs led the way—though as he embraced Lev with brotherly affection, Lev felt a sharp pain on his arm. Looking down to examine it, he was sure he had been bitten by a bedbug that had emerged from this illustrious personage's sleeve.

The residence that the minister offered, the best of their properties, presented the same problem. "I could not become accustomed to life among bugs and unwashed women," Lev remembered. The fabled "East" did not seem so appealing in its unvarnished Central Asian form, and he begged his father to find them a new place to stay. So the Nussimbaums moved into the only lodging that had a European toilet and a level of cleanliness not offensive to gentlemen from the other side of the Caspian: the Kizel-Su motion-picture cinema.

Looking back on the experience later, Lev recalled that in the next few years, he would sleep on billiard tables, under the belly of a Karabakhian donkey, on the humps of a camel, and in a synagogue, yet the cinema in Kizel-Su was the most beautiful and most peculiar accommodation he would ever experience. The cinema, "perhaps the only one between the Caspian Sea and the grave of Timur," Lev recalled, didn't present many movies anyway, and the government discontinued them in honor of the foreign guests. This ultimately caused problems, as "the people demanded their picture-plays" back. So the city's governing body "asked for permission to allow this source of public amusement to be used from time to time." Given the troubled nature of the times, Lev recalled, "we bowed to the will of the people."

Life in the cinema was monotonous, despite the occasional picture. The locals occupied themselves largely with the diversion of buck fights, whereby fat rams butted each other to the amusement and speculation of the crowds in their long multicolored robes and white turbans. These basically cowardly animals were not as obliging as cocks or bulls and had to be goaded into a fight with red-hot pokers and sharp iron spikes; thus provoked, they would attack each other, but then they would quickly retreat, their heads bleeding, and try to escape from the "field of honor" by slipping out through the crowd. Somehow a winning ram was declared and the victor decorated with flowers.

Lev spent much of his time chatting with the sole European in the city, an old German named Baron von Osten-Sacken, who had spent the past thirty years of his retirement, along with his German wife, in Kizel-Su. Since he did not associate with "colored" people of any kind, a group that included the entire local population, the baron seldom left his house. He was happy to talk to the young refugee from Baku. Indeed, Lev would say that these were some of his earliest discussions about Germany. They rarely spoke about their present situation, Turkestan, or Muslim Russia at all; the baron wanted to chat only about his fatherland, though, like many of the most adamant German nationalists, he had not been born there himself.

Lev also made the acquaintance, through his father, of the police chief of Kizel-Su, a Georgian named Prince Alania, who in the wake of the czar's fall had turned himself into a radical minority socialist, allied with the forces who controlled the Republic of the Red Water. The prince introduced Lev to the various law-enforcement problems of the area. The economic situation in Kizel-Su was grim—the paper money that fueled domestic commerce was printed on only one side, to save ink (Lev recalled writing satiric verses on the flip side of the nearly worthless bills to pass the time), and the government was constantly dealing with troubles posed by forgeries. One particularly good batch of banknotes came in from Persia, confounding the local minister of finance. He dealt with it by issuing a statement that summed up the sorry state of things: he instructed people to dampen any suspected banknote with water. If it bled, it was genuine; if not, a forgery.

During their time there, Kizel-Su became more and more cut off. Since Azerbaijan was now in the hands of the Bolsheviks, port traffic had almost ceased. Abraham had a small interest in the local alabaster quarries, along with his rental properties, but there was virtually no trade, since the ports of export in Russia and Baku were closed. Only tiny Turkoman boats now sailed to Persia, and the government survived largely on the income of taxing nomadic clans who did business exchanging furs with Persian merchants for ammunition and bread. The cities in the interior belonged to the hostile governments of competing clans, or else to the Bolsheviks.

The cafés and bazaars filled with news about the distant Great War. Lev heard of fantastic new weapons, like a massive gun the Germans had built for the Turks, which, it was said, would fire a shell from Constantinople to Baku. In fact, there was no gun, but such Munchausen-esque fantasies were hardly stranger than the realities all around them. Two summers before, the czar had commanded the largest army in the world in battle. Now he had been murdered by his own subjects, and the great Russian Army had blown to the winds.

Lev heard that the new Soviet government, in an all-out effort to appease the Turks, was promising that Soviet Russia would introduce the Islamic prohibition on alcohol into Russia along with the harem. In those wild days of 1918, anything was possible. An element of genuine confusion existed within the Bolshevik party about its proper attitude toward the former subject peoples of the czar. Would Soviet Russia become a new incarnation of the Russian Empire? Or would it, according to its own principles, oppose imperialism in all its forms and set Russia's former subjects on their own course of socialism? Stalin saw no need ever to liberate the subject peoples. Lenin disagreed—in theory. But Lenin argued that the Muslim peoples could achieve independence only after they had developed an industrial proletariat, and since territories like Turkestan were sparsely populated badlands whose inhabitants were either nomadic hunters or primitive farmers, the Muslims were unlikely to be on the Bolshevik roster for independence for at least another century.

Besides, the Bolsheviks operated secure in the knowledge that treaties were only scraps of paper, and as their triumph over more popular parties in the revolution had shown, murder overwrote all promissory notes. But as fate would have it, the city of Kizel-Su became famous for a cold-blooded act of violence committed against the Bolsheviks, not by them— and Lev would gain some fame himself when he wrote about it in *Blood and Oil*. This was the murder of the twenty-six Baku commissars, who had led the first Baku Soviet and been responsible for the brutal repression that Abraham and Lev had fled—until a sudden reversal of fortune sent the commissars on the very same escape route.

A group that included Russians, Armenians, Georgians, and one Muslim Azeri, the commissars had been members of Stalin's loyal group of followers who terrorized the Caucasus in 1917–18; at least two of them were personal friends of Lenin's. But when Baku came under siege by German and Turkish troops as well as Azeri nationalist forces, they decided to "make themselves secure for the sake of the world proletariat," as Lev put it, and hightailed it out of the Azeri capital. The escaping commissars followed the same course Lev and his father had taken just weeks before, but they commandeered a considerably larger vessel—an oil tanker—for the purpose. (They could choose no other route than by sea, since the nationalist forces surrounded Baku on all sides by land.) Once safely under way, the commissars wanted to go north, to where the Caspian meets the mouth of the Volga, Soviet Russian territory. But the seamen who took them aboard refused to sail to Russia, fearing the chaos of the revolution. This left only the route south to Persia, which was occupied by the British, therefore not an option, or the route due east to Turkestan and the port of Kizel-Su. "The entire dialectic of Marxism was now employed to persuade the sailors at least to choose the harbor of Kizel-Su," Lev wrote, "if they absolutely refused to go to Russia."

Lev said he was standing with Prince Alania on the shore as the oil transport steamer arrived in port. It was a welcome, and rare, sight in those days to see the familiar hull of an oil tanker. At first everyone assumed there were only refugees aboard. But as the ship unloaded the men, disguised as sailors who had sustained injuries fighting the Bolsheviks, the prince turned to Lev with delighted recognition and a smirk: "Do you know who is on that steamer? The Communist government of Azerbaijan!"

Upon orders from Alania, the police promptly replaced the commissars' bandages with shackles. (Alternate accounts tell a different story: for one thing, the arresting officer is said to be a Cossack officer rather than a Georgian prince turned radical socialist revolutionary.) Lev said he followed the captives down to the small makeshift prison erected in back of the courthouse—since the regular prison was full—and though he was not allowed inside, from where he stood, he could hear the thudding of rifle butts and screaming and shouting as the interrogation began. He was later told that the government had decided to transport the commissars to the interior of the country, where they would be handed over to the English or the White Russians, whichever opportunity arose first. Most other accounts describe the commissars being locked up in tiny cells, in appalling conditions, for several days, until the radical socialist faction government of Kizel-Su received word from another radical socialist faction government in another city, slightly higher in the pecking order, as to how to deal with their important Bolshevik prisoners.

Lev claimed that he saw the condemned men when they were led out of the prison at night, handcuffed, surrounded by guards. "Most of them were pale but calm," he wrote. "They had been rulers long enough to know what such a nocturnal deportation meant in the Orient. Only one—he was a relative of mine—did not want to go; the soldiers had to drag him by the collar like a steer to the butcher. Every three steps he stood still, and said monotonously, distractedly, dully: 'I won't—I won't— I won't.' I can still hear those soft words today, their tortured, no longer human, almost beastlike sound." Lev found out only later what had happened: the twenty-six had to dig their own graves in sand and were then shot one after another and thrown in.* That night he wandered the streets, unable to go back to the cinema. He met the police chief the next morning, but the prince did not tell him about the execution; he talked about his girlfriend in Persia and how he hoped to bring her to Turkestan soon so they could be married.

Lev put his eyewitness account in *Blood and Oil* when he was twenty-three, recalling events that happened when he was twelve, so there is good reason to be skeptical of the details. What does one make, for example, of the offhand remark that one of the Bolsheviks' most famous martyrs was one of Lev's relatives? One doubts it should be taken seriously, and yet, given his mother's activities, the man *could* have been a family member, certainly a family friend. Notably, the scene of the condemned men leaving the prison appears over and over again in Lev's writings, and is there again in his deathbed notebooks, where he remembers the "bleating" of the man he recognized as he was led off.

The Soviets considered the twenty-six Baku commissars honored martyrs, and Lev's report provoked controversy when it was published in *Blood and Oil.* (Lev's account may have been the first thing to bring him to the attention of Trotsky, who was obsessed with tracking down the murderers of the commissars and wrote a book about it.) The official Soviet version of events put the blame mostly on a British secret agent

---

* Some accounts say that the commissars were hacked or bayoneted to death. There is no argument about the fact that they were killed in cold blood.

named Reginald Teague-Jones, even though documents showed him to have been two hundred miles away on the night of the killing. The Soviet world network put out an assassination order on Teague-Jones, and the Englishman spent the rest of his life under an assumed name, Ronald Sinclair. It was only when he died, in 1988, that *The Times* of London revealed his true identity and told the story of how he had been hiding for seventy years because he was blamed for the murder of the commissars.

The facts of Lev's account were debated by all those except the parties who had been directly involved, for the prince, the sailors, and indeed nearly everyone involved with the commissars' murder were killed in the chaotic first years of the revolution, or, like Teague-Jones, disappeared from view. The British spy's own diaries, published posthumously in 1991, reinforce much of Lev's account—though Teague-Jones fixes the blame for the killing on the rival committee of socialist revolutionaries, who, he makes clear, were receiving logistical support from the British Army at the time. This British aid to their leftist enemies infuriated the Bolsheviks, and it is likely one of the reasons why Trotsky fixated on Teague-Jones as the man who supposedly gave the order to have the twenty-six executed. For his part, Teague-Jones, in the diaries he kept secret for seventy years, matter-of-factly recalled being informed by his socialist contact, several days after the commissars came to Kizel-Su, "that the majority of the prisoners had been quietly shot."

By October, Lev and Abraham appear to have continued on their journey away from the Bolsheviks and the other radical socialists, due east into the desert. They were heading for the remaining stronghold of the Old East: the capital city of Bukhara, where the emir still held fast. One of the last preservers of the old order with any power left, he could be counted on to welcome them. Lev and his father normally would have traveled by train, but with the revolution, the railways had become a dangerous means of travel. The railway workers were among the first to join the Bolsheviks— along with the machine-gun corps—and the so-called Railway Cheka was more ferocious than the secret police elsewhere. Many contemporary accounts describe the railway bureaucracy itself as a huge, mechanized tyranny, aware that it controlled what was now the most precious commodity: movement. In 1918 in the Russian Empire, the ability to escape, and thus to search for work and food, was in very short supply. Then there was the problem of fuel. Oil shortages caused by the disruptions in Baku meant that the railways had reverted to wood-burning engines. But the lack of wood in the desert led to the burning of other substances, and at the time that Lev and his father were in Turkestan, the favorite substitute was dried, salted fish. It turned out to be decent fuel for the trains, and the rock-hard stuff was confiscated in great quantities to fuel the traffic away from the coast. Some locals even claimed to see roasted fish occasionally pop out of the chimneys of moving locomotives, and starving people rushing out to grab it for their meals.

Abraham Nussimbaum wanted no part of the Railway Cheka, so they instead took the tried-and-true route—camel caravan. "The wild tribes of the desert, the sandstorms, the seasickness on the humps of camels, the great thirst, were all to be preferred to the railroad," Lev recalled. A hired band of armed nomads would get them around many treacherous checkpoints between Kizel-Su and Bukhara. So they set out into the deserts of Turkestan. They covered most of the trip on camels and a donkey, avoiding cities whenever possible, as these were often under the influence of the Bolsheviks. In the wilderness, his father's reputation sometimes helped them; at other times, the general hospitality of the desert people toward strangers was enough.

They traveled in a fifty-camel caravan with a group of Russian families who, Lev noted disdainfully, "till then, except for the desert scenery of the imperial opera, had seen nothing of the Orient." He developed a great respect, however, for the caravan leader, whom he called the *chalwadar.* Lev would later assure his European readers that this man felt safer in the desert than the European did within his four walls. "To get lost in the desert, to lose the way once entered upon, is impossible . . . for infinite distances he feels a contact between himself and all the oases and clans." Lev noted how the *chalwadar* discerned recent events and the position of the caravan by the color of the sands, and how he seemed to smell water at enormous distances, like an animal. He also managed to avoid the dreaded sandpits, where the desert sand was too thin to bear the weight of the camels and caravans could sink into the depths. Lev remembered the gruesome sight of a dog drowning in such a pit. He watched as the *chalwadar* wrapped a few fresh loaves of bread in damp rags and buried them deep in the sand; a stake would mark the spot for some unknown caravan that might come by, lacking food. Lev's caravan continually came across such stakes, and sometimes the *chalwadar* dug them out and replaced the hidden provisions with fresh ones. He also cut signs into the loaves in what Lev took to be a kind of secret code, passing on news of the desert. "No doubt [this is] the most curious newspaper of mankind," he observed. Lev found himself chatting on about "all sorts of philosophic topics, religion, war, beautiful girls, even literature," in hopes of drawing out the *chalwadar* about his method of guiding, but all his efforts ended in defeat. "I have rarely seen such inaccessibility and reticence," he wrote. "It seemed as though he really possessed few human characteristics, and vegetated in dull omniscience, his whole attention centered on the desert."

At first Lev swooned to see his Arabesque dreams becoming reality. But before long the monotony of the desert set in, and he often cried for it to end and for some new adventure to pull them aside from their straight, unvarying course. Though his flight across Turkestan would later seem romantic from an apartment in Berlin, Vienna, or New York, much of the actual time Lev spent traveling with the caravan was a torment. Aside from getting the cold shoulder from the *chalwadar,* the young scion of Baku was continually shocked by the coarseness of desert life, the way the nomads, lacking water, cleaned themselves by simply rubbing down their hands and face in the sand. How tired one became of the desert's "tediousness, melancholy, and suffering, derived from hunger, work, and disease." He was awed, however, by the powers of the hakims, whose talents seemed to him astonishing, almost supernatural. The hakim was a doctor in the medieval sense; rather than learning the traditional medical sciences, he studied theology, literary history, logic, and grammar. "Often he is a member of a pious society of dervishes, at times a student of the Koran and a poet." Lev witnessed cures of various local diseases—for example, one called *pindinka,* a horrible skin disease that would begin with one red spot and then spread to engulf the face in a flaming red mask of scabs. If a hakim treated the first spot, rubbing a native salve on it, the disease could be controlled. The spot remained but did not grow, and gradually disappeared, leaving only a scar. If it went untreated, however, the disease could spread to the conjunctiva and cause the loss of an eye. "I had an insane fear of *pindinka,* but luckily was spared its suffering," remarked Lev—eerily foreshadowing his own illness, still years away, that would begin with a dark spot on his foot.

The caravan ride was often precarious, as the strength of the bandit bands in the desert increased at a corresponding rate with that of their competitors, the various Bolshevik factions. Turkestan would eventually be split, with much of the country declaring an independent nationalist Muslim government while the rest went Bolshevik. Eventually the Bolsheviks won, but the nomads, based in the hills and dunes, remained indomitable for years.

From his palace in Bukhara, an ancient city of pinnacles and domes, the emir survived by ruthlessness. Some accounts say that he had recently revived the medieval practice of taking prisoners to the top of the Kalyan Minaret, the infamous "Tower of Death," from which they were pushed. As a descendant of the Tatar khans who had ruled Russia for centuries, the emir tended to believe that he, not the czar, was the legitimate sovereign of all Russians. However, he wore a general's uniform in the imperial army and raised no barrier to Russian immigration and cultural imperialism in Bukhara. He could not, for the emir was up to his ears in debt to imperial Russia. Bukhara depended on St. Petersburg for economic and military aid the way a modern Third World nation depends on Washington.

All this changed with the revolution. "When the Czar was dethroned by the revolution, the Emir became thoughtful," wrote Lev. "He took off his general's uniform and called the royal council together. When the dignitaries had gathered, the Emir greeted them and ordered them to murder all the Russians in his country within twenty-four hours. As an argument in favor of his sentence, he explained that Russia was now weakened and that there would scarcely ever be such an opportunity again."

The chilling suggestion to "kill all these foreigners who talk and pray differently from us" is at the heart of Lev's small masterpiece, *Ali and Nino.* It is why Lev came to hate revolution on principle: it was too easy a pretext for mass murder. The Russian inhabitants of the capital were confined to their quarter of the city and guarded by heavily armed soldiers. For three days, they were trapped while some in the government argued for their safety. According to one version of the event, the minister of finance knelt before the emir's throne and refused to get up unless the Russians were spared; Lev would hear the minister himself proudly tell the story years later, when they were both refugees in Berlin. The Bolsheviks would show no such restraint, and "with the help of a few hundred Soviet soldiers, Bucharia was made a free, independent, sovereign republic," Lev would remark with cool irony. "The Emir fled to Afghanistan; the new and old princes, the ministers . . . the courtiers, governors each ran where he could."

Lev would come to meet some of these princes and ministers in the 1920s in Berlin, where the remnants of Bukharan court society joined the thousands of White Russian aristocrats who made the German city their new capital. By then Lev Nussimbaum would be a Muslim like them and, under the name Essad Bey, would have become the celebrated chronicler of their splendors, corruptions, and petty falls. Given the indignity of their exit from history's stage and the usual resentments of emigrant society, it is no surprise that these exiles all came to mistrust this young man, whom they first met as a Jewish refugee in a camel caravan.

As the emir fled to Afghanistan, a ragtag group of nationalist Muslim and White Russian forces scattered across the deserts, fighting with the Bolsheviks and each other. The only thing containing the struggle was the presence of the British Indian Army, and it was soon to depart. That perpetual voice in the wilderness Winston Churchill had called for England to stay to defend the old Muslim kingdoms of Central Asia, no matter how venal or obscure they might be. But the British military machine could not move from fighting the kaiser to fighting Bolshevism overnight, and the project was deemed too vast to be risked. A lieutenant colonel in the British-Indian Army, just returned from Turkestan in 1920, published a heart-rending description of what the country's abandonment meant to the Muslims of Asia. As the lieutenant colonel and his men were preparing to withdraw, a deputation from Bukhara came down to beg him to stay:

> "Leave us a thousand men, only a thousand men, and we can hold the enemy." It was pointed out that our soldiers were due for rest and relief; and he continued, "Leave us 500 then: surely the great British Empire can spare 500 men to protect us." "It is impossible to leave 500 men" was the reply. He then made his final and most touching appeal: "Leave us at least one Englishman here; then my people will know that Great Britain will never abandon them, and we will continue to oppose the Bolshevists." On being told that even this was impossible, and that orders had been received for the withdrawal of all troops, the chief made a despairing gesture and said, "In that case there remains no hope for us in Turkomans. We shall not be able to hold out by ourselves. . . ."

Now that Russia is gone up in flames, Great Britain would have been in a position to influence not only all Persia, but also Turkestan, probably without employing a single soldier, had she continued to back the Turkomans during those critical days. We should have gained the lasting friendship of 2,000,000 sturdy Mohammedans (against whom we have never fought, and whom we should never need to fight). . . . This opportunity is lost to us.

To add to the confusion, forty thousand half-starving German and Austrian prisoners of war, captured by the czar's armies and shipped to camps in Bukhara to keep them out of trouble, were now set free by the Bolsheviks. The POWs, marooned in the middle of Muslim Central Asia with no way to return home, were a volatile force. Some of them married local women and settled down to work at their pre-military trades, building houses and the like, but many found it easier to practice their newer skills, becoming mercenaries and executioners for hire. The Bolsheviks paid them well, though sometimes in never-to-be-fulfilled promises. (The Austrian POWs who helped the Reds take Bukhara's capital were executed en masse when they tried to collect their payment.)

Bukhara was clearly no longer a place for Abraham and Lev. The capital city resounded with machine-gun fire. Eyewitnesses reported seeing men with white shirts stained a perpetual grimy red, like butchers' smocks, wandering through the streets. If the violence was not bad enough, the arrival of the influenza epidemic, more deadly because of all the human chaos, threatened to take those who were not machine-gunned or hacked to pieces first. The years 1918–20 represented almost as close to a global apocalypse as the world had ever come. Most of the important monarchies of Europe and Asia, having provided stability for hundreds of years, suddenly ceased to exist. The khanates of Central Asia were distant backwaters, but Lev was deeply struck by the spectacle of "those glorious old kingdoms," collapsing one after another, as "the desert fell beneath the power of the red star."

Abraham contemplated the next move. Afghanistan, to the east, was a stronghold against the Bolsheviks, but it held its own dangers for those without local influence. It was also farther east than these citizens of Baku, the "easternmost city in Europe," wanted to go. China and India were out of the question for the same reason. Yet Bolsheviks now blocked the route back west at every turn. The defeated bands of czarist Whites were at least as dangerous, since, like the Reds, they were rumored to be attacking any caravan they stopped. There was nowhere to flee but south, so the Nussimbaums joined a caravan of Russian and Muslim refugees heading for Persia.*

The desert borderland between Bukhara and Persia was still quiet, and the caravan crossed into the nominal domains of the shah without incident. Like Turkestan, northern Persia was largely unsettled, but the culture was older and more civilized. The caravan traveled for days across the desert, coming occasionally upon luxuriant oases and the ruins of old cities and forts, dusty and lonely, like some sprawling string of elegant ghost towns. The inhabited cities were surrounded by walls six feet deep and twenty feet high, made of pounded clay; as in the Middle Ages, city gates were opened in the morning and closed at night. The walls could not withstand modern artillery but served to keep out tribes of marauding bandits and nomads. The Kurds were common raiders in northern Persia, but, along with the ethnic Azerbaijanis, they also provided the bulk of the Persian Army. The native Persians did not like to fight. In this class-bound society, they thought it déclassé to take up arms. Lev would create a comic scene in *Ali and Nino* in which Ali tells his Persian cousins about his plans to defend Baku against the Bolsheviks. The Persians recoil in disgust, saying that they did not know there were soldiers in the family:

> I had forgotten [reflects Ali] that in the eyes of a noble Persian to be a soldier is to be low class. . . . Iran was under God's special protection, and did not need the Sword any more to shine in the world. It had proved its valor in days long gone by. . . . The Prince preferred a poem to a machine-gun, maybe because he knew more about poems than about machine-guns.

This land where poetry and art mattered more than ideology and weapons was a revelation to Lev. As the caravan lumbered on, he felt he

---

* The nation would become Iran only in 1935, as part of a Nazi-influenced name change. As some Iranians will still proudly tell you, they are more closely related by blood to the Germans than to their Semitic neighbors: Iran meant "land of the Aryans," a notion that pleased Reza Shah Pahlavi, the country's dictator at the time, and founder of a dynasty that would end with his son's overthrow by the Ayatollah Khomeini in 1978.

was being transported back through time. "Nothing is alive in Persia," Lev wrote admiringly, "neither the degenerate Kajar-princes nor the farmers who follow the plough and recite five-hundred-year-old stanzas by Hafiz or Saadi. It is the true country of the old poets and thinkers, considering its present tattered garment unworthy of a glance, and proudly studying the versification of the divine tent-maker."

Of course, Persia was full of life—its forests were filled with wolves, tigers, foxes, and wild boars, while lions roamed the deserts along with Persian horses, which were famed for their beauty, even if they were not as fleet-footed as the Arabians. The country was also known for its agricultural wealth—some of the world's finest wheat, cotton, sugar, grapes, and tobacco. Everywhere Lev went, he smelled tobacco and hashish, as well as the famous roses of Persian love poetry that bloomed in so many varieties in the gardens and oases. The kingdom of the Qajar shahs seemed like a sanctuary from history, where the people lived among the fig trees and orchards, spending their time distilling roses into precious perfumes, weaving rugs, guarding harems, and composing poetry. In this literary graveyard of versifying tent-makers, he found a land yet to be set upon by the modern world.

The caravan's journey through post–First World War Persia sometimes sounds like a swing through the American Bible Belt. "In Persia religion alone is alive," Lev wrote, but it was a religion of many strange branches, sects, and secret societies. He encountered Ismailis, devil worshippers, Babists, and Bahaists, a sect of universalist Muslims who believed that a Muslim messiah had returned to earth sometime in the mid-nineteenth century—around the same time Joseph Smith found the Books of Mormon—and that we were living in a millennium when all religions could come together. Mainstream Muslims despised the Bahaists as blasphemers, and they often persecuted them.* Islam's original triumph in Persia in the seventh century had represented the defeat and banishment of the local religion, Zoroastrianism, whose dualistic creed had prevailed in the Persian court for hundreds of years. But along with the Muslim conquerors came another kind of Koranic proselytizer—refugees, not conquerors—who called themselves *Shi'Ali,* "the Partisans of Ali," or sim-

---

* Until the 1980s, in fact, anti-Semitism was uncommon in Persia, whereas anti-Bahaism was rampant. In the minds of many of today's mullahs, the two seem to be merged, so that the disciples of the Ayatollah Khomeini have warned of Zionist-Bahaist-American plots.

ply the Shiites. The Shiites taught the Persians not to trust the Arab con-querors, who claimed to represent the way revealed by the Prophet Muhammad.

The Shiites believed that the right to be caliph, or spiritual leader, of Islam should have fallen after Muhammad's death to his cousin and son-in-law, Ali. Ali was chosen caliph for a short time, just four years, but then he was murdered with a poisoned sword. A few years after Ali's assassi-nation, his sons Hassan and Hussein tried to assert their family's rights and were similarly dispatched: Hassan by poison, Hussein in a heroic last stand in the desert, near the town of Karbala, in modern-day Iraq, where, like Ali, he was killed by the Sunni warriors who opposed him. The mar-tyrdom of Hussein, in which the grandson of the Prophet Muhammad sacrificed himself for the true message of God, was for his followers some-thing like the crucifixion of Jesus was for Christians (though Hussein was not considered divine): in the eyes of the Shiites, Hussein's death is Islam's central tragedy. Shiite ideology was complex and kaleidoscopic, varying from place to place, but it all came down to one belief: the Prophet's right-ful successors were murdered, injustice ruled in the House of Islam, and the world would not be made right until the Mahdi, the Shiite messiah, arrived to implement the Divine Kingdom on earth.

The hills and towns of Persia were filled with songs detailing Hussein's suffering for their sins, and the leading form of theater in the country was passion plays commemorating the martyrdom. Lev got glimpses of this fervor wherever the caravan went, but it all came to a head the day the caravan paused in its tracks as the city it was visiting exploded in the an-nual Muharram passion festival. Men walked in the streets, and it seemed that there was no one, at any level of society, who did not join in the ac-tivities of the crowds. Music was in the air everywhere, like a Middle East-ern version of a New Orleans jazz funeral. The musicians played their dirges on drums, flutes, and cymbals, and young men no older than Lev marched bare-chested, beating themselves and chanting: "Hassan, Hus-sein, Hassan, Hussein." The procession was followed by crowds egging the flagellants on. The Shiite clergy positioned themselves throughout the city to direct religious traffic and give speeches.

In a land where suffering for the martyred Hussein was the highest measure of devotion, the most remarkable figures Lev witnessed were odd long-haired men whom he at first mistook for women. Over their luxurious locks, some of them wore pointed orange caps. All were barefoot, and during the religious festivals, many of them carried little whips made of iron strands and cruel blades, with which they abused their backs and shoulders, wailing and chanting. Others had knotty clubs bristling with nails and bits of brass. In their right hands, some carried what looked like little tomahawks with a verse of poetry written on the blade. These were the dervishes—pursuers of religious truth who did not seek material reward and were hence seen as incorruptible. The sacred orders of these dancing beggars had spread with the Sufi movement all across Asia—a Gnostic, ecstatic tradition in Islam that transcended all partisan divisions. Lev noted that "merchants, warriors, princes, even foreigners, can be seen in their company. One need not be surprised at being addressed in German, French, or English, by a ragged, long-haired beggar in the street. In the Orient education and wealth are separated. The dervish must be a beggar, even if his order is the chief creditor of the government. . . . Ceaselessly they travel from one city to another, preach of the approaching end of the world in the bazaars, and assert with pride that the best people in the country are to be found in their ranks."

Lev found Persia's Shiite Muslims theatrical and seductive. It was Islam in its most intoxicating form—a self-sacrificial dance of outsiders and rebels. He loved the raw religious fervor all around him, which he had never experienced in Baku. Shiism's encouragement of the underdog nurtured Lev's view of Islam as a bastion of heroic resistance in a world of brute force and injustice.

Shiite passion might rule the Persian heart, but this was still a land of infinite petty tyrannies. While crossing the provinces of Mazandaran and Gilan, the caravan was stopped by a Persian rider in gaily colored clothes. He introduced himself as the messenger of the Jafar Khan, the ruler of the region. The khan sent his greetings, the messenger announced, and wished to inform the travelers that they were all to be killed. They were please to wait until the khan arrived to carry out the sentence himself.

Lev had a sinking feeling that, after surviving the civil wars in Azerbaijan and Bukhara, and having just witnessed the passion of Hussein's martyrdom at Karbala, they would now die at the hands of a picturesque lunatic out of *The Arabian Nights*. But Abraham Nussimbaum knew better. Lev listened as much torturously friendly and banal banter ensued.

The messenger was so courteous and circumspect that it was impossible to understand what he was driving at. But Abraham continued talking, and all became clear when the messenger finally said: "Of what use is your money, if you are dead?"

The refugees breathed a sigh of relief: the man was merely trying to elicit a bribe, something only too familiar to anyone brought up in the Caucasus. But the style of this bribe was so baroque that they had almost sacrificed their lives without knowing the simple price to save them. They had offended the khan by walking through his territory without making any sort of offering, the messenger explained, and they must not think the bribe was any crude matter of money. "But what will be said abroad when it is discovered that even highly esteemed people refuse to give the Khan a present?" said the messenger.

"For this reason he wished to kill us," reflected Lev, noting the comic-operetta aspect of the thing. Abraham did not laugh but instead made a serious offer, which was conveyed by the messenger to the court. A furious back-and-forth of horse traffic ensued. The reply finally came that "upon the recommendation of his financial adviser, and in view of the fact that enough blood was already being spilled, [the khan] had decided, if . . . and so on." Lev and Abraham sent the khan a flowery letter with a cash "gift" enclosed, via the messenger, who rode off dashingly like a medieval knight. When he next caught up with the caravan, the messenger bore an invitation for Lev and Abraham to stay as the guests of His Highness the Jafar Khan.

With the caravan, Lev had learned about Persia's religious life. Now, at the court of the Jafar Khan, he would learn about Persia's political life. Beginning at ten every morning, Lev attended the khan's governmental meetings, which consisted almost solely in accepting bribes from his many subjects. The bribes ran the spectrum from gold and silver coins to live hens and sacks of flour. Everything and anything was accepted. Sometimes the serious business of the government was interrupted by a bit of levity: a flock of doves was once set free in the yard, and Lev watched the khan shoot them down one after another. But even here, there was a serious tax-collecting purpose: each time the fat potentate hit a bird, a courtier walked up and congratulated him with a few coins for the royal kitty.

Lev found that the Persians favored pompous titles. The number of titles seemed infinite, and since each one needed to be personally bestowed by the shah, they were constantly changing. Lev had great fun trying to keep all of this straight and for years afterward liked to entertain his Western audience with tales of court etiquette:

> For example, when the bearer of the title "Pillar of Justice" dies, a "Sword of the Fatherland" is raised to the rank of "Pillar of Justice"; a "Pearl of Wisdom" may become a "Sword of the Fatherland" and so on. Even without death, however, a transference often takes place, so that one can never know with certainty whether a letter of recommendation addressed to "The Shield of Faith" really does reach the person intended and not some former "Protector of the Hidden."

Lev wondered when he and his father would leave the court. They could not really decide whether they were guests or prisoners of the khan, and it seemed impolitic to ask. Indeed, Lev had an honorary bodyguard of two heavily armed but barefoot soldiers who followed him everywhere. They carried him over particularly dirty streets in their arms, as his own servants once had in Baku.

For Lev, the Old East, especially sensual Persia, was a repository of antique sexual ambiguities as well as the mysteries of the true religion. He memorably describes how one night the khan sent a *bitscho,* or pleasure boy, to the room where he and his father were staying. Lev explained to the servant accompanying the boy that they could not accept the honor "since our interests lay on another plane." The moment was awkward. The servant apologized profusely and retreated. Scarcely had they laid themselves down on the floor pillows and rugs to sleep when the servant was back. Now two young girls, who looked curiously at the travelers through their gauzy veils, accompanied him. As Lev capped off the tale, in *Blood and Oil,* now a refusal was impossible "from the point of view of good manners."

> Nevertheless the Khan was hurt by our forgoing the pleasure of delighting ourselves with the youthful charms of his Bitscho. He visited us the next morning and acted as though he were now convinced that he had to do with wild barbarians who could not appreciate his more cultivated feelings. He told me endless stories about the beauties of the Persian

past which were entirely in accord with his taste, complained about the corruption of the present youth that was enthusiastic only about the low pleasures of existence, and brought to light a rather comprehensive body of knowledge.

Since as I have said, I showed appreciation for everything classical except the Bitschos, he soon became reconciled, and even proposed that I should dine with him in his harem. I was careful enough not to enter his harem, for there, from sheer devotion to the treasures of the past, he might possibly have treated me as a Bitscho, too. Outside the harem, where his power was limited by the conventions of hospitality, I could feel safe. When we departed, he gave me a Hafiz manuscript, pulled a long face, and, naturally in verses, made a formal declaration of love, to which I naturally also responded with a declaration of love. But I am sure that his love would not have remained platonic if our caravan had not been protected by armed riders.

Lev's account of the khan's overtures was similar in its vague implications to many of the stories he would tell of the Orient: it was not that he, Lev Nussimbaum, had ever been tempted by a *bitscho* himself, or by any other homoerotic encounter; rather, everywhere they went on this journey, young Lev felt himself the object of men's desires. The Jafar Khan's were not the only erotic embraces he would narrowly escape. Lev found this "Persian-Greek tradition" of polymorphous embrace to be yet one more charmingly preserved aspect of the Old East that decadent Persia had preserved intact from modern civilization. It seemed to excite in him a robust anthropological and poetic interest, and he took it as a matter of form, rather than substance.

After days of suffocating hospitality, Lev and Abraham at last secured their leave. The caravan now set off to the northwest, hoping to reach the port of Enzeli on the coast of the Caspian. From there they would return by boat to Azerbaijan, which was occupied by the Turks, who had just driven out the English. The Turks were the ideal occupying force, as far as the Nussimbaums were concerned—Azerbaijan was a Turkic nation, after all. Abraham was eager to reclaim their property, and they both yearned for their native city of Baku. They had not traveled far, however, before they encountered problems.

———

All across northern Persia, as the Jafar Khan warned them, the revolt of the Jangalis was raging. The Jangalis, or "Forest Brothers," were a fanatical Shiite sect who had decided to break with the local custom of inaction and take up arms against the foreigners on Persian soil. Yet even this apparently indigenous Muslim hostility to the West was merely another brush fire lit by the spark of the Russian Revolution. The Jangalis were strongest in the north of Persia, along the Azerbaijani border, and with good reason: the border was the main conduit for revolutionary propaganda.

Inspired by the calls for revolution that swept Russia and the Caucasus in 1905, some Persians also founded a revolutionary movement that was at first moderate and liberal. In 1906 the shah granted a constitution that mandated voting rights, a constitutional monarchy, and a parliament. But in a foreshadowing of American CIA interference in the 1950s, the British and the Russians helped the shah stage a bloody counterrevolution, burning down the newly built parliament building—with many deputies still inside it. By 1911 the liberal Constitutional Revolution had been suppressed.

European interference changed the central goal of the Persian revolutionaries from constitutional democracy to anti-Western jihad. In 1912, at the height of the reaction against liberalization, an itinerant dervish founded the so-called Unity of Islam party, whose goal was to kick all foreigners out of Persia. Six years later, inspired by the Bolsheviks' use of violence in Russia, he took his Unity of Islam party to the countryside, transforming it into the Jangalis sect. Their followers were a terrifying sight to behold, for they had sworn to "let their hair and nails grow until the last unbeliever had left the holy soil of Iran." The Jangalis were joined by fanatics of every stripe who simply wanted the chance to murder unbelievers, or to murder period. Lev and Abraham's caravan started to pass deserted villages; sometimes they spotted human corpses and rusted weapons lying about.

When the caravan was set upon by a band of ugly, sword-wielding rogues who identified themselves as the Jangalis, Lev thought they looked more like plain robbers than revolutionaries of any kind. The robbers' leader, a young Persian with flashing dark eyes, advanced and said: "Unbelievers, step to the side and surrender your property to the true believers." The camel driver tried to negotiate a bribe, but the robbers silenced him. The robber chief addressed himself to the learned foreigners, inquiring about their journey. Then he announced that all who wished to were invited to join the band. Lev and Abraham declined "most politely" and were stripped of their valuables. The robbers searched everyone.

"When it came to my turn," Lev recalled later, "the chief asked me whether I would like to become his lover; he would then promise me a particularly rosy future." Unaware of native custom on this point, Lev made up a story that he was already the lover of a holy imam from Meshed, and in the name of Allah did not want to leave the wise man in the lurch. "The authority of the servant of God saved me," he said. At the last moment, when the robbers were about to leave with all the caravan's camels in tow, the camel drivers joined them. Lev and Abraham remained in the desert alone, without guides. They set off to seek the next settlement on foot. They did not catch sight of the first houses until daybreak.

The exhausted father and son wandered into town. They had no money, no camels, no companions. They decided to visit the local mosque. Unlike a modern church or synagogue, a mosque will often be one part of an entire compound, with courtyards, meeting halls, and cafés. Here the Jews raised among Muslims knew they could find shelter. Indeed, they found not only shelter but enough money and food to continue on to Enzeli, a day's journey away—but as they were on the point of leaving town (on horses or camels Lev doesn't say), a messenger rode up to them, announcing that he was from the Committee of Iron. This was a proto-fascist organization run by Reza Kuli—the man who would later become Reza Shah Pahlavi. The committee was reputed to wield increasing power in the country, and it functioned as a self-appointed enforcer and keeper of the peace.

The messenger brought out a sealed leather bag. He opened it, and sand began pouring out. He fished around and came up with a blood-encrusted object the size of a melon. A human head.

"That is the head of the villain who caused you the discomfort on the way here," he explained. It was an offering of respect, the messenger said, from the Committee of Iron, which wished them a very pleasant journey.

Lev and Abraham had trouble convincing the man that they did not want the head. Merely to have seen the head offered deep satisfaction, they assured him, and they could not think of accepting it. They eventually left the messenger standing there, no doubt trying to decide whether to dispose of the thing or risk returning the gift undelivered.

At last, father and son arrived in the port city of Enzeli. There they heard confirmation of a favorable political situation in Baku: a highly esteemed lawyer who Lev felt was "one of ours" was in power; now they knew they could return with confidence. The revolution was over. The restoration had begun.

They found other Caucasian refugees milling about the port city and joined a group of oil-well owners with their families and their Kotschi bodyguards. This group would sail back across the Caspian together. They pooled their money and bought a boat that looked suspiciously old. It was meant for fifty people at most, but two hundred got on board.

They hired a crew of four captains, including two who had worked on Abraham's oil tankers. The Kotschis and some other rough men served as sailors. The normal steamer trip from Enzeli to Baku was about twelve hours, but they allowed for twice that. They had enough food and water aboard for about two days. They decided to sail out of port in total darkness, in order not to be seen by the English soldiers. The most difficult thing, Lev recalled, was boarding the ship unnoticed. The passengers had to row out silently in small boats and climb up rope ladders to the deck, and it took hours to get all of them on board. "At last the four captains and the robber-sailors raised the sails, and we began our joyous return home. No one could tell later how many bottles of wine the home-comers emptied during that night."

After evading the English searchlights at Enzeli and safely leaving the port, they had a huge feast, and most people fell asleep. Lev slept in the cabin with the women and got an earful of their vengeful talk. He found it much more gruesome than anything the men were discussing. The women gossiped about all the punishments they thought should be inflicted on 90 percent of the population of Azerbaijan. When Lev slept, he, too, dreamed about Bolsheviks suffering. He heard them moaning before their avengers—but the moans were not only in his dreams. At last he woke up and saw that his cabin was filled with frightened people, for outside a tempest was raging. The rickety ship had run into one of the notorious storms that swept over the Caspian every few months and were avoided by real seamen.

Then, as the storm was abating, a mysterious ship appeared out of the darkness—a warship, by the look of its guns. Oddly, it was still flying the old imperial battle flag of the czarist navy.

The sailors on this ship recognized no revolution. Even though the czar had been shot months before, both officers and men still swore their allegiance to him. Fanatical monarchists, admitting no other possible organizing principle for life, they manned a battleship patrol of the Imperial Russian Navy and had been at sea continuously since 1917, likely staying alive by plundering ships just like the one the refugees had hired. The monarchist crew boarded the hapless refugee boat and announced that they were steaming to Baku to bombard the anti-imperial forces anchored in the harbor there. But the Germans and Turks now controlled Baku, the passengers explained. It did not matter a whit to the imperial sailors, for they did not recognize the peace treaty among Russia and Germany and Turkey, which had been signed by the Bolsheviks. As far as they were concerned, nothing had changed except that now they were at war with more parties rather than fewer: the Germans, the Turks, the Bulgarians, the Austrians . . . and their own Bolshevik countrymen.

They regarded Lev, Abraham, and all the other passengers on the boat who wanted to return to Baku as traitors, and they announced that they were within their rights to sink the ship with everyone on board. The refugees were to stay put while they decided what to do with them. In the meantime, as it was the birthday of some grand duke or other, the sailors returned to their battleship to celebrate it. The captains of the refugee ship watched through telescopes as the fierce czarist sailors got plastered. And then the immigrant ship quietly pulled up anchor and sailed away.

Soon enough, however, the passengers had to deal with another problem: a large leak in their bow and only one modest hand pump on the whole ship. As the men confronted that challenge, it was discovered that some of the children on board had started getting hideous black spots on their skin. One child died. The captains called the disease black smallpox, though Lev thought it could just as well have been the plague. And the pump didn't work properly. A human chain with buckets took to bailing. The ship was gradually sinking. Fear and chaos set in on the darkened, buffeted ship. The Kotschis began robbing people and assaulting the maidservants. Lev and Abraham took shelter on the floor of a lifeboat. They heard gunfire.

"The ship was like an insane asylum," Lev wrote in his memoirs. "We sailed starving, freezing, and semiconscious over the waves." He tried to distract himself by reading the only book they had with them: a Russian edition of *Don Quixote*. For a time, father and son quietly discussed the problem of death. The Baku harbor was not far off in the darkness, but between the sinking of the ship and the rising of disease on board, there seemed little chance they could survive the short voyage.

Their rescue came suddenly, like something out of a cheap novel. On the afternoon of their fifth day at sea, the passengers caught sight of a steamer on the horizon, flying the imperial German flag.

The conduct of the German sailors was most respectful, Lev noted. The refugees were all invited to leave their sinking ship and board the German vessel, while its crew immediately emptied their cabins, even the captain's cabin, to make room for the princes, oil magnates, and politicians among them. The captain reassured them that the situation in Baku was stable, the oil derricks were unharmed, and the enemy had fled the city, whether Bolshevik or British.

The next day, the German ship sailed into the Baku harbor. Lev saw the old city, the palaces, the medieval ramparts, all as it had been. It was truly a magical, fairy-tale city, more wondrous, he thought, than all the places they had seen on their travels. The new prime minister, the respected Baku lawyer, arrived with his bodyguards and a soldier holding the new flag of independent Azerbaijan. As they stepped off the boat, after all the dangerous months, Lev saw his first division of German soldiers. He heard them singing and could follow the words: "The birds in the forest sing so very beautifully. At home, in my native land, we shall meet again."

Lev and his father found two Turkish soldiers standing guard at their front door. A German officer and a Turkish officer were billeted inside. When Abraham introduced himself as the owner of the house, the Germans assured them that they would move immediately. Abraham begged the officers to stay with them, as there was plenty of room. But the Germans refused.

The tables had been turned. Lev did not know what was to come next; he knew only that they were finally home. The Nussimbaums had returned to their "native land."

Chapter 4

Escape

❧

THE NUSSIMBAUMS' FLIGHT ACROSS TURKESTAN AND PERSIA seems to have lasted only a few months, but in that time Baku had undergone a dizzying number of political transformations, sieges, and alliances involving the Soviets, the British, the Cossacks, the Social Revolutionaries, the Germans, and the Turkish "Army of Islam."* The Armenian population had been decimated by massacres. At the moment of Lev's return, Baku was, for the time being, in the hands of ten thousand Turkish troops and hundreds of Prussians.

Though its medieval fortress walls had undergone bombardment by at least three different armies, Lev found Baku's cosmopolitan jumble of European and Asian architecture oddly intact. The carts with the corpses were gone. The chilly October winds off the Caspian blew through the alleyways of the khan's palace and the medieval mosques, and scattered leaves down the boulevards lined with the oil barons' Beaux Arts mansions and opera houses. The old buildings were ventilated by bullet holes here and there, and everywhere Lev went, he found a new structure that marked the months of feverish "political activity" that had so recently absorbed the city: gallows.

---

* A bizarre British–Cossack–Social Revolutionary coalition so alarmed Lenin that he made a secret deal with the kaiser's forces, offering to link them with his Bolshevik troops to retake Baku. It would have pitted two of the most unlikely coalitions in history against each other: the Bolshevik-kaiser coalition versus the czarists–monarchists–Social Revolutionaries.

Residents said that the gallows had been erected by the German and Turk authorities to restore order after the siege. Corpses were hung with placards announcing their crimes: "Hanged for theft of a pound of nuts." The signs were effective. "Before the conquest," Lev recounted, "Baku was swarming with criminals of all kinds; five days after the capture, the city was a model of honesty, security, and order." In a city recovering from months under siege, food-hoarding and price-gouging were the highest levels of offense.

The days of riot ended. The oil fields began pumping again. On the balcony of the Hotel Metropole, looking out over the Caspian, the oilmen in their evening clothes once more smoked cigars and drank champagne, now chatting with the stiff-necked Prussian and Turkish officers. "One of the first who appeared was the Turkish pasha, the conqueror of Baku," remembered Lev. "He was surrounded by a circle of German officers who outdid each other in felicitations and friendliness. I acted as interpreter between them and my father." Lev enjoyed translating for the German officers, who made a great impression on him with their insistence on doing things properly and refusal to take the customary gifts and bribes from the population. "According to the general view it was not proper for a conqueror to pay for something that belonged to him, but they could not be convinced," he wrote. "Never before had one seen such strange conquerors in the Orient."

The Turks were somewhat less alien than the Germans in this respect. Both were a relief from the Bolsheviks. Had the revolution been simply a bad dream that he and his father had avoided by taking a desert trip? Would he now return to his life of bodyguards, library books, costume parties, and dreamy strolls along the gray ramparts of the old city?

The German-Turkish occupation lasted just weeks. In October 1918, as the Bulgarian front collapsed, leaving the Central Powers impossibly exposed, both the Turkish and the German general staffs began suing for peace. At the beginning of November 1918, the Germans were forced to turn over the administration of Baku to the British, who moved their forces back from Persia. The British troops were not amused by their new assignment, particularly since the municipal government of the oil city was the same one that had helped the Turks and Germans throw them out just weeks before. If the British had been somewhat haughty on their first stay in Baku, they were downright contemptuous this time.

But for a few months, the Caucasus enjoyed a respite from war and revolution. Indeed, Azerbaijan became the first functioning democracy in the Islamic world, and for the first time in the history of Muslim society, women were allowed to vote. The uniquely progressive, productive blend of East and West that had marked oil-boom Baku once more began to take hold. Though corruption and backroom deals were always part of the oil city's style, so, too, was a measure of practical pluralism that now allowed a lively political scene. Even the skeptical British commander was won over by the leadership of the Azeri statesmen, especially the parliament's new speaker, the professorial and mustachioed Rasulzade. At the 1919 Paris Peace Conference, President Wilson took note of Rasulzade, a "very dignified and interesting gentleman from Azerbaijan . . . who talked the same language that I did in respect of ideals, conceptions of liberty and conceptions of right and justice."

Despite the improved relations between the occupiers and the Azeris, Lev found that whenever the English didn't like something, they would ask that the practice be ended because it "violated the principles of civilization." The implied threat: the British troops would pull up stakes and go home, leaving Azerbaijan to its own devices. And in August 1919, they did leave. The elected government made a show of welcoming their impending independence, but the obvious question was on everyone's mind: could democratic Azerbaijan defend itself from the Bolshevik behemoth to the north? Still, there was excitement when the British evacuated the city. Businessmen like Abraham Nussimbaum could now operate in the capital of their own independent country, no longer an outpost of the Russian Empire or a protectorate of the British. "For the oil lords, who now came into power, this time was the best time of their lives," Lev recalled.

Lev would always look back on this yearlong period of the independent Azeri republic as an unusually optimistic time. My interviews with Zuleika Asadullayeva, the younger sister of Lev's schoolmate Asad, confirmed that many felt this way. "We were all proud of our independent, modern Muslim republic," she told me. "We had the vote for women, something unheard of in the Muslim world. . . . We had a reasonably uncorrupt government with educated statesmen. It seemed too good to be true—and it was! Our leaders did not realize that we were utterly defenseless."

The Azeri Parliament negotiated political and economic treaties with its neighbors. It signed an exclusive oil-exploration deal with Dutch Shell (though not entirely to its advantage). Russia was embroiled in a civil war, while a productive peace settled on the Caucasus. But it was to be a brief lull.

In one of the more improbably apt coincidences in *Blood and Oil,* Lev writes about a small dinner party his father hosted for members of the Azeri government one night. The discussion over cigars turned to troop deployment. The minister of commerce and the military governor of Baku had stayed on later than the other guests, and they were talking about the problem of disturbances along the Armenian frontier. The Armenian frontier of Azerbaijan is in the southwest, and in order to adequately defend it, most of the republic's small army, including its border patrols, had been relocated away from the country's northern frontier. Did it really make sense to leave one border unguarded to protect another, wondered Abraham, especially when the more powerful enemy was on the unprotected border?

The republic had only so many resources, the military governor countered, and there were priorities that had been carefully weighed. Besides, the other minister said, the republic had just concluded an important new treaty with Soviet Russia. After the dignitaries finished their cigars, Lev watched from his balcony as the military governor got into his car. "I could still see the night-patrol which was just passing greet the governor and call out the customary 'long live.' "

Several armed men approached the minister when he arrived home that night, declaring that he was under arrest. "By whose authority?" he asked.

"By order of the Cheka of the Socialist Soviet Republic of Azerbaijan."

Servants awakened Lev and his father with the news that the Bolsheviks had taken the city. "Through the window I saw the entrance of the Red troops, saw the brutal faces, tattered figures, the wicked Bolshevik grimaces, and the envious, hungry Russian eyes which coveted the riches of the oil-city."

During the night, trainloads of Soviet soldiers had crossed the Russian-Azeri border, taken night trains down to the coast, and quietly surrounded Baku. They brought the Bolsheviks' most fearsome weapon: the All-Russian Extraordinary Commission for Combating Counterrevolution and Sabotage, or the Cheka. These "Chekists" in their trademark black leather jackets, with Mauser pistols strapped to one side, would murder more people in the next five years than the czar's secret police had in the previous century. As one of Russia's most distinguished socialist authors, Vladimir Korolenko, who had himself spent much of his life in the czar's Siberian prisons, put it at the time: "If under the Czar's regime the district police bureaus had been given the right not only to exile to Siberia but also to execute, it would have been similar to what we see now." The Cheka's preferred weapon was a small handheld machine gun that they used to mow down anyone trying to "escape."

The Azeri government quickly decided that resistance was hopeless and drafted a deed of capitulation. In the document, the conquering Communists "expressly bound themselves not to persecute a single minister, member of parliament or oil-magnate in any way, but to grant them free withdrawal from the country." Yet less than a month after the overthrow of Baku, the killing began. Following the pattern it had established elsewhere, the Cheka carried out "liquidations" methodically—rather than a reason to be killed, a reason to be spared was required as evidence—and most victims dug their own graves. The oil magnates mostly went to prison (the better to entice bribes from relatives), except those needed for the export industry; they remained at large under strict supervision.

The first time Lev watched the world being destroyed, he had felt fear and confusion. The second time, his predominant emotions were disgust and anger. The amazingly pure destructive force of the new regime was already legend—its contempt for everything that had existed before it. The Mongols, Lev knew, had killed as ruthlessly in their conquest of these regions—they were perhaps the only pre-twentieth-century force comparable to the Bolsheviks—but the Mongols were also a perfect example of the old paradigm, which had lasted for at least twenty centuries, until 1917: even when they demanded absolute submission from defeated peoples, they absorbed elements of their cultures. The Bolsheviks did not believe in the past, except as a formulaic stage that had been passed through and was now to be discarded like a dirty lab solution.

The Cheka was the central organ of the new Communist government. It arrested anyone who could not indisputably prove his "decent" convictions or his indispensability to the oil industry. Lev saw victims of the purge being led through the streets. An officer recognized him, waved his hand, and pointed to his neck in a sign of his own impending fate. Lev later heard that these men had concealed iron rods in their clothing and had attacked the soldiers escorting them; their formal execution turned into a brawl in which both prisoners and guards were literally beaten to death.

From this modest beginning, the pace of the murders increased. Every day, hundreds were arrested—bankers, nobles, teachers, students, journalists, and Kotschis were thrown into prison. The head of the Baku Cheka was a Russian sailor who "made use of his marine experiences." Prisoners arrested in Baku were taken out in boats to the small island of Nargen, where the Cheka had established its official headquarters. To save time, Cheka officers often simply shot prisoners on the way and threw them overboard. Everywhere, people disappeared without a trace, and even their nearest relatives didn't dare question their fate. If they did, they might be promised a meeting on the island of Nargen. Besides arrests and murders, the Cheka revived the revolutionary spirit in Baku in other ways. The square outside Lev's house became the stage for a regular auto-da-fé in the style of the Inquisition. The Cheka used wax figures made up to resemble famous "bloodsuckers": President Woodrow Wilson, French president Georges Clemenceau, and British prime minister David Lloyd George, in their dress suits and monocles, "were thrown on a huge pyre and burned solemnly during the singing of the *Internationale.*" Lev watched as the Bolsheviks filmed these exhibitions in order to show them around the country. Years later, he would see one of the films in a Berlin cinema. He recalled that it received good reviews in the German press for its direction.

When Lev's recollections of the Bolshevik persecutions were first published, at the end of the 1920s, he—and his German readers—believed such things could never happen in a modern European country like Germany. Yet three years after the publication of *Blood and Oil*, the Nazi Revolution brought arrests, murders, and autos-da-fé to Berlin on a far grander scale than the Bolshevik burnings in Baku. The new Nazi "secret political police," the Gestapo, would take the Cheka as its model and avidly study its methods and tradecraft.

It did not take long before representatives of the Cheka showed up at the Nussimbaum house. They explained to Abraham Nussimbaum that "as an 'old bandit, bloodsucker, and criminal' " he was sentenced to death.

However, the sentence would be postponed indefinitely if he would agree—under supervision, of course—to assist with the oil industry "until experienced successors had arisen from the ranks of the proletariat." The prospect of a full pardon was held out, with special consideration for help with the transport sector of the economy; the Bolsheviks needed to get the oil flowing north to Russia in a hurry. Abraham consented to work for the new Baku Soviet. Summoned in front of the board of directors of the new government oil industry, he was no longer a "bloodsucker" and a "criminal," but had received a lifesaving demotion to "suspicious but temporarily irreplaceable bandit."

It was during this period, Lev told Pima, that Stalin came to stay. (Stalin was briefly in Baku in 1920; though it's impossible to verify where he stayed, the Bolsheviks did seize mansions for their headquarters.) Lev told a journalist from the *New York Herald Tribune* in 1934 that this was when he first began gathering material for his biography of Stalin, when they were under the same roof. At times, the scene suggests a kind of black comedy, with Stalin the ultimate unwanted houseguest: "I often sat opposite him. He usually read a stupid book that said the world revolution was close at hand." Another time, Lev says, he protested: " 'My God, haven't they committed enough murders?' . . . To which [Stalin] replied, 'What do you want, we let you live!' " And, if all this is to be believed, Stalin stayed up late at night talking with Lev about his mother.

"Only when the *Pockennarbige* lived with us did he tell me many things about my mother," Lev tells Pima. "He was by then already an important character"—*ein ganz hohes Tier*, or "a pretty big animal"—"and he told me how my mother had helped him often in the past. . . . We spoke almost all night long. . . . 'She was a wonderful human being, a saint that had to suffocate. . . . She sacrificed everything and it's not her fault she despaired of victory.' " Could this be what his aunt Sofia had meant when she told Lev, "She was right back then. . . . Time showed it to be an error"? That Lev's mother had despaired just as the Bolsheviks were on the brink of success?

If indeed Stalin was for a time their "protection" in Baku, eventually the Nussimbaums lost that protection. In another foreshadowing of Nazi measures, the Bolsheviks introduced an official "week of plundering," in which they encouraged the "awakened proletariat" to invade the homes of all bourgeois owners and take whatever they liked. The "non-proletariat" population was expected to watch and keep silent. Any opposition would be a revolt against the state, punishable by death. "Proletarians" in rags strolled down the street carrying elegant furniture and rugs, food and liquor, laundry and samovars, and assorted antiques. People were expected to give up all but the clothes on their backs if demanded, and sometimes these. Lev was struck by the way the plundering affected the truly rich, his own social class, least of all:

> To the owners of oil-land, this week of plunder seemed like play. People who had lost millions after the taking over of the oil industry by government and confiscation of the banks, and who were in daily danger of being shot, had small interest in cooking utensils and other dishes. The middle class came off worst, for they were deprived of their last property, and, when all is considered, had never been substantially richer than a good worker. Many men killed themselves as dishonoured because their harems had been invaded. In the homes of the middle class a harem is the room that the woman of the house, usually only one, occupies with her children.

The harem in poorer Muslim families contained the household's most valuable property: the silk sheets and pillow covers on which the family slept. As symbols of domesticity and female honor, these sheets might absorb a significant share of a household's income. Now they were stolen "for the purposes of the world revolution."

A raiding party confiscated everything at the Nussimbaums' house, but Lev and his father remained fairly indifferent to the thieving because it seemed like the least of their troubles. "We knew that either the Bolshevists would be chased away and we could then establish ourselves again, or we should be shot. . . . Perhaps too, we might be able to get away. We could do without our furniture in any event."

A Cheka man returned after the plundering, carrying a paper he said ordered the Nussimbaums to clear out "within twenty-four minutes"—a standard Bolshevik eviction notice; the functionary had simply crossed out "hours" and substituted "minutes." The Cheka allowed them to move into Abraham's offices, where they could occupy only one room. They had almost no possessions left to fill it with, regardless.

Lev writes that around this time a manifesto was published that announced: "The Proletariat can stand no dirt!" All "class enemies of the

Revolution" were made to sweep and wash the streets of Baku. The spectacle of elegant old men and women on their hands and knees was yet another that was to carry over smoothly from the Bolshevik to the Nazi revolutions. Brutalities on a scale that no autocratic czar or sultan had begun to imagine were taking shape in the minds of those now in power.

Lev, now almost fifteen, and his father made a plan. This time they would go west, escaping overland to Georgia, which was still independent. Since they were always watched when together, and since it was assumed that father would never flee without son, they would leave separately. Under less scrutiny, Lev would go first. He would travel to Ganja, the old city in the interior of Azerbaijan, close to the Georgian border, where the family had many friends and where the nationalist opposition was based. A few months after his son's flight, Abraham would make a tour of inspection of the oil fields outside Baku, and during the tour, he would also disappear and head to Ganja. They would meet up at the Azerbaijani-Georgian border.

As soon as he could, Lev caught a freight train out of Baku across the open desert—a cattle car he shared with peasants—avoiding the riskier passenger trains. Sitting on the floor like some hobo in a Steinbeck novel, traveling across the plains and deserts and mountains, Lev felt at home. The peasants "all cursed the communists, so that I almost felt as though I was among owners of oil land." Every so often, the train would creak to a stop and soldiers would get on to ransack the cars in search of "Whites," curse the "stupid natives," and threaten everyone with the Cheka, but, like the conductors, they were generally drunk.

Lev knew that if he and his father could both make it to the Azerbaijani-Georgian border, they could get a freighter across the Black Sea and be in Europe. There they would be safe. After the deserts, they passed through lush villages and gardens, away from the oil fields. Occasionally, Lev got off the train at stops; he picked fruit and shared it with his fellow riders. "At that moment the land of Zarathustra seemed as though still untouched by the Reds; it was spring."

When he arrived in Ganja, the former capital of Azerbaijan, Lev found the place already quite Bolshevized, though it was supposedly the center of "nationalist" activity. He saw the same signs and military notices that he knew from Baku. But something was happening here that felt distinct from Baku, especially in the Muslim half of the city, where in the bazaars people loudly cursed their Red "liberators." The mood excited Lev, and, free from his father's cautious influence, he had his first taste of what would be a lifetime of plots and intrigue. A friendly merchant introduced him to a group of conspirators who thought it worthwhile to have a member who knew Baku, which would be the main object of the nationalist assault. At first Lev was flattered to be brought into the inner circle. Once on the inside, he realized that almost everyone was being brought in, so that eventually, "we worked almost publicly at the plot." Lev marveled at the inefficiency of the authorities that the unwieldy group was not immediately found out and liquidated.

Amazingly enough, the nationalist plotters were not caught, and on the appointed day, a citywide uprising took the leaders of the Russian Bolshevik forces by surprise and overwhelmed them. The plotters received help from White Russian exiles, eager for a chance to kill Reds, and since there weren't many Bolshevik soldiers in Ganja in the first place, the plot was much easier to carry out than it might have been in Baku. Lev claimed to have taken part in manning machine-gun posts on a key bridge, but whether or not he actually saw action, his military career lasted no more than a day.

In describing these events in *Blood and Oil*, as in describing his entire childhood and flight, Lev Nussimbaum wrote as if he were the Muslim Essad Bey—as if Abraham, his father, were a Muslim lord—so it is interesting to note the few places where his own preoccupations as a Jew seem to break through the façade. Remembering the Ganja uprising, for example, he writes:

> The Russian Whites who had allied themselves with us, in accordance with the tradition of their country, suggested a pogrom against the Jews. This suggestion, however, we curtly rejected, although the Russians had already had notices printed with the inscription: "Beat the Jews, save Azerbaijan!"

Lev made a point of the fact that, while the "other" Muslims refused the suggestion, he personally went around and took down the notices calling for the murder of the Jews, and destroyed them. He declared to the Russians "that they must not forget they were in cultivated Azerbaijan and not in wild Russia, whereupon the Russians suggested a pogrom against the Armenians." Lev claimed that his countrymen rejected this idea, too, because the Muslim Azeris killed only when called to by honor and revenge; as they had already taken revenge against the Armenians in their massacre in Baku, so they "now wanted to spill no blood needlessly." (Years later, in Berlin, Lev concluded: "It was not easy to move the Russians to continue to work sensibly.")

The plotters and their growing group of hangers-on prepared themselves "with Oriental calm"—that is, slowly and inefficiently—to bring the battle to the rest of the country. In the meantime, however, the Bolshevik leadership in Baku got word of the coup in Ganja and sent twenty thousand troops to surround the city. Before they could make plans to take their rebellion any further, the plotters were effectively cut off from the rest of the country and the outside world. The Bolsheviks gradually drew the circle tighter. The plotters didn't know that similar revolts were happening in other parts of the country, revolts the Bolsheviks were dealing with in similar fashion. This was the pattern all over Central Asia and Russia: encircle, isolate, and destroy resisting cities or towns. In Ganja, the Bolsheviks first reoccupied the Armenian section of town and then approached the bridge separating the Armenian from the Muslim quarter. The river, which had once given the city its name, had not existed for many years, but there was still a riverbed where a small stream sometimes ran in springtime. This bridge was to play a central role in Lev's imagination: it was where his alter ego, Ali Khan, made his last stand against the Russians in *Ali and Nino,* manning a machine-gun post—"the bullets gliding through [his] hands like rosary beads"—until he was finally cut down by the advancing Bolshevik troops, falling over the railing into the dry riverbed. Many Bolsheviks did die charging the Ganja bridge, whether or not Lev was among the defenders, but they succeeded in capturing it when they managed to break through on the Muslim side as well, so that the guardians of the bridge found themselves cut off on both sides.

I traveled all around Ganja with Fuad, my friend from Interpol, looking for the bridge. After seventy years of Soviet rule, no one could tell us where it was anymore, and we were guided to more than half a dozen bridges that day. But at last we found it, looking out of place and useless, spanning a patch of muddy riverbed. Its stone façade was still scored with bullet holes from the revolution. On the street corner next to the bridge, on the old Armenian side from which the Bolsheviks advanced, stood a mental hospital.

When the fighting was over, the Cheka "investigated" the revolt. "The court procedure was as simple as one can imagine," wrote Lev. "Name, profession, and age were quickly demanded, the answers noted down, and in ninety cases out of a hundred the sentence 'Shoot!' was executed on the spot. . . . It was organized mass murder, which one cannot even soften by calling it 'terror.' "

Lev never explained exactly how he made his escape after the coup failed. (Or how, as an inexperienced teenaged bookworm, he managed to join the plotters in the first place.) When he first published his memoirs, in Germany in 1929, his stories of intrigues and close calls during this period were generally accepted by liberals and widely scorned by the anti-Semitic right, who took his concealment of his Jewish background as a sign that his stories of escaping the Bolsheviks were also a fraud. Though Lev's first memoir, published when he was only twenty-four, is filled with dubious flourishes—moments described with bravado that almost certainly would have found him paralyzed with fear at the time—he later proved he was capable of a strange courage, and continued to take absurd risks with the Fascists in his early thirties. His main survival skill—his imagination— was uniquely appropriate to someone who had lived in a gilded cage, dreaming of adventure, until events more dramatic than he ever could have imagined suddenly erupted around him.

There was also an aspect of unreality to the Bolshevik Revolution, no doubt heightened in the borderlands of Turkestan and the Caucasus. Most of the revolutionaries must have operated in a state of shock at their own successes, unable to believe that they were actually tearing asunder centuries of social and political custom in the course of a few bloody days or weeks. In his deathbed notebooks, Lev wrote,

When I was arrested by the Cheka, I laughed. God knows why. But I laughed. I was fourteen years old. An adult by the standards of the Orient. But the whole thing was an adventure, a funny, exciting adventure. It was obvious, of course, that in a few weeks, in a few months, all traces [of the revolution] were going to vanish. Everyone thought so, even the Reds themselves.

Lev's account of evading the dragnet in Ganja does indeed read like a funny, exciting adventure—one whose characters and themes were to sustain him through the darker and more dangerous events that were to follow.

After some days hiding in a cellar, he thought of a plan. He approached a passing soldier in the street and asked him how he could reach the offices of the Cheka. The surprised soldier—no one ever *asked* to find the Cheka—gave him the information.

Lev went to the Cheka and asked to see the presiding officer. "Comrade, please make out a permit for me to leave the city," he said in Russian. The agent demanded to know who Lev was. "Young communist from Astrakhan, son of a workman," he replied. "I was in Ganja on behalf of the Communist Youth Organization and was attacked by enemies of the proletariat, and want to return home to re-enter the ranks of the fighting workers." (Lev claimed he was helped in his ruse by the fact that his Russian was flawless, his composure held, and he was too young to be any sort of "White" officer.)

"Papers?" demanded the officer of the Cheka.

"Have destroyed them in accordance with the general instructions of the party congress after the White revolt."

The man examined me curiously, considered a little, and asked: "What did Comrade Lenin say about the right of self-government of the peoples?"

"Self-government till independence!" I answered.

"What does communism lead to, economically speaking?"

"From the domain of temporary economical anarchy to that of systematic production," I answered fluently, according to the ABC of the communists of Bucharin, which I had already learned by heart at the time of the first Bolshevist invasion.

Lev passed the examination. The man smirked and made out the permit for him.

But when Lev got to the railway station, the agent there was unimpressed. "The Cheka of Ganja may merely give permits to leave the city. For the trip on the railroad, the approval of the railroad-Cheka is required," the bureaucrat barked. When Lev tried to leave the station, the

Railroad Cheka man would not give him his paper back. He told Lev that he looked suspicious and he could either surrender the papers or stay behind personally. Lev chose to leave without the papers.

All alone, knowing nothing of the surrounding villages or how he might get to the Georgian border to meet his father, Lev had to get out of the city on foot. He walked a full day without meeting anyone. Toward evening he began to pass gardens and neatly planted rows of trees and bushes. Suddenly, he saw something in a bush—a flash of a gun muzzle— and a voice said, "There goes some boy."

The sentence was striking because of the language in which it was uttered: German. Lev put his hands over his head and called back in German, asking the voice what it wanted.

"Defense-guard of the district of Helenendorf," replied the voice, and commanded him to approach the bush.

Several thousand prosperous Germans, Lev discovered, were living in what appeared to be a perfect replica of a Black Forest community nestled between the Azeri desert and the foothills of the Caucasus. The founders of Helenendorf had emigrated more than a hundred years before, fleeing famine and religious oppression in their native Swabia in the wake of the Napoleonic wars. Czar Alexander I offered them parcels of land in the Caucasus, to help populate this frontier region and secure it from the Muslims. The sturdy pilgrims had traveled the length of Europe, from the border of France to the borders of Georgia and Armenia, to create a model German colony here among the Aisors and Kipta, Ossetians, and Chani nomads. According to a German study published in 1910, fifteen wagon trains of Swabian pioneers traveled to the Caucasus in 1816 and 1817, believing the Russian frontier to be "a land of freedom and happiness." They paid no mind to the ceaseless clan feuds and ancient soup of Oriental customs all around them. They grew rich through hard work and through the cultivation of Azerbaijan's only cognac and wine industry.

The German colonists had no stake in Azeri politics; they simply paid their taxes to whoever was in power. But they had to keep their eye on the local tribes, who coveted the well-stocked wine cellars. And now they had the nationalist uprising and Bolshevik repression in nearby Ganja to worry about. It was no wonder they sent out an advance guard. Had the Bolsheviks tried, they would have had no easy time taking the town; the

Helenendorf defense force was efficient and vigilant. Still, it was lucky for the Germans that the Bolsheviks were too busy for the moment to bother with them.

For Lev, coming into the sanctuary of this village, it was as if he were suddenly in Germany. The inhabitants did not speak perfect "High German," but they were fluent in the Swabian dialect of their ancestors, which was remarkably pure considering that they had lived in the Caucasus for more than a hundred years. To keep it up, they sent members of the town to Germany on research trips, to make sure they were in no way behind any good German village there. They brought in their schoolteachers from Germany, employed German physicians, and insisted that their pastors be educated German theologians.

From the moment the guards escorted Lev into town, everyone was welcoming to him. They might not have been so open to all those who came seeking shelter, but he was helped by the fact that he could speak German. The Helenendorfers enjoyed his attempts at mastering their dialect. Lev recalled that for weeks he led a "holiday life"; he drank the colonists' wine, went to church with them, and "paid court" to the German girls. He attended the Sunday-afternoon concerts and coffee klatches that made an odd contrast with the lives of the surrounding nomads, in their *yourtas* and tiny clay huts. Though the townspeople knew Lev was fleeing the Bolsheviks, they never asked him about it, treating him instead like a summer visitor who had decided to stay awhile, albeit with little money—whatever he had managed to conceal—to pay his bills.

Years later, as an exile in a Germany increasingly hostile to minorities, Lev would look back on the people of Helenendorf as less representative of German than of Caucasian culture, and as an example of how the mountainous middle land between Europe and Asia opened itself to outsiders. This town, where a tiny minority managed to defend itself while remaining hospitable to refugees and strangers, became Lev's ideal—the Caucasus of his imagination.

The Azerbaijani peasants from the surrounding towns looked up to the enterprising German "colonists," who cultivated their own land and had many conveniences the peasants themselves did not have. The Helenendorfers built solid two- and three-story houses in traditional Swabian style, with steeply slanting roofs and traditional brick construction, and stone-finished cellars that their neighbors marveled at. Lev found that, while remaining culturally aloof, some of the Germans appeared to have taken one thing from their neighbors—their dark hair and coloring. Many, by appearance alone, might be taken for Azerbaijanis. Yet the residents of Helenendorf were strictly and vocally above intermingling with the natives. Lev treated this subject with his usual comic irony:

> The German colonists, who want to have nothing to do with the "coloured" natives, will soon be "coloured" themselves. Everyone who knows the life of the German colonists will confirm the fact that no "race-shame" is at the bottom of this. Mixture between natives and colonists is highly improbable; it is most likely that the climate influences the hue of the skin. But it is remarkable that blond children are found among the new generation of the Aisors who live near Helenendorf, for a German would never degrade himself by contact with an Aisor woman.

The conclusion that there was no "race shame" behind the mixing of the Germans and the locals would have had particular pungency when Lev published his autobiography—in a Germany on the verge of Nazi takeover, when a rising tide of public opinion held that race determined destiny.

In 2000, I made my way with Fuad to the village of Helenendorf. We got lost trying to find it and were stopped by a group of heavily armed Azeri soldiers. The village sits almost directly on the border with Armenia, where Azeri and Armenian troops were sporadically exchanging fire over a line that never moved. It was as though the First World War had been frozen here by the Bolshevik Revolution and had remained dormant like a virus for eighty years, waiting for the fall of the Soviet Union to become active again.

We finally found Helenendorf, looking very much as Lev had described it, with one difference: the Germans were gone. In 1941 Stalin deported the hardy colonists en masse to Siberia. (Most died there, though a small remnant was repatriated to Germany in 1991.) If there was even a minuscule hope of finding someone who remembered a refugee boy from Baku, this erased it. The buildings were as solid as ever, but the people were long gone.

Only one person showed any recognition when I spoke German to her, an ancient lady who explained, in halting German laced with much Azeri Turkish, that her father had been one of the original colonists; her mother was from one of the local tribes, so she had managed to keep from being deported. All the others I met were descendants of the Azeri families who were relocated here after the forced departure of the inhabitants. These families did their best to keep up the beautiful village they had not built. They were fiercely proud of their finished basements, unique in this desert country. I was led down many an old wooden staircase into a cool brick room lined with shelves, stocked with wine and liquor and fruit preserves.

I found the church Lev had described, where the village had done most of its socializing, from Sunday sermons to daily coffee klatches. A sturdy redbrick Lutheran affair, it was remarkably well preserved on the outside. But when I went inside, I found that the pews had been ripped up and the building had been turned into a sports center. A group of young Azeris ran around vigorously, dribbling and blocking and dunking basketballs into a hoop hung above the pulpit.

It was in the church one night that Lev says he overheard another refugee, an Armenian, reverently praying that he might leave the country alive. Other refugees had found their way to the village, but this man caught his attention. He was in the oil business, like Lev's father, and he had driven all the way from Baku in an old truck loaded with only one possession, his samovar. The teapot and the truck were everything he had left in the world. Lev found the truck interesting.

Lev and the Armenian discussed their common objective: how best to reach the border. The Armenian was carrying a paper that supposedly commissioned him to buy up fishnets all over the country and abroad, wherever he thought necessary. This paper had been enough to convince the "road" Cheka to let him travel by truck from Baku, but now the truck was on its last legs. The border was too far to reach on foot, and the ferocious Railway Cheka worried him. Besides, the businessman did not dare travel alone, for he might be killed as an Armenian by the Muslims, if he was not first arrested by the Cheka as a social parasite. If he and Lev traveled together, they reasoned, each one could provide the other with protection: Lev could protect the Armenian from ethnic troubles with the Muslims, and the Armenian could return the favor. The Armenian's "fishery certificate" would have to protect them both from class genocide.

They practiced their story: the Armenian was a proletarian expert from the Ministry of Fisheries, sent to buy up nets; Lev was his trusty secretary and expert on netting. The Armenian forged a document for Lev, backing up this story. When the time was right, they would attempt to drive on back roads to the border.

The plan had to wait for a while because the countryside had suddenly gotten too dangerous. The Bolshevik forces had consolidated their power in the cities and were fanning out across the countryside to expand their reign of terror. Everywhere villages were forced to "give up the aristocrat" or face artillery bombardment, burning, or mass execution for sheltering "bloodsuckers." According to Lev, in villages that were too small to have a noble, khan, or "capitalist shark," some unlucky peasant was chosen to pretend to be a landowner and sacrifice himself for the sake of the town. In other towns, where they actually did have a local aristocrat, the inhabitants often refused to give him up, and the towns were razed. Lev wrote that many provincial noblemen reported to the local Cheka, risking execution rather than putting their villages in peril.

Indeed, while he was staying in Helenendorf, the Cheka attempted to bolshevize the village. Covert agitators arrived and mixed in among the genuine refugees. It became unsafe to befriend anyone, but the police spy who caused Lev and his new friend to hasten their departure was not undercover. This man was obvious because he was not from anywhere in the Caucasus or even southern Russia. He was a Latvian. He soon arranged a "social evening" that began with dancing. In the course of the evening, stray supporters planted in the crowd started singing Bolshevist songs, and at the end the Latvian mounted the stage and made a speech. After this supposed rousing affair, everyone was expected to rise and sing "The Internationale."

Soldiers arrested Lev after the show and brought him to see the Latvian, who was, of course, a Cheka officer. The Latvian accused Lev of staying seated during "The Internationale" and of being a counterrevolutionary. Lev gamely offered up the story of how he was on a mission to scout fishing nets for the Association for the Promotion of Fishery in Azerbaijan. The Latvian looked as though he thought this was about the most ludicrous invention anyone could come up with—in the mountains, surrounded by deserts, in the middle of a civil war. But he couldn't be sure, given the fact that caviar was Azerbaijan's second-largest industry. He demanded the name and address of the association, and Lev gave it to him.

If telephones and faxes had existed in Azerbaijan in 1920, Lev would have been done for. As it was, the Latvian Cheka promised to inform the association of the comrade's disloyal conduct and to make inquiries about Lev himself. He ordered Lev not to leave the colony until he received word about him from Baku. Of course, that was the cue to leave immediately. Lev went and woke up the Armenian. They departed that night in the old truck, not forgetting to take the samovar. But the truck lasted barely to the next village before breaking down. Lev and the Armenian managed to buy horses and rode the rest of the way to the border, hoping that they could still manage to defend the fishnet story while riding about like two lost cowboys.

The borderland of Azerbaijan and Georgia is a country of verdant fields of orchids, where wild horses graze and flocks of sheep are apt to wander into the road. I did my best to follow in Lev's footsteps, in an old BMW driven by Fuad's uncle—once the head of pediatric surgery in Baku, now a chauffeur and real-estate agent. Dr. Rauf was happy for a reason to drive through this country, which holds some of the finest food and drink in the Caucasus.

Lev recalled riding into villages where the elders would make a speech welcoming their guests and offering them gold, women, or sheep—everything the village had, because the guests were clearly nobles. When they refused the offerings, the people kissed their hands and made a feast in honor of "the guests who did not rob anything." The plan that Lev and the Armenian had come up with worked better than they expected. In the Muslim villages Lev vouched for the Armenian, and in the Armenian villages the Armenian vouched for Lev. Of course, the two Bakuvians had more in common with each other than they did with the mountain folk.

I would have doubted Lev's accounts of the overwhelming hospitality he encountered had I not traveled through this countryside myself, the old BMW making me, Fuad, and Uncle Rauf into something like nobles as well. People offered us everything they had, though they had almost nothing. There were no restaurants, but every tiny village was a feast waiting to happen; every dirt road revealed a man who could fetch you the freshest fruit from the trees, pull some trout from a pond, or slaughter a lamb or a goat for your supper. (Or, as Lev described Caucasian hospitality in *Ali and Nino,* "If a guest enters your house holding the severed head of your only son in his hands, you must still receive him, offer him food and drink.") The people of the Caucasus showed the hospitality that must have greeted the armies of Alexander when they came this way, more than two thousand years ago. It is easy to understand the growing affection Lev felt for his native land, even as he tried to escape it. At their campfire feasts, Lev and the Armenian heard songs about the old khans, about the nightingale that died for the love of the rose, songs from the Persian poets Hafiz and Saadi sung to the music of the *saz,* a kind of violin with three strings that is held like a cello. He watched the knife dance, which involved ten daggers and a beautiful woman but was somehow also supposed to remind one of the Holy Hussein and the martyrdom of Karbala: The man, holding all the daggers, circles the woman, driving away her enemies and trying to embrace her. The woman withdraws, setting him further tasks to fulfill, all to the rhythm of the music. First the man must put down one of the daggers and invite the woman to step on it, as a sign of the power she has over him. Then she throws coins into the air that he must catch without dropping any daggers.

Though illiterate, the peasants of Lev's time were steeped in the traditions of their language. Wandering poets traveled from village to village, as they did in Persia, passing out verses in exchange for gifts, treats, and affection. They composed verses on the spot and could recite something appropriate for any mood or occasion, whether pious or obscene. Lev found that the poorest peasants appreciated fine poetry and were willing to trade whatever they had to hear some and learn the verses if they could. And he discovered the last of the "poetry contests," which came to represent for him everything noble about the Caucasian culture. The contests drew competitors from all the surrounding villages. There were no restrictions of rank or wealth: only skill counted. The contestants would meet in an open square and face off in every genre. Often the audience would be called on to suggest a theme, and the poets would improvise on it. Lev's most famous description of the contests is in *Ali and Nino,* where he uses the dueling poets to show the struggle of the old mountain traditions in the face of the dissolution of honor in the modern world. Lev also cap-

tures the surprisingly cosmopolitan vibrancy to be found in these "mountains of poetry," where masters of the art composed poems in the winter
months, only to emerge in the spring to recite them to audiences in arenas
ranging from the meanest huts to the khans' palaces, and to fight their famous bloodless duels. When they did, the villages of the "fighting poets"
would fill up with an equal mix of Christians and Moslems, all there to
witness the occasions, much the way medieval European towns would fill
up on the day of the joust. Scholars of the Caucasus still quote these passages, though they come from a novel, as the finest example of the unique,
bygone culture of this borderland region. Lev's most vivid description begins as two "valiant lords of song," wearing their hair ostentatiously long
and dressed in silken robes, strut in front of the crowd, eyeing each other
suspiciously, until one of them lets loose a volley of verse:

"Your clothes stink of dung, your face is that of a pig, your talent is as
thin as the hair on a virgin's stomach, and for a little money you would
compose a poem on your own shame."

The other answered, barking grimly: "You wear the robe of a pimp,
you have the voice of a eunuch. You cannot sell your talent, because you
never had any. You live off the crumbs that fall from the festive table of
my genius."

. . . Then an old grey-haired man with the face of an apostle arrived
and announced the two themes for the competition: "The moon over
the river Araxes" and "The death of Aga Mohammed Shah." . . .

Then the more soft-spoken one cried out: "What is like the moon
over the Araxes?"

"The face of thy beloved," interrupted the grim one.

"Mild is the moon's gold!" cried the soft-spoken one.

"No, it is like a fallen warrior's shield," replied the grim one. In time
they exhausted their similes. Then each of them sang a song about the
beauty of the moon, of the river Araxes, that winds like a maiden's plait
through the plain. . . .

Riding in the mountains—"in the regions which have no oil and which
know no Kotschis, no Cheka"—Lev felt truly at ease for the first time
since the revolution. In his time, the foothills were dotted with high stone

towers, centuries old, where the peasants could retreat from their clay huts in case a neighboring headman made war on the area, or it was beset by robbers. Over the centuries, the towers became sanctuaries: it was understood that in times of battle, people hiding in the towers were to be left alone. When the fighting was finished, after all, the peasants would form the new tax base for whoever emerged victorious. The Bolsheviks, when they finally took this area, ordered that the towers be razed as "remnants of feudalism." You can still see a crumbling foundation here and there, sitting abandoned in a meadow.

Much as Lev's caravan trip across Turkestan would inspire his books and articles on the desert and Islam, his journey on horseback along the Georgian-Azeri border would lay the foundation for his works on the Caucasus. These two influences, the desert and the mountains, would merge into a spiritual alternative to the flattening oppression of revolution, totalitarianism, and world war. While the rest of the Caucasus was embroiled in the civil war between Bolsheviks and nationalists, the folk in this border area still fought symbolic medieval battles, acted out with homemade weapons and surrounded by an unlikely mythic calm. Whether they wore crosses and chain-mail armor, like the Khevsurs, or held jousting tournaments and gladiatorial battles using sticks and improvised clubs, like the Pehlewans, the local knights and warriors seemed to Lev like overgrown children, safe in their enchanted woods, ignorant of the outside world, furiously and comically at play. Even the animals had fallen through the looking glass: Lev witnessed "cow races," where the locals spurred the sluggish producers of their sweet cream and butter to act like fiery steeds.

He also met the "devil worshippers," or Jezids, who inspired fear in neighboring villages but turned out to be rather harmless, peaceful, and shy. The Jezids did not proclaim against God, as European Satanists did, but rather held to a dualist view of the universe that believed in appeasing the devil as well as God. Their tradition held that God, being good, was more easily appeased, and that therefore more time must be devoted to pacifying the devil. The Jezids worshipped the devil in the form of a golden peacock, which represented the most important of seven angels holy to their sect. They considered the golden peacock to be the devil, yet somehow he had repented and his tears were said to have doused the everlasting fires of hell. It was important to appease the golden peacock so that his repentance did not cease and the fires flare up again. Lev witnessed a ritual where the Jezids gathered around the grave of their founder, and dancers dressed in white gowns held torches and sang songs praising the devil from sundown to sunrise. A holy man, the ruler of the Jezids, presided over the scene, and he was recognized as the official representative of the devil on earth.

The village of the Jezids added another key bit of evidence to Lev's view of the Caucasus as a sanctuary from the dogmas of the modern world. Ethnically, the Jezids were Kurdish. Religiously, they were a kind of synthetic hybrid of all the major faiths of the Caucasus: Islam, Judaism, Christianity, and Zoroastrianism, with the last influence being paramount. The Jezids feared the sunlight, feeling closer to the darkness, but they also worshipped the sun as the eye of God and fire as the life force of the universe. They practiced baptism and circumcision. Their dietary taboos were vast and extended to vegetables as well as meats. Their scriptures were purely oral and as such were like the poetry of the mountains, subtly changing with each speaker and telling.

In a land where ancient mistrust was so unavoidable that an Armenian and an Azeri had to vouch for each other in every village they went to, the village of the Jezids was the one place where no questions were asked of Lev or his companion. This persecuted, despised sect had no trouble admitting either an Armenian or an Azeri into their midst—worshippers of the golden peacock, it was all the same to them.

In his works on the Caucasus, published mostly in Nazi Europe, Lev sometimes seemed to write about the religious and ethnic minorities of the region as a way of making points about the Jews. The Jezids, mistrusted by everyone, the subject of assorted irrational prejudices, were the supreme example. The Christians took them for Satanists. The Shiites accused them of being descendants of the Caliph Yazid, who murdered the Holy Hussein; hence they saw the Jezids as devils themselves. Their rumored sexual perversions drew contempt from all the surrounding religions, and the Turks even accused them of being a race of homosexuals who reproduced in some unnatural way, inspired by the devil.

When at last the travelers came to the river separating Azerbaijan and Georgia, the Armenian wanted to cross it immediately to the freedom of the Georgian side. But being a loyal companion who had agreed to help Lev find his father, he rode on with Lev to the point at the river where he and Abraham were to meet. They avoided the road by the river itself, assuming that even if the Bolsheviks had not yet arrived in strength, they would at least move quickly to secure the border.

Trouble arrived not in the form of Bolshevik troops but quite the opposite. A group of local peasants who had formed a makeshift anti-Bolshevik militia stopped the riders and accused them of being revolutionaries themselves. Lev and the Armenian met cold stares when they protested that they were in fact capitalists and oil magnates from Baku, the enemies of the revolution. The peasant militia was not convinced, and the situation further deteriorated when the self-appointed guards searched the travelers and discovered the supposed fishery papers. The peasants reserved judgment on the papers because they could not read, but when the only literate person in the area was found, he confirmed that the documents identified the prisoners as Bolshevik agents. The peasant militia began suggesting various medieval punishments to find out the truth.

Shortly before they were led off, a village elder appeared and said that a noble Bey, a highborn gentleman, from Baku had arrived, and since he knew everyone of importance in the city, he had offered to examine the prisoners. Lev and the Armenian brightened, for surely they could prove their credentials to any prominent citizen of Baku. They could not have hoped, however, for the sight that greeted them when the local headman led the distinguished guest into the hut where they were being held. Dressed in the national gear of the Caucasus—the high fur hat, double bandolier, and dagger that ingratiated one from Batum to Baku—was Abraham Nussimbaum. Though in chains, Lev had arrived inadvertently at the meeting place on the border.

After much rejoicing, the Nussimbaums crossed the river and left Azerbaijan behind.

Wherever I went in Georgia, I felt constantly at the edge of a precipice, gorge, or valley. When I visited the country in 2000, I was struck by the presence of enormous statues of medieval Georgian saints and crusader knights, wielding shields and crosses that were indistinguishable from swords. They seemed out of place in these mountains of Shiite shrines and Sufi warrior saints. Yet somehow it was part of the same thing. This was a permanently unsettled frontier, and all these cultures had sent tribes out ahead, who somehow got lost in the hills and staked their claim, jealously guarding it for centuries against all competing tribes. In the bazaar of the Georgian capital, Tiflis, Lev found "Armenian peddlers, Kurdish fortune-tellers, Persian cooks, Ossetian priests, Russians, Arabs, Ingushes, Indians."

Georgians speak an ancient and bizarre language, unrelated to any major linguistic grouping (though philologists have tried to link it to Finno-Ugric and Japanese).* The inhabitants of the tiny mountain kingdom get along with their powerful neighbors so well perhaps because of their experience of foreign relations within the confines of their own borders. They are beloved for their nobility, their independence, their joviality, and their ability to drink everyone else in the region under the table. Georgia is the Scotland of the Caucasus. "Here they drank wine, danced, laughed and sang, were pliant and hard like a steel spring," wrote Lev in *Ali and Nino*. "Was this the gate to Europe? No, of course not. This was part of us, and yet so very different from the rest of us. A gate but leading where?"

Georgia is the third-oldest Christian country in the world, and unlike the region's other Christian kingdom, Armenia, it usually has had good relations with its Muslim neighbors. The Georgians converted to the Cross in the fourth century, a hundred years before the Romans. When wandering crusader knights arrived in the Caucasus from Jerusalem in the eleventh century, the Georgians welcomed them home to their fabled kingdom. Lev was fascinated his whole life with the remnants of the crusader culture to be found in Khevsuria, the region of Georgia to the northeast of Tiflis. He would make much of it as a symbol of the chivalry and hospitality of the country, a place where lost tribes and noble customs survived.

The Ottoman expansions of the sixteenth and seventeenth centuries threatened this remnant of antique Christianity in the Caucasus, and many Georgian nobles took up Islam in order to appease their powerful neighbor to the south. The Georgians might have been scattered to the winds, like the Armenians. Instead, they selectively absorbed Islamic influences, producing their queer mix of Europe and Asia, Christianity and Islam, and remained independent.

Abraham remembered Tiflis from his childhood, but Lev had never

---

* Georgian is one of four languages—along with Mingrelian, Laz, and Suan—that composes a microlinguistic family spoken only within the borders of the country.

lived in a Christian country. Years later, he would remember Georgia as a last gasp of heroic feudal life. But the reality of his experiences there was harsher than his published accounts let on. Unlike the adventures escaping the Bolsheviks in Turkestan, Persia, and Azerbaijan, these hardships were of a new and less swashbuckling sort: poverty and passport troubles in a foreign land. ("It was only in exile that I experienced what money is— the chain-mail shirt that protects its wearer from life.") Lev and his father were at least in good company. In 1920, besieged by the Bolsheviks but still clinging to its independence, the Republic of Georgia became the transit stop for thousands of former citizens of the czar's empire. Like the Nussimbaums, they were headed for Batum, Georgia's main deepwater port on the Black Sea. During the last forty years of the oil boom, Batum had been the main port for exporting Azeri oil to Europe—and also a flashpoint of worker unrest, thanks to the Bolsheviks. (The pipeline connecting Baku to Batum had been the first oil pipeline in the world; it still functions today and is the linchpin of the post-Soviet oil boom.) Before the revolution, steamers plied the Black Sea, entering at the Bosporus; great ships sailing under German, Italian, French, Greek, and Russian flags all stopped at Batum. But in 1921 the main outlet for Russia's oil wealth now became the outlet for its refugees.

The Black Sea oil port became a kind of czarist Casablanca—the bottleneck for all those fleeing west; the gateway to Turkey, to the Mediterranean, to Europe. Lev's memoirs record his horror at the crush of exiles crammed into the city—"the sad gaze of the refugees"—waiting for permission and papers to move on. "Swindlers and millionaires from all over Russia sat here on the border to the old world and waited for the steamer that would take them to Europe. Strange people, formerly hidden in dark alleys. We stayed with relatives, [with] former employees, we shared an apartment with a demimondaine and waited, waited, waited. For what? Either for the collapse of Bolshevism, or for the steamer to Europe like everyone else."

From the seaside where he walked, Lev could see the white peaks of the Caucasus Mountains over the rooftops. The familiar scent of petroleum, which he had known his whole life, hung in the air. But stranded tanker ships, with no cargo to carry, stood idle in the harbor, and the train yards held trains with empty tanks. Across it, out of sight, lay Constantinople! Europe! The World! "I can remember only one dream of Europe that would haunt me back then," he wrote. "A broad, clean street. It is evening, and people are out for a stroll, myself included. All unarmed, for it is Europe, a land where there is no shooting. I approach a house. I take a simple little key and open the door. No iron bolts on the door, no bars, no sentry—it is Europe, a land where no one breaks into the houses. . . . Everything within me yearned to be . . . on the right side of the sea."

But to get out they needed passports, as the old imperial ones and those of the short-lived Azeri Republic were now both useless. Lev and his father had joined the fastest-growing nation of the interwar years—that of the "stateless person." Abraham set about remedying the situation. They were not completely without resources; the problem was, half the city was toting smuggled gold bars and jewelry. It was a buyer's market.

Yet Lev also found a more pleasant side to the situation. He had discovered "an inordinate number of beautiful women—in cafés, on the street, under the palm trees, everywhere." Georgian women were so renowned for their beauty that Lev half believed a tale he had once heard, that the Turkish sultan would not let his subjects visit certain provinces of Georgia for fear they would be enchanted by the women and never return. In Russia, Georgian women were equally famed for their wild temperament, with a reputation as warriors rivaling the women of the Celtic tribes. Lermontov publicized the exotic danger in his 1841 poem "Tamara," dedicated to the fornications and murders of a Georgian queen who lures her lovers past the eunuch guarding her chambers and each morning has their decapitated bodies thrown into the Terek River. The poem was based on the legend of Tamar, a man-killing sorceress, but the image of the Georgian woman as a hellion was also backed by a memorable incident: during the Russian annexation of Georgia at the beginning of the nineteenth century, the Georgian queen Miriam assassinated the czarist general I. P. Lazarev by plunging a dagger into his breast after luring him into her bedroom.

The women along the strand who awakened Lev's heart with their audacious looks, however, were mostly not Georgian beauties. They were fellow exiles. In Baku, outside the set of liberated rich girls who were his friends, the women Lev had seen his whole life in the street had still worn the veil. It shocked him to see so many unveiled women, and twenty years later, he wrote that he could "still see the delicate faces of the women, faces which depending on their temperament looked down with a smile, with boredom, or with indignation at the boy staring at them, at these apparitions from another world."

Lev found a companion in girl-watching—a Georgian boy whose father, the former imperial governor of Batum, Zachariah Mdivani, was an acquaintance of Abraham's. The boy's name was Alexei Mdivani. The two fifteen-year-old boys got drunk in the beachfront cafés of the city and chased the daughters of the Russian exiles until they had their faces slapped or worse. In fact, Lev managed to get involved in his first duel, though I take his account of it—written in a letter to Pima Andreae—with a grain of salt. Lev said he was sitting in a café when the door opened and "an angelic being walked in, beautiful beyond any praise or description." She was escorted by her brother. Falling "instantly and passionately in love," Lev followed the Russian beauty all over Batum without working up the courage to speak to her. One day he followed her into a café and found himself watching her adjust her hat in a mirror. He apparently paused too long, because suddenly, "her wonderful lips opened and she puffed in the mirror, 'You awful Caucasian lad.'" Lev was embarrassed and left immediately.

Some hours later, he lay on the beachfront beneath the moonlit palms, dreaming of the Russian girl and the European cities on the opposite coast and "whether the Bolsheviks would fall after three or six months." Suddenly he felt two hands reach out of the dark and begin throttling him, enormous hands of some robber or bandit. The man held his neck so tightly he could not call for help. But Lev had an old pistol that his father had given him, if only he could reach for it. He managed this, and when he had the gun trained on his attacker, he recognized that it was none other than the brother of the Russian girl. Lev writes that he called out,

"I provoke you." At that, the man had a laughing fit and said, "You provoke me? Are you then old enough, are you of age? I doubt whether you can understand the expression. I'm chamberlain of the Highest Royal Court." But, being armed, I remained calm and answered, "If you are simply a coward and all you can do is attack people from behind, then I'm well capable of seeking revenge for the insult." . . .

In the end, the man . . . admitted that I was capable of demanding a duel, but that unfortunately he was not armed. . . .

"What weapon can one talk about in this wilderness (Batum he thought of as wilderness). We'd better do it like they do it here, this must be a manner unknown to you—a dagger and a veil over the left hand."

They met on the beach an hour later. Alexei Mdivani and his brother David were Lev's witnesses, while the Russian had brought with him a pair of Persians with fancy titles. Lev recalled how odd it was that the Russian had Persian friends, and even odder that they spoke Russian as though they, too, had come from the court in St. Petersburg. They agreed to fight in the local Georgian manner, with the dagger and veil. There was some boasting of fighting to the death, but then they settled on fighting till the "first bleed," which, as Lev bragged to Pima, came when he gave the Russian a gash on the arm. They made up after that, and the Russian's sister even wanted to get to know the "awful Caucasian lad." But by that time, Lev had taken offense and wasn't interested—or so he said.*

In any case, Lev's cavorting came to an end some days later when his father successfully bribed a doctor for inoculation certificates and purchased steamer tickets on an Italian liner named the *Kleopatra*. Wielding his still-considerable influence in the Batum government, Zachariah Mdivani arranged Lev and Abraham Georgian passports. Then he and his sons, the Mdivani "princes," boarded the *Kleopatra* as well, and they and hundreds of other exiles set out on the four-day journey to Constantinople (now Istanbul). "Strange, how seldom a person knows which days of his life are tragic and which are happy," Lev would later think. "The gates of Europe opened wide" before him, and the day seemed like the beginning of happiness.

On board the *Kleopatra,* he and his father joined the world of refugees

---

* While this was the beginning of a romantic career that often seemed to involve as much bluster as actual lovemaking (and let us not forget that Valentino said he preferred a good plate of pasta to a woman any day), the amours of Lev's companion Alexei Mdivani would become world-famous. He became known as an international ladies' man when he married Barbara Hutton, the Woolworth heiress—and drove her to divorce less than a year later. She consoled herself with various European royals and the actor Cary Grant; Alexei took his million-dollar settlement and drove his Mercedes into a tree in Budapest. American high society blamed the Caucasian prince for ruining Hutton's life, but Lev always defended his friend against charges of cruelty (comparing Alexei's unhappy alliance to his own disastrous marriage to an heiress—though he would also somewhat pettily expose the fact that Alexei was not really a prince).

that would be their new society, a shabby yet elegant crowd that echoed their old oil society of Baku. In some ways it was as though they'd made a roundabout return to their home on the Caspian, only this time it was a mobile city moving west with its possessions sewn into its suits: politicians, princes, Bolshevik haters of every stripe. It seemed as if the whole world was on the ship.

Lev was reunited with the Armenian from Helenendorf who had helped him make his escape in search of "fishing nets." He found as well an old acquaintance from Baku who had "somehow become a Dutch consul somewhere." The speeches and gossip of exile began—a constant conversation that would be carried on for years as these dignitaries from a dead empire survived as gigolos and doormen, con artists and toilet sweepers and tradesmen. The debates about counterrevolution! And strategy! And geopolitics! And finance! About the strategic significance of the Caucasus and how the West would not let the Bolsheviks hold the region for long.

Once the *Kleopatra* left Georgian coastal waters, the crew insisted that the passengers pay for their food and drink in gold currency. Lev wandered about the ship "as though in a dream," gaping at the bars, the orchestras, the brightly lit staterooms that were the floating symbols of his new continent. He was tired—mentally, emotionally, physically—and the sight of "the clean stewards, the illuminated passages, the orderly meals" were like a collapse onto starched white sheets after months spent in the dirt, sweat, and blood of running away.

CHAPTER 5

Constantinople, 1921

L EV WAS IN HIGH SPIRITS as the boat left the Caucasus behind and steamed toward the capital of the tottering Ottoman Empire. The *Kleopatra* hugged the Black Sea coast of Anatolia for a few more days, but at last Lev glimpsed the fabled mosques, churches, and palaces he had read so much about: the Golden Horn.

This flooded river valley was said to sparkle like gold because the Byzantines had thrown all their valuables into it when they knew the Turks were coming. (The Turks did not give them much reason to run, though—soon after taking the city on May 29, 1453, Sultan Mehmed the Conqueror ordered construction of dozens of synagogues and churches and invited more foreigners to stay in the city than were allowed in any great European capital of the time.) The Horn's unusual pontoon bridges—on which a line of white-robed men assembled, forcing pedestrians to hand over a coin as toll before letting them pass—connected old Stamboul, the Turkish capital of palaces and mosques, with Galata, the "Frankish" trading port. Thousands of Jews had fled here from the Spanish Inquisition, settling among the Arabs, Greeks, and Armenians. Looking down from Galata's highest point was the stone watchtower, built by the Genoese traders who had first established the district in the fourteenth century.

Most great cities are built next to bodies of water, but Constantinople appeared to exist virtually in a waterway. You could steam or sail through

Constantinople from both north and south. The riches and innovations of two thousand years packed its shores. To control its waters was to control all passage of commerce and arms between Europe and Asia, and the Ottoman Turks had ruled it for nearly five hundred years.

Now everywhere Lev looked, as the *Kleopatra* sailed into the harbor, he saw the gray gleam of modern gunboats topped by the fluttering red, white, and blue of the Union Jack. The Ottoman Empire had joined the war on the German side in 1914 and in 1921 was still paying for the decision. Constantinople was now divided, much as Berlin would be after the Second World War, into zones: the French controlled Stamboul; the British were in Galata and Pera, the so-called Frankish quarters (the Turks still referred to Christian Europeans by the name of the invading Crusader tribes from a millennium earlier); the Italians and the Greeks occupied smaller parts of the city. There were even a number of Japanese soldiers, since Japan had joined the anti–German-Turk coalition toward the end of the First World War.

The alliance with Germany had been a sudden about-face in Turkish strategy engineered by the Young Turks, a cabal of nationalist strongmen who had seized power from the sultan in a violent coup in 1908. The Young Turks spoke a lot, at first, about the universal rights of man and racial and religious equality, promising to bring the Ottoman Empire, with its many ethnic groups—Armenians, Greeks, Jews, Arabs, and Kurds—into the modern age. "Whether one goes to a synagogue or another to a church or the third to a mosque," declared Enver Pasha, the leader of the junta, "we are all, who live under this blue sky, proud to call ourselves Ottomans."

But the spirit of universal Ottoman brotherhood soon melted away, revealing a harder, more exclusive ideology. The Young Turks embraced something called "pan-Turanianism"—the notion that all Turks from the Russian steppes to Anatolia came from a single ancestral land called "Turan." In this view, the entire historical orientation of the Ottoman Empire toward Europe and the Middle East had been misplaced. Instead, the empire should be focused on reuniting the Turanic peoples in Russia and Central Asia. In his book *Allah Is Great,* Lev compared the Turanian obsession to "blood and soil" ideas in Germany. In a kind of Turkish parallel to the German idea of lebensraum, the future was to be found in the

East—in an invasion of Russia to reclaim ancestral lands from the thirteenth century and earlier, not only those of the Ottomans but of the other great Turanians, the Mongols and the Huns.*

What clinched the Turkish-German axis in the First World War was really the personality of Enver Pasha. A dark fireplug of a man who had served as the Ottoman military attaché in Berlin, Enver had embraced all the pointed helmets and polished boots and talk of Wagnerian Götterdämmerung-cum-Jihad. (Kaiser Wilhelm did his part by spreading the rumor that he had converted to Islam.) When Enver led the Young Turks to power in 1908, as war minister, he was sporting a Kaiser Wilhelm mustache, which should have been a clue as to which way things would go. What ensued may have amounted to the most dramatic "self-colonization" in history: in the name of achieving instant modernization and international power, the Young Turk junta turned the Ottoman Empire into a virtual military colony of the German Reich. *"Deutschland über Allah,"* said some diplomatic wags. But it was a dead serious maneuver, and it happened with lightning speed. Enver turned over the entire Ottoman officer corps to the Germans; more than *twenty-five thousand* German officers and NCOs assumed positions of direct command. A Prussian officer founded the Turkish Air Force, and two German battleships arrived in the Golden Horn. The German crew brazenly donned fezzes and sang *"Deutschland über Alles"* beneath the seaside villa of the Russian ambassador.

The Young Turks had launched the Ottoman Empire off a cliff. It is hardly remembered now what a large role Turkey played in the First World War, except for the storied Gallipoli landing, where the defending Turks slaughtered British, Australian, and New Zealander expeditionary forces. Almost everywhere else, it was the Turkish soldiers who were slaughtered. More than three hundred thousand Turkish soldiers died fighting the Russians in the Caucasus alone, as a result of Enver's plan to begin a great reconquest of the ancient Turkish heartland. The plan was to take Baku so

---

* Since the eighteenth century, Russian foreign ministers had referred to the Ottoman capital not as Constantinople but as Czargrad, in anticipation of it becoming the new capital of the world-dominating Super Russian Empire. The counter-theory of the pan-Turanian principle meant that if the Russians wanted to reconquer Constantinople, the Turks would do them one better, reconquering half of Russia.

as to launch Turkish armies across the Caspian in oil tankers, landing at Kizel-Su and crossing Turkestan, conquering Bukhara, Samarkand, and eventually, even Mongolia. On the eve of the revolution, the czar's forces poised for a final attack on Constantinople. Had Russia stayed in the war and the Bolsheviks not prevailed, Istanbul might today be called Czargrad and the Middle East might be an imperial Russian federation. The Turkish rout was the fault of poor planning and bluster—Enver sent Turkish troops to fight in the Caucasus in winter with no overcoats and without even boots—but the increasingly fanatical Young Turk junta looked for someone else to blame for the failure of the Turanian dream. Thus, the infamous Armenian massacres of 1915 were set in motion.

As they had in Azerbaijan, the Armenians had always done rather well under the sultans, often controlling important business and political positions. In the late nineteenth century, however, Russia proclaimed itself protector of the Armenians, as fellow Christians, and began arming and encouraging an Armenian separatist movement. Under this pretext, Sultan Abdul Hamid ("Abdul the Red") orchestrated the murder of tens of thousands in pogroms, far deadlier than the czarist pogroms against Jews in Russia. During the First World War, a similar cycle of Russian provocation and Turkish reprisal hit the Armenians, but the persecutions by the Young Turk regime were a different sort of beast. The regime declared a secret war against its own Armenian subjects and, in the spring of 1915, began to order the rounding up and deportation of Armenian men, women, and children. Almost all the killing and dying took place in remote areas of eastern Anatolia and Syria. The majority of the victims were sent on forced marches into the desert where they died of thirst and starvation, but Kurdish bandits, traditional enemies of the Armenians, attacked them on the marches as well. Many Turkish officers protested, and a number were executed for treason. There are no firm figures on the number of deaths, but estimates suggest hundreds of thousands of victims to possibly 1.5 million in hardly more than a year. By 1916 the Young Turk government had prepared an elaborate diplomatic defense of the action, which explained the killings as a "defensive" maneuver against an internal insurrection. With slight variation, this has remained the official Turkish position to this day. But even if military reasoning could justify murdering so many civilians, the arguments the Young Turks offered for their actions—though too often accepted by First World War historians—were obviously false. While there had been an Armenian separatist movement of importance in Ottoman Turkey, it was a minority movement, and most Armenians staunchly supported the imperial state, especially during the war (not least for fear of being accused of disloyalty).

By 1918, ten years after their ascent to power, the Young Turk government had destroyed the Ottoman Empire, led millions of Turkish soldiers to their deaths, and visited mass murder on their own civilian population.* As Allied forces drew closer to Constantinople, a group of liberal parliamentarians and Ottoman royals banded together to arrest the Young Turk leaders, but they escaped to Berlin on German torpedo boats. A pro-Allied government installed itself and immediately sued for peace. The new Ottoman sultan, Mehmed VI, and his grand vizier thought they could renew the special relationship with the English and the French that had sustained the empire for the previous two hundred years.

The British answered the overtures of the liberal Ottomans by sending a warship, the provocatively named *Agamemnon,* to drop anchor in the Golden Horn, and a joint international force occupied Constantinople and began dismantling the "sick man of Europe." (The phrase had first been used by Czar Nicholas I in the 1850s, at a time when Russia seemed in the pinnacle of health; as it turned out, the Russian Empire suddenly expired of its own illness in 1917, leaving the Ottoman "sick man" to linger on for a while.) The Ottomans pointed out that the occupation of Constantinople by British, French, and Italian troops was a violation of the armistice they had signed, but to no avail. Lord Curzon, the British secretary of war and former viceroy of India, favored making Constantinople an international city. He led a campaign to strip the Hagia Sofia of its Koranic inscriptions and turn the world's most famous mosque back into a Christian church.† The Vatican wanted in on the action, and soon the Ital-

---

* Today the phrase "young Turk" means someone with a brash desire to shake things up, but this is surely a case of a term entering the language that should have been thought better of, considering that the Young Turks' main distinction would be introducing genocide to the modern world. The phrase "storm trooper" could denote the same sort of youthful dynamic energy.

† One of the myths about the Turkish conquest of Constantinople in 1453 was that the Ottomans destroyed St. Sofia, the world's most magnificent Christian church, in order to turn it into Hagia Sofia, the world's biggest mosque. It is true that the Turks converted the church into a mosque, but it is not true that they sacked or destroyed it. That honor belongs to the "Latin Crusaders," as the Byzantine Christians called them—the Catholic

ian government was arguing that since Constantinople had been founded by a Roman emperor, the entire city should once again be ceded to Italy.

An immediate postwar map of the region shows the Ottoman Empire whittled away to a tiny seed of its former self, with much of even its Turkish heartland in the hands of Greeks, French, even Italians. The Ottomans might still have found a creative way out of their dilemma at the bargaining table had the Armenian massacres not permanently alienated the most important potential ally at the Versailles conference: the United States. By 1919 the fate of Armenia had taken on a significance for Americans and their government that probably has no comparison. "Suffering Armenia," as it was called, was the largest foreign-policy fund-raising cause in the history of the United States. In 1917, President Wilson delayed the entrance of America into the First World War solely to avoid obstructing the transfers of America's most popular charity. The sultan's representatives at the Versailles peace conference condemned the massacres and starvation marches—arguing that the empire had been hijacked by the Young Turk junta and the Germans—but the Allies took the new Ottoman government's conciliatory overtures as signs of weakness. Instead of reaching an agreement with the Ottomans—preserving some sort of constitutional monarchy favorable to Western interests—the Allies humiliated the Turks at every turn and allowed Greece to invade parts of Turkey in a hapless attempt to reconstitute a Hellenic Empire à la Alexander.

The situation gave a golden chance to the one man who could take up the nationalist cause: General Mustafa Kemal, who had defeated the British at Gallipoli but had always been an enemy as well of the pro-German Young Turks. He was the more moderate kind of nationalist. He did not sport a Kaiser Wilhelm mustache or excel at massacring Armenian civilians. General Kemal met with the sultan a number of times between November 1918, when the Allies occupied Constantinople, and April 1919, giving the impression that he was merely a loyal defender of the Ottoman throne. On April 30, 1919, General Kemal obtained an appointment to go to Anatolia to "pacify" the region and assure the observance of the Allied

---

crusaders from France and Germany who stopped by the Christian city of Constantinople on their way to fight the Muslims and sacked every Orthodox Christian monument in sight. The Ottomans in fact took possession of the world's greatest Christian church that had been sacked by . . . Christians.

armistice. Of course, he did just the opposite. Once in Anatolia, he started a civil war that would lead to the birth of an independent, post-Ottoman Turkish state. Ataturk would end up in Constantinople, though Lev and his father—and a hundred thousand more refugees from the new Soviet Union—would beat him to it.

Representatives of the inter-allied administration, with a pliant Turkish official coming along for form, boarded the *Kleopatra*. A dozen doctors and many more policemen followed. The doctors carried a long list of diseases the passengers might be bringing in from dirty Asia that could exclude them from entry. The multinational police carried equally long lists of political and other offenses. To their relief, the Nussimbaums found that the British, who led the inspections, conducted the entire process along strict class lines. Lev marveled that there was no question of bribery, since mere rank sufficed to exempt one from true examination. The third-class passengers were taken into quarantine or put under arrest, questions to be asked later; they were presumed to pose some threat or another. The second-class passengers were sent through the gauntlet of doctors and, if they passed unscathed, were subjected to endless questioning by the police.

In the first-class saloon, where Lev and his father waited, a gray-haired professor heartily shook hands with all the travelers, handing them medical certificates certifying that they were free of plague, typhoid, and cholera. The political commission next stamped the passengers' traveling papers certifying that they were of proper background and above political suspicion. Abraham commented on the backwardness of Asia and the smooth, modern ways of the West.

The Nussimbaums left the steamer and went to an international hotel. On the way, they saw khaki-clad soldiers everywhere, many of them with black and brown faces. As the Allies had gotten increasingly worried about the threat of a nationalist siege, they poured more troops into guarding it; thousands of soldiers from Egypt and Palestine had joined nearly ten thousand Indian regulars. The British had recently convinced the sultan, in his role as caliph of all Muslims, to issue a fatwa against Ataturk, and a British-backed "Army of the Caliphate" was marching westward to besiege Ankara.

Lev was oddly touched by the plight of the musty, embattled Ottoman monarchy—at this point resented by nearly all sides—and enraptured by its ancient imperial city. Constantinople had long been the capital of Muslim tolerance, and now it was also, as Lev would discover, the capital of Muslim modernism, Orientalist enlightenment, and an exiled empire of refugees.

In November 1920, General Pyot Nikolayevich Wrangel, widely considered the most decent of the White Russian commanders, had sailed 126 ships into the Golden Horn, bringing more than one hundred thousand Russians into the heart of Constantinople. Slavic expansionists had dreamed for years of seeing Russians overrun Constantinople ("Czargrad"), but when the czar's army at last arrived at the city gates, they came not as conquerors but as refugees. More than half the Russians that General Wrangel had with him were not even soldiers but civilians—peasants, professionals, monarchists, Jews, and anti-Semites—who had managed to climb aboard his motley flotilla as it evacuated from the Crimea, final stronghold of the Whites in Russia. General Wrangel and his men found the Ottoman authorities, their traditional enemies, surprisingly welcoming. The logistical show was run by the Allied occupation authorities—the British and French billeted more than twenty-five thousand Russians in their old camp on Gallipoli—but the reaction of the Ottomans to the fleeing Russians was in part an act of kindness from one dying imperial dynasty for another. Constantinople became the temporary headquarters of "Russia abroad," or simply the Emigration, as the refugees called their new, portable motherland. The size of the White Russian Army in the city was staggering—more than five times larger than the Allied occupation force of English, French, and Italians combined. There were rumors that the White Russians were going to try to seize control from the Allies, but these were baseless. The Russian soldiers were now merely refugees, people whose whole world had just gone up in smoke and who didn't know where they would be in a month. The Bolshevik government would soon revoke their passports, turning them, like Lev and Abraham, into that pariah figure of the era, the stateless citizen. The city's great boulevards and alleyways were soon crowded with Russian officers driving taxis and selling clothing, books, and gold coins at the bazaars. Many went hungry, and many wore increasingly tattered trousers and shoes, with no money to replace them.

In his book *White Russia: Men Without a Homeland,* published in

Berlin in 1932, Lev would remember the desperate inventiveness of some of the refugees, and the "strange businesses" that flourished on the sly. (One entrepreneurial type "invented a new sport, which soon became common all over the city: cockroach races," Lev wrote. "The Russians gathered especially strong exemplars, placed them in an empty cigarette carton, covered the carton with glass and arranged races. An audience gathered and paid admission.") Constantinople's theaters and nightclubs soon became a virtual Russian monopoly. The exiles ran clubs like the Black Rose and the Petrograd Patisserie, where the Russian waitresses were as much of a draw as the music, food, or liquor (at Turkish restaurants, only men were allowed to wait tables). The women were tall and fair-haired, and many were aristocrats, or said they were—thus at Le Grand Cercle Moscovite, a voguish restaurant, the waitresses were referred to as "duchesses." Lev's fellow Azeri Banine Asadullayeva captures the scene in her 1945 memoir, *Jours Caucasians:*

> One of the great attractions in Constantinople were the Russian clubs, which step by step advanced toward "the West" until they finally landed in Paris. The city was brimming with Russian emigrants. The men argued with one another, sold jewelry or took on any old job. The women attempted mainly to become courtesans. . . . The most elegant nightclub was the Black Rose. My husband often took me there. . . . One Russian song was sung after another. One after another, bottles of champagne were drunk. . . . In all sincerity I was told, "One comes here not to laugh, but rather to cry," by one of the regulars.

Now that the exiles had lost everything and given up the fight against the Reds, it was all one long party for survival. The duchesses posed perhaps the most immediate problem for the authorities. A leading Turkish wives' and widows' association soon petitioned the governor of Constantinople that the city's men were "worn out by the habit of consuming lethal poisons such as morphine, cocaine, ether and alcohol and this is entirely because of the baleful influence of these Russian women." The Russian restaurants, bars, and *cafés chantants* were places, according to the petition, where "hundreds of young Turks drag their health, wealth and honor into the whirlpool of calamity every night." Hardly less scandalous were the jazz clubs, one of them run by a black American entrepreneur who was himself a kind of White Russian exile. He was said to have opened his first jazz club in St. Petersburg, and when the revolution hit, he followed his clientele of czarist jazz fans down to their new stomping ground on the Bosporus. He soon had Constantinople dancing the Charleston and the fox-trot.

By day, Lev wandered alone among the "stone fairy tales" of Constantinople as if he had found a living version of his parents' library. To Lev, the city was Baku on an infinitely larger scale. He realized what a miniature he had inhabited before—in a way, it had been perfect for a child, to whom the khan's palace was vast—but now he felt he was at the center of everything.

Lev had imagined he was taking the final leap west—and had found himself at the heart of the East. This was the paradox of Constantinople. And it seemed to Lev that it was the Muslim character underlying the basically European city that encouraged a respect for all traditions, a fundamental tolerance.

When Ataturk overran the city in 1923, after Lev and his father had moved on, the White Russian "government in exile" beat a hasty retreat. It evacuated the Russian embassy, and Soviet representatives arrived. Constantinople's years as a high-living international capital were over, and two years later, Constantinople itself would be gone, renamed Istanbul. The émigrés left and took their duchesses, their jewels, and their *cafés chantants* with them. Many would die destitute in Paris, São Paulo, and New York.

The Allied occupation of Constantinople would largely be forgotten after the British retreated and belatedly embraced Ataturk. But the resentment that the Allies stirred up in Turkey was to reverberate throughout the century, crystallizing into a generalized Muslim resentment against the West. Lord Curzon's move to re-Christianize the Hagia Sofia and abolish the caliphate showed the potential to spark Islamic protest even then. From 1919 to 1924, the "Khilafat" movement, a pan-Islamic, anti-British ideology, swept South Asia, largely stoked up by fear and outrage over what the occupiers were doing in Constantinople. Mass rallies were held in Delhi, Bombay, Karachi, and the South Indian Muslim province of Kerala. The Khilafat leaders said that the British, who had most of the world's Muslims under their control already, were now about to wipe out

the caliphate itself. The idea took root that the West was some sort of dia-
bolical machine bent on destroying Islam, and that a millennial battle was
in the making. To be sure, moderate Muslim leaders like the Aga Khan,
leader of India's Ismaili Shia sect, also expressed outrage. The British Indian administration sent desperate cables to London, warning that India
would be lost if certain people did not moderate their administration of
Constantinople.

It was a bitter irony that when Ataturk, not the British, disbanded the
caliphate two years later, one of his stated reasons was the Islamic leaders'
international protest movement. He regarded the outcry as a gross interference in Turkey's internal affairs.

I didn't know much about the Ottoman Empire when I first returned
from Baku, but when I got back to my apartment in New York, the perfect source presented itself to me across the hallway. As was so often the
case in my search for Kurban Said, aka Lev Nussimbaum, a startling coincidence presented history to me in the form of a charming elderly person,
happy to find someone interested in events that had meant so much back
before the world wars. Invited to dinner one night by our neighbor, a
raven-haired, blue-eyed Turkish English New Yorker named April, my
wife and I were introduced to her cousin by marriage—an older man im-
peccably but modestly dressed in a Brooks Brothers suit of uncertain vintage. Thus, I found myself shaking hands with Mr. Ertugrul Osman, the
rightful heir to the Ottoman Empire. He was the eldest male member of
the ancient house that had ruled the Muslim world for six centuries, and
had things gone differently, he would now be the sultan of Turkey.

Mr. Osman had the unmistakable sleepy-lidded eyes and pointed eyebrows that I knew from the portraits of Süleyman the Magnificent and the
other sultans, though he was thinner and wore a black knit tie rather than
a silk turban. Ertugrul had been the name of the semi-mythical first
Osman (the origin of the word "Ottoman"), who defeated the Seljuk
Turks on the field of battle in 1290. The current Mr. Osman's gestures
seemed youthful for an octogenarian; I felt I was speaking with Süleyman
the Magnificent as an old-fashioned Harvard man.

Mr. Osman's wife was a relative of the deposed Afghan king, but she
was far prouder of her husband's lineage. "What is the Afghan kingdom?"

she said to me. "Nothing that old, really. This man here, my husband, is the rightful heir to the longest existing empire in the history of mankind."

"It is true about the empire," said Mr. Osman with a disarming smile, "but I'm not the rightful heir, darling, since the empire does not exist. I am the pretender to the throne, technically, but even that does not interest me."

While my two-year-old daughter pulled the hair of the pretender to the Ottoman throne, and April served us one delicious Turkish dish after another, I received a tutorial from Mr. Osman in Ottoman history. Everything was a bit different from the history books. He cited comparisons of different sultans as if they were ballplayers: the sizes of their harems, the percentages of the royal treasury their wives spent on clothes, their attitudes toward Europe and their ways of handling the West. He recalled his great-great-uncle, whose wives suddenly became enamored of European clothes and "went to Paris and bought out every store in St. Germain des Prés and nearly bankrupted the treasury! In 1860 in Istanbul, no member of the harem would be seen except in the newest, fanciest Parisian outfit." He was particularly adamant about history's misunderstanding of his grandfather, the infamous Abdul Hamid, Abdul the Red—scourge of liberals and Armenians and the last sultan to hold the empire firmly in his grasp.

"One reason they wanted to depose my grandfather was that he refused the alliance with Germany because he knew it would be a disaster. My grandfather was very good friends with the kaiser. There is a letter in Turkey, from the kaiser to the sultan, where he calls him my brother and says that if we have a war, you will be together, you will be on my side." This letter was part of the campaign of wooing the Turks over to the German side begun in the 1890s, when the sultan's international reputation was at an all-time low. There is a wonderful picture of Hajji Wilhelm perched on an Arabian horse in the desert, his omnipresent spiked helmet wrapped in traditional Islamic headgear. "My grandfather very politely said that he wouldn't. No thank you, in other words," explained Mr. Osman. "He knew that if there was a war, the Germans would lose and then we would lose." According to Mr. Osman, all the great mistakes had been made by his grandfather's successor, "Uncle Mehmed," who had listened to the Young Turks and steered the empire away from England and

France and toward Germany. There was a series of sultans in those years, none very successful, he went on, all uncles, ending with his cousin Abdul Mejid, who became only caliph, not sultan, in 1922.

Mr. Osman didn't make too much of it, but after the disastrous Young Turk flirtation with Germany, the last Ottomans were in fact cosmopolitan and progressive. The brief "jazz years" of Constantinople saw the throne reject its recent disastrous leap into ethnic nationalism and resurrect its centuries-old tradition of tolerance. The city got a Kurdish chief of police and a flowering of Kurdish newspapers. The Armenians were left in peace. Women's hemlines were rising and the veils were falling. Yet these last Ottomans were enormously unpopular. It was not that the Turkish people weren't ready for liberalization of all kinds, as Ataturk would prove shortly thereafter. It was rather that the last Ottomans had shown a love for all things modern, liberal, and Western—fast cars, fast women, "high life," as Mr. Osman called it—just as their empire was being picked apart by the European powers. They were seen, quite simply, as traitors.

Ataturk was firmly in control of the "new" nation of Turkey by 1922, though it was unclear what his official position was. He had moved the seat of government to Ankara, a small, barren city in Anatolia, in order to insulate Turkish politics from the intrigues of Constantinople. He had removed the temporal rights from the Ottoman throne—that is, detached the title of sultan from caliph—turning the position, for the first time in history, into a purely religious one, but he was not prepared to abolish it yet. To end the caliphate at the same time as the sultanate might have been too much for the hidebound Turks, especially the religious establishment. Ataturk did not want a civil war, so he ended the sultanate first, and then looked around for the cleverest, most honorable Osman to become caliph.

He chose Mr. Osman's cousin, Abdul Mejid, who was a serious-minded Renaissance man—an accomplished scholar, painter, musician, and poet—and perhaps the most progressive ruler ever to have sat on the throne. An American magazine profile in 1924 noted that the caliph "read a great deal . . . German and French philosophers . . . he regretted his inability to read English well enough to understand the English philosophers. He found politics distasteful, because it is 'the cause of so much hardship and unhappiness.'" Mr. Mejid had told the magazine that he counted on foreigners to come to Turkey. "Their coming here should be of great assistance to this country," he said. "Their money will enable us to build schools and enlighten the people of this unfortunate nation, who until now have been nothing but excellent warriors, though they have all the aptitudes for becoming philosophers and scientists."

Most astonishingly, perhaps, the spiritual leader of all the world's Sunni Muslims flatly denied the superiority of Islam. The scholar-sultan told the American reporter that he dreamed of a world "where all human beings will call one another brothers, racial and religious considerations will disappear, and people will live obeying the true word of God as it was brought to them by His prophets, Moses, Christ, Confucius, Buddha and Mahomet."

Then, on March 3, 1924, Ataturk suddenly abolished the position of caliph, a little more than a year after convincing the enlightened Mr. Mejid to take the job. On March 23, the *vali* of Constantinople, a sort of lord high chamberlain, received instructions from Ankara that "the Caliph should be treated with utmost courtesy but must be out of Turkey before dawn." All male descendants of the Osmans were to be given twenty-four hours to leave. Princesses and others had three days. The caliph would receive $7,500 in cash, and $500 each would go to the other members of the Osman family. The Osmans had never handled money before, as their servants had always had unlimited access to the country's treasury on behalf of their material wishes. Many barely knew how to dress themselves. The family's passports were to be stamped to bar them from ever returning to Turkey; they were to be permitted to live wherever they chose in the West, but no Osman was to take up residence in a Muslim country, for fear that he could resurrect himself as either sultan or caliph.

When the high chamberlain came to inform Abdul Mejid of his fate, he found the caliph of all Muslims lying on his couch reading Montaigne. (I did not need to take Mr. Osman's word for this delightful anecdote, for a transcription of the high chamberlain's testimony was put into the public record the following day: "His Majesty was reading Montaigne's *Essays* when I informed him that the Vali and three other police officials insisted on seeing him at once.") The chamberlain regretfully informed the caliph that he had been given a maximum of four hours to dress and prepare himself for exile.

Contemporary news reports describe how the palace was suddenly bustling with fevered action: the women of the harem, most of whom were over seventy by this point, ran around wailing with distress. The eunuchs wailed even louder, drowning them out. Hundreds of servants carted out old-fashioned carpetbags and luxurious gold dressing cases and piled into them everything they could see: vases, antique coffee cups, lamps, ancient uniforms, silk gowns, manuscripts, weapons. . . . How do you wrap up a six-hundred-year-old dynasty like it was a convention site? What do you do with the centuries of gifts that had been laid at the feet of the world's oldest imperial family? The servants clearly had no idea and were throwing things into the carpetbags in a kind of hysteria. Eventually, the commissioner of the police and his men intervened and helped them pack more mundane suitcases full of Western clothes and bed linens.

At four in the morning, the caliph and his family walked out of the palace of their ancestors. In a few hours' time, they would join the thousands of other royal exiles who were flooding Europe, and His Imperial Majesty, the Light of the World, etc., etc., would become plain Mr. Osman, like my dinner companion, his cousin. Abdul Mejid could soon sit in quiet anonymity in a Paris café and read his Montaigne unmolested by the troubles of 100 million souls.

"How did you feel," I said, asking the current Mr. Osman the American newscaster's question, "knowing that you would never be sultan or caliph of all Muslims?"

"I wasn't too much affected, really," he said. "I didn't need to go into exile, because I was already out of the country, in boarding school—the Theresiana, in Vienna. Of course, the whole world was in turmoil— the Austrian Empire had just collapsed as well, which probably affected me as much as the Ottoman Empire's collapse. . . . But to tell the truth, I was mostly concerned with soccer. You see, I was the captain of my team that year at the Theresiana." Mr. Osman recalled for me the names of his soccer teammates of seventy years ago. "They were almost all Austrians, except me," he said, chuckling.

I asked what it had been like to be at a high school with only aristocrats—who could they play against in soccer matches, for example?

"Oh, it wasn't only aristocrats. In fact, just before the collapse, they had instituted a program to try to recruit more non-royal and non-noble boys—it was sort of like affirmative action in your country."

But what did he think about losing his right to become sultan? Could Turkey have been better off if the sultanate had survived?

"Monarchy is dead," said Mr. Osman. "As King Farouk said after he was dethroned, 'Pretty soon there'll be only five kings left in the world: the king of spades, the king of hearts, the king of clubs, the king of diamonds, and the king of England.' "

His wife agreed but expressed her concern that people were so uninformed now about the Ottoman Empire that its legacy had been forgotten and misunderstood.

Mr. Osman shrugged and inquired about the health of my wife's cat, which, at thirteen, and in decline, had also been invited across the hall. Mr. Osman apparently liked cats. We discussed the enormous tiger tomcat for the rest of the evening while he sat comfortably nearby. The pretender to the Ottoman throne and his sympathetic wife inquired gravely into his eating habits, his sleep, and his attitude toward strangers, and later, they offered to cat-sit for us. We took them up on it.

Before we left, Mrs. Osman returned to the topic uppermost in her mind. "It is a shame that after my husband is gone, the line of Ottomans becomes much more diluted, and nobody knows as much of the history as he does."

"I wouldn't say that," said Mr. Osman modestly.

"Tell me, who knows a thing!" his wife snapped, meaning in her husband's family. "Who cares anything about the history, this great empire, the oldest in the world, who *cares* about it at all?"

Lev cared about it all desperately. When he wandered the streets of occupied Constantinople in 1921—at a time when even the Turks were rejecting their Ottoman complexity for the simplicity of nationalism, when the ever collapsing capital of the world seemed destitute and decadent—Lev believed he had discovered the meaning of his life in the racial and religious melting pot of the world's oldest empire. He wandered around in a kind of daze, leaving his father at the hotel to plot with the exiles and make plans for further escapes. Lev needed no further escape. He had entered the world of his childhood daydreams.

"I think I went mad for days," he would recall in his deathbed notebooks, dreaming of seeing it all again: "Walking among the palaces, the viziers and court officials . . . I was nearly reeling with ecstasy, walking through the streets of the Caliph city. . . . Was that even I? A stranger with different feelings, different thoughts. . . . I believe that my life began in Istanbul. I was 15 then. I saw the life of the Orient and I knew that as much as I yearned for Europe, I would be forever captivated by this life."

CHAPTER 6

Minarets and Silk Stockings

A FTER A FEW WEEKS AMONG THE MOSQUES AND THE NIGHT-clubs, the Nussimbaums were on the move again. Like their fel-low White Russian émigrés, most of the Baku exiles treated Constantinople as a stopping point on the way to their real destination, the unofficial capital of the Emigration: Paris. Elite Russians spoke and read French, and France had been the main investor in czarist Russia's cap-italist schemes. (This had led to the unusual spectacle of the last czar, who scorned even the idea of a constitution, standing and saluting next to the civilian French president as the Marseillaise was played.)* Before the revo-lution, the Bolsheviks made the grittier quartiers of Paris their global nerve center of operations. The revolution would mean merely a changing of the guard—the Reds leaving to take power, the Whites arriving.

Some émigrés took the Orient Express overland through Bulgaria, as the exiled family of the imperial house of Osman would do. Banine Asadullayeva recalled making the trip alone and locking herself into her train compartment, terrified that "one or more of the men" on board would be so overcome by lust that they would attack her. By the time she reached the outskirts of Paris, she had taken off her veil—symbolically and

---

* France's investments in czarist Russia (as well as in the Ottoman Empire) largely account for why, though it was "victorious" in the First World War, France in the years between 1919 and 1939 tottered on the verge of financial collapse. The Bolshevik and Turkish revo-lutions ruined many French investors, contributing to France's insistence on receiving massive financial reparations from Germany after 1918.

literally—and went on to live the life of a modern independent woman in the West. The Nussimbaums did not take the overland route but instead boarded a ship bound for the Adriatic coast of Italy. The other central destination for the Russian exiles was Berlin, and they decided that they would make their way up the Italian boot of the "real Europe" and leave their options open. Crowds of refugees, desperate to get from Constantinople to any European port as quickly as possible, had replaced the line's former pleasure traffic between Europe and the Orient. Many of the Italian sailors sold space in their cabins to travelers who could not afford regular passage, but the Nussimbaums managed to get a legal berth.

Back aboard the floating world of the exiles, Lev was overtaken by a nostalgia for the "East" as he'd just experienced it in Constantinople. His sympathies were with the sultan and his court. It seemed to him a grand institution—the sultanate, the caliphate—and there was something in the mosques and bazaars of the great Islamic capital that made Lev feel as though he had found his purpose in life. As he traveled west, dressed in his European suit, he was increasingly sure that no matter how he might appear to people on the outside or what it said in his Georgian passport, inwardly he was a Man from the East, a realm of lost glory and mystery. He began to fantasize about a pan-Islamic spirit that would preserve everything from revolutionary upheaval. All revolutionaries and passionate political movements—indeed, all modern politics—disgusted and alarmed him. So he sought a retreat into the permanent institutions whose foundations lay in the distant past.

Monarchism, even absolutism, held a distinct appeal. He had grown up in a time and place when an almost American style of dynamism had flourished under a backward, absolutist regime. Despite the virulent anti-Semitism of czarist Russia, Lev had grown up with a curious affection for what he dreamed the monarchy could be rather than what it ever was or had been. In some ways, what Lev wanted from monarchism was not so different from what the modern American wants from liberal democracy: the right to be left alone. Lev was at heart a conservative, in the old liberal sense of the word. To be conservative could be a hard thing for a Jew in Europe—where the old order had so often favored tyranny and persecution. But for children of the great empires early in the twentieth century, it was becoming an increasingly attractive outlook. When Woodrow Wilson won the day in 1918 with his vision of imperial identities being swept away in favor of national "self-determination," the aspiring nations within the Ottoman and Hapsburg empires leaped at the chance—and at each other's throats. The end of the imperial system in Europe and the Near East unleashed a string of little genocides all across the continent. In this landscape a not insignificant number of Jews mourned the lost emperors who had kept life relatively civilized and safe. Much like the Hapsburg Empire, the most tolerant of the great empires destroyed by the First World War, the Ottoman Empire was finally a loosely run federation of dozens of different ethnic groups who were forced to live in relative harmony by their subservience to imperial power.

The dozens of Christian nationalities didn't miss their fallen imperial houses: they knew exactly what they were going to do when they controlled their ancestral spot on the map. The Jews hadn't a clue what would become of them once old monarchies fell, but they guessed it would be nothing good. They were the only group, besides the Gypsies, who couldn't claim a patch of ground as their ancestral right.* So the Jews supported both the Hapsburgs and the Ottomans to the very end, and even after the end, many continued to carry the torch for multiethnic monarchism.

"From the day of the abdication of the Czar, I became a confirmed monarchist," Lev would write. "At first only for sentimental reasons, out of sympathy for fallen greatness, then more and more consciously." Such loyalty among Russian Jews was rare—after all, the court in St. Petersburg had often spoken openly about murdering them—and all citizens of the Caucasus, no matter what their background, had had mixed feelings about the Russian imperial house. But though he would soon attach himself to perhaps the strangest of the neo-czarist supporters—the Eurasian–Young Russian sect, led by a half-Persian ex-czarist officer in Paris—Lev's emerging monarchist loyalties were never directly to the fallen czar.

At some point during his journey to Italy, Lev decided that he would adopt an Ottoman identity—just as everyone else was rejecting it, even many of the Turks. He was struck by a kind of instant nostalgia, having

---

* Palestine was an Ottoman province, but the Jews of the Ottoman Empire had virtually no connection to it, since they were centered in Constantinople, Smyrna, and Baghdad; the Zionist project was the dream of European and Russian Jews.

met the culture he felt he was born for, too late: for him and for the culture. The Ottoman Empire had hung on for more than half a millennium, and now, just as Lev's destiny washed him up on its shores, it was all coming to an end. Still, Lev found his newfound identification comforting. He was becoming a believer in a kind of monarchy of his own imagining that was a blend of the Ottoman and czarist legacies with those of the ancient Jewish kingdom of the Khazars and the Crusader clans of Khevsuria. It would be a monarchy that existed in an unreal space between Europe and Asia. The new identity that was taking shape in his mind had the pedigree of a Caucasian warrior, half Persian, half who knows what. He would not arrive in Europe as a stateless Jew from the East, he would come dressed in an Ottoman fez or, when he felt like it, as a Cossack.

"To understand my cousin's attitude," Noam Hermont would tell me in Paris, "you must read Pushkin. Liovoschka did, like all Russian educated boys. Who were the heroes of those books? The Russian soldiers and the Caucasian warriors, the Khazars! Liovoschka could not become a Russian officer; he was a Jew. So he became a Khazar!"

The passage to Italy was mostly uneventful, but one day Lev went belowdecks, exploring in the dark steam tunnels, curious to see where the sailors lived. He passed a number of shipman's quarters, nothing remarkable. Then he followed a damp metallic corridor to a door with grates on the window. He peered into a long room.

It seemed to be some sort of dining room or meeting room, judging from the long table and chairs. But the walls were not plastered with nautical charts or the sailors' favorite actresses or dancing girls. Instead, they held giant portraits of Lenin and Trotsky. Lev also saw Bolshevik slogans, like the ones he remembered from Baku, only in Italian.

He returned on deck and asked a sailor about what he'd seen, casually mentioning the pictures.

"Ah, you've seen our Communist Bastille," said the sailor proudly.

Before the ship had reached the shore, Lev already regarded Italy as a lost cause. To him, the sailors' room belowdecks was a sign that the revolutionary violence had spread faster than the exiles could escape it. (He was hardly alone in thinking this. At the time, exporting the revolution to Europe was still Lenin's pronounced policy.) Even the White Army, backed by the might of the British and American allies, had turned en masse and fled through Constantinople like Lev, Abraham, and all the other refugees.

After three days afloat, the passengers disembarked at Brindisi, Italy, a southern Adriatic port. Lev got off the ship with his father and "gazed long and hard at everyone as they walked past. They were Europeans . . . just walking down the street. Europeans sat in bistros, ate and drank just like Eurasians. So this was the other world." It was the spring of 1921. Lev was amazed that they landed "without seeing any street battles or hearing any screams." But they soon made their way to Rome, where his apprehension returned. He and his father temporarily moved into a hotel in the center of the city, and as in Constantinople, he was drawn to the history around him; Rome had held out for centuries against the Barbarians, after all. But one afternoon he was standing on the Via Veneto with another Russian exile when he saw a troop of young men come marching up the street. They were walking fast in military file and swinging heavy sticks in front of them. As they marched, they sang some sort of anthem and shouted out slogans.

It was clear. The Communists had taken over Rome. They must have seized the army, the police, and the municipal buildings. Lev could imagine what would happen next: the Rome soviet would begin confiscating property and arresting people. The heaps of books would pile up for burning in the Coliseum. Lev clutched his companion's hand and tried to pull him away. In his deathbed memoir, he transcribes a scene as though writing a play, one with more than an element of farce to it:

"Where to?" said his friend.
  "To pack our bags."
  "What for?"
  "Maybe we can still catch the last train to France."
  "What do you mean? Why?"
  "God in heaven, don't you see. . . . This is how it always starts. The Bolsheviks. I had a hunch when I was on the steamer. It's over for Italy. Poor country! We must flee."

The Russian laughed like Lev had rarely seen anyone laugh before. "But they're fascists!" he said.

Lev glanced around nervously. What did he care what the Reds called themselves in Italy? His companion was an idiot. Lev had never heard the word "fascist" before. Neither had Europe, for that matter—it was derived from *fasces,* which in ancient Rome denoted bundles of rods in which an ax was placed and borne before Roman magistrates as a badge of authority; a *fascio,* or bundle, in modern Italian, had been brought into the modern nationalist lexicon to emphasize the solidarity of "brothers in action" and to push for Italian entry into the First World War. By 1919, Mussolini had adapted the term for his own new movement, coining the term *fascismo*—fascism. The winter of 1920–21 was a crucial time for this new movement, and the march Lev was witnessing was one of the Fascists' first appearances on the national stage.

Patiently, his fellow exile explained to Lev that his understanding of the Fascists was exactly backward. The black-shirted young men claimed that they would save the country from communism, not impose it. The Fascists stood for the preservation of private enterprise and property, and all the old traditions and customs of the country.

Lev watched the marchers parade in lockstep down the Via Veneto. The anti-Bolsheviks he had previously met had all been remnants of the old order, like czarist officers or Muslim tribesmen, or mild-mannered liberal patriots like his father's friends. The organized youth groups he had seen, forward-looking and modern, had all been the preserve of the Reds. Yet here in Italy, it was the youths who were standing up against the menace, and they looked like a force to be reckoned with.

A few nights later, Lev witnessed another Fascist demonstration. A well-known Bolshevik leader was rumored to be staying in a hotel across from the one Lev was in. Suddenly it was surrounded by young men chanting, "Down, down, down!" Lev leaned out his hotel window and began chanting along with them: "Down, down, down!"

A strange feeling came over me. I felt . . . welded into a unity with these people, about whom I knew nothing but that they were called fascists and were against the Bolshevists. A warm, gratifying feeling of inner solidarity with a mass of people whose language I did not understand, whose thoughts were foreign to me. It was the first time I had the feeling that I wasn't alone. The feeling only lasted a few moments. Then reality returned: the little room, the suitcases half unpacked, my worried father—the first stage of emigration.

In years to come, contempt for civilized institutions and individual rights would become part of the internationally recognized definition of fascism. But in 1921, sheer destructiveness, as far as Lev or most other observers yet knew, was the monopoly of the leftist revolutionaries. (While countless thousands had already been murdered by the Cheka, the entire death toll from the fighting around the Fascist coup in Italy the following year would not reach into the hundreds, with fewer than a dozen killed in the March on Rome itself.) In addition to the better-known endorsements of Winston Churchill and George Bernard Shaw, American newspapers from *The New York Times* to the Cleveland *Plain Dealer* would write admiringly of Mussolini's brilliant leadership and humanitarian aims. A 1925 article in the *Times* compared Mussolini with Caesar and Napoleon and declared that in marching on Rome, his Black Shirts had "driven out the politicians as money changers were once driven from the temple." One *Times* reporter, Walter Littlefield, was decorated by the Mussolini government. Mussolini had been a journalist by profession and always had a high regard for writers and newsmen.

The positive reviews reflected American establishment opinion in general. Mussolini was widely compared to Theodore Roosevelt, with the Black Shirts seen as a kind of Fascist Rough Riders. Will Rogers took a much publicized trip to Italy to interview Mussolini and declared, "Dictator government is the greatest form of government . . . that is, if you have the right Dictator." The 1920s Republican administrations in Washington openly endorsed Mussolini, and with the aid of J. P. Morgan, they helped engineer hundreds of millions of dollars' worth of credits and loans to the Fascist government. The relationship between Mussolini and the Republicans was so embarrassingly close that President Coolidge's ambassador to Italy, Richard Washburn Child, helped ghostwrite Il Duce's "autobiography," surely one of the odder and more (deliberately) forgotten moments in U.S. diplomatic history. Just as incongruously, Ida Tarbell, the famous populist journalist who spent her career demonizing Rockefeller, went to Italy for *McCall's* in 1926 and came home with glowing appreciation for Mussolini's "admirable social experiment."

In the 1920s the United States and Europe were nearly hysterical with fear that the revolution would spread from the new Soviet Union to destabilize the Western democracies. Democracy seemed a risky proposition against bolshevism. In February 1917, when Czar Nicholas was overthrown bloodlessly and the rule of law came to Russia, the United States had celebrated the Russian Revolution, likening it to 1776. Washington had been the first great power to recognize the new Russian democracy. But the basic decency of those February revolutionaries had spelled their doom. The Russian liberals' rigorous interpretation of American-style constitutional rights—applied to a more absolute extent than they had ever been in the United States—turned the world's most extreme autocracy into its most extreme democracy overnight. Within eight months of the February 1917 declaration of constitutional government in Russia, the Bolsheviks mounted one putsch, failed, then succeeded with another. While Lenin rallied his commissars, Trotsky led a ruthless attack with armored cars, machine guns, and artillery on the new democratic government offices in the Winter Palace.*

The West got the message. Constitutional theorists and senators might not have what it took to defeat the Reds, whereas a strong new movement on the Italian model might be just the ally the democracies needed. In the end, of course, it would be Nazism that played the role of the Red Menace, ending democracy in Europe, but even here, the Communists would have a hand. In the fall of 1932, the German Communists and the Nazis, who hated only moderate democrats more than they hated each other, would band together to bring down the Weimar Republic. Lev Nussimbaum would play a prominent role in helping to give substance to fears in the West with his bestselling exposés of Stalin, Lenin, and the early Communist death squads.

But in the spring of 1921, Lev and Abraham did not stay long in the capital of fascism. They moved on, as most Russian émigrés did, to Paris.

In the French capital, the Nussimbaums were forced to live on "dead souls." This was the term used by the men of the foreign commodities exchanges—likely a reference to Gogol's famous novel, only here the "souls" were oil wells that had been expropriated by the Bolsheviks rather than deceased serfs. Dead souls they might have been, but the brisk trade in them kept exiled oilmen like Abraham very much alive in Paris. The haggling took place mostly in the elegant cafés along the St. Germain des

---

* The defenders of Russian democracy that day happened to be one of Russia's first all-female army detachments, stationed around the palace in a largely formal capacity; the Bolshevik machine gunners made short work of them.

Prés. Agents of Standard Oil, Royal Dutch, and Anglo-Persian were the main buyers. An English count or baron might come in to spice up the bidding, or perhaps a man from Texas or his agent. The defeat of Wrangel's army in the fall of 1920 had pretty much ended the civil war, but the Soviet regime was just entering a period of famine and economic collapse, and its permanence seemed anything but assured.

Most White Russians were poor, but in those early days, the Emigration was living high off the proceeds of its pant seams, so to speak: there were still diamond necklaces to be hocked, assets to negotiate. The days when every Berlin doorman was a Russian grand duke and every Paris cabbie a White Russian officer—Vladimir Nabokov's Colonel Taxovich (who later migrates to America in *Lolita*)—had not quite arrived.

The oil barons from Baku held a special trump card. Imperial Russian money might be worthless, czarist stock bills so much scrap paper. But the deeds the Baku oilmen held were still seen by many as the key to one of the great industrial treasure troves in the world. And Paris was the place to sell them. Sugar, coal, and steel were also the object of café-house business—all the Russian commodities were still in play in some hopelessly abstract game—but Caucasian oil was king. The game hinged, of course, on whether one thought bolshevism was a temporary phenomenon, and if so, how long it would last. Most émigrés believed with the deepest fiber of their being that it would be defeated—they could face no other prospect—and they passionately conveyed their convictions to all who would listen. Westerners were more skeptical, especially after the humiliating decampment of Wrangel's army to the Bosporus earlier that year. But the émigrés' initial reluctance to sell their assets—whether out of hope for the future or stubborn patriotism—helped convince foreign businesses that they had heard something, or knew something, and that the Bolshis would soon be gone. This in turn made foreign interests more eager to buy, which made the Caucasians more reluctant, which drove the market speculation steadily higher.

Paris was not yet the capital of the Russian emigration in 1921. For the time being, that distinction still belonged to Constantinople, if one measured sheer numbers, and it was rapidly passing to Berlin, with its rock-bottom prices, cheap rents, and a vigorous publishing industry. The intelligentsia, especially the writers, flocked to Berlin, where artists' ateliers could be rented for a wheelbarrow full of worthless money and printing presses had for a song. But the ex-captains of Russian industry, like Abraham Nussimbaum, gathered in Paris because this was closer to the great markets of the West. Berlin was a ruined capital, Paris a victorious one. The delegates of the Versailles conference were still straggling home from their long stays, along with the remnants of international armies.

For Lev, used to the czar's empire and an aristocratic Muslim society, the adjustment to bourgeois Paris was a social education. He was probably being only slightly facetious when he recalled his discovery on the metro that "there are people who ride second and even third class. . . . Previously I had been convinced that normal people who lived in average, normal circumstances only rode first class." The original émigrés—the few thousand nobles of the ancien régime who fled the French Revolution—gave the word an optimistic connotation, since they eventually returned in triumph. But the émigrés of 1921 were different, and represented a vast group. Nobody could put their finger on the exact number: one population expert in 1921 calculated 2,935,600; the American Red Cross said 1,963,500 around the same time. It was impossible to be exact because the refugees traveled on such a patchwork of papers, most of them expired or worthless.

The mass Emigration from Russia created the first refugee crisis of modern times, and it established many unfortunate patterns that were to play out through the rest of the century. Past European exiles had been small and specific, mostly religious in nature, resulting from the schisms caused by Protestantism, such as the Puritans or the Huguenots. The only forced emigration that could compare to the White Russians' in size or significance was the expulsion of the Jews from Spain in 1492. There, too, a world that had existed for centuries had been suddenly "shipwrecked," in the phrase the Whites liked to use. Of course, there was a historic irony in that the Russians now found themselves in a position mirroring that of the Jews throughout the millennia, for entering the twentieth century, Russia had been the capital of world anti-Semitism.

The term "White Russians" first referred to a group of czarist army officers who formed in the spring of 1917 to fight the democratic revolution that had overthrown Nicholas. These included sundry religious fanatics and a core of ultra-reactionaries, many of whom had been involved with the Black Hundreds, the anti-Semitic secret society that had fomented pogroms as a way of fighting westernization and reform. Such groups believed that not only bolshevism but also democracy, constitutional monarchy, any limited government at all, was a mark of a worldwide Jewish-Masonic conspiracy that had been taking over the world since 1789. (A more interesting version came to include even the Mongols and the Chinese in the conspiracy.) Yet the White Russian Emigration embodied far more than these extremists. The Bolsheviks had usurped democratic government in Russia, and almost every political party, including most socialists, vehemently opposed them.

General Wrangel's command of the Southern Army in early 1920 gave a brief glimpse of what might have been had the best of the anti-Bolshevik cause been victorious. Unlike the other White leaders, Wrangel himself was above reproach, and he declared that "the absence of a strong, legal government and of a law-abiding spirit" had brought ruin to the White cause. When he established his short-lived White Russian homeland in the Ukraine and the Crimea, he deliberately removed its ultra-reactionary cast and focused on providing security to Russians of all social backgrounds. Wrangel's surprisingly flexible and visionary political ideas are often forgotten. He pushed through a series of basic reforms that granted private property to the peasants and initiated radical agrarian reforms. As a result of his creative policies, every sort of Russian sought shelter in the Crimea under his provisional government—monarchists, Mensheviks, Jews, Uzbeks, Armenians, whoever could get there—and when that government was forced to make for the ships and then steam and sail its jury-rigged flotilla to Constantinople, a broad cross section of Russia went with them. Many Russian citizens of an intellectual or professional background had been leaving any way they could since 1918, but Wrangel's flotilla was the real beginning of the Emigration. It represented the dashed hopes of millions: had the Bolsheviks not sealed the borders in 1921, it might have climbed from the millions to the tens of millions.

Everywhere, Lev noticed among the exiles in Paris the ritual of leaving bags half-unpacked to symbolize the imminent return. "Next year in Baku" or Petrograd or Moscow was the gist of many a drunken toast. The elegance of Paris and the distance from the events in Russia allowed the émigrés to believe even more easily that the counterrevolution was around the corner. They continued to live in grand hotels on the strength of their pawned assets, assuming that somehow they would soon be able to reclaim their rightful properties back home.

The feeling that their fate was temporary also encouraged the Russians to stick to themselves and kept them from integrating into French society. They were not genuine immigrants but refugees, temporarily seeking shelter from revolution, war, and politics. After enough vodka and café life, they would regroup their regiments and return to the fight. Some of the officers of Wrangel's former army tried to keep their units in existence by arranging regular meetings at bars and cafés. Only the Cossack regiments really succeeded in this—martial traditions went back centuries and were linked intricately to their identity. Still, even the Cossacks lost something in translation, especially as they began to disperse. "Around Cannes there were many Cossacks who kept chicken farms," recalled an exiled countess, Natalya Sumarakov-Elston. "They never learned French."*

In 1921 the millions of young Frenchmen dead or crippled from the war and the influenza epidemic had produced an acute labor shortage. Manual workers were in high demand, both miners and factory workers, but there was little need for the professions so much commoner among the exiles—the so-called liberal professions: medicine, law, teaching. In this way, the Russian émigrés were like the German Jews who would come after them: too qualified to find work. Like my grandfather who came from Heidelberg, they would find themselves putting up shingles that said things like CHILD PSYCHOLOGY AND GRAPHOLOGY, ALL AGES, only to find that no one in their new neighborhoods had the foggiest idea what they were talking about.

Ex-czarist officers chose taxi driving and chauffeuring above other professions because these offered freedom of movement, the chance to be in

---

* In 1926 the League of Nations and various French charitable organizations made a push to get some of these unassimilated mountain men to move to South America. Ads appeared in the Russian newspapers and bars advertising land to be had in the interior of Paraguay, Bolivia, and Peru. About five hundred French-based Cossacks responded to these offers, but came back a few months later with stories of battling snakes, vampire bats, and mosquitoes. A Cossack colonel wrote a series of articles called "Why I Returned from Paraguay," concluding that he hoped to get back his old job driving a taxi. He recommended Paraguay to fellow émigrés only if the sole alternative was to jump off the Alexander III Bridge—the favored method among exiles of committing suicide in interwar Paris.

charge of one's own ship, and, not least, fancy uniforms. One exiled countess recalled that her fellow aristocrats quite literally became shabby chic: "The Russian dustmen of Cannes were famous," she recalled. "They were very elegant and glamorous in their military tunics! Everyone loved them. I knew an English woman who lived below a Russian colonel who was working as a dustman, and he used to give her copies of the *Tattler* every week. She asked him why on earth he got the *Tattler*—'Oh, to keep track of my friends.'" The countess's father went to work for the gas and electric company. "His friend Baron Prittwitz read the meters." Perhaps the only time they really felt at home in France was during a glorious two weeks when a film company re-created a Caucasian village in the mountains above Cannes and the émigrés all got to work as extras.

To work in France, the émigrés needed to put their hands on the indispensable *carte d'identité,* which came in a rainbow of significant colors: gray-blue for *travailleur* (worker); yellow for agricultural *travailleur;* orange for entrepreneur; green for "liberal professional," student, or unemployed. The French identity card, an extensive and remarkably specific document, was actually nineteen pages long and filled with details about the holder's life and background, including all the information the French police would need to round up Jews twenty years later. Along with the *carte d'identité,* one needed special permission from the local police to work—the coveted *avis favorable* that became increasingly more difficult to come by.*

For Lev in 1921, Paris was fortunately more like a vacation, however brief. He was sixteen, and as long as his father's luck in dead souls held out, he was still the son of a millionaire. But as Abraham read the stock market ta-

---

* By the 1930s Depression years, the situation would become so bad for the Russian émigrés in France that they were being deported for minor traffic violations, anything to get rid of them. Neighboring countries often refused them entry, so the émigré would end up walking back across the border into France, where he would be sent to jail or to an internment camp. The horrors and heartbreak of the stateless émigré—a subject of countless films and novels in the 1920s—were largely forgotten because the situation of the stateless Jew in the 1930s was so much worse. But they did not deserve to be forgotten. In the late 1930s the Jewish Socialist French prime minster Léon Blum liberalized all the laws under his Popular Front government—creating the irony that the White Russians were most benefited by a French communist politician—but soon the Nazis would be in charge and Blum himself would be in Buchenwald.

bles, Lev took to reading the classifieds, just to pretend he was doing something purposeful and related to work. He would run his finger down the list of want ads, circling positions with the most interesting-sounding addresses, especially names with historic or mythic references. He would then take a taxi someplace, as if going to a job interview. Once there he would get out and walk up and down the street. "Sometimes I took a taxi and gave the driver the name of a street and a number and let him drive me there and then I stood in front of a house and told myself, 'So that's the Rue Bonaparte in Paris,' and felt so happy about it."

But despite the relief of being out of danger and more or less carefree, Lev was not really so happy. Though the city was filled with other Caucasian émigrés, including many of his own relatives, he did not mix well with them. After all the excitement and danger of his early life, he stumbled through Paris abstractedly and soon grew isolated in this luxurious refuge (even though, as he noted dryly, "A person who is born on a train can hardly feel ill at ease in a hotel").

I don't know why, but although in Paris I went out without an armed guard of course and completely alone, I used this freedom for nothing, for nothing at all. While my father got together with emigrants from everywhere, I, despite my newfound freedom, was always alone. I didn't particularly like the few new people I met, and they apparently didn't think much of me either.

Around this time his relatives no doubt began to realize that young Lev was a bit odd. He never accepted their invitations to the cinema, the theater, or museums. When they dragged him along to something, he would sit silently and stare into space, seeming intense and off-putting. By his own confession, he was regarded by his family as rather an idiot.

He did, however, enjoy sitting on a park bench and gazing at the tall, slender *Parisiennes* in their sheer silk stockings. He affected an air of knowing sophistication. Yet when he actually managed to meet a girl his own age, almost always a fellow émigré, he lost all ability to talk to her. "Once I spent an entire hour with one of the most beautiful girls in Emigration," he later recalled, but he could manage not a word. They sat "alone, in one room. During this whole hour I read the newspaper!" Not daring to think "profane" thoughts about the women he saw on the street,

Lev decided that their silken legs reminded him of "the slender prayer towers" of Istanbul.

It's not hard to imagine that Lev failed to find much of a home among his Parisian relatives—for example, his wealthiest cousins, on his mother's side of the family, the Leiteses, who had converted to Russian Orthodoxy in the 1890s (perhaps Lev's inspiration for later turning his mother into a purebred Russian aristocrat). They were living in a particularly grand hotel on the Champs-Elysées. One of the Leites boys had served in the czarist cavalry and indeed had passed through Constantinople as part of Wrangel's White Army, rather than as a civilian. One of Lev's female cousins had lived in Paris since before the war, and served as a kind of guide for the rest of the family.

But "among the dozens of relatives," Lev would tell Pima, "there is only one whom I love and who loves me. She is Tamara and she is married to an Italian. She is the only one in the clan who is not rich. This will sound very strange, but I am not sure whether she is my aunt or my sister. She is only a few years older than I am. We grew up together. Some say she is my sister, others say she is my aunt. My father sometimes says one thing, and at other times another."

Tamara was in fact Lev's aunt—Berta's younger sister, and not much older than Lev when she came to stay in Baku. The "Italian" she married was another Russian Jewish refugee, who was lucky enough to have acquired Italian citizenship in Constantinople. It was a peculiar thing for a Russian to have acquired Italian citizenship in 1920; most of the occupying Allied powers were not offering citizenship to the émigrés, though some of Wrangel's officers managed to obtain it. Twenty years later, this vagary of fate would save Tamara, her husband, and their son, Noam, from the gas chambers.

When I met Noam Hermont in Paris, his resemblance to pictures of Lev was immediately striking. After all these years of piecing together Lev's story from letters and memoirs and the occasional police file, I had almost started to feel like I was his only family. It was shocking to meet someone who was the spitting image of his portraits, though aged. The face was very distinct, with a prominent nose and enigmatic smile that must have been inherited from the mother's side of the family.

Noam and I talked for hours and looked at old photographs. There were none of Lev's mother, disappointingly, but many of Tamara. (There again, that look—the face was well suited to a woman, just as it always looked to me a bit feminine on Lev.) Noam had never been to Baku himself, but he had heard many stories about it from his mother. It had been a strange experience for a ten-year-old girl newly arrived from a shtetl in the Pale of Settlement, living under the roof of her "revolutionary" sister and her millionaire husband. And then, after Berta killed herself and Baku began to be torn apart by unrest, life had been very hard. Noam recalled his mother saying that during the Armenian-Azeri riots, Abraham had offered his house to people under attack. Tamara remembered the faces of terrified Armenians who came to seek shelter from Muslim mobs. But she also remembered Muslims who came to seek shelter from Armenian mobs. "The point was that since Nussimbaum's was a Jewish house, it was a kind of neutral house," said Noam. "They left the Jewish houses alone, no matter which side was rioting. Mr. Nussimbaum could offer shelter to anyone who needed it."

We discussed some of Lev's books, and Noam expressed skepticism for Lev's Muslim alter ego in the novel *Ali and Nino*. He said he found the picture of ethnic and cultural relations in the novel "a bit romantic . . . perhaps Liovoschka's idea of how he thought it had been in old Baku." Noam recalled that in the circle of Caucasian émigrés in Paris—his mother got out of Baku around 1919 and married in Constantinople—his parents were friendly with the prima donna of the Baku opera house and her husband, who was also a popular singer. The prima donna was Jewish, and her husband was Armenian. "But their house was a great social center for all the Caucasians and many of the other émigrés as well," Noam recalled. "Every year for the birthday of the prima donna, there was a party, and people played in Paris, piano, opera, singing . . . the Gukosoffs were very popular in the Paris Emigration." Tamara had been one of those rare refugees for whom the Emigration was probably more pleasant than life in the Russian Empire had been. She was married, and though they were not well-off compared to Lev's other relatives, she and her husband lived in a hotel overlooking the Jardin des Plantes.

Now that he was among his mother's relatives, Lev was thinking about his childhood. It was as though he and his father had escaped the inferno of the revolution but had left his mother behind. Of course, she had left them behind, years before. But somehow everyone in the family regarded her as a casualty of the revolution. He tried to confront his relatives about her fate, since his father had maintained his silence on the subject. Tamara was living in the house at the time of her death, and later told her son that Berta died by swallowing acid, but she did not share this with her sixteen-year-old nephew. Lucky for him, probably, but it haunted him that no one would talk about her. "The four princes in Paris," as he called his richest cousins, on the Champs-Elysées, "were like lumps of ice in this respect. They looked out the window and talked about the weather."

His father must have known the truth but never told him. It was more than he could bear to discuss, or perhaps he felt responsible somehow. Abraham often dreamed about his late wife, that much Lev knew. Lev himself never did.

By 1921, weighty decisions were being made about Lev's future. His father and various relatives contemplated his education, and for reasons that were never made clear, they were all against the most obvious idea—that of Lev entering a French lyceum. Abraham Nussimbaum especially would not hear of it, perhaps in part because of the influence he saw Paris having on his son. The boy would go abroad to be educated in a "serious" country.

The first option considered was England. In all parts of the East, an English education was considered the pinnacle of what a father could do for his son. Lev recalled his rich relatives' logic on the matter: "English education had to be good, for after all, the English ruled the world." Vladimir Nabokov, Sr., had sent his son to school in England. But Lev's relatives questioned whether "a sixteen-year-old boy from Baku, who had never before seen real snow, was equal to such rigors." Besides, Abraham Nussimbaum had never cared for the English—blaming them in part for the defeat and dismemberment of the Ottoman Empire, or possibly, as Noam Hermont speculated to me, simply the result of some dispute about an oil deal. (Along with the Dutch and the Nobels, the British were serious competitors for Caucasian oil.)

But something entirely different clinched the decision, at least as Lev remembered it. A prominent Baku citizen had sent his twelve-year-old son to England at the beginning of the war. The war and revolution separated them for seven years, and in 1921 the son, now grown and with a complete English education, was reunited with his father in Paris. "The general curiosity was great; great too was the initial pride of the father," Lev recalled in his memoirs. The curiosity of the family and the father's pride both turned quickly to dismay, as it became clear that by the standards of old Baku, the boy had become an idiot. He had forgotten Russian and Azeri, and the father needed an interpreter to speak with his own son. The son, named Jusef, insisted on being called "Joe" and burst into laughter whenever anyone called him by his given name. "While Jusef or Joe was very modest and well-bred," Lev recalled,

> what he said was more than strange. He spoke with deep seriousness about football and horse racing, but fell silent when asked a question that went beyond such trivialities. When one nonetheless wished to know his opinion on Bolshevism, the war and the like, he expressed views that resembled those of a five-year-old. On top of this, he dressed himself in a perplexing and unnatural fashion, and one got the impression that his trousers . . . appeared to be somehow attached to his collar.

Since Jusef had been clever and intelligent as a child, everyone in the Baku émigré circle concluded that this calamity must have been the result of his English education.

One encounter with the young man was enough to put Abraham Nussimbaum off the idea of England. (Though it may sound unlikely that such an important decision could be guided by such evidence, anyone who comes from a family of refugees might recognize the tendency. Among my own "exiled" relatives, I had the impression that as a refugee's practical experience narrowed with his resources and job opportunities, as his fear of missteps in the new life increased, anecdotes from fellow refugees took on a disproportionate power. If one refugee's son failed trying something, it must be a lesson to all: that way led to failure and defeat! Avoid it for another!) France and England were thus ruled out. Abraham looked around for another country to send Lev to in order to complete his studies.

As fate would have it, an uncle who had spent his youth in Germany arrived in Paris at about this time. The uncle could not praise highly enough a secondary school that he had attended, located on one of the many small islands of the North Sea coast, not far from Hamburg. Abraham and the other relatives were entranced by the description of the uncle's education, the lofty ideals and high discipline. Men of the Russian nobility had always come to Germany to study, and Jews in particular held a German education above all others. A few years of Germanic virtues and culture might be just the thing, Abraham thought. The relatives agreed. Lev was fluent in German, thanks to Alice, and Germany was swimming in Russians who, like the uncle, raved about the opportunities for education and the literary life.

And there was the issue of money, which "was becoming tighter in spite of the trade in dead souls and the help my relatives gave each other." England was fabulously expensive and France was no bargain, whereas Germany was cheap. It was settled. No further discussion was necessary, certainly not to consult the boy. Lev's relatives agreed that he would leave Paris shortly to head for the North Sea island so highly recommended.

In preparation for the trip, Lev said he bought a single new item: a monocle, for, as he later wrote in his deathbed memoir, "I was convinced that, in Germany, a monocle was as necessary for a gentleman as an umbrella in England." Practicing squinting to hold his new eyewear in place, Lev took to the road again with his father, this time traveling by first-class sleeping car, east to Germany. It was a fateful decision for them both.

PART 2

Berlin, 1919

CHAPTER 7

The German Revolution

A S THEY CROSSED THE FRENCH BORDER into Germany in the late spring of 1921, Lev turned his monocle nervously between his fingers. He could think of only one thing as he looked out at the gray landscape that had so recently been the site of massive trench battles: revolution! They had escaped one, and now it seemed they were rolling right back into another. Were they mad? Many Russians said that Germany was the heart of revolution—more revolutionary even than Russia itself. Lev had been obsessed by the subject of Germany's political upheaval ever since the family had decided on his future schooling. He consoled himself that he "could always leave if things got too bad. It wasn't my revolution, it wasn't my country." Still, the reports from Germany kept him on edge.

Lev's fear of revolution had become a kind of hysteria, which surely dated back to the things he had seen in Baku. But sometimes it took hysteria to interpret the events of those years—the exposed moral nerves without which ordinary people let deeply ominous signs pass as just another week's bad news. A violent revolution *had* raged in Germany for more than two years, and it remained somewhat obscured from international view by the insane swirl of changes around the globe: the triumph of the Soviet colossus and flight of the Whites; the collapse of the Ottoman Empire and the Turkish Civil War; the Versailles Treaty, the collapse of the Hapsburg monarchy and the emergence of a dozen new states and alliances throughout Europe; the influenza pandemic that was even now taking tens of thousands of lives a week throughout Europe, Asia, and America. All these events took the world's attention away from the German Revolution.

Frau Schulte would have comforted Lev, told him stories of Germany as she had when he was a child, but she was not here—where was she? Stuck God-knew-where between Baku and the Balkans. Her German nationality had kept her behind in Baku, though it might help her now, if she could only meet up with the family again. Abraham had taught Lev to have a high opinion of German culture and German people. The Nussimbaums had sheltered German prisoners of war during the siege of Baku, and Lev and his father both had found the German officers to be decent fellows. But Lev's thoughts stayed dark as he neared the border.

The initial events of revolutionary change in Germany and Russia had been similar: disaster on the battlefield had led to the abdication of an emperor and the replacement of an entire monarchical system by a democratic coalition government; that coalition had then immediately come under attack by radicals from both left and right and had chosen to play one extreme against the other. The main difference between how the revolution proceeded in Germany and in Russia was that in Russia the moderates indulged the extreme left because they perceived the danger coming from the extreme right; in Germany the moderates indulged the extreme right because they perceived the danger from the extreme left. In both cases, the strategy backfired: in Russia the result was a murderous totalitarian takeover from the left; in Germany it would be a murderous totalitarian takeover from the right. The leaders of the new German democracy, much like Lev, could see only the specter of Red Revolution, of bolshevism, ascendant in Russia and threatening to spread westward. The Revolution of the Right—fascism, Nazism—had not yet taken form. Just as the centrist democrats in Moscow had allowed Lenin to operate in Russia in the hope that he would defend constitutional government, so the democrats in Berlin unleashed equally anti-democratic right-wing forces in the hope that they, too, would defend a constitution they in fact wished only to destroy. A right-wing Lenin did not yet exist, though he was soon to emerge out of the bloody chaos.

But in 1918–19, no one worried about a right-wing Lenin. All eyes were out for another messianic demagogue of the left. Some mistook an outspoken dissident socialist named Karl Liebknecht for the German Lenin, supported by his female accomplice in revolution, Rosa Luxembourg (though she grew up dreaming of emulating Vera Zasulich and Sofya Perovskaya, she never actually tried shooting anyone). By the standards of the Bolsheviks, even the most radical German socialists were not "real" revolutionaries—they had no tradition of terrorism or armed uprising— as Lenin said, they wouldn't storm a train station unless they had first purchased tickets. He had tried organizing in Munich for years, but had eventually given up on German socialists entirely and moved to Zurich to await the revolution there. That bane of the Bolsheviks known as the "Second International"—the moderate revision of Marx's First International that transformed socialism into an evolutionary rather than a revolutionary movement, and focused on trade unionism and parliamentary action—was a German affair. Theoretically, the socialist parties in Europe, and around the globe, were all linked in the cause of worldwide Marxist revolution. But parties like the German Social Democrats had grown so conciliatory that, to many, they hardly seemed like Marxists at all.

In Berlin, Lenin came to rely on Liebknecht and Luxembourg and the breakaway faction of the Social Democratic party they led: the Spartacists.* On arriving at the Finland Station in Petrograd in 1917, conveyed there by the German General Staff in a special sealed train—like a bacillus, as Churchill famously put it, or, as we would say, a biological weapon—Lenin had immediately turned on his benefactors and declared that he hoped Liebknecht would stage a revolution to overthrow the kaiser. But the Spartacists would have none of the ruthless flair of the Bolsheviks, and though revolution would soon spread to Germany, there it would take a dramatically different turn.

In 1917–18, Germany's government was a quasi-military dictatorship run by its most famous military men: General Ludendorff (who would arrange Hitler's unsuccessful, illegal grab for power in 1923) and Field Marshal Hindenburg (who would help in Hitler's legal seizure of power in

---

* The name originated in January 1916 when, on the occasion of the kaiser's birthday, a series of open letters and handbills circulated calling for violent revolution, signed "Spartacus." Evoking the first-century Roman slave Spartacus, who had nearly overthrown the Roman Empire with his insurrection, the letters caused a scandal among the mainstream, "patriotic" Social Democrats. It would later become clear that "Spartacus" was the outspoken, oft-imprisoned Liebknecht.

1933). Ludendorff was the more proto-Nazi in outlook—though the word had not yet been invented, his dreams for a vast Teutonic lebensraum, or "living space," in the East and, later, views of a global Zionist conspiracy fit the bill—and he was also the more brilliant tactician. Most Germans backed the Ludendorff-Hindenburg government, with the kaiser as its front man, so long as it held out the promise of total victory in the Great War, complete with annexations of territory in the East. By the spring of 1918, they seemed to have made good on that promise, forcing Russia to give up enormous territories in exchange for a negotiated peace: the Treaty of Brest Litovsk, signed by Bolshevik Russia on March 3, 1918, surrendered to Germany a swath of Russian territory that, as the historian A.J.P. Taylor estimated, was "nearly as large as Austria-Hungary and Turkey combined." In addition to gaining land, the German Empire virtually doubled its population, adding 56 million new inhabitants from these formerly Russian territories, and more than doubled its stock of key raw materials. Much of Estonia, Finland, Lithuania, Latvia, Poland, Russia, Romania, and Ukraine became part of a new German Empire that, on paper at least, rivaled Napoleon's conquests in size and diversity, and surpassed those of any previous German empire.*

This great Second Reich would last less than six months. It cost Germany a million soldiers, stationed from Finland to Azerbaijan, to try to secure and squeeze the material rewards out of it. The German people were half-starved, isolated from materials by a British naval blockade, and unable to exploit their new empire in time to make a difference. By the end of the summer of 1918, the German Army was spread thin, malnourished, and beginning to suffer from Spanish influenza, which was to kill perhaps 20 million people worldwide over the course of the next year—more than

---

* The Second Reich, as Kaiser Wilhelm's Germany was known, thus also rivaled the future Third Reich, and Ludendorff's spike-helmeted troops briefly attained a "living space in the East" to make Hitler swoon. Yet, oddly, the 1917–18 *Drang nach Osten,* or "drive east," drew added impetus from a principle entirely anathema to the Nazis: philo-Semitism. In 1918 hundreds of thousands of German soldiers occupied the shtetls of the Russian Pale as liberators—from both czarist oppression and local anti-Semitism. Ludendorff believed this strategy would secure the aid of Russian and World Jewry for Germany's cause, and though this did not occur, the strategy did contribute to the tragic confusion in 1941 when some village Jews in Eastern Europe and Russia actually welcomed the invading Nazi armies, thinking they would act as the benign 1918 German occupiers had done.

the war itself and, indeed, any cataclysm, human or natural, until the Second World War. The surrender of the Bulgarians in late September 1918 left Germany's southern flank unprotected and cut off the land route to its other main ally, the Ottoman Turks. Like his cousin the czar in 1917, the kaiser was ever more convinced that a vast Jewish-Masonic conspiracy was afoot. Ludendorff, architect of the "pro-Jewish" occupation in the East, and now showing signs of mental instability, vigorously agreed. The kaiser and Ludendorff hastily endorsed the Zionist plan for Palestine in a desperate attempt to win the aid of the Jewish World Conspiracy . . . but too late! They were beaten!

Ludendorff, the brains of the outfit, looked desperately for a way out. At the beginning of October 1918, he instituted negotiations with the Allies for an immediate armistice, in order to save the German Army from total destruction. When the Allies would not deal with a military dictatorship, Ludendorff dictated steps to transform Germany, immediately, into a liberal constitutional monarchy and persuaded a liberal relative of the kaiser to become its first chancellor. But still the Allies doubted German intentions, and the armistice negotiations dragged on through October 1918. When the Turks signed a separate armistice on October 30, and the Austrians declared a unilateral cease-fire on November 3, the Second Reich—the paper empire stretching from Baku to Brussels—was suddenly fighting all alone. Though the military leaders had known for weeks that the war was lost, they had neglected to tell the German public, or the millions of soldiers at the front, continuing instead to issue reassuring bulletins of steady advances and imminent victory. But rumors abounded.

As in Russia, armed revolution began with the sailors: on November 3, the Imperial German Fleet, rather than follow its officers' orders to steam out to sea for a final (likely suicidal) battle with the British Fleet, mutinied. Red flags were hoisted on the kaiser's battleships, officers were thrown overboard, and machine guns were mounted on supply trucks, creating the vehicle of choice of the German Revolution. Within three days, workers' and sailors' soviets had taken over the important port cities of northern Germany and were threatening to march on Berlin. In the south, with the Austrian front collapsed, the Bavarians panicked, fearing howitzer shells in their beer gardens, and a bloodless revolution raised the Red flag in Munich, on November 7. The fatherland was falling apart.

By the evening of Saturday, November 9, Ludendorff and his fellow generals had a plan. They would hand over the whole mess to some democrats. Preferably left-wing democrats. The head of the Majority Social Democratic party, the largest left-wing party in parliament, Friedrich Ebert, was contacted, and he replied that he would meet his patriotic duty. Raimund Pretzel, who was eleven years old at the time—and who would later become a prominent anti-Nazi journalist under the name Sebastian Haffner—recalled the scene in the streets that weekend:

> That Sunday I heard shots fired for the first time. During the whole of the war I had not heard a single shot. Yet now, when it was over, they began shooting in Berlin. . . . Someone explained the difference between the sounds of heavy and light machine guns. We tried to guess where the fighting was taking place. . . . It turned out to have been a rather pointless brawl between rival revolutionary groups, each claiming possession of the royal stables. . . . The revolution had clearly triumphed.

During four years of war, patriotic young Pretzel had eagerly followed the news of Germany's glorious victories posted daily on the police precinct bulletin board, and remarkably,

> On November 9 and 10 army bulletins of the usual kind still appeared: "enemy breakthrough attempts repulsed," "after courageous resistance, our troops withdrew into previously prepared positions." On the eleventh there was no army bulletin on the notice board at my local police station when I appeared there at the usual time. Empty and blank, the board yawned at me. Horror overcame me to think that the board, which had sustained my spirit and nourished my dreams every day for years, would remain empty and black forevermore. I walked on. There must be some news from the front somewhere. . . . The neighborhood became less familiar. . . . How shall I describe my feelings—the feelings of an eleven-year-old boy whose entire inner world has collapsed. . . . Like these streets, the whole world had become strange and unsettling. . . . The great game had clearly had other secret rules that I had failed to grasp. There must have been something deceitful and false about it. Where could one find stability and security, faith and confidence, if world events could be so deceptive?

On Monday, November 11, delegates from the new Social Democratic government of Germany officially signed the armistice, ending Germany's involvement in the Great War. The kaiser rode a gold-and-ivory-plated train car to comfortable exile in Holland. In Berlin chaos ruled. Emil Eichhorn, a firebrand from a leftist faction known as the Independent Socialists—somewhere between the Majority Social Democrats and the Spartacists—walked into police headquarters at the head of a mob. He freed some 650 prisoners, armed them, and declared himself chief of the "People's Revolutionary Berlin Police Department." All over the German capital, left-wing mobs seized newspaper offices, government buildings, stores, and telegraph offices. Installed in the former quarters of the kaiser and drunk on their first draft of real power, Ebert and his parliamentary colleagues negotiated, both publicly and in secret: publicly, they negotiated with the Allied powers about how to arrange terms; secretly, on a special hotline in their new offices, they negotiated with right-wing generals in the German Army about how to quell the revolutionary unrest in the streets and reestablish order. The generals agreed not to oppose the new government if it agreed not to oppose them in using "whatever force necessary" to suppress leftist revolution. Germany's first democratic government managed thus to take upon themselves all the responsibility and blame for the humiliating surrender, while simultaneously giving up all real political power to rightist military men who would eventually tar and destroy them.

Throughout December 1918, German soldiers returned home from the front and marched into Berlin, with bands of confused revolutionary sailors—who thought the "Marxist" parliamentary government was on their side—looking on. The city the soldiers returned to bore little resemblance to the iron-disciplined, orderly Prussian capital they had left behind. "All moral restraint seems to have melted away," recalled the artist George Grosz, one of those soldiers returning from the front, and whose autobiography is one of the grimmest and most graphic reminiscences of Berlin in revolution and its aftermath:

The city was dark, cold and full of rumours. The streets were wild ravines haunted by murderers and cocaine peddlers. . . . People denied all knowledge but whispered about secret maneuvers by the Black *Reichswehr* or a newly formed Red Army.

Bands of armed men wrapped in flags of all colors and political messages cruised the streets. Not only shots but also bursts of machine-gun fire and hand-grenade explosions were common. Grosz recalled:

> Inhabitants, half-crazed with fear, could not stand the confinement of their own four walls, so they went up on the roof to shoot pigeons and people. Their sense of proportion, or size, somehow got misplaced. When one of those roof hunters was picked up and shown a man whom he had hit, he said, "But officer, I thought he was a large pigeon!"

The influenza pandemic was killing even more Germans than had died in the trenches; in Berlin alone, three hundred people perished of the disease each day that December.

Soldiers who had had enough of war left their weapons in their barracks and went home. Or they sold them on the open market. "You could buy guns and ammunition everywhere," Grosz wrote. "My cousin, who was discharged a little later, offered me a complete machine gun. He assured me that I could pay for it in installments, and didn't I know anybody who might be interested in two other machine guns and a small field gun."

Those who had *not* had enough of war kept their weapons and followed their unit commanders into a Mafia-style world of loosely connected militias, the Freikorps, or "free corps." The Freikorps attracted the most hardened German trench soldiers, often members of famous elite battalions that had led suicide missions across no-man's-land to French and British trenches. The young officers who led these attacks were courageous, physically powerful, and fanatical—they would later be taken as prototypes by the Nazi Waffen SS men of the next generation. But many of the Freikorps members had seen barely any action at all; indeed, some joined these newly formed units because they felt they had missed out on the purifying blood rituals of trench warfare.

The Western powers assembled the legal framework to restrict the German military, but allowed the Freikorps to stay armed and operational, perhaps in no small measure because of the perceived threat from Soviet Russia. In the fall of 1918 and the winter of 1919, new Freikorps units spontaneously made the journey eastward—to the new front against bolshevism. Blood-red recruiting posters screamed HILF MIR! (HELP ME!), whether in real or in manufactured fear of a Soviet invasion. Without official orders, Freikorps units headed straight to Poland, Lithuania, Latvia—all the same areas that the Nazis would reinvade in 1941. In fact, the nearly forgotten "Freikorps front" of 1918–19 was in many ways the birthplace and testing ground for the future Nazi invasion.

More than anxiety over the Red Menace drove the new fighting. A deep historical identification was at work. The original Freikorps had been volunteers in the Wars of Liberation against Napoleon in 1813–15. As Napoleon's empire crumbled, volunteer armies sprang up all across Europe calling themselves the Vienna Freikorps, the Potsdam Freikorps, the Italian Freikorps, and so on, to roll back the forces of the French Revolution. But the Freikorps phenomenon was itself revolutionary—in 1813 as in 1918—for it implied the power of the soldier-citizen to rise up and remake society through the force of his own arms and decisions of a small-group leader. The original Freikorps were the ancestors of all guerrilla fighters and revolutionary insurgents of the next century.

And an even earlier identification attracted the soldiers who joined the *Ritt gen Osten,* the ride against the East. When the Freikorps embarked on their adventure in the Baltic states, they insisted on referring to them not as Estonia, Latvia, and Lithuania but by their Germanic names: Kurland, Livonia, and so on. This was to invoke the medieval crusade of the Teutonic knights, who, starting in the thirteenth century, had marched against the barbarians as far as Moscow and established lasting feudal kingdoms in the Baltic provinces (medieval castles built by the German invaders stand there to this day). As far as the new crusaders were concerned, they were fighting to reclaim their rightful territory. Until the Russian Revolution, hundreds of thousands of so-called Baltic Germans—German-speaking but loyal Russian subjects—had remained ensconced in semi-feudal provinces a few hundred miles from St. Petersburg. An elite handful of these Baltic or "Russian" Germans would become truly obsessed enemies of bolshevism and, as exiles in Germany, central actors in the Nazi rise to power.

The Freikorps'goal, as one soldier put it, was to prove itself "worthy of the battles of the Knights of the Order against Poles and Tartars." The men kept copious diaries and wrote memoirs, poems, and novels about their experiences fighting the Red Army. These would later become the favorite reading of SS recruits, both in Germany and in translation in foreign countries. "I had to think of the past," wrote a typical Freikorps memoirist. "A Knight of the Order, who had come back to life. It seemed to me as if all the intervening ages had been extinguished." In the classic Freikorps bestseller *Riders in the East,* Ernst von Salomon described how, as he arrived on the eastern front as a volunteer, ready to do battle against the Reds, he felt overwhelmed by a sense that he had been there in another life. The smell of the soil moved him, seeming "to unite everything in it-self, the hope and danger," and he "was transported by the dangerous for-eignness of this land, to which I stood in a peculiar relationship." Another Freikorps veteran wondered as his armored car drove past the ruins of Germanic castles: "Were they surprised at the little flag with the black cross, which snapped up and down below them? Did they recognize the badge on our caps, which they had once seen on the white cloaks of their inhabitants?"

When they arrived on the ever-shifting front of the Russian Civil War, the Freikorps men proved remarkably adaptable. The presence of German troops was against the armistice terms, and even though it was backing the Whites, France threatened to send a division against the Freikorps if they did not leave Polish and Baltic soil at once. The Freikorps commanders simply ordered their men to don Russian feather caps and fur hats and Caucasian bandoliers and to call themselves Russian, which they did. Miraculously, the White armies in the Baltic suddenly increased by tens of thousands of new and highly disciplined troops, who marched into battle against the Red Army while alternating between renditions of German and Russian folk songs.

Despite their efforts, the Freikorps could not turn the military tide for the White armies, who had been outnumbered and outmaneuvered. But as the Whites fled, the junior Teutonic knights returned home, bitter and armed to the teeth, to wreak havoc on the new republic.

"This morning Christmas Eve began with an artillery action," noted Count Harry Kessler in his diary. "Government troops tried to bombard the sailors out of the Palace and the Imperial Stables. . . . The Christmas Fair carried on throughout the blood-letting." Count Kessler remains one of the best guides to the German Revolution and the grotesque aftermath during which one of the world's great cultures slid back, in less than a dozen years, into the lowest form of barbarism. Kessler, a half-Irish, half-German aristocrat of liberal convictions and Oscar Wildean snobbishness, witnessed the events of those years both from street level and in the social company of most of the political and revolutionary figures of the age, as well as leading intellectuals like Albert Einstein and Jean Cocteau. On January 5, 1919, the government's decision to arrest Chief of Police Eichhorn brought the German Revolution in Berlin to its next phase. This is when the best-known news photographs of revolutionary Berlin appeared around the world: the mutinied sailors and civilians crouching side by side behind barricades made of massive rolls of newsprint, aiming their carbines through the paper to fire at the Freikorps with their heavy weapons. But the Spartacists had a great many machine guns as well. In his diary entry for Wednesday, January 8, 1919, Count Kessler provides a priceless log of a typical day during the first week of Berlin's "real Marxist Revolution":

> The machine-gun on top of the Brandenburger Tor was firing into the Tiergarten crowd, which dispersed amidst agonized screams. Then silence. It was a quarter to one. When the shooting began again, I was proceeding towards the Reichstag. That was also Spartacus's line of fire. Bullets whizzed past my ear. . . . At half past seven I had a meal in the Fürstenhof. The iron gates were just being shut because a Spartacus attack was expected on the Potsdamer Railway Station opposite. Single shots were dropping all the time. I looked for a moment into the boldly lit Café Vaterland. Despite the fact that at any moment bullets might whistle through the windows, the band was playing, the tables were full, and the lady in the cigarette-booth smiled as winsomely at her customers as in the sunniest days of peace.

The Freikorps attacked the revolutionary neighborhoods of Berlin with armored cars, tanks, flamethrowers, heavy machine guns, and field howitzers. Photographs of the time show the street barricades, now manned by disturbingly boyish rightist soldiers, with signs that read: HALT! ANYONE WHO WALKS BEYOND THIS POINT WILL BE SHOT! The Freikorps assaulted civilians without restraint, especially anyone who looked like he or she might be a Bolshevik sympathizer. In effect, they brought the front back to civilian society. German culture blurred the boundaries between the military and the political, and these fanatical soldiers were herded together by officers who had an interest in maintaining the fantasy that the war had not really ended. Members of the civilian population were now the enemy, but as civilians, they were not prepared or armed. For members of the Freikorps, it was a lesson in local brutality and cold-bloodedness that prepared many of them for work as storm troopers or concentration-camp guards in the years to come.*

The Spartacists took to the rooftops with sniper rifles, doing whatever they could to disrupt both bourgeois normalcy and Freikorps brutality now that the major Red effort had been suppressed. But a Freikorps unit stormed and occupied the Spartacist headquarters at Spandau, and on January 15, 1919, Karl Liebknecht, Berlin's Lenin, was shot in the back while "trying to escape." The words "shot while trying to escape" would become almost a propaganda slogan of sorts for the rightist revolutionaries as the decade wore on. It was a warning of their lack of "moral squeamishness" and "bourgeois sentimentality," two of the many terms they used that were almost literal translations from Lenin—to which the Nazis would merely prefix "Jewish" or "Judeo-Bolshevik" to avoid any possible confusion of them with the Red revolutionaries. It was not immediately clear what the Freikorps members had done with "Red Rosa," who had disappeared while in their custody on the same day as Liebknecht. "Allegedly she was killed," wrote Count Kessler in his diary. "Her body has at any rate disappeared."

The revolution continued in Berlin, even though its leaders were dead or among the missing. The Spartacists employed sniper rifles and machine guns; the government and Freikorps also used these weapons but added heavy artillery, tanks, and airplanes. Each side would seize municipal buildings, churches, and schools, and turn them into armed fortresses. In March 1919, the Berlin papers reported hundreds dying in street battles every day. Ben Hecht, the American reporter—and future screenwriter of *The Front Page*—arrived in Germany around this time to cover the events for the *Chicago Tribune;* like a character from *Scoop,* he cabled home: "Germany is having a nervous breakdown. There is nothing sane to re-

---

* Many returning soldiers, no matter their political disposition, would display signs of sociopathy. Homicides and rapes became commonplace in postwar Berlin, brutal acts committed by men with no previous criminal records. The most famous German painters, all front veterans themselves, showed a disturbing compulsion to paint grisly scenes of sex murder and dismemberment, often working from police photographs. Otto Dix told a friend that if he had not been able to render these sex murders in art, he would have been compelled to commit one himself.

port." But Hecht, who would become one of the lone voices in the American press to protest the Holocaust two decades later, got a first glimpse of its tactics here in Berlin in the crazy spring of 1919. In the yard of the Moabit Prison, the Freikorps took revenge on those they picked up for making revolutionary gestures or appearing in Spartacist clothing: "Units of twenty-five men, women and boys chained to one another were marched across the prison yard," Hecht wrote. "Three machine guns opened fire on them and kept up the firing until the bodies had stopped moving." Hecht got the description of the massacre from a distraught lieutenant who himself commanded one of the machine-gun crews, and the former Chicago crime reporter then climbed a tree across the street from the Moabit Prison and confirmed the story with his own eyes.

The panic evoked in Germany by the fate of Russia drove so deeply into the psyche of ordinary Germans that they could not see that the forces of the new right were equally hostile to bourgeois values like law, order, and moral restraint. The Freikorps ethic, every bit as revolutionary as that of the Bolsheviks, masqueraded behind a false aura of conservatism and pacification. Real conservatives believed in the value of traditions, but the Freikorps believed exactly the opposite—for them, the Great War had proved that the morality and social structure of peacetime were corrupt and meaningless. The politics behind the war had been a fraud, but the fighting had been real, and in this reality, the "New Man" of the right-wing revolution was born. In his bestsellers of 1920 and '22, *Storm of Steel* and *Battle As Inner Experience,* Ernst Jünger hailed this "New Man, the storm soldier." Jünger welcomed the coming of "a whole new race, smart, strong, and filled with will," to save Europe from its liberal delusions. For this New Man, as for the Red revolutionaries, the legal and moral foundations of society were mere bourgeois squeamishness. At the front, only the values of bravery, ruthlessness, and camaraderie mattered—and the fundamental precept of Freikorps ideology: all society is the front.

A country driven nearly hysterical by the fear of one sort of terrorism thus legalized another, ensuring that if its enemies did not destroy it, its new friends certainly would. In 1919 the German supreme court passed a ruling that defined a new sort of "supra-legal" emergency—essentially, society under threat of revolution—under which the normal prohibitions against murder would not apply. The high court gave as an example political murders committed by the Freikorps in their voluntary war in Poland

and the Baltic provinces to fight bolshevism. The New Man of the Freikorps and the emerging Nazi movement would take full advantage of the precedent set by this ruling.

Yet the more latitude the Social Democratic leadership gave to the Freikorps to suppress the revolution, the faster it spread around the country. The Communists established soviets—Bolshevik cells or revolutionary councils—in towns and cities across Germany. After Berlin the other great German experiment in revolutionary communism was the Munich Soviet, which in its first incarnation was surreally comical and almost harmless. While revolutionaries of left and right machine-gunned each other in the streets of Berlin, the genial theater critic Kurt Eisner led a Dadaist revolution that seemed to amuse even many of the city's nonrevolutionary bourgeois residents—amused them, that is, until Eisner was gunned down one day in broad daylight by a half-Jewish anti-Semite who apparently shot Eisner in an effort to "prove" his own Aryan credentials—essentially, as a kind of proto-Nazi fraternity initiation stunt. It was doubly absurd since Eisner had been on his way to the Munich Soviet that day to announce his resignation. The post-Eisner Bavarian Revolution got increasingly radical but retained its eccentric flavor. Its new leaders were cabaretists like Erich Mühsam and Ernst Toller. The Munich Soviet's foreign minister, Dr. Franz Lipp, was a former mental patient who sent threatening telegrams to the pope and declared war on Switzerland for failing to provide the soviet with a shipment of locomotives. Toller, the president of the Bavarian Central Committee, recalled in his autobiography how all manner of cranks seemed drawn to the revolution, "believing that at last their much-scorned ideas would have a chance to turn the earth into Paradise. . . . Some believed that the root of all evil was cooked food, others the gold standard, others unhygienic underwear, or machinery, or the lack of a compulsory universal language, or multiple stores, or birth control."

In April 1919 the "Bolshevik triumvirate," led by hard-boiled associates of Lenin, overthrew the fairy-tale revolution and attempted to launch a Red Terror. Members of the bourgeoisie and aristocrats of all kinds were thrown in jail, property was confiscated, opposition presses were smashed, and schools were closed—though even this was not a real Red Terror but more of a Red Terror manqué. But in the absence of sufficient ruthlessness on the part of the German left, the German right was only too happy to fill the void. The Freikorps attacked Munich as though it were a city in France or Belgium, blasting it with heavy artillery and bombing it from airplanes. Munich's Red defenders held out for three days. When the Freikorps took over the city, they shot more than a thousand people, including not only communists but socialists and even seminary students. Anyone in a group of three or more was suspected of comprising a soviet.

The next year brought more revolution to Germany, this time from both the right and the left. In March 1920, Dr. Wolfgang Kapp, a former officer in the imperial foreign ministry, staged a putsch with the help of General Ludendorff. The Ehrhardt Brigade, one of the most revolutionary of the Freikorps formations—which had begun putting the swastika on its members' helmets before even Hitler had the idea—marched through the Brandenburg Gate. The Social Democratic government fled, and since they could not call out the Freikorps against the Freikorps, they retaliated by calling a nationwide general strike. Remarkably, the workers complied, and starting on Monday, everything in the country stopped: newspapers, electric power, water faucets. German workers were disciplined, and a strike was a strike. Kapp's gang fled to Sweden in frustration.* In the wake of the failed Kapp putsch, the Communists tried to seize hold of the German Revolution once again. After the nationwide strike drove the right-wing revolutionaries out of power, the Spartacists raised an eighty-thousand-man "Red Army of the Ruhr" to seize Germany's mining and heavy industry. Lenin had sent a crop of agents to lead the job, and the Spartacists systematically attacked police and military installations. But as it always did against its own left flank, the Social Democratic government in Berlin hit back with the ferocious Freikorps, who took on the task of revolutionary street fighting as if they were staging an assault on Verdun. The same swastika-sporting troops who had just tried to stage a right-wing revolution in Berlin crushed the left-wing one in the Ruhr Valley.

---

* Hitler, while still serving as a soldier, supposedly flew all the way from Munich to Berlin in a biplane to participate, only to be met by Kapp's personal secretary, a Hungarian Jew named Trebitsch Lincoln. According to Lincoln, he informed the future führer that the coup was over, the plotters were all running to Sweden, and he'd best get back to Munich if he didn't want to be caught. "Don't let them find you here," the Jewish plotter advised Hitler, "unless you want to get yourself arrested. Sorry I can't stay and talk with you. Good luck!"

Finally, the major disturbances ended, though street battles and small uprisings continued to break out in towns across the fatherland.

In the spring of 1921, as Lev crossed the border into Germany with his father, the country had fallen into uneasy quiet. The Nussimbaums were also going to a region as far from the political violence as you could get—a place that likely had seen no disturbance even at the height of the turmoil. The school Lev had enrolled in was on one of the exclusive islands off the North Sea coast that even today remain vacation paradises for Germany's rich, something like European versions of Nantucket, or perhaps the islands off the Carolina coast.

As the Nussimbaums arrived in the small station at Aachen, at the frontier where Germany, Holland, and Belgium meet, Lev braced himself for agitated masses of people, flag-waving workers, soldiers, shouting, or at the very least rough questioning and teeth-baring suspicion. "The usual image of a train station in the throes of a revolution," he wrote, but,

> instead, a porter came, took my things and carried them calmly into the other station. I was so surprised, my monocle fell out. They call this a revolution? I had not yet arrived in Hamburg when I was already better off by a tad—every nation seems to carry out revolution in its own way. There was no doubt: in this land, about which I had heard the most terrible things, one could live quite nicely.

Lev and his father journeyed for two more days before reaching the beautiful island with the model school of which his uncle had spoken so highly. Lev swooned with joy for every mile they encountered no angry workers or stone-faced soldiers. He soaked in every timeless glimpse of German fastidiousness and bourgeois, flowerpotted order. He could barely control his jubilance at how little was going on.

The island (which Lev never names) did not actually contain a boarding school per se but rather a sanatorium, a kind of exclusive hospital-cum-spa of the sort so popular in Germany and Central Europe before the war. It was exactly the kind of institution where rich oil folk from Baku spent most of their time while visiting Germany, so the Nussimbaums immediately felt at home. A large park took up much of the island. At the center was a cluster of small living quarters and two main buildings: the sanatorium and what was called the "pedagogium," where children "in need of rest" could keep up with school. The island bustled with purposeful activity. Doctors, nurses, teachers, servants, and administrators rushed around, busily caring for the health, education, and recreation of their guests.

Nussimbaum *père et fils* were hurried off to meet the directors, the jovial elderly physician who ran the sanatorium and the lean young academic who ran the pedagogium. The administrators knew from the uncle that they would be receiving an oilman and his teenage son from Baku, via Paris, and that the boy was to continue his education here. They were not prepared for the monocled Parisian dandy in patent-leather pumps who introduced himself as "the child" and presented his father with halting, stilted formality. Abraham Nussimbaum spoke no German whatsoever, so he was confined to maintaining an enigmatic silence as his son spoke.

Lev first expressed profound gratitude and relief, on behalf of both his father and himself, that the revolution was being handled so brilliantly here in northern Germany. Never had he seen such a fine display of aristocratic and bourgeois brilliance in the face of general disorder. It was truly a marvel "that there was no shooting going on in spite of the revolution," said Lev, "and that the policemen all stood dutifully at their posts."

By Lev's own account, as the directors took in the old gentleman and his monocled son, they could barely disguise their puzzlement. Lev did not take it amiss. He was too delighted at the benign aspect of his new country to be bothered by an odd look. This was the Germany of the orderly colony at Helenendorf and the biannual tours of Europe— prerevolutionary luxury of white-jacketed staff, newly mowed grass, and polite conversation.

The directors held lengthy discussions and consultations, at first with Lev and his father and then privately. At length they informed the monocled "child" that he was "too mature" to live together with the German boys his age, and that his education was "too distinctive" for him to study with them. ("Only later did I realize what a sensation my appearance had caused," Lev would recall. "The discrepancy between me and the 15-year-old German boys was simply too enormous.") The directors decided to treat Lev as an "amphibian—half spa patron, half pupil." He would live in the sanatorium and receive private tutoring from the teachers at the pedagogium, until such time as he "could be regarded as a normal 16-year-old."

Such a time was unlikely to come, but it was all a bit unclear to the Nussimbaums, who did not exactly comprehend the distinction between a sanatorium and a pedagogium. The arrangement sounded fine to them. Abraham took the train back to Paris, where he had dead souls to attend to.

Lev registered in the sanatorium, and almost immediately, his total ignorance of European culture helped him make an impression. He was assigned a room next door to a famous violinist. Occasionally, the violinist would practice, and in the garden below his window, enraptured guests would gather to listen. Lev knew nothing of the man's fame, nor did he have any ear for music. "I regarded the listeners as fools," he recalled. "But the violinist would practice when I wanted to take my afternoon nap." Lev adjusted his monocle and went to complain to the director. Couldn't he do something about the racket? The director only laughed. But a few hours later, Lev ran into the violinist. The great man approached him with seriousness and pressed his hand. "Splendid chap," he said, "you had the courage to be objective and to stand up for your own opinion." From then on, Lev and the violinist played checkers, which only added to the eccentric reputation of the young man with the Asiatic appearance and the peculiar wardrobe.

Lev loved the island. He enjoyed sports for the first time in his life—tennis and swimming. He lay on the hot black beach and imagined that the North Sea was a rolling blue desert. He did not concentrate much on his studies, but he perfected the one skill that was to be the basis of his career—a solid if idiosyncratic command of the German language. He got to mix with all manner of rich Europeans who met on the island. Lev felt he'd stumbled on "the best face of Europe. Its summery, radiant, carefree, eternally satisfied, cultivated countenance." Here on the island, life was "light as a feather." Lev found his dark mood lifted. "Suddenly I stopped being silent. I talked and listened. It turned out that I had something to say, and that the other guests were able to give me something. It was a short, happy stopping point in an existence which to that point had been lonely and confused."

As with most teenagers, the basis for the lifting of this burden, the fence separating him from other people, was a connection with the opposite sex. At last Lev found a sweetheart—sort of. Or rather, he discovered that he *could* have one, which can amount to almost the same thing for a young person. Remembering his first real encounter with girls, he always came back to the distinction between Eastern and Western courtship, the question of veils and invisible barriers that separated the sexes. In Baku many women in Lev's social set had not worn veils, yet they were "as good as veiled," Lev felt:

> One spoke with them as little as possible and only with expressions of the greatest shyness and the greatest respect, as if one were dealing with very fragile but also very dangerous beings. Actually, aside from immediate relatives, there were no women in the European sense. There were distant living statues, which one must never touch.
>
> Of course I knew that there were other women whom one could touch, and not only touch. But in our consciousness they were not women, not humans. Perhaps animals, they were for the sailors from the docks and for the savages, with whom one should not associate.

In Batum he had discovered that women of good backgrounds, educated women from the blond and blue-eyed Christian parts of Russia, could also make themselves available to men for a price. The Emigration was filled with such women, even more so in Constantinople and in Paris, where it was all he could do to suppress his feelings by imagining minarets while he watched the silk-clad legs go by. But even in Paris, these women were "like beautiful pictures, and it didn't even enter my head to speak to them, much less to touch them. I was after all no drunken sailor and no savage. I knew what women were for. Someday, when I had returned home, I would marry one and have children with her—very simple—that was all.

"On the green island everything was different: women were suddenly not distant creatures." They were no longer cousins or sisters, either his own or other people's, to be defended and circumvented. German women were among the most liberated in the world. Most of the girls at the sanatorium school were from Hamburg, which meant they were even more liberated than most German girls, with a sporty English outlook. Lev was shocked that women could be talkative, sports-loving "flesh-and-blood people." He played tennis and danced with them, watched them jump around "half naked"—that is, in a 1920s bathing costume—in the waves, and ate dinner with them at the same table. Most shocking for him was the way he felt they looked at him—"with undisguised curiosity."

He was also shocked by their blondness. The girls on the island seemed like dolls from a wax museum. He had never been around so many blond women, never really seen blondness up close. It struck him as an awkward absence or lack of something essential: "At first it seemed a bit ridiculous to me: they were colorless, as it were, and incomplete. I recall that I couldn't help laughing when I encountered flaxen-haired girls." He also had trouble telling them apart, for it seemed as if all these young women had the same face with minor variations. Even as he did learn to tell them apart, they were still too strange to excite him with anything beyond nervousness. After sunset, the young men and women sneaked off for rendezvous to the garden, and Lev watched the blond couples kissing happily in the moonlight.

His nerves kept him from approaching the girls for anything more than a game of tennis, but they soon approached him. He began to go out with groups of young Germans to the pubs in the local town. For the first time in his life, Lev mixed easily with people his own age. He was hardly one of them, and that was his entrée: "I was a strange creature, a wild Oriental who had come straight from Paris." (It may also have helped that he dressed in dark suits, wore a monocle, and lived in the sanatorium, rather than in the quarters with the other students.)

Whether in a real or an imagined way, Lev felt himself watched by everyone on the beach. In a world of healthy blondes, he was the skinny dark one, the mysterious foreigner. His musings on the deserts of Azerbaijan and their relationship to the North Sea, a "mystical unity," were a reflection of sexual confusion as much as nascent Orientalism: "Chaotic visions tormented me, while half-naked women and girls crawled about me in the sand and gazed at me with lust, for I was . . . a sensation."

Lev still couldn't imagine kissing a blond girl. But he got to know a girl from Berlin, beautiful and two years older, with brown eyes and thick brown hair. He went rowing and played tennis with her, and went into town with her in the evening to go dancing. On the way home one night, Lev drew up the courage to embrace her. They stopped under a tree by the seafront, the waves roaring in the background. "She resisted in jest and with a smile. Then she didn't resist anymore."

The girl kissed Lev's hair, kissed his eyes. She breathed heavily as he kissed her and threw back her head in delight. Lev looked up at her tender half-open lips, and as he caught a glimpse of her teeth, glinting in the moonlight, he lost control of his thoughts, found them sinking some-where away from romance. There was something almost horrible about this girl. The lips were voracious, the teeth . . . and the eyes. Lev suddenly felt that the brown German eyes looking at him were something foreign, far away, lifeless. "There was something inhuman in this face, in these eyes, something inhuman, unfathomably deep."

Lev gently extricated himself from the girl's embrace. She was quiet. He felt confused at his own reaction, confused that he felt no animal passion for her—she was really beautiful, he knew, one of the most beautiful girls on the island, or so he had thought. He took her home, acting his most courtly, kissing her hand. Back alone, he broke down into nervous laugh-ter, then tears, and washed himself obsessively for the next hour. He felt dirty and so lonely. But he also felt as if he had escaped some oppressive danger. The brown-haired girl looked at him from then on with the deep-est hatred, but Lev felt he had done the only thing possible, remembering "the horror of her nocturnal, craving eyes."

Lev would lead a succession of German girls to the trees by the seafront. His Oriental fascination proved durably attractive, and the mystique of the previous spurned women only seemed to attract new ones to the futile task. Lev's prudish insult was meted out equally to each of his charming quasi-conquests: a sudden retreat from tenderness into stiff formality and politeness. It was not for want of trying. He wanted to be a great lover and enjoyed the first steps. But each time he and the new girl locked in em-braces, the girl's lips and eyes appeared "ravenous" to him, and each time he recoiled from the "nocturnal cravings." He could not adjust to the overtly displayed passion of German girls. "Yet every time, every time, I recoiled at the sight of the unfamiliar lust, and it ended with a kiss on the hand and a bow." He later looked back on this as the first sign of his trou-ble with Western women.

Because of the number of girls he brought to the seaside, Lev acquired an entirely undeserved reputation as an Oriental seducer, though he seems to have stayed free of any real experience during the entire summer he spent on the island. He eventually moved on to blondes, but nothing much ever happened. He spent his days playing checkers, studying hardly at all, and dreaming of camels walking up the rocky beaches below.

At the beginning of autumn 1921, the pedagogium directors wrote to Lev's father that perhaps his son's education would be better taken up in a more traditional environment. By that time Abraham had relocated his dead-souls business from Paris to Berlin, which was now where most of the Russian immigrants were. Lev was sad to leave his comfortable room in the sanatorium—checkers with the violinist, and the romantic, if aborted, moonlit strolls with the beautiful girls.

But during the two days he spent in Hamburg on his way to Berlin, the world still seemed light and free. Lev explored the harbor city and saw the shipyards from which so many Russian Jews had pressed off and away from Germany, making the passage on one of the vast liners to America. (The man who had built the Hamburg-America line, the Jewish shipping magnate Albert Ballin, had committed suicide in November 1918, unable to bear the grief of Germany's surrender.) The spell of the island and the young women and nights spent by the moonlit waves still insulated Lev from his former gloomy thoughts and paranoias. But once again he was unprepared for the world outside his imagination. Abruptly, "everything changed completely—as if a strange magician had pressed a button and had given my life a whole new direction," he wrote in his deathbed manuscript. "I came to Berlin and laughed as well, thinking it was another green island on the northern sea. I was very mistaken. . . . The city received me with the indifference with which a giant glances down at a dwarf."

Lev would come to love the uniquely twentieth-century sooty modernity of Berlin—"the straightness of the streets . . . a beautiful, self-created austerity" enraptured him in a way that contrasted starkly with his love of ancient crumbling walls, winding souks and minarets—but there was a particular austerity to his big-city greeting that fall. Lev's arrival in Berlin was overshadowed by the news of the dead souls: they had not been doing so well. In fact, the market had become deeply depressed, as the prospects rose ever higher that the Soviet government would endure and the oil deeds would become worthless. Indeed, Abraham may have withdrawn Lev from school to save money. (When Germany and Russia signed the Rapallo Treaty in 1922, granting each other most-favored trading and military status—by which the Bolsheviks would allow the Germans to secretly rearm—the dead-souls market collapsed entirely.)

The old man was as elegant as always, never going out without perfectly polished boots and a walking stick. Lev matched him with greased hair, three-piece suits, and a monocle now worn with a natural panache. But

Lev saw his father for the first time as less than the master of all he surveyed, and the scales of his sheltered upbringing finally fell from his eyes, in a way that all the adventures of his "desert days" never could have done. "I saw now what was more important than all the wisdom of the green island. I learned that besides camels, deserts . . . besides teachers, beautiful women, and the green sea, there existed something else, the flip-side of life: money."

CHAPTER 8
___

The Berlin Wall

❧

W HILE POVERTY WAS A FACT OF LIFE for most Berliners in 1921, postwar inflation and the hopelessness of the Germans made all foreigners, including even the Russian émigrés, seem well-off by comparison. The mark, which before the war had an exchange rate of 4 to the dollar, by 1921 was 75 to the dollar (and things would get much worse: two years later, it would be 440,000,000 to the dollar). If the Russians still had jewels to pawn or accounts in Switzerland, they could make a killing at the current rate of exchange. But former industrialists with properties in Russia were in trouble. And Abraham had almost no money left at all, though he still filed his claims regularly in Paris. These were now merely petitions for the record, rather than leverage for sale and negotiation. The Nussimbaums were broke.

It would have been humiliating to return to Paris, to live off Lev's mother's relatives, while returning "home" was obviously not an option. And oddly enough, Lev found himself in a surreal, transplanted version of home, as though he and his father had been trudging around the known world, fleeing the collapsing Russian Empire, only to find themselves back at the heart of it. That was what Germans were calling Berlin in the fall of 1921—the second capital of Russia.

Like most other émigrés, Lev and Abraham moved into a flat in Charlottenburg, the formerly posh western area of the city that was now referred to by Germans as Charlottengrad (the Russians called it Petersburg). Berlin had been going Russian since 1918, when those escaping the revolution began gathering in the capital in such numbers that when the tram drivers reached the Bülowstrasse, they yelled: "Russia!" It had been geographically the closest capital to the Russian Empire, entry visas to Germany were easy to get, and life was cheap. Most of the émigrés in Charlottenburg were not from the exotic "Oriental" parts of Russia and had not taken the circuitous southern route, via Constantinople, Rome, and Paris, to get there. They were from St. Petersburg and Moscow and had crossed directly through Poland by train or car or whatever would carry them.

"At every step, you could hear Russian spoken," recalled the writer Ilya Ehrenburg, who arrived from Moscow that fall. "Dozens of Russian restaurants were opened—with balalaikas, and zurnas, with gypsies, pancakes, shashliks and naturally, the inevitable heartbreak." Jobs were tough to find, but savings or payments from international welfare agencies stretched a long way in a town where Germans carried their inflationary pay home in water buckets. "Shopkeepers changed their price-tickets every day, the mark was falling," Ehrenburg recalled of 1921 in his memoirs. "Herds of foreigners wandered along the *Kurfürstendamm:* they were buying up the remnants of former luxury for a song." The surrealist poet Andrei Belyi wrote a few years later, "If one were to hear German there would be great disbelief: How? German? What are they looking for in 'our' city? . . . In front of the ornate stores sit beggars, who have no arms, no legs, the invalids from the war, from '14, from '18, many of them decorated with the iron cross . . . they display their stumps to the passersby."

As a metropolis, Berlin had grown up during much the same time as the American city it was most often compared to, Chicago. It had risen fast and fallen even faster.

At the beginning of the nineteenth century, the sleepy city on the Spree River had been a mere garrison town, the administrative capital of the kingdom of Prussia, where almost everyone worked for the government. Yet the Francophile king Frederick the Great had begun to acquire culture for the capital with the efficiency of a military campaign: he had invited the persecuted French Huguenots and radical thinkers like Voltaire to bring in new ideas and even cultivated "the best" local Jews like Moses Mendelssohn, who received partial dispensation from Prussian anti-Jewish laws because of his genius (and his politics). As tolerated Jews and foreigners opened French-speaking literary salons, the city acquired the nickname "Athens on the Spree," though critics said this was just a reference to all the neoclassical buildings its autocratic rulers commissioned. Everyone knew Berlin was really "Sparta on the Spree," the capital of an austere, fiercely militaristic state.

Whatever formula for growth the Prussian kings had hit upon, it worked. By the turn of the twentieth century, Berlin was the capital of the second-greatest industrial nation after the United States. The city's population had gone from one million in 1877 to two million in 1905 to four million by 1920, not counting the Russians, who added another half million. The government solved its fantastic prewar housing shortage in classic Prussian military style, building vast "rental barracks," army-style makeshift housing where 90 percent of the population lived by 1910. An early-twentieth-century architecture critic disparaged Berlin as "a stone coffin" where an average of eighty people lived in a space that in New York would house just twenty. But that underestimated the appeal of the gritty metropolis. Added to the Athenian architecture of columns and open spaces was something grand and exciting, a city with a pace like nowhere else in the Old World. Political expression in the kaiser's capital was surprisingly free in these years. Berlin's famed political cabaret developed alongside steel-helmeted horse parades and imperial pomp, and it was by many accounts almost as radical as its more famous Weimar-era successor. It was all buoyed by seemingly endless growth and productivity and the sense that Germany's situation could only get better.

As Lev and Abraham arrived in the wake of war, inflation, and shortages, Berlin was transforming itself again. "It seemed as though everything was bound to collapse," wrote Ilya Ehrenburg,

> but factory chimneys went on smoking, bank-clerks neatly wrote out astronomical figures, prostitutes painstakingly made up their faces. . . . At every turn there were small *Diele,* dance halls where lean couples conscientiously jigged up and down. Jazz blared. I remember two popular songs: "Yes, we have no bananas" and "Tomorrow's the end of the world." However, the end of the world was postponed from one day to the next.

Speculators built fortunes by buying up properties and industries on credit and then waiting to pay back their loans a month or a week later with vastly depreciated currency. In this atmosphere, anyone with any money at all was a millionaire and soon could be a billionaire. The atmosphere of excess contributed to the obsession with gambling, drugs, and drink that the 1919 revolution had brought to Berlin.* Berliners were changing metaphors again, and the building dynamism of émigrés and expats, radical politics and radical lifestyles, would soon give Berlin its new nickname: "Manhattan on the Spree." By which was meant a wild mix of Harlem and Greenwich Village, as the swirl of collapsing European empires around the Weimar Republic sucked the world's most creative artists, writers, philosophers, musicians, and scientists into the city's maelstrom. Indeed, German society's free fall seemed to achieve the kind of cultural gravitational pull that Berlin's rulers had never really managed when they tried to create it deliberately. The city was becoming white hot, and at the core of this new transformation were the Russians.

All this Russian culture only drove home to Lev the degree of his isolation. Rooms in Charlottenburg were not hard to secure, as the German tenants had all fled to even cheaper digs, but the ones Lev and his father found were dispiriting, and the landlord, who seemed to be pimping his daughters as well as half the girls in the building, became aggressive when he was not paid on time. But at least they had a roof over their heads. Finding a school for Lev proved more challenging. They spent the first dreary weeks trudging around the city looking for one, and Lev was demoralized by the responses they got, now that they were poor stateless refugees rather than itinerant oil millionaires. Headmasters were critical of Lev's previous education: some subjects he knew too little about, some too much. His education was not German, and hence barbaric. The months at the sanatorium school hardly counted. Finally, when they were despairing that any decent school would take Lev, they found one that welcomed them with open arms.

The Russian gymnasium in Charlottenburg was one of two Russian high schools in Berlin at the time catering mainly to children of the émigrés. It was housed in a private German girls' school, and the Russians

---

* An American Red Cross worker in Berlin during the 1919 revolution noted: "An interesting phenomenon associated with the revolution and apparently typical of all revolutions, for I understand that it occurred in Russia, as well as in France, . . . is the great increase in dancing. Practically all cabarets and many of the cafés schedule dances beginning early in the afternoon and continuing throughout most of the night."

were allowed to use the building only starting at three in the afternoon. The curriculum was carefully developed to follow monarchist pedagogical principles and to transmit the traditional culture of imperial Russia. The émigré community, both in Berlin and in Paris, donated whatever they could to support the school; their greatest fear was that the young would assimilate into the local cultures and forget the motherland. Most of the classes were in Russian, both because the students, like many of the professors, could not have managed them in German, and as a political statement. Lev had begun his studies at an imperial czarist high school in Russia's "near abroad," the Caucasus, and now he would finish them at one in "Russia abroad"—that is, the Emigration. He found it both familiar and disconcerting to be surrounded by "the children of the best Russian families" now that he and his father were broke.

And soon enough, he felt the old alienation he had known as a boy— the feeling of being different from the other children and knowing that the difference was not due to some identifiable reason like ethnicity or religious background but simply something deep and indefinable in his soul that separated him from the group. On the green island, Lev had fit in because his outsider status was classifiable. His overt foreignness had allowed him to become a type: a consumable weirdo, the dark kid from Paris with the monocle whose father owned oil wells. But in Berlin, in a class full of Russian émigrés, many of them Jews whose parents had also gotten out with their wealth sewn in their suits, Lev suddenly felt the old gap that separated him from other people.

"Perhaps it was the wall of money as well," Lev remembered. The Nussimbaums' landlord took to letting himself into the apartment in drunken rages to demand payment instantly, and the visits so disturbed Lev that he would sometimes sleep in the courtyard in order to avoid them. Though all of Germany was suffering, poverty was acutely embarrassing to the young man who had known only its opposite.

But while a psychological wall certainly separated Lev from his classmates—and from most people anywhere—the "wall of money" was in some sense a neurosis, a token of his difficulty adjusting to diminished circumstances. Destitute though they were, the Nussimbaums were no poorer than most of the other émigrés they knew, not to mention the population of Berlin at large. Lev's classmates were an interesting bunch, and it was not surprising that he would look back at the end of his life and realize that "the few friends I still have in the world come for the most part from that school." One of them, Alexander Brailowsky, was perhaps the first to break through Lev's defenses. A Russian Jew, he had escaped with his family via the White Russian enclave in Crimea, and had enough happy memories of the kindness he'd been shown by Turks there and in Constantinople to become an interpreter of Lev's Turkish pretensions to the rest of the class. Another good friend would be Anatoly Zaderman, also Russian Jewish, who liked to paint and recite poetry; he would later move to Paraguay, then Argentina, and become a well-known South American news photographer (as Anatole Saderman). Both Zaderman and Brailowsky would live into the later part of the twentieth century and, looking back on their time in Berlin, both would recall Lev's eccentricities and antics in tales told to their children and grandchildren.

Some of the other boys in the class had even odder backgrounds than did Lev. Boris Alekin grew up in Japan and passed through Paris before arriving in Berlin; he would eventually die fighting in Nazi uniform against the Communists. Myron Isacharowitsch also joined the nationalist Germans to fight communism, only in quite a different sense. Rebelling against his father, a Russian Talmud scholar, Myron ran away from home to join the Freikorps, who were with the Whites in Lithuania. That the son of a Talmud scholar would think of joining a band of aspiring Teutonic knights—and that they would accept him—would have been unthinkable if not for the hole the Bolshevik Revolution had blown in Western life. Among the girls in Lev's class were Zozefina and Lydia Pasternak, the sisters of the novelist and poet Boris, whose parents would come to act as foster parents for the whole class. Their father, Leonid, had been a famous painter in Russia, and his wife was a former concert pianist. Lev spent many happy hours at the Pasternaks', entertaining the others with his "Oriental tales" and flirting with the young women.

Another one of these was a raven-haired girl named Valentina Brodskaya, who, under her later name Vava Brodsky, would become Mrs. Marc Chagall. Vava's best friend, the great blond beauty of the class, was Elena Nabokov, the beloved younger sister of the novelist. Sixty years later, Alexander Brailowsky would still remember her stunning looks, not without some excess of interest: "blue-eyed and pink-cheeked (what used to be described in Russian folklore as a 'blood and milk' complexion), with a straight little nose, a generous mouth, long and heavy blond braids and a luscious body."

Elena's family was the most illustrious of Lev's circle—not because of her brother yet, but because of her father, Vladimir Nabokov, Sr. He was a real hero of the émigré world, a man who represented everything that was best about liberal pre-revolutionary Russia. In 1905 he had helped found the Constitutional Democratic Party, nicknamed the Kadets, which became the largest political party in Imperial Russia prior to 1917. After a decade spent as a parliamentarian, criminologist, journalist, and army officer—as well as a convict in the czar's prisons—the multitalented Nabokov had joined the brief constitutional government of Kerensky in 1917. When the Kadets were declared "the Party of the People's Enemies" by Lenin and the Cheka were given free rein to assassinate and imprison them, the Nabokovs had made their way, via the Crimea and Constantinople, to England.

Nabokov *père* had moved his large family from London to Berlin in the fall of 1920, to be closer to the heart of "Russia Abroad." (His eldest son, Vladimir, Jr., stayed on to finish his degree at Cambridge.) Nabokov assumed the editorship of the new émigré daily *Rul* (*The Rudder*), and the first issue, appropriately enough, went to press just as the news of Wrangel's defeat hit Berlin. Like the Kadet Party and Nabokov himself, *The Rudder* stayed constant in the middle of the storm, veering neither to the extreme right nor the left, providing the émigrés with an objective view of their situation. It became something like *The New York Times* of the Emigration. Its role in connecting and informing the émigré community in Berlin was illustrated by a cartoon it published, simultaneously self-mocking and boasting: the drawing showed a dejected violinist onstage before an empty auditorium; the caption read, "A concert that was not announced in *Rul.*" Lev and Abraham probably would have read *The Rudder* regularly—the latter in no small part because it reported daily stock market tables and featured extensive business coverage of former imperial assets, including the dead souls. The paper took the position that Russian democrats must avoid making deals with extremists of either side to keep the hope of a real Russian revolution, in the best Western tradition, alive.

On March 28, 1922, Nabokov and another liberal leader, Dr. Pavel Miliukov, visiting from Paris, hired the Berlin Philharmonia Hall for a benefit to aid famine victims. The audience had little in common with the ultra-radical, anti-Semitic fanatics who were associated in the popular mind with the White Emigration. But two of these latter types arrived that night. And as Miliukov was known for taking the position that reconciliation with the new Soviet regime was best, he made a good target. The ultra-radicals burst into the hall as Miliukov was speaking and fired at him, but missed; one of the bullets hit Vladimir Nabokov in the heart, killing him.

Nabokov's killers were pawns—one of them was apparently nearly insane with fury at the murder of his fiancée by the Bolsheviks—but they were under the influence of the darkest and most lethal legacy of the Russian Emigration in Germany. They were followers of Fyodor Vinberg, a Baltic German who was obsessed with Jews and dedicated to proving that the overthrow of the czar was their work alone. A publisher whose sole business appears to have been distributing anti-Semitic materials, Vinberg printed lists of Jewish Soviet officials, much like the anti-Semitic dictionaries that had been popular in Germany and Austria since the end of the nineteenth century. Lev would appear in one in the early 1930s under the profession "Jewish story swindler," or fabulist.

Along with a handful of other Baltic Germans, Vinberg would help Hitler revolutionize German anti-Semitism, making Jews an explanation for the worldwide plague of social upheaval. To make their case, they relied on *The Protocols of the Learned Elders of Zion,* which fused together every revolution from 1789 to 1917 into a single Jew-run plot to destroy the world. The *Protocols,* which had been around in one form or another for almost thirty years, were likely first concocted in the late 1890s by the Paris office of the Okhrana. The book's conceit was that the secret graveyard meetings of these "Elders of Zion" had been infiltrated by an Okhrana spy and that the spy had managed to take notes. These notes supposedly revealed how the Jews fomented strife among Christians via war, moral depravity, revolutionary thought, and market capitalism, with the ruin of Christian civilization and the rise of a Jewish world police state as their ultimate goal. In order to keep them docile, the Elders of Zion planned to give the gentiles social benefits like full employment and food and medical care. Thus, all forms of socialism were part of the plot.

The *Protocols* presented the Jewish conspiracy as both a communist plot and a capitalist cabal, both of which were masks for Jewish power. The Jews were behind everything and would use whatever worked. If you bought into this theory, suddenly all things could be explained as part of a vast plot so cold-blooded and inhuman that it seemed as if Jews were aliens from another planet who had arrived to dominate the earth. The *Protocols* were first published as a series of newspaper articles in St. Petersburg in 1903, but their real "debut" was during the 1905 revolutionary disturbances in Russia. A mystical Russian Orthodox cleric named Sergei Nilus, a competitor of the monk Rasputin for the czar's attention, added the *Protocols* as an appendix to his book *The Great in the Small, or the Advent of the Antichrist and the Approaching Rule of the Devil on Earth*. Nilus was part of a long tradition of extreme religious figures in Russia who sought apocalyptic explanations for world events. The murderous violence of 1905 seemed to confirm many of the *Protocols'* predictions, and the disastrous First World War and the revolution of 1917 that followed practically made the writings seem like a scientific explanation of the state of the world. Nilus continued to bring out editions of his strange work, with the *Protocols* attached as a "primary-source" appendix after 1905, and in 1917 he updated the title to the timely *He Is Near, at the Door . . . Here Comes Antichrist and the Reign of the Devil on Earth*. In this 1917 edition, Nilus stated for the first time that Theodor Herzl, the founder of Zionism, had been at the center of the Jews' plot and was somehow also responsible for the upheavals in Russia.

After the czar's family was shot in Ekaterinburg in 1917, there were three books found belonging to the czarina: the Bible, *War and Peace,* and Nilus's work with the *Protocols* appendix. According to the czarina's diary, while they were imprisoned, awaiting their fate, Nicholas would read aloud to the whole family passages from the *Protocols* to explain what was happening to them and to Russia. (Apparently deeply moved, the czarina Alexandra had carved a swastika—already popular as an anti-Semitic symbol—on her windowsill.) When they were published in English in 1920, *The Times* of London asked gravely: "What are these Protocols? Are they authentic? If so, what malevolent assembly concocted these plans, and gloated over their exposition? Are they a forgery? If so, whence comes the uncanny note of prophecy, prophecy in parts fulfilled, in parts far gone in the way of fulfillment? . . . Have we, by straining every fibre of our national body, escaped a 'Pax Germanica' only to fall into a 'Pax Judaica'?"*

It was in Germany that the *Protocols* would have their greatest impact. Collaborating with a high German army officer named Ludwig Müller von Hausen (alias Gottfried zur Beek), Vinberg brought out the first German translation in January 1920. It was a runaway bestseller. By the time Hitler took power in 1933, there were more than thirty German editions in print, with hundreds of thousands of copies in circulation. The *Protocols* and the many related pamphlets and books that Vinberg and his colleagues published struck a deep chord with the public. Some used them to argue that bolshevism was but a mask for a vast Asiatic devil plot led by Jews, Freemasons, Muslims, and a host of other "Eastern" bogeymen. Vinberg himself claimed to have "documentary proof" that the New York banking houses had financed the Russian Revolution: in 1905 it was supposedly Jacob Schiff and Max Warburg pulling the strings, while in 1917 the Bolsheviks were supposedly backed by Kuhn, Loeb, and Company. Crazy as they sound, these stories were picked up by many respectable world papers. Jacob Schiff sued, only drawing more attention to the idea. The lie had grown from a few seeds of half-truth: along with other wealthy Jewish philanthropists, Schiff had lobbied the American government to intervene during the 1905 violence in Russia—not to help the revolution but to try to stop the pogroms that broke out as a result of it. He became involved in Russian affairs again in 1917, this time trying to help Nabokov and Miliukov, when their liberal Kadet party was struggling to hold together the parliamentary government; along with the U.S. government itself, Schiff and the other forces of "Jewish Wall Street" had involved themselves in Russia to stop the Bolsheviks, not help them.†

As Vinberg's disciple, Alfred Rosenberg, an architecture student in Mu-

---

* In 1921 *The Times* would reverse itself, publishing a groundbreaking series of articles by Philip Graves, exposing the *Protocols* as a forgery. The young reporter said he had been approached by a "Mr. X," a "Constitutional Monarchist" who had fled with the White Russian exodus in 1920 and had gotten his proof from officials of the czarist secret police. Among the documents "Mr. X" handed Graves was a pamphlet, a nineteenth-century French satire of Napoleon III called *Dialogues in Hell Between Machiavelli and Montesquieu,* which contained verbatim many of the scenes in the *Protocols,* minus the Jews.

† Like so many Baltic German ideas, the "fact" that Jewish banking houses had financed the Russian Revolution was adopted into the Nazi canon. But the story's bizarre resurrection in communist propaganda best demonstrated the power of such nonsense within the

nich, brought the *Protocols* to its most important audience, with another Baltic German, Max Erwin von Scheubner-Richter, providing the financial backing and connections. The audience was Adolf Hitler, and he perhaps never paid such close attention to anyone again in his life as he did to this small group of German-Russian émigrés who showed up in Munich in 1919 and 1920. The botched attempt to murder Miliukov, which resulted in Nabokov's death, had been planned in part by Vinberg, most likely with help from Scheubner-Richter and Rosenberg. These "German Russians" feared the Eastern influence more than most real Germans were likely to. They brought to German anti-Semitism the idea of the Final Solution and mass demographic engineering in the East, of recolonizing areas once conquered by the Teutonic knights, and bringing the borders of Germany up to the gates of Moscow. The Baltic German faction hoped that the Nazis would help them regain Russia for the Russian ruling classes. Instead, they helped develop the Nazi ideology of Russia as a phantasmagoric land where ultimate violence was necessary to confront Asiatic Judeo-bolshevism in an apocalyptic race war. In a twist that would confound his Baltic German friends, Hitler would insist on taking Lenin and Stalin as his models as well, seeing in bolshevism the key to the methods that would defeat it. In a similar manner, though Hitler would never publicly admit it, and only rarely spoke of it in private, the idea of the Elders of Zion itself would provide the model for his race war: he would beat the Jewish world conspiracy with an Aryan world conspiracy, just as he would fight bolshevism with the methods first suggested and employed by Lenin.

But for the time being, the Russian émigrés would provide Hitler's greatest source of funding, new ideas, and friends in high places.

Elena Nabokov's personal tragedy was shared by the class that spring at the Russian gymnasium. It signaled the fragility of life here in "stable" Germany, which had supposedly suppressed its revolution but had in fact redirected it in new and more ominous directions. Almost all the classmates regarded themselves as Russians, but nearly all were also Jews or liberals or both. Vladimir Nabokov's assassination emphasized the vulner-

---

context of the *Protocols*: inverting the charges, the Soviets alleged that the Jewish Wall Street banking houses—again Schiff and Kuhn, Loeb, and Company were invoked— were the main financial backers of Nazism.

ability of bourgeois German constitutionalism, and of the liberal monarchist movement, the majority in the Emigration, against its far-right fringe.

This would be a spring of assassinations in Berlin, and the murder of Nabokov was only the prelude to one of far greater significance, which would put the deathblow to any hope that Lev and his father had escaped the specter of revolutionary violence. The historian E. J. Gumbel calculated that between 1918 and 1922, there were 376 political assassinations carried out in Germany, the vast majority by the radical right. The figure does not seem so high compared to the horrors that would later descend upon Germany through state-sponsored violence. But a few hundred political assassinations in four years is a tremendous number. (Think what the 1960s would have felt like if not three but three hundred American leaders were shot dead.) The murders of public figures had an effect similar to the assassinations by the radical left in Russia in the late nineteenth century: they made society itself seem vulnerable to some cataclysmic change.

The assassinations of the spring of 1922 demonstrated the power of the radical new anti-Semitism sweeping in from Russia, and the movement being built around the nascent Nazi party in Munich. But the party would have gotten nowhere if not for the growth of the Freikorps and the bizarre cults of youth and honor-murder its members set loose on Germany. In many ways, the Freikorps' nihilistic violence was as much of a necessity for the triumph of Nazism as the bomb-throwing of the Social Revolutionaries in the 1870s had been a condition for the rise of Lenin. The Freikorps was the last crucial ingredient necessary to create the Nazi movement— without it there would never have been more than a collection of plotters, politicians, and their occasional hired assassins. As with the Bolsheviks, the Nazis would eventually have to put down this radical current—youth-oriented, unpredictable, paradoxical—in order to take power. But before it did put down the Freikorps leaders, or banish them to safe positions outside the centers of power, it would benefit from the sheer force of their anarchic violence.

These young men would not campaign for power. In fact, they would barely explain themselves without an ironic smile. Their Germany was an extension of the world of the front—a place where at any moment the skies could burst open, in Ernst Jünger's famous phrase, in a storm of steel. One clear motive for the assassinations can be discerned from their targets: the majority of those murdered between 1918 and 1922 were Jews (Nabokov being an exception), and not only those on the radical left. Members of various ruling liberal coalitions were also shot or bombed, as were Jews from conservative and nationalist parties. Anyone with a Jewish name or background, of whatever party, could be a target. A new attitude was emerging in Germany—something foreshadowing Nazism but still quite different from it, more than a decade before Hitler would seize power. This attitude would coalesce on a sunny day in June 1922, when three youths murdered a man many considered to be the greatest German of his generation, and certainly the most important Jewish German ever to serve his nation in high office. The pistol shots and explosion that killed Walther Rathenau on his way to work that morning heralded the arrival of a new and terrible kind of revolution.

Walther Rathenau was the heir of the AEG empire, Europe's version of General Electric. His father, Emil Rathenau, had bought the European patents for Edison's electric lightbulb at a trade show in the early 1880s after witnessing its presentation at the Paris Exhibition of 1881. Typifying the fin de siècle generation of German Jews for whom no goal was high enough, young Walther Rathenau studied chemistry, physics, and electrical engineering, and he became a well-known literary essayist before taking over the department that led his family company's global construction of power stations, including the one in Baku. The Rathenaus aimed to make AEG the biggest supplier of electricity in the world. Walther joined the boards of almost one hundred different companies, while continuing all the while to publish literary and cultural criticism, including famous essays on Jewish assimilation—he was for it—and on the evolution of Berlin into "Chicago on the Spree." By the outbreak of the First World War, Rathenau was one of the most important industrialists in Germany, yet he was also a serious intellectual and, paradoxically, a critic of unbridled industrial capitalism, arguing for a more rationalized yet humane and egalitarian economic order. A frequent adviser to the government and acquaintance of the kaiser, though his Jewishness always kept him marginalized, he criticized the emperor's policies when he thought they endangered prosperity and sanity. When almost everyone in Germany went delirious with joy on the outbreak of the First World War, friends recorded that Rathenau broke into tears.

Though not a convert to Christianity, Rathenau represented a Jewish apostasy more typical of his time: the conversion to Wagnerian Teuton-ism. In this generation the first name Siegfried was almost a sure indica-tion of Jewish background. "My religion [is] that Germanic faith which is above all else religious," Rathenau wrote. Part of what made the postwar "stab-in-the-back theory" so maniacally insane—and what made German Jews so slow to realize its dangers—was that, viewed from the outside, it often seemed like the only people who actually *were* protecting Germany's interests during these years were its prominent Jewish citizens.* Though he had opposed the war, after it started, Rathenau went to the generals and to the kaiser to raise a crucial point: Germany would run out of raw materials—food, fuel, ammunition—after a year of fighting, two at most. The generals laughed. Everyone assumed the war would be over in months, why bother planning? These Jews are always such hoarders. In the face of much ridicule, Rathenau established the Imperial War Raw Materials Office with almost no funding or support, and First World War historians agree that his tiny department enabled Germany to go on fight-ing at least two years after it otherwise would have run out of chemicals, cotton (necessary for guns as well as uniforms), wool, and rubber.

After the war, Rathenau became the most respected and the most hated man in the new German Republic. He came to doubt capitalism and pub-lished a bizarre pair of nonfiction bestsellers, one of which, *Tomorrow's So-cialization,* was adopted by the Munich socialist revolutionary Ernst Toller as "a guide for the redistribution of Bavaria's wealth and industry." Yet the conservative post-kaiser German governments wanted nothing more than to have Rathenau on board their ship of state, hoping that the internation-ally respected industrialist could extract Germany from the mess of Ver-sailles. Rathenau demurred. It was not any inherent modesty, lack of patriotism, or lack of desire to serve in a high position. It was clear to him that it was dangerous for a Jew to climb too high publicly in Germany. Fi-

---

* In 1915, Hermann Cohen, the famed neo-Kantian who is even today often regarded as the most important Jewish philosopher of the nineteenth century, published an essay in which he argued that it was the special duty of the modern Jew to spread the supremacy of German culture. Cohen was the ultimate establishment Jewish figure. As late as 1930, with anti-Semitism rampant and the Nazi party scoring mass successes at the ballot box, German Jewish Rabbi Max Dinemann could give a sermon, on the occasion of French military withdrawal from the Rhineland, that compared the event to the deliverance of the ancient Hebrews from their wanderings in the desert.

nally, in March 1922, a few weeks before Vladimir Nabokov's assassination, Rathenau agreed to become foreign minister, the highest post a Jew had ever taken in a German government. All his mother could say was "Why have you done this to me?"

"I really had to, Mama," Rathenau replied, "they could not find anyone else."

At the world economic conference in Italy, Rathenau charmed and negotiated around the clock, trying everything to press the Allies for some concessions on reparations. He wanted Germany to deal with the West, but France was adamantly opposed—and Rathenau was not the sort of man to let the company collapse just because it was unsuccessful in one market. If the Western democracies would not help Germany, he was determined to "play the Russian card." In a midnight phone call with the Russian delegation, Rathenau arranged a secret meeting in the nearby seaside town of Rapallo. There, he entered into negotiations with none other than Leonid Krasin, the elegant bomb-maker of Baku who had once sat at the Nussimbaums' dinner table. Krasin's terrorist days were over, and he was now helping bolshevism with his smooth negotiating skills and wide knowledge of the oil business. (In fact, his main brief was to sell Baku oil concessions to Western companies on behalf of the new Bolshevik regime, and thus render worthless the "dead souls" that men such as Abraham Nussimbaum still pinned their hopes on.)

The new special relationship between Germany and Soviet Russia was based on their purely negative common affinity—a hatred for the West and the "victors of Versailles"—and would have terrible unforeseen consequences. Its secret codicils would allow the German Army to illegally rearm and train on Russian territory throughout the twenties and thirties. Tens of thousands of German "work commandos" would come to Russia in 1923 and begin experimenting in the new, still theoretical technique of the blitzkrieg, the idea that small, high-quality, mobile forces backed by airpower could overcome a country before it could react. Under the treaty, the Germans built aircraft outside Moscow and manufactured poison gas in a plant in the Russian provinces. Red and German armies trained their aviators and tank officers together at a series of new schools throughout the Soviet Union. Thus, the armies that would slaughter each other in the 1940s in the most massive mechanized battles in history trained together in the 1920s.

When he'd gone to visit Rathenau at the Ministry of Foreign Affairs in Berlin, Count Harry Kessler had found his old friend straining under "his own countrymen's vindictive hostility." ("His most cordial relations are with the British, followed by the French, Italians, Japanese, and so on; his worst, with the Germans.") Rathenau told Kessler that he received threatening letters daily and that the police urged him to accept protection. He refused. "As he said this," recalled Kessler, "he pulled a Browning from his pocket." In April 1922, word of a plot to assassinate him was passed to the government by Papal Nuncio Pacelli (who would later become Pope Pius XII), who said that he knew of a plot to kill the foreign minister but could divulge nothing further. British colleagues said Rathenau sometimes mused about his impending assassination.

A shadowy network of conspirators and ultra-nationalists backed the three young men who carried out the plot, but, like the Russian terrorists of the 1870s, they acted essentially alone. "What motive shall I give if we're caught?" asked Ernst von Salomon, one of the terrorists, who would later become a leading intellectual and hero of the Freikorps movement. "For all I care, you can say he's one of the Wise Men of Zion or . . . anything you like," the other replied. "They'll never understand our real motives."*

The morning of June 24, three terrorists trailed the minister's open car. At 10:45 A.M. they pulled up close to it and emptied a pistol into Rathenau; they then threw a hand grenade into the car for good measure. Though two of them died in the attempt to escape (one killed by the police, the other by suicide), the authorities eventually put the entire terrorist cell on trial. Dutifully, the driver of the getaway car testified that he'd heard that Rathenau, Germany's leading industrialist, was actually the leader of an underground Bolshevik movement, which—of course—was an arm of the Elders of Zion Jewish World Conspiracy. His testimony was

---

* After the Second World War, von Salomon published a bestseller called *The Questionnaire,* a sprawling quasi-novel satirizing American efforts to de-Nazify Germany. The format is ostensibly his responses to his de-Nazification questionnaire, only the responses get crazier and crazier, becoming laced with intricate running jokes and impenetrable commentaries on Nietzsche, modern appliances, and his own family's geneology. The book implies that the author and his friends are "above" simple political definitions like "Nazi." Throughout their lives, he explains, the conspirators argued about why they'd killed Rathenau, some maintaining that "it was pure chance" that they chose the Jewish foreign minister, though von Salomon himself believes the murder was foreordained and deeply worthwhile on philosophical grounds.

so convincing to the Weimar-era jury that after getting out of prison four years later, the young nihilist decided to go back to law school and eventually became a successful trial attorney.

After doing five years, von Salomon emerged from prison and wrote a bestselling novel about life as a terrorist called *The Outlaws*. He became the hero of Germany's "conservative revolutionaries" and a friend of Ernst Jünger and Martin Heidegger, as well as some left-wing writers and artists. Martha Dodd, the very liberal—ultimately Communist—daughter of the American ambassador William Dodd, gushed in her memoir: "At my last party I produced much to the astonishment (there was a little hushed gasping and whispering behind hands from the oh so proper gathering) of the diplomatic right set Ernst von Salomon, accomplice in the Rathenau murder and author of *The Outlaws*. He is much worthwhile." Von Salomon maintained his distance from the Nazis—so beneath his Nietzschean ideals—but his novels of Freikorps adventures and terrorism became favorite recruiting tools and pleasure reading for the Waffen SS.*

Years later, when the body count was in the millions, many would write volumes trying to untangle the mess of ideas that motivated the young "revolutionaries from the right" in these first years. The possibility that the bad winds had come from the East was almost commonplace in the 1920s but has been dismissed by most later historians, who see it as a variation of the Nazi argument about a Judeo-Bolshevik conspiracy threatening Europe. But it should not be so quickly dismissed. The Russian Revolution and the Emigration had unleashed vast new currents into Europe. The Baltic Germans saw the Eastern problem in terms of Jews, Mongols, Muslims, and Slavs encroaching on the West, while others saw the so-called Eastern problem in the reactionary vanguard itself.

The death of Rathenau caused many, notably Thomas Mann, to rethink all previous statements on the superiority of Germanic culture—the idea, going back to the late eighteenth century, that the fundamental genius of Western society was embodied in German *Kultur*, which was spir-

---

* Von Salomon also had a rich postwar career writing for the movies, with such highlights as the 1956 feature *Liana, the Jungle Goddess*, a "sex tease jungle-woman movie [about] a beautiful blond jungle girl" who is kidnapped and taken to Germany, where she is joined by "Tonga, a faithful native warrior, and Simba the lion, [and] where she wears sexy nightgowns and a bikini"—according to *The Psychotronic Video Guide to Film*. A mix of "topless native footage and out-of-place jazzy big band music," the guide concludes.

itual and deep, in contrast to the superficial materialism of Roman, French, or Anglo-American society. But the true extent of what primitive beastliness was being unleashed between the Rhine and the Elbe was best understood by outsiders. D. H. Lawrence, for one, saw a frightening new force emerging, a kind of spiritual combination of Russian and Germanic barbarism, a resurrection of the Eurasian savagery of the Huns with an edge of nihilism and modern aimlessness. Lawrence toured Germany two years after the Nabokov and Rathenau assassinations and described his apprehensions in a letter home:

> It is as if all the life had retreated eastwards. As if the Germanic life were slowly ebbing away from contact with western Europe. Germany feels empty and somehow menacing. So must the Roman soldiers have watched the black massive hills: with a certain fear and with the knowledge that they were at their own limits. . . . Germany is very different from what it was two and a half years ago, when I was here. Then it was still open to Europe. Then it still looked to western Europe for a reunion, for a sort of reconciliation. Now that is over. The barrier has fallen.
>
> The great leaning of the Germanic spirit is once more eastwards, towards Russia, towards Tartary. The strange vortex of Tartary has become the positive centre again, the positivity of western Europe is broken. . . . Returning again to the fascination of the destructive east that produced Attila.
>
> These queer gangs of Young Socialists [by which he meant National Socialists], youths and girls, with their non-material professions, their half-mystic assertions, they strike one as strange. Something primitive, like loose roving gangs of broken, scattered tribes. . . . As if everything and everybody recoiled from the old unison, as barbarians lurking in a wood recoil out of sight. . . .
>
> Something has happened which has not yet eventuated. The old spell of the world has broken, and the old, bristling, savage spirit has set in. . . . And it is a happening of far more profound import than any actual event. It is the father of the next phase of events.

CHAPTER 9

A Hundred Kinds of Hunger

ITH THE SOVIET UNION CRAWLING with German engineers, instructing Soviet generals on the uses of poison gas and the intricacies of tank warfare, it was clear that there would be no imminent restoration of the old order in Russia. Lev dreamed of taking revenge on Leonid Krasin, who he believed had been in league with his mother and who was now ensuring the liquidation of his father's rightful assets.

Because of Walther Rathenau's deal-making and the new Russian-German alliance, Berlin became the only city in the Emigration where Whites and Reds mixed on more or less cordial terms. Among the pro-Soviet writers were Leonid Pasternak, Alexei Tolstoy, and Ilya Ehrenburg. Vladimir Mayakovski and Maksim Gorky also came through, for who could avoid Berlin in 1922, capital of the New Russia. Sergey Eisenstein received a hero's welcome from Berlin's film fans, and Konstantin Stanislavski brought the Moscow Art Theatre to Berlin on tour.

For a while, the alliance elevated the view of all Russians in the minds of regular Germans. In this sense alone, perhaps, the émigrés indirectly benefited from the Rapallo Treaty. One of Lev's classmates recalled:

Some of my friends and I were riding in the subway and talking. Perhaps we were speaking a little louder than ordinarily in order to overcome the noise. The people in the car immediately began to grumble, and one said: "You are making yourself at home here, forgetting how

Germany is suffering." I answered: "Russia is suffering not less," to which there was an unexpected reaction from several people saying: "If they are speaking Russian, let them."

In official ways, however, the treaty made the émigrés' lives more difficult. With the active ties between Berlin and Moscow—partners against the "victors of Versailles"—government support for the exiles became muted. (Ironically, the group least affected by the German-Soviet friendship was the ultra-monarchist, ultra-racist cabal in Munich—the men who killed Nabokov—because they didn't care what the democratic government thought: their alliances were with the growing Nazi movement.) The Soviet Russians had already issued decrees stating that all refugees who had left Russia without a Soviet visa after November 7, 1917, or had lived abroad for more than five years, forfeited their rights to Russian citizenship. The German government began enforcing these decrees. Whatever documents the émigrés had been using from one of the interim White governments during the civil war were now treated as scrap paper by the authorities.

Lev and Abraham lived with just such expired documents—the papers issued to them in Batum by the Menshevik Georgian government. The Germans had always tried to stay on good terms with any Georgian government because they considered the small Christian nation the key to the Caucasus, and German industrialists coveted Georgia's diverse mineral deposits. In 1916, Georgian monarchists had been allowed to establish a kind of government in exile in Berlin, the German-Georgian Society, under the guidance of the aging Prince Matchabelli. Then, for a time, the Germans backed the independent Menshevik Republic of Georgia against the Bolsheviks.* But when the Red armies overran Georgia in 1921 and murdered its leadership, while Lev was in his island "pedagogium," the Nussimbaums' Georgian documents became worthless.

The police informed Lev and his father that they must obtain valid papers or leave Germany immediately. If they had had money, they no doubt could have solved the documents question with little trouble; for the time being, anything was still possible with money. As one of Lev's classmates

* Prince Matchabelli himself soon gave up the struggle for the Georgian monarchy and moved to New York, where he amassed a fortune by putting his name and family crest on a line of perfumes.

said, people were simply going to the suburbs, where "the petty officials were frequently accepting bribes." But fate provided a more affordable solution.

As so often happened to Lev, a chance encounter with someone from the past temporarily saved the day, or at least perked up his spirits enough so he felt it had. During the First World War, the Russians had run a POW camp on one of the islands in the Caspian. The commandant, a Baltic German, was said to be especially cruel to his prisoners in order not to be accused of having any fellow-German sympathy for them. Everyone in Baku heard about the appalling conditions. Lev and Alice, who felt kinship with these suffering Germans, convinced Lev's father to intercede on their behalf. The governor joked that their house was a "spies' nest," but allowed them to turn the first floor into a kind of temporary barracks to house some of the prisoners. Lev recalled that approximately twenty-five Austrians, Germans, and Turks stayed with them, including one woman who was "the wife of a German officer who had been traveling, intending to visit relatives in the Caucasus and taken unawares by the war." Their charity was repaid—Lev got piano, violin, swordsmanship, and riding lessons from the "guests"—but the bigger payoff came five years later. "I was walking through the Tiergarten one day," he wrote Pima, "when I bumped into the wife of the German officer. . . . I told her the situation I was in and she went with me to police headquarters. She found another few people who had been living with us in Baku and I got a passport and residence permit and could even study at the university."

It is unclear what sort of papers Lev was able to arrange, for he had a habit of lying about citizenship documents his entire life—his final feat being turning steamship tickets into an American passport, and then announcing to his Fascist patrons that he "voluntarily renounced his American citizenship"—but he did receive some substitute for the Georgian papers that spring. He and his father also got from the police what every émigré was entitled to in the first place: a Nansen passport. It's likely that Lev obtained one in March 1922, and at least as late as 1930, according to a Berlin investigative reporter who looked into his story that year, Lev Nussimbaum was receiving annual renewals of his Nansen paperwork from the representative of the High Commissariats of the League of Nations for Refugees in Germany. I never found Lev's Nansen passport, but it must have looked a good deal like the one used by his fellow student

Alexander Brailowsky, which I did see, when his widow, Norma, dug it out of an ancient box of papers for me. It was in there along with his photographs of the 1920s, of young Lev and the other Russian students in Berlin—Lev looking as cheerful as any high school senior, although a lot thinner.

The passport was a sad document, its multicolored inks and faded watermarks evoking the failed ideals of the League of Nations itself—strange, anachronistic, ultimately useless. The Nansen Passes tended to be one-way documents: a holder could often get a visa to enter a country to look for work, but then he would have no place to return to, if he found none. In theory, holders should have received more lenient treatment regarding the regulations, but the reverse was true. The Nansen Passes carried a stigma, and what status they conferred steadily eroded as the reputation and power of the League of Nations eroded. (The first blow had been dealt by the United States, which, after essentially inventing the League, refused to ratify its creation or join it.) I unfolded and unfolded the pass of Alex Brailow—as he called himself once he got to America—until it was the size of a treasure map, covering the kitchen table, depicting a dense landscape of bureaucratic stamps and residence permits and visas its bearer had acquired, including the official "Nansen tax" stamps from the League of Nations. It was a map to a treasure you knew had been revealed to the bearer, years ago, as fool's gold.

"There are a hundred different kinds of hunger, and there are a hundred ways to conceal it," Lev would write, remembering the bitterness of his first Berlin years. "And I had to conceal it. I myself don't even know why anymore. It was rarely naked bodily hunger, even if this form was certainly not lacking."

Lev defined the various sorts of hunger that he sought to conceal from his classmates—for example, "clothing hunger," which did more than strike at his dandy's soul. Lev had never seen his father, a man of expensively understated elegance, go a day without a freshly pressed suit and perfectly shined black boots. Now both looked worn and could not be replaced. Lev, too, appreciated the power of dressing: the monocle he had chosen for the trip to Germany had been a pointed affectation, since nothing more cartoonishly invoked the image of the aristocrat. Clothes, on some level, had saved them: even in the most precarious moments of their travels, the old man always seemed to have an oil bond or gold ruble in his pant seams. But the seams were finally empty, and the Nussimbaums had landed in a place that did not look kindly on poor foreigners from the East.

When overcome by circumstances, Lev remembered, "I would lie down in bed and sleep. But another form is the hunger for a place to live, whereby the landlord, acting completely within his rights, wants to evict the non-paying, suspicious foreigner, and I, the suspicious foreigner, have nothing to say to him but that I have millions at home." Lev learned that landlords have limited imaginations. And he noticed the transparency of creditors' emotions in a way that only the indebted would: "How obsequious, how submissive they were when one happened to throw them the money and how devilish when one didn't."*

But Lev was young, and he had a young man's problems. The hardship that really stood out in his memories was, of all things, what he called "cinema hunger." It was in part a matter of pride: if the other Russian students went to the movies, Lev felt ashamed not to go. The worst jam was when he agreed to go to a film with friends but then had to make excuses at the last minute because the price of the ticket had suddenly become too much. Or he had agreed to go only because he couldn't bring himself not to, knowing that he could never actually dip into his father's tiny resources. But still, the other students from the gymnasium went to the cinema a lot. Everyone in Berlin went to the cinema a lot. Like the passion for cabarets and dance halls, "cinema hunger" in Berlin in the early twenties was more intense than a mere fad; it amounted to spiritual longing.

During the chaos of the German Revolution, Berlin had emerged as Europe's Hollywood and Broadway in one. Berliners flocked to the UFA dream temples on the Ku Damm, the posh shopping avenue. UFA, Germany's leading film production company, had been founded in 1917 to nationalize the industry and produce propaganda. (By the end of the war, the Germans had built close to five hundred cinemas on the western front and three hundred in the east, but UFA would truly fulfill its intended

---

* An entire minor literature of Russian émigrés complaining about their German landlords exists, preserved for posterity in the Berlin novels of Nabokov, especially *The Gift*.

role under Joseph Goebbels's direction in the 1940s.) In the early 1920s, it became Europe's leading entertainment production company, with ties to MGM and Paramount, whose films it distributed. The premier cinema in all Berlin was the UFA Palace *am Zoo.* It could accommodate two thousand patrons and a seventy-piece symphony orchestra to accompany the films.

Though conceived to broadcast war propaganda, in the end UFA offered escape from the chaos the war had brought. The vast back lots in Babelsberg, a Berlin suburb, rivaled Hollywood in producing cinematic spectacles. Ernst Lubitsch, the son of a Polish Jewish tailor, became the first of a long line of German and Austrian directors to hone their skills in Weimar-era Berlin before going on to Hollywood. They also produced complex reflections of the disturbing times through neo-expressionist films like Robert Wiene's *Cabinet of Dr. Caligari* and Fritz Lang's *Metropolis*—though Lev's contemporaries more likely would have rushed to see grand historical epics like Ernst Lubitsch's *Madame Du Barry, Anne Boleyn,* and *The Loves of Pharoah.**

"I had long ago set aside the habit of seeing in every Berlin mosque a Muhammadan house of worship," wrote the Austrian novelist Joseph Roth for a German newspaper, in a column about the UFA Palaces and the Berlin film scene. "I knew that the mosques here are movie theaters, and the Orient is a movie."

But not all Berlin mosques were movie theaters. At some point during this time, Lev put aside his angst about not keeping up with his friends and went off in search of the real thing.

He hadn't forgotten the Orient he had glimpsed in Constantinople, with its marvelous past. He had experienced desert wanderings and

---

* Lang, Lubitsch, Erich Pommer, and most of the other luminaries of Berlin film were Jewish, to one degree or another, and so the German Hollywood was a mirror of the real thing. This applied to many of the actors as well. The most famous movie version of a Nazi officer—Major Strasser in *Casablanca*—was played by Conrad Veidt, a Berlin Jew often typecast as a Nazi. Veidt, who cried real tears when playing the title role in *Jew Süss,* the iconic persecuted Jew, in 1933, donated much of his salary from *Casablanca* to the British War Relief Fund, no doubt conscious that, had he been in Europe at the time, he would have died in a camp. (Instead, Veidt died playing golf in Hollywood in 1943.) Erich von Stroheim, the world's image of a Prussian officer, mostly for 1937's *Grand Illusion,* was the son of a Viennese Jewish haberdasher.

strange tribes. But what now set him apart from any teenage dreamer who went to see the adventures of Sinbad or Valentino at the cinema, except of course that he couldn't afford the price of admission?

And yet the modern world sometimes did offer dreams around every corner, for after surviving the wretched year of 1922, that year of assassinations, Lev at last found his Orient in Berlin—and best of all, it was playing for free. "In Berlin I learned that everything that had to do with camels, deserts, Arabs, dilapidated archways and the people who had once erected them is taught at the university, at the Seminar for Oriental Languages."

This discovery filled him with hope and ambition. He suddenly knew what to do with his time, for the gates of this "mosque" had been flung open to him, and it was filled with what true Muslims valued more than any image: words.

> There was no holding me back. I went to the rector, I went to the dean, I went to the director of the institute, begged for them to let me study there and I was successful. . . . I tore my way into the discipline like a starved dog who'd suddenly come on a piece of meat.

On October 17, 1922, Lev enrolled as a student in classes in Turkish and Arabic in the Seminar for Oriental Languages at the Friedrich-Wilhelms-Universität. On his application, he wrote his name as "Essad Bey Nousimbaoum," from Georgia. This was the first recorded official use of his new name—which was essentially "Mr. Leo Nussimbaum" transposed into Turkish. (The word "Bey" had once had connotations of Turkish nobility, but here it was simply a way of saying "Mr." or "sir.")

The inconvenient detail that Lev had not yet graduated from high school was not mentioned, and it became his great secret for the next year and a half. At first he was slightly disturbed by the university lectures, for he found that "the professors spoke about their subject matter as though they were speaking about completely ordinary things." But gradually, he understood that the professors saw the Orient as a professional pursuit, while he was driven by "a mysterious compulsion." Lev started to figure something out—a neat trick, in fact; a mental survival skill. He found that his love of ancient crumbling walls and winding souks was a guiding light he could shine on almost any landscape, no matter how bleak and intimidating it might seem. He would learn to carry a portable "Orient" inside him, one that he could unpack whenever he found a comfortable spot and the right audience.

He began to keep a crazy schedule. He was determined that no one in the Russian gymnasium find out that he was attending the university (under false pretenses), and at the same time no one at the university must realize that he was still in high school. At 6 A.M. each day, he set out from Charlottenburg and walked all the way to the other side of the city to the university. He would spend the morning in seminars while the gymnasium was still full of German girls. When the Russian school opened, at 3 P.M., he would be there just as if he had been loafing all day like his classmates. "While the teacher was explaining a geometric theorem, the Arabic grammar lay on my knees."

After school got out, at 8 P.M., while his classmates went off to cafés or the movies, Lev walked quickly back across Berlin to attend the last evening lectures at the university. "I almost always went on foot, for I suffered from a particular species of hunger—carfare hunger," he wrote. He returned home and did his homework for school and his reading for university late into the night, until he fell asleep, only to wake up a few hours later at 6 A.M. to start all over again. He lived like this for two years, cramming his head full of the mysteries of the East.

Lev's capacity for hard work and mental focus was something that would drive the rest of his short life. The émigré writers were known for drinking and working like fiends, but Lev would soon astound even them. His clandestine academic activities made him feel at times like he was in an "exclusive club," and at other times as though he lived in another world. He was glad to have a reason for being separate, however. Both the work and the schedule were a sort of emotional survival strategy. "Most likely I would have perished from this leap into poverty, if it had not been for the love of the ancient Orient that kept me going," he recalled. Lev also found he enjoyed having a secret life. He was different, he knew, because of what he had done and what he was doing. He was now an Orientalist.

In the box of Alex Brailow's things, among the pictures of students horsing around Weimar Berlin, there were at least a dozen of Lev. He was surprisingly handsome—taller than most of his classmates and better dressed (the favored style of the day, at least for Russian girls, suggested harvest time at the old dacha)—and he had a faintly tragicomic expression, like a more urbane Buster Keaton. He seemed to live in these pictures like a movie actor playing a part, while the others were simply real people being photographed. By now his social awkwardness had departed, since in almost all the snapshots he looked contented, confident, and very much part of the group. One shot of a summer's day on a lawn showed Lev with his friends Adia Voronov (arms wrapped tightly around him), Tossia Peschkowsky, Zhenia Voronov, and a blond baby of about a year old. The baby, Alex Brailow had told his wife, was Michael Igor Peschkowsky, who would later become a U.S. citizen and change his name to Mike Nichols. Born in Berlin in 1931, Nichols had managed to get out of Germany with his family in 1938 and later went on to a career as a pathbreaking stage comedian and Hollywood director, a sort of 1960s version of the great German and Austrian Jewish émigrés who remade American entertainment in the 1930s and '40s.*

But of greatest interest to me was a handful of other portraits: Lev alone, a bit older and more filled out—after university?—in full Muslim drag. In one he wears a white turban with a stone ornament and a spraying feather in the center, enormous multi-hoop earrings and rings on his pudgy fingers. He appears to have on eyeshadow and lipstick and even a painted mole above his lip, and he regards the camera with campy, Mesmer-like intensity. Another shot I had already seen, because it became the author photo for *Twelve Secrets of the Caucasus*—Lev in profile dressed as a Caucasian warrior knight, with black sheepskin hat and scimitar at his waist.

Most of the students and teachers at the Russian high school got used to calling Lev "Essad," as he insisted. In addition, Brailow noted in his memoir, his Caucasian accent seemed to get thicker as the year wore on, "with excessively broad a's, emphasis on k's and kh's." Some students couldn't resist teasing Lev about it, and about his "Islamic" identity in general, which included proclaiming himself to be "a theocratist in the Is-

* When my article on Lev appeared in *The New Yorker* with a reproduction of this photograph, Mike Nichols wrote in complaining that the baby was in fact *not* him and that lady friends could swear he was a "much cuter baby." Alex Brailow, who frequently mentions the Peschkowskys in his memoir, had written the names on a piece of paper clipped to the photo.

lamic tradition" one day and a liberal constitutional czarist the next. Brailow found that Lev's "romantic immersion in Islam" progressed "to the point of an almost complete oblivion of everything around him" and sometimes provoked not only incredulity but even hostility from his classmates. He recalled that frequently Lev "would join the teasers and would provoke a general relaxed laughter by clowning and exaggerating. Sometimes he would emphasize the irony of his statements, so that it would be impossible to tell whether he was serious or joking. But sometimes he would fly into a rage, become physically violent and would have to be restrained and calmed down."

One classmate in particular delighted in provoking Lev and never letting him "forget his origins." Norma Brailow showed me pictures of this boy, Georgie Litauer, whom all the Russians called "Zhorzhik." He was a strikingly good-looking, wiry kid who seemed to be jumping out of every black-and-white frame he was in, even if he was only shadowboxing on a Berlin street corner. Georgie was taking dancing lessons with a former ballerina of the imperial ballet, and after school supported himself as a paid ballroom dancer. He found it especially funny how seriously Lev took his transformation into "Essad Bey"—or "Assad Bej," as Lev still wrote it, following the Azeri Turkish spelling. Georgie never missed a chance to remind his classmate that he was only another Russian Jew like himself. Not knowing about the secret routine at the university, how Lev was spending every spare ounce of energy to study without going home, Georgie didn't realize what a sore spot he was touching.

The horsing around and taunts about his name change so got to Lev that one day he pulled a knife on his tormentor and threatened to cut his throat. Brailow recalled that "Essad, besides being a nervous type, seemed to indulge in outbursts of murderous rage, perhaps because he felt that this was his obligation as an 'Oriental' for whom revenge would be a sacred duty." Brailow intervened to prevent his friend's "Caucasian temper" from leading to murder. (Sadly, Georgie didn't need anyone else to do him in; he died of carbon monoxide poisoning, a probable suicide, in Paris barely five years later.)

The rivalry between Georgie and Lev also had another, more classic component. Both were stuck on the same girl—a green-eyed, copperhaired beauty named Zhenia Flatt. Brailow remembered that Zhenia "hardly read anything, was rather indolent and very preoccupied with her

looks" and held down a job as a store model for "very fashionable and expensive bras and corsets." I later saw a reproduction of Zhenia's "tenderly
beautiful profile," drawn by Leonid Pasternak, the father of their classmate Lydia and her brother Boris. In Pasternak's pastel sketch, at least, she
was truly lovely. Georgie and Lev fought for Zhenia's affections, but she
kept them both guessing—until she transferred her affections outside
the group, to an older man named Yashenka, "fat, urbane, very intelligent
and witty," who eventually moved with her to New York. There, reversing
all the ideals of the Emigration, they became fervent Stalin supporters.
Brailow always believed that Yasha was Lev's model for Nachararyan, the
"evil Armenian" in *Ali and Nino,* who is Ali's rival for Nino's love. In the
novel, rather than take the girl away to America and turn her into a Stalinist, the fat rival Nachararyan kidnaps Nino in his motor car and tries to
drive her "into the West," stealing her away from her beloved Caucasus
and her prince—but Ali (Lev) manages to chase the car down on a white
horse and stabs his rival to death. (It is a ridiculous-sounding scene that
nevertheless comes off rather well in the book.) As Brailow saw it,

> The whole love affair, including the elopement of Nino and the sub-
> sequent pursuit and killing of Nachararyan, is as much of a wish-
> fulfillment as is the autobiography of Ali whose adolescence and youth
> are a curious mixture of Essad's own and of what he would have liked
> them to be.

In his letters to Pima, Lev referred to the girl he had loved in Berlin—
unrequited though his passion was—as "Su Su Haman," a fellow Muslim
native of Baku. Of course, he could not reveal to Pima that he'd been in
love with a Russian Jewish girl. In fact, Lev knew no Azeris his own age in
Berlin, and almost all his friends were Jews, either from St. Petersburg or
from the Pale of Settlement. It must have been a great paradox to him,
what became of his émigré love.

After Zhenia, Lev went out with a succession of German girls, "usually
pink-cheeked blondes, to whose fluffy golden hair he would invariably
draw attention," Brailow wrote. It was a repeat of life on the green island.
Lev would draw close to the girls but then draw away. He was almost disappointed to be back among Russians again, though, where the proper
"18-year-old girls and boys sat next to each other [but] no kissing went on;

indeed it wouldn't have occurred to anyone to treat the girl he studied with any differently than was customary in old Russia: with reserved politeness."

On the day of his final examination at the Russian gymnasium, Lev felt lost and hopeless. He had spent far too much time at night school, studying Arabic, Turkish dialects, and Uzbek geography. There was no hope he could pass in his basic subjects—especially Latin and mathematics. He felt a fool and imagined how his and his father's prospects would become even worse when he flunked the exam. He would not be able to face the old man, who had experienced so much hardship. It would be more than he could bear.

The chairman of the examination committee, a wrinkled old Romanov prince with a monocle sunk impossibly deep into his face, seemed to take barely any notice of Lev during his exam. Then Lev saw he had written on his pad, "in his melancholy aristocratic handwriting" next to the name Nussimbaum, "a very poor candidate." During the history examination, the old chairman practically seemed asleep as Lev was quizzed, sitting there indifferently and gazing off into the distance. Suddenly, he raised his head, fixed Lev through his monocle, and said: "Tell us something about the dominion of the Tartars and Mongols over Russia."

The question would already have been the ultimate gift to Lev, even if he wasn't in his third semester at the Friedrich-Wilhelms-Universität. "I saw before us the wide Mongolian steppes and the horsemen . . . and there was no stopping me," Lev recalled.

I think I even forgot that I was in the middle of the examination. I spoke and spoke, I quoted Arabic, Turkish, Persian authors in the original languages. Indeed, I even knew some Mongolian. The committee was dumbstruck—the prince dropped his monocle. Then suddenly he started posing questions, and lo and behold!—he posed questions in Persian, in Mongolian, he even quoted the classics of Oriental literature. . . .

Only later did I find out that the prince was one of the most renowned Orientalists of Russia. The examination committee sweated; the whole thing went beyond their imagination. The teacher suddenly looked like a little schoolboy. What started out as an examination turned into a discussion in all different languages about all sorts of Oriental problems. I think it lasted two hours and it would have continued into the evening if the person sitting next to the prince, a former Russian privy councilor, hadn't given him a nudge.

The discussion saved Lev. Whatever other mistakes he made on his examinations, the old prince saw his talent and would not let him fail. In place of "a very poor candidate," the chairman made sure that all his examiners marked Lev as "average." He could graduate.

At night the school friends continued to gather, often for literary evenings at one another's apartments. "What made Essad a temporary center of that group, which often met at the home of his lady-love"—Zhenia—"was his talent for telling stories," Brailow recalled. The stories were in the popular style of ironic or psychologically challenging fairy or folktales, which combined the early-twentieth-century German craze for fairy tales with the Weimar urge to turn everything into a kind of black humor. Lev found in the tales an early outlet for his romantic Orientalism, drawing on both his Baku childhood memories and his university night-school training, as well as a way to play around in a voguish style of European literature. Alex apparently copied them down in Russian at the time, and had produced typescript translations of them decades later. I read them, and, though clearly juvenilia, they had an irony that was instantly recognizable as the raw material of *Ali and Nino* and so many of the Caucasian books Lev would write.

What most of Lev's classmates didn't realize was that he was ready to shed the identity of Lev Nussimbaum altogether by this point. In August 1922 he converted to Islam in the presence of the imam of the Turkish embassy in Berlin and became Essad Bey—or Assad-Bej, in Russian. When his schoolmates found out, particularly the Jewish ones, they were more amused than anything else, as we can gather from their reminiscences, not only Alex Brailow's but Anatoly Zaderman's.* This was an attitude that

---

* Lev also told Brailow about his first attempt to convert when he was fifteen, in Constantinople. During his brief stay in the city, he asked the mullah of a neighboring mosque to accept him formally into Islam. After a "comic interlude" based on the mullah's ignorance of the similarity between Judaism and Islam as far as circumcision was concerned, an interlude that Lev "recounted with his customary mixture of earnestness and burlesque," he supposedly became a Muslim but perhaps believed it didn't really take.

would be perpetuated by many of Lev's future café-house friends. The existence of "Essad Bey" was never intended as a joke, but it did not mean that Lev Nussimbaum, who continued to exist, could not on occasion laugh about it.

Why did he do it? Brailow believed that, having grown up in a cosmopolitan, Russified Jewish household, Lev was searching for authenticity, and found it in "the world of native servants whose roots were right there, in the Muslim villages, or 'aouls' nestling in the mountains of Baku's hinterland." That is probably true—but in any case, I don't believe it had to do with escaping persecution for his Jewishness. The truth seems far more complicated—as connected to his feelings about modernity and history as to any imminent threat (which was not quite imminent in 1923, if you weren't Walther Rathenau). When Lev walked into the Turkish embassy, it was an Ottoman embassy, still under the titular authority of the Montaigne-reading caliph and the modernist Orientals who were the last of the old Osman line. It may be closer to the truth to say that he converted as a way of rediscovering the multiethnic hope that he had as a young Jew from Baku.

The new identity would later become a racial and religious alibi, and he would use it to stay alive. But it was a cultural shelter he was seeking when he walked into that embassy, and it was no coincidence that he did it while it was still Ottoman. In one of his first portraits as "Essad Bey," Lev sits posed in a worn leather armchair that seems to be sitting outside in an alley or courtyard. He stares enigmatically at the camera, his legs crossed; he wears a well-cut suit, spats, and that symbol of Ottoman refinement, a fez.

Less than a year later, the caliph would be reading his enlightenment novels in Paris and spending his time at the opera, and both the fez and the term "bey" would be officially banned in Turkey. Lev thus traded one dying identity—son of a Jewish cosmopolitan from Baku—for another.

Lev was taking other steps to connect with Islam outside the world of the Oriental Institute. In 1923 his name turned up on a list of founding members of the Islamic community in Berlin, as "Essad Bey," and in 1924 he helped found its affiliated student group, Islamia. His accounts of this time, however, mainly stress the (in his view) pettiness and political infighting he encountered. In an autobiographical article in 1931, he rather melodramatically described the scene:

In a dark, smoky pub on the north side of Berlin, the few panislamists gather. Our numbers grow, all the languages of the Orient are spoken in the smoky room, and now and then some German as well. Probably half of those present are English or Russian spies. The leader is an Indian eunuch, who likewise will later enter into the service of the English. All of us together engage in politics, war has somehow led all of us astray. Conspiracies are planned, assassinations prepared and not carried out, proclamations written. I hold lectures about the Caliphate and write poems. . . . Practical politics begins to disgust me. Practical panislamism begins to degenerate into gossip, mutual backbiting, and mistrust.

The smoky room may have been located near Hannoverstrasse, where the community under Abdel Jabbar Kheiri—who was undoubtedly the "Indian eunuch"—was also based. Lev quickly became an active participant, both socially and politically; elected to the delegates' assembly, he spoke out about the wretched situation of Muslims in the colonial world, and he was eager to add his thoughts to those of the many disaffected Muslim students and professionals in the room.

These were among the first actual Muslims, as opposed to German and Russian scholars studying Islam, that Lev had spent any time with since escaping from Azerbaijan. They gave him some of his first adult glimpses of the Islamic world, at least of its grittier, more modern side. Many of them had come to Germany before the First World War, as teachers, doctors, and merchants; many others were political emigrants. The anticolonial movement was strong in Berlin in the 1920s, and the general German sympathy for Muslim independence was encouraged by the revolts of the Syrians from French colonial rule and the Moroccans from the Spanish.

Unfortunately for Lev, the Islamic community in Germany was also more nationalistic, especially ethnic nationalistic, than it was in some other places. And this exacerbated the old personal alienation: in smoky rooms with real Easterners, it was harder for Lev to be "the man from the East." Much as he experienced culture shock on returning to an all-Russian environment after the island of healthy blondes, he now felt out of place among his fellow exiles from Muslim countries, many of them like himself, from now Soviet, formerly Russian, territories. Social life in refugee communities is often filled with backstabbing and bitterness, but things were especially rocky for a lone Jew in a sea of disenfranchised Muslim activists. It was not even a question of religion, since Lev had converted and was a staunch defender of the progressive pan-Islamist agenda common to the group.

The problem was that ethnic nationalism with a Muslim flavor was fast becoming the favored method for opposing Soviet domination from afar. Azeri "national pride," for example, was far stronger among Azeri exiles than it had ever been in the cosmopolitan Baku of Lev's youth. Cosmopolitan Ottomanism, as one might describe Lev's loyalties, did not actually win him many allies among the Muslim exiles. Lev would find that it appealed to a different group—of liberal Europeans and "Orientalist" Jews—but he did not yet know these people. The smattering of converts in these groups took a backseat to the Arabs, Turks, Iranians, Afghanis, and Indians in the room, not to mention the other Soviet exiles. And on the whole, Lev's relationship with these "countrymen" was less than a smooth one. It was helped not at all by his emerging career as a writer.

CHAPTER 10

Weimar Media Star

L EV NUSSIMBAUM—writing under the name Essad Bey—was just twenty-four when *Blood and Oil in the Orient,* his first book, was published. By the time he died, twelve years later at age thirty-six, he had written at least fourteen more books, not counting the two novels by Kurban Said—an average of one book every ten months. I found it hard to develop a complete bibliography from library catalogs and the Internet, since new titles were always popping up: the biographies of Lenin and Stalin, one of Czar Nicholas II, a history of the world oil industry, a study of the Russian secret police. Lev wrote a kind of contemporary social and historical romance—a genre still possible before the mass horrors of the late 1930s and the 1940s made contemporary history seem distinctly unromantic.

As a twenty-six-year-old, Lev tackled biographies of Muhammad and Stalin simultaneously, and both were in bookstores before he was twenty-seven. They were international bestsellers and were warmly received for their colorful writing style and for their insights into these two world-historical figures. The biography of Muhammad is the only one of Lev's books that has always remained in print in one language or another, and the original *New York Times* review of it sums up the idiosyncratic nature of his work:

the texture of this fine book is as a Persian carpet. There is material underfoot. But it is magic to the eye. We walk firmly on what we are bound to believe, we look at what transcends belief, and the question is how we can rend the credible from the incredible without tearing asunder the whole design.

The books are readable seventy years after they were written, in no small part because Lev narrated even the driest analysis of oil-pricing mechanisms as though it were a Caucasian folktale. His Stalin is like no other Stalin one can find anywhere, and when his next book on the Soviet Union appeared, in 1933, less than a year later, the *Times* ran a news story under the headline BOOK SEES RUSSIA IN GRIP OF CRUELTY; ESSAD-BEY TELLS OF COMPULSORY PARADISE . . . BOLSHEVIKS, IN ZEAL TO FOUND A NEW RELIGION, BECOME SLAVES DRIVEN TO DOOM, HE SAYS.*

Drinking, writing, and publishing seem to have been the main Russian émigré occupations in Weimar Berlin. The city was the capital of émigré publishing until 1924, fueled by cheap paper, ink, and vodka, as well as the availability of Cyrillic typefaces from the revolutionary presses of pre-1917, when *they* were the ones in exile. But after inflation cleared out the landscape and sent much of the Emigration on to Paris and Prague, those left were a more intimate circle—largely liberal, largely Jewish, more willing to find a voice for themselves in German. Lev was perhaps the most successful example of this group.

But before he found his voice in German, Lev honed his style by giving readings in Russian, at first to his classmates from the Russian gymnasium and then to others he met at the university. At literary evenings at the Voronovs or the Pasternaks, Lev tried out his poems and "Oriental tales"— cleverly written, punning stories that stretch the genre of folktales.

Lev quickly graduated from the living-room circuit to various public "culture circles" and émigré coffeehouses. He read at the same "literary club" as young Vladimir Nabokov—a place the émigrés called *Na cerdake,*

---

* Curious that the *Times's* own Walter Duranty, its man in Moscow, would get caught up in a scandal decades after his death, when the Pulitzer Prize board in 2003 formally considered withdrawing its 1932 award to him. Almost ever since it was given, critics had protested that Duranty's upbeat reporting on the Ukraine famine and other disasters in Stalin's Russia had to have been willfully in error; other journalists, like Lev, had not missed the rising oppression and death count. In the end, however, the prize stood.

or "In the Attic." It's possible he got his introduction from Nabokov's sister, his school friend Helen.* (Press reports from the time noted that Lev received healthy applause from the audiences at In the Attic.) The following year, he joined the Poets' and Writers' Club, a forum for young émigré authors that Nabokov also joined.

But Lev had his sights set on a much wider audience, and these coffeehouse readings were the last things he would ever produce in Russian. He wanted to be a German writer. By December 1931, when the Poets' and Writers' Club gave its second public literary soiree, "Essad Bey" was among the authors featured in the publicity—but Lev did not show up. By that point, poetry and fiction were taking a backseat to other kinds of writing. He would leave fiction behind for many years, but when he finally returned to the form—combining the vigor of his journalism with the ironic atmosphere and subtlety of the Oriental tales—he would produce his one enduring masterpiece.

Even before the arrival of the Russians, Germany had been the world's leading book publisher. The Germans had the best typesetting, printing, and distribution, though the real secret weapon of the German book trade was an absolutely voracious reading public. German was not a colonial language—hence, not a world language—so the domestic market had to absorb most of the production. In 1913, the last year before the war, there were thirty-five thousand books published in Germany. Almost incredibly, by 1920, amid the chaos of recovery, disease, and revolution, the German book trade had almost returned to its prewar levels, managing to bring out thirty thousand volumes that year. And the diversity of the trade exploded: including the Russian presses, there were 895 new German publishers that opened their doors in the early Weimar years. Like everything that made Berlin wild just after the war, the phenomenon was partly a matter of cost: paper and presses and ink were cheap, talented editors and writers and typesetters were plentiful—and no matter what misfortunes befell them, Germans never stopped reading.

Yet by the fall of 1923, hyper-inflation had devastated commercial activ-

* Nabokov, just out of university in England and joining his devastated family in Berlin, also hid behind a mysterious, Eastern-sounding name, "Sirin." He was not yet the literary star of the Emigration; that title still belonged to Ivan Bunin, who would soon win the Nobel Prize.

ity of every kind, including émigré Russian presses, cafés, and theater companies. Inflation destroyed not only the German middle class, it also wiped out many Russians' savings, especially those who had bought anything much in Berlin. From then on, Paris would be the new center for émigré writing, while Prague would become the new center of émigré scientific and scholarly publishing. As the broader Russian Emigration moved to Paris after 1923, the predominance of Jews among the remaining exiles turned Berlin for a time into a center for Jewish culture. The YIVO Institute for Jewish Research relocated its headquarters to Berlin from Geneva; on the political front, the Zionist socialists ramped up their Berlin operations, as did the old Russian Jewish Bund.

Lev came of age in this new émigré environment, where assimilation into German culture was becoming more common. And for once he had good timing. In 1923–24, when Berlin was in the depths of economic ruin, Lev was in school. By 1925 and '26, when he was ready to put his hard-earned knowledge to work building a career—offering his services as an expert on everything Eastern—German publishing was recovering and about to enter its Golden Twenties period. From 1926 to 1930, Berlin was the center of literary activity in Europe, with dozens of serious newspapers and one of the best literary magazines of the day: *Die Literarische Welt* (*The Literary World*), a magically eclectic weekly that was Germany's equivalent of *The New York Review of Books,* where every week you could find Alfred Döblin musing about urban aesthetics, Bertolt Brecht trashing bourgeois theater, and Walter Benjamin analyzing the latest foreign movies. ("Having discovered the dynamite of tenths of a second, film exploded this old world of incarceration . . . forcing from a petit-bourgeois apartment the same beauty one admires in an Alfa Romeo.")

At twenty-one, Lev had a young writer's classic lucky break: perhaps through the Pasternaks, he got an introduction to *Die Literarische Welt*'s powerful editor, Willy Haas. In no time he was one of the favorites, part of the inner circle around the charismatic Haas, who gave Lev top billing when most of the columnists were twice his age or older. Haas called him the paper's "expert on the East," and that was a timely thing to be. Whatever the reason for Haas's initial patronage—and spotting an improbable hurricane of talent and energy had to have been the main thing—Lev, or rather "Essad Bey," became one of the journal's three most prolific contributors.

Lev's first article, appropriately enough, was "From the East," in 1926—a discussion of newspaper journalism in Malaysia and Azerbaijan. His contributions would range from a consideration of the poetry of Genghis Khan (Genghis got a positive review) to "Film and the Prestige of the White Race," a seemingly frivolous but actually prescient consideration of how images of European and American immorality were lowering the status of the West in the eyes of Easterners, Muslims in particular. Lev prescribed some positive images of Western culture on the double, if the "white race" did not want to permanently lose the respect of the increasingly independence-minded peoples of Asia. He reported on curiosities like "The Eunuch Congress," describing how the former palace and harem eunuchs of the Ottoman sultan had recently held a trade organization meeting in Constantinople. And he wrote a positive review of the first German biography of Ataturk, concluding that Mustafa Kemal is the "least Turkish of all Turks, who aided the victory of the West with Eastern methods, with cunning, tyranny and deception."

In these early pieces, Lev pays particular attention to Eastern leaders who know how to use the West to their advantage, like Ataturk and, later, Reza Shah Pahlavi, who becomes a subject of particular fascination. During the 1930s Lev would become obsessed with Peter the Great, the monarch who, more than any other, united East and West in his realignment of Russia to absorb the European Enlightenment. Lev loved and hated Peter, but in the end he was overwhelmed by his subject and could not finish the book. For another author that might have meant wasted years; for Lev it meant bringing his study of Peter to biographies of Czar Nicholas and Reza Shah. (Lev believed that the dictator of Persia came much closer to ruling like Peter the Great than the last czar, Nicholas, ever did.) But in a droller vein, Lev also covered the glamour of the East. In one feature, "Buchara at the Hotel Adlon: The Last Emir, Fairytales from 1,001 Nights in the 20th Century," he describes in amusing detail how the royal courts of Central Asia, defeated by the Bolsheviks, are now living rather well in the heart of the Potsdamer Platz, entertaining and going to formal parties.

The series of articles Lev wrote for *Die Literarische Welt* and other papers about the visit of the dynamic Afghan monarch King Amanullah to the German capital in 1928 allowed him to combine his nose for East-meets-West drama with critical political analysis. Though the articles paint a picture of the bleakness of both the geographical and social climate of Afghanistan (it "is inhabited by wild, mutually alien clans . . . who hate everything foreign [and] patrol their borders on small ugly horses, stare greedily at the armed caravans that come from far away, and show them pyramids of skulls that until recently marked the borders"), Lev also conveys the bright hope that characterized Afghanistan in the twenties, where "in contrast with the other Islamic countries that found a rather humble present on a glorious past, it is a country without a past but with a great future." Lev ends his portrait with an Afghan poem written in tribute to the modernizing king ("America is our friend, and Germany too has become Afghanistan's honest friend. . . . O homeland, we are the moths around your light / We would perish for thee, O Afghanistan").

This mélange of reporting, free-floating political commentary, and Central Asian metered verse was just the sort of thing *Die Literarische Welt* thrived on. Essad Bey was their "man on the East," and he had a fairly free range in that landscape.

Among the other regulars at the journal were such fascinating Weimar types as Egon Erwin Kisch, Valeriu Marcu, and Walter Mehring, the deeply sarcastic Dada cabaretist and literary intellectual who became a close friend of Lev's. Radical experimental cabaret had peaked in Berlin in the early twenties, when revolutionary bullets were still whizzing through the air. After that it retreated into the cafés, those places where, as Mehring put it in his remarkable 1951 memoir, *The Lost Library: The Autobiography of a Culture,* "more books, and often greater ones, have been planned than are housed in all the libraries of the world put together—and more deeds than have been committed in world history."

Not only after work but also before and during it, the writers for *Die Literarische Welt* would repair to the "Café Megalomania," their nickname for the Café des Westens ("Café of the West") on the Kurfürstendamm, where a "red-haired, hunchbacked" waiter named Richard "was the go-between among all these conceited, difficult guests who took their talents as seriously as army officers take their decorations." Mehring's descriptions capture the atmosphere of flamboyant exoticism that welcomed the most peculiar behavior in Café Megalomania.

One of the most striking figures in this subculture—and close to Lev in her obsessions—was Else Lasker-Schüler, a German Jewish poet known to go around Berlin calling herself "the Prince of Thebes" (where she claimed, in her CV, to have been born). Reactions to Lasker-Schüler were always intense: the cabaretist Erich Mühsam thought her poetry "glowed with the fire of Oriental fantasy." But Count Harry Kessler said in his diary, "I have been trying to avoid this woman for years," and Kafka thought her poems "indiscriminate spasms of the brain of an overexcitable urbanite." Karl Kraus dubbed her a combination of "archangel and fish-wife." Certainly, no one failed to notice her.

Lasker-Schüler claimed she could speak "Asiatic," approximating the original language of the biblical Jews, whom she called "Wild Jews." She was arrested in a church in Prague for giving a sermon in "Asiatic" to a bewildered crowd. Her concept of the Wild Jews—freed of the debilitating effects of two millennia in the Diaspora—became quite popular. Her first-person narrators were almost always Arabs, whereas her third-person voices often told the stories of Jews.*

The painter Oskar Kokoschka, a friend of Lasker-Schüler's, recalled walking through the streets of Bonn with Else dressed in her Wild Jew costume: "harem pants, a turban, and with long, black hair, with a cigarette in a long holder. [We] were of course laughed at and derided by the crowds of passers-by that gathered, cheered by the children, and nearly beaten up by the irritated students." Lasker-Schüler gave her friends silly nicknames like the Great Caliph and the Dalai Lama. The philosopher Martin Buber was Herr von Zion and the poet Gottfried Benn was the Nibelung, or simply the Barbarian. She referred to her friends collectively as *die Indianer* (that is, Native Americans). At the Megalomania, she also

---

* When Lasker-Schüler later emigrated to Palestine, she found that she did not actually enjoy living in the Holy Land. "It is too hard for me among the people here," she wrote. "Even King David would have moved on." One of her final projects was to try to convince the Jews and the Arabs in Palestine to build an amusement park, so they could learn to have fun together. At the twenty-first Zionist Congress, she rose and declared to the assembled somber representatives: "Do you know how we can solve the Jewish-Arab problem? There's only one way: by creating joy. We will found an amusement park for Jews and Arabs, to which both peoples will come and eat the same *Reibepfannkuchen,* ride the same carousels, and play the same wheel of fortune. . . . But over the entrance there must be a sign: 'For God.' "

hung around with the millionaire futurist poet F. T. Marinetti, whom everyone called Tom and whom she liked because he had been born in Alexandria.

In these smoke-filled rooms of wild ideas and even wilder poses, a turbaned, dagger-toting Azeri *literato* named Essad Bey, whom somehow everyone also knew as Leo Nussimbaum, fit right in. The world of the café-house travelers was really the perfect place for Lev to hone his Orientalist act. This is not to say that the act was for anyone else's benefit but his own. This was the very point of café-house life—that the ultimate audience was one's own fragile sense of self—and it also helped that no one cared about money or academic credentials.

Mehring was already a famous man, ten years Lev's senior, and he likely helped give Lev entrée to the café scene. But Lev gave his often depressive friend a boost, too. Mehring had been the chief practitioner of the type of cabaret songs and patter imitated by Joel Grey in the Broadway play and movie *Cabaret* (though the film's depiction was actually an anachronism, for already by the late twenties, during the rise of Nazism, such intimate, political, and harshly satirical cabaret was practically dead). Political theater had perhaps been strongest in the kaiser's Berlin, as unlikely as that now seems; imperial censorship made the jokes funnier. Mehring had reigned during cabaret's most celebrated caustic heyday, from the time of the revolution of 1919 through the end of the "inflation year" of 1923. After that, Berlin's cabaret acts had their own version of vaudeville's slide into burlesque, as the kick-line musical revue—with girls dressed as soldiers, doctors, convicts, and Eskimos—replaced the more thought-provoking entertainment of earlier years. The main competition to the dancing-girl revues came not from cabaret but from an even lower entertainment: the naked-girl revue. By 1927, Lev's Berlin positively screamed with neon signs advertising shows like THE WORLD WITHOUT VEILS, EVERYONE'S NAKED, and BY THUNDER: 1000 NAKED WOMEN! Lev's colleagues Walter Benjamin and Siegfried Kracauer spent happy hours analyzing—critically, of course—the various aspects of mechanical reproduction evident in such human displays.

By the mid-1920s, true cabaret in Berlin had moved into the realm of the ultra-political, with shows put on by communist agitprop groups on the one side and proto-Nazi *völkisch* entertainers on the other. The original Dada cabaretists like Mehring had had *die Schnauze voll!*—meaning they'd had enough.* Perhaps it was Lev who suggested to Mehring that he leave Berlin and make a journey around Algeria. However he got the idea, the trip proved reinvigorating and produced Mehring's first prose work, *Algeria, or The Thirteen Miracles of the Oasis.* "The Book of Exodus accompanied me to the Saharan pyramid city of Ghardaïa, in the Algerian Mzab, where the Abadites live their Islamic *golus,*" Mehring reminisced. "Among them dwell the last authentic Israelites, who call themselves Ishuruni—the Upright." (It is noteworthy that wherever the café-house Orientalist went, he found strange Jews, especially if he himself was as self-camouflaging a Jew as Lev or Walter Mehring.)

Lev enthusiastically reviewed his friend's work for *Die Literarische Welt,* maintaining that while Europeans were being deceived by guidebooks that sapped the East of its soul, in this book by a wiseacre who'd never ventured farther east than Budapest before that year, the "true Orient" could be found. The key was that Walter Mehring saw and heard poetry everywhere, and "there is no longer an Orient, or there is very little left of it, or it has hidden itself and is visible only to the eyes of a poet. . . . Those who have never been in the Orient, those who can only dream of the land of the crescent moon, they should not read travel accounts, or the reports of the numerous royal and non-royal academies of science—they should read *The Thirteen Miracles of the Oasis* by Walter Mehring."

But they did not read Walter Mehring. They read Essad Bey.

Before he left *Die Literarische Welt,* at twenty-eight, Lev had published 144 articles in the journal—even more than Walter Benjamin, who was another of Willy Haas's favorites—and he had published half a dozen bestselling books as well. His friend and future collaborator George Sylvester Viereck would write that Essad Bey could walk into a room and come out a matter of hours later with a mostly finished manuscript. Exaggerated as that description may have been, Lev wrote so much and so flu-

---

* In the kaiser's day, many of the jokes had been Jewish jokes, often told by gentile entertainers, and at the expense of the ultra-assimilationist German Jew—the man who had been "baptized several times." Now that anti-Semitism was turning serious, Jewish jokes were no longer considered so funny, and they declined along with political humor, which was all becoming "too disturbing" for the public. Hitler's rise to power in 1933 would cause an exodus of Jewish cabaret stars from Germany, though some who went to Austria, Czechoslovakia, France, and Holland would return to the German stage against their will: in the concentration camps of Westerbork and Theresienstadt, among others, they put on their final performances in elaborate, SS-supervised cabarets.

idly that it was considered almost unseemly. By 1934 his business manager, Werner Schendell, would write what is surely one of the rarer requests an agent has ever made to an author, especially a bestselling one with seventeen international editions to his credit. Schendell begged his client "not to publish too many more books. . . . One mustn't be considered [too] prolific. . . . take a year-long break between books."

As Essad Bey, Lev became an expert on the "East" in both of the radically different meanings the word had at the time: the mysterious "Asiatic" East, the world of Islam and the other non-European religions, and also the Russian East, now the Soviet Union. Both were places of mystery and danger but also fascination—populated by fanatics and potentates, whether czars and commissars or sultans and shahs. There were also ample opportunities for writing anti-French pieces when one covered the Middle East, which was always popular in Germany.

Haas and Mehring and Lev's other colleagues presumably knew about his real background—they certainly knew by the 1930s—but no one spoke of it publicly. When his first "autobiographical" work, *Blood and Oil in the Orient,* appeared, *Die Literarische Welt* began its unsigned review of its regular contributor, "We know Essad-Bey from the 'L.W.,' but we didn't really know him until today. Until now, we thought of his name as a pseudonym, and we stand amazed before these strange biographical sketches of an Asian born in Baku, Azerbaijan, son of a Muslim aristocrat and a Russian revolutionary intellectual." Whether this was Haas being coy or whether the editors were truly confused by the background of their Russian refugee colleague with the Caucasian costumes is impossible to tell. For most of his life, until fortune threw him to a place where he could no longer joke about such things, Lev would keep up a kind of comic dialogue with his writer friends about his "transformation" from Lev to Essad. It was not that he mocked his conversion or allowed others to. But among those he felt could understand, and these were mostly his fellow Jews, he seemed to think it fair to reveal the transformation. With anyone else, he grew circumspect, neither denying nor accepting the suggestion that he was covering up something. Rather than trying to refute anything, he responded by diving deeper into his identity and becoming more and more the Orientalist—more and more Essad Bey.

In his books and his articles, as in his self-image, what Lev cared about was Truth—intellectual and emotional—which he distinguished from mere facts.* In a memorable article for *Die Literarische Welt,* "The Oriental Lenin Myth," he places Lenin in the context of three thousand years of Eastern idols and mythmaking. For him the late leader of the Russian Revolution is "a djin, an immortal ghost. . . . And in Russia itself, too, Lenin has become a popular saint in spite of the Third International. In many villages, one can find his image next to those of the customary saints." And Lev would be the one who picked up on the Caucasus Stalin, the ruthless mafioso from wild Georgia, in his *Stalin: The Career of a Fanatic* (1931); another early biographer mistakenly saw Stalin as the essential Russian, even though he had barely mastered the language before adulthood. If Lev's portrait of Stalin was "suggestive of the life of a Chicago gangster—and not very different in atmosphere," as an American reviewer noted, Lev seemed to get at something few other journalists yet did. (A surprised F.D.R. would remark, on meeting Stalin, that he had expected the head of the Soviet government to be a gentleman, not a Caucasian bandit.) And when reviewers complained that Essad Bey's writing was overly colorful or implausible, it was sometimes they who were in the wrong. A reviewer of *Stalin* in *The Times Literary Supplement,* in 1932, commented that as journalism the book was "brilliant" but that Essad failed "in persuading us (as he seems to intend to do) that Stalin is capable of continuing indefinitely to hold the power he now wields. . . . Eastern rulers have overstepped themselves before; in proportion as Russia becomes industrialized it will become more and more difficult to control by that simple application of force." The reviewer's incredulity was typical of the response to both Stalin and Hitler in their early years, though the illusions about Stalin lasted far longer, outliving even his reign of terror. Lev's books and articles were among the first to convey his implacable nature, and the essential criminality of the system he helped build.

The mistakes Lev did make were probably the result of sheer speed. In

---

* As he would write in his deathbed manuscript: "It is apparently difficult, particularly difficult for a 'literary man,' to 'photograph' instead of forming. The temptations of literature are enormous. In the memory, perspective shifts. Involuntarily, the writer begins to prefer the truth of atmosphere to the simple truth of facts. . . . But today, in the face of death, I want to try to capture once again only the truth, at least in these lines [text struck out: 'that are meant only for me'], even if it is not the full truth. For my wretched life, which is now culminating in the great torment of suffering, strikes me as typical for our days and our time, for this time of upheaval and cataclysm."

the space of four years, between 1929 and 1933, he would publish most of his major works: after the memoir, *Blood and Oil,* there were *Twelve Secrets of the Caucasus, Mohammed, Stalin,* and *OGPU: The Plot Against the World*—a history of the Russian secret police under the Bolsheviks. And this was while continuing to publish articles in *Die Literarische Welt, Deutsche Allgemeine Zeitung,* and *Prager Tageblatt*—as well as in American magazines such as the *Saturday Review of Literature, Asia,* and *The Living Age.* Some, like *OGPU,* were heavily sourced; others were not or, like *Stalin,* combined scholarly research with vivid anecdote, some of it admittedly hearsay. All his nonfiction works were ambitious, sweeping, and full of grand notions of history as well as unforgettable spot portraits of their subjects.

With the imprimatur of *Die Literarische Welt,* Lev fashioned himself as a Weimar media star—a professional "Man of the Caucasus." Though he received much attention on this side of the Atlantic, it was always German readers who mattered most to him. There were favorable German reactions: Kurt Aram, a well-known author of historical novels, called *Blood and Oil* "one of the most interesting, entertaining and informative books of our time," and Karl Hoffmann, another well-known author, applauded the memoir's "political romanticism" and the author's "orientally fervent and at the same time drastic art of presentation, which in parts is of a shuddering urgency." The book sold very well in Germany and was soon an international hit.

The book received favorable reviews from most papers in Britain and Europe, and did well in France, Holland, Spain, and, especially, Fascist Italy; widespread appreciation for Lev's work there would eventually have decisive influence on his life. Reviewing *Petrolio e Sangue in Oriente,* the *Bibliografia fascista,* a leading literary magazine in Rome, found its author to be "a really capable and likable storyteller" with "a good sense of humor." American reviewers liked the work and also found Lev's ongoing self-invention charming—it was as American as apple pie. This aspect of the book, however, elicited a much harsher reaction in Germany.

Almost as soon as *Blood and Oil* appeared, a few politically driven German reviewers took it upon themselves not merely to warn the public away from the book but, in a sense, to "out" the author. Lev was perceived as a kind of ethnic cross-dresser, as well as something far more devious.

Else Lasker-Schüler might dress up as Tino of Baghdad, but she was clearly a German Jewish poet. Many Jewish journalists and scholars were writing books on the Middle East at the time, often out of a deep and sympathetic knowledge of the Muslim world, but they did not tramp around Berlin dressed in turbans, speak of their filial ties to warrior chieftains, and call themselves by fancy Turkish names.

The following article, from the influential right-wing journal *Der Nahe Osten* (*The Near East*), is typical:

> This book is one of the most miserable publications of recent years. . . . The author, who introduces himself as "Mohammad Essad-Bey" and pretends to be the son of a Tartar oil magnate from Baku, has turned out to be a Jewish dissident named Leo (Lob) Nussimbaum, born in Kiev in 1905, son of a Jew named Abraham Nussimbaum from Tiflis. When one compares the accounts in the book, according to which the author was threatening Russian ministers at the age of ten, and in which the author pretends to be a relative of the Emir of Bukhara and an expert on Muslim customs, one gets a clear idea of the whole grotesquerie. . . . The Muslims will presumably firmly reject their alleged fellow believer "Mohammad Essad-Bey." (Essad=in Arabic asad, esed=lion=Lob=Leo?)

The reviewer concluded that no Jew could possibly paint a real picture of the East, and that "the various states abused in this book, such as Azerbaijan, Armenia and Turkey etc., will presumably not put up with the slander and insults" of this "Jewish dissident."

While anti-Semitism was at the heart of most of the attacks, not all critics of the book thought it too distant from the "Eastern" point of view. One reviewer, on the contrary, complained that the faults of the book came from the fact that it was "too Asiatic" rather than not Asiatic enough—and that this "Oriental quality" threw doubt on the narrative. Everyone knew that Orientals in general were devious, the reviewer explained, and hence, though Asian and European lived together in the author, "the first is the stronger, unfortunately not to the benefit of the work."

In addition to the right-wingers, the campaign to "out" the author behind the name Essad Bey was driven primarily by a group of "real"—that is, non-Jewish—Islamic exiles from the Soviet Union. Various Arab and Persian emigrant organizations in Berlin added their voices to the public denunciations. Werner Schendell, Lev's business manager, was the author of the foreword to the memoir, and he also came in for blame. Schendell should have prevented the publication of this "filthy work," the critics admonished, and thus he, too, was guilty of endorsing an attack on "the East." A Persian émigré paper ran a front-page article denouncing this "unprecedented slander against Germany by a Russian swindler." The Islamic organizations got together and issued a one-page "PROTEST" that they sent to the leading newspapers:

> The entire contents of this "memoir" are directed against the orient in the most undignified way, and attacks with hate-filled contempt and blind rage the eastern lands and peoples with their cultures, national traditions, ways of life, moral concepts and even religious rites.
>
> We declare, for the general record, that the ostensibly-named "Essad Bey," with his descriptions, is pursuing the sole purpose of discrediting the orient in the eyes of Europeans. His pornographic book bears the stamp of the filthiest agitation and the statements contained therein are lies from beginning to end and the basest form of slander. . . .
>
> He is no Oriental, and also isn't really called Essad Bey. In reality his name is Leo Noussimbaum and he was born on October 20, 1905, in Kiev, Ukraine, as reliable German authorities have been able to confirm. With that, enough said!

The protest was signed by a long list that included one representative each of a dozen Muslim countries with exile or nationalist groups based in Berlin.

Lev's old club the Islamic Institute joined the campaign against him. In the spring of 1930, its board accused Essad Bey of having insulted "the feelings of the Islamic world [with his] literary scams" and announced it wanted nothing more to do with this devious trickster who had passed himself off "as a native Muslim, contrary to the facts." Its business manager, Mohammed Hoffman, himself a convert, attacked Lev for trying "to pass for a born Muslim," and he even threw doubt on the veracity of Lev's conversion to Islam, suggesting it had been a ploy, and that his knowledge of Azeri and Turkish was doubtful. It was all part of the growing argument that Essad Bey ("Essad=in Arabic asad, esed=lion=Lob=Leo?"—as the German debunker writing in *The Near East* had so proudly elucidated) was a "Kievan Jew"—the lowest of the low—not even from the "noble Orient," the Caucasus, but a simple shtetl Jew.

And the ire of émigré Muslims was not confined to Germany. In the Parisian journal *Prométhée,* a review entitled *"Une mystification dé-masquée,"* by a critic named Ibrahim bey Tchoulik, denounced *Blood and Oil* as "a pornographic tableau of 'oriental culture.' " A Muslim newspaper in Prague would see "sharp and subtle attacks against our brothers in faith in Asia and Africa" in Lev's biography of Muhammad, while another de-clared Essad Bey's books "arrogant acts of sabotage against Islam." Every-where in the Muslim press, his Jewish identity was pointed out, whereas other foreign reviewers ignored or were unaware of it.

The leading point man in the Islamic faction of the assault on Lev was an Azeri nationalist living in Constantinople named Hilal Munschi. Mun-schi summed up the attacks on Essad Bey's character in a series of pam-phlets he published in German and Turkish. In addition to the usual questions about his "origins" and intentions, Munschi attacked Lev's pre-cociousness, disparaging the fact that "the great, controversial author" of so much troublesome material turned out to be only twenty-five years old and was "living with his 'aristocratic' father, Abraham Noussimbaum (dis-sident, born in 1875)"; Munschi exposed the fact that Essad had "matricu-lated [to the University of Berlin] using falsified papers, without proof of having finished high school or comparable preparation" and registered under the obviously suspect moniker "Assed Bey-Noussenbaum."*

---

* When I visited Baku for a second time, in 2000, specifically to interview the various Azeri partisans of the Kurban Said "debate"—who clustered around the theory that Josef Vezir, not Nussimbaum, wrote *Ali and Nino*—I was actually handed copies of Munschi's attacks on Lev's character and background, in Azeri, as though they were contemporary news reports. I was shocked by the vehemence of the language—until I realized that I was reading anti-Semitic attack literature from the 1930s, resurrected seventy years later as "evidence." "You see! You see!" shouted one prominent Azeri professor, waving his finger in the air, "it is all the proof we need! Right there in Munschi's article, he exposed the swindler for what he was! This Nussimbaum could not possibly have written a sub-lime work like *Ali and Nino.*" My article in *The New Yorker* had apparently sparked a

The Islamic nationalists tried contacting the powerful *Deutschnationale Volkspartei,* the "German National People's Party," which was the main racist right-wing party in the Reichstag, more powerful than the Nazis at that time, to ask them to take "action" in the case of this Essad Bey Nussimbaum. The DNVP apparently had more pressing business in 1930, when they were fighting off a frontal assault from the Nazis for the right-wing vote. But while they hit a dead end in parliament, the enraged Muslims found an unexpected new ally in their fight against Lev: the German Army.

The former chief of staff of the Eastern Army in the Caucasus, Lieutenant-Colonel Ernst von Paraquin, had been deeply insulted by *Blood and Oil.* For von Paraquin, the offending passages largely concerned eight pages in which Lev describes the massacres that took place in Baku when it fell to the Turkish-German siege in September 1918. The events are some of the few depicted in the memoir where Lev states that he was not there at the time—he and Abraham got back to Baku from their Persian adventure only *after* the massacres had happened—and he fully admits that he is drawing on secondary sources to reconstruct what likely happened in the days before they arrived.

Though filled with sympathy for the Armenian victims of the massacres, Lev's description does not blame the German high command; rather, he presents their role during the siege of Baku, correctly, as a militarily minor one compared to that of the Turks. Furthermore, the Turkish "Army of Islam" was commanded by none other than Nuri Pasha, the twenty-seven-year-old brother of the Young Turk dictator Enver, the man behind the Armenian genocide. General Nuri Pasha was marching to Baku in September 1918 as part of his older brother's planned "Turanian" conquest of Central Asia. Lev points out that the Germans actually reined

renewed debate, as prominent Azeris had to deal with the suggestion that their "national novel" had been written by a Jew. Literature is taken very seriously in small countries like Azerbaijan—countries that have so few military or political heroes to celebrate, where a statue of a poet or playwright stands in every street square—so passions were higher than they would have been elsewhere. *Ali and Nino* was Azerbaijan's best-known literary achievement, and, to some, it seemed as though I was trying to take it away. These partisans were eager to set me straight, and the work of Munschi, freshly translated into Azeri, was considered a prime piece of evidence.

in some of the bloodshed in Baku that September, but he presents them as largely looking the other way while the Armenian massacres happened. In fact, he states that the Germans ordered the Turks to stop the massacres after three days, implying that they could have done so sooner had they chosen to. It is a very small section in *Blood and Oil,* yet it aroused a big response from the German military veterans of the Caucasian front, who were especially sensitive to any hints that they had had a hand in the fate of the Armenians.

Von Paraquin rattled off attacks on Lev in major newspapers in Berlin, Hamburg, and Munich. "Everyone knows how Germans of all persuasions have been honestly striving for many long years to wash their nation clean of false accusations," he stated in the *Berliner Börsen-Courier.* "It is highly deplorable that a prestigious German publisher allows itself to be used to broadcast to the world unsubstantiated, fabricated accusations against the German Command." In contrast to those of the Muslim émigrés, von Paraquin's attacks on Lev were sober, starched-shirt military rebuttals.* German politicians and military figures spent much time and effort in the 1920s attempting to save their honor from the many atrocity stories leveled at them during the First World War—somewhat ironic considering the far uglier depths into which events were about to descend.

To the military man's straightforward objections were added the increasingly low blows of the racialist pan-German press. Various right-wing journalists picked up on the article in *Der Nahe Osten* parsing Lev's name, combined it with the accusations of von Paraquin, and used it all as the basis for pieces exposing "this Jewish falsifier of history," who had be-

---

* Von Paraquin's role is fascinating because it exposes the ambiguous relationship between the German presence in the Turkish Army and the Armenian genocide that occurred in those years. There is a paper trail indicating approval among highly placed German racialists for the exterminations, but there was also a movement against genocide led by Germans in Turkey, including members of the army high command. Von Paraquin himself got into a public argument with Nuri Pasha in a Baku hotel lobby about the massacres, which caused him to resign his command. After the war, he filed a report on his (failed) efforts to "personally put a stop to the murders." Still, the German Army was so deeply "embedded" in the Turkish command structure during these years that it is impossible to absolve them of all guilt. Von Paraquin's official title is indicative: chief of general staff of Ottoman Army Group East.

smirched the honor of the German Army. Everyone knew that German soldiers and officers would never harm civilians! They would have no part in ethnic persecution of such a low and primitive nature! That the critics constantly denounced Lev as a "Jewish forger" and his book as a "Jewish forgery" suggested a certain surreality to their claims. Lev's picture of the German Army on the eastern front was rather tame for a description of the events of 1918, and very soon the attempts of "Germans of all persuasions . . . to wash their nation clean of false accusations of atrocities in the east" would become entirely moot.

The Berlin police launched an investigation of the "literary story swindler," but they found nothing illegal in his past. The Union of German Writers put out an *Ehrenerklärung* ("statement of honor")—written by Werner Schendell, who, fortunately, was an important figure in the organization—defending "the member Mr. Essad-Bey Leo Nussimbaum" from any wrongdoing. Unfortunately for Lev, "Essad Bey" would never be officially accepted as his name. It is difficult to change one's name legally in Germany under any circumstances; even today, the government insists that petitioners pick from a list of "accepted German names."

In an article entitled "Oil Sensations" in the *Deutsche Rundschau*, a centrist publication, in October 1930, the investigative journalist Karl Hoffmann attempted to put the growing "Essad Bey scandal" in some perspective and to bring some basic facts into the flurry of accusations and counteraccusations:

> Since its publication, it has been claimed that [*Blood and Oil*] contains boldfaced lies and that Essad Bey does not exist at all. . . . There is indeed an Essad Bey. There is a certificate concerning his identity dated March 18, 1930, a certificate from the "Representative of the High Commissariats of the League of Nations for Refugees in Germany." Essad Bey was not born "Essad Bey," but rather Leo Nussimbaum. The family is not what one generally understands to be *ostjüdisch*, nor is it Muslim—instead, they belong to an Asian-Israelite tribe of an oriental lifestyle. The father, Abraham Nussimbaum, who comes from Tiflis . . . [has property] estimated to be a few million. . . . [Leo Nussimbaum] first converted to Islam in Berlin. A document from August 13, 1922, from the religious representatives of what was then still the Ottoman Turkish Imperial Embassy states that he was baptized [*sic*] as Essad. He proba-

bly fibbed about his heritage and his standard of living, elaborated on the truth and exaggerated, but it is not really a falsification.

The motley assortment of refugee Muslim nationalists, German Army officers, and racialist critics was hardly satisfied. Having failed in parliament, they brought the campaign against the "Kievan Jew" and "story swindler" to the attention of the German Foreign Ministry, claiming that Essad Bey's work was likely "to damage the reputation of Germany in the Orient, to disturb friendly relations . . . and to unleash abroad a new witch hunt based on lies." They demanded "that this literary mystification be put to an end through appropriate measures against the further distribution of the book and against the author."

Lev was summoned to the foreign ministry at the end of March 1930, and brought before *Legationsrat* Kurt Ziemke. He brought along an impressive recommendation from the head of the Literary Section of the Academy of Arts and president of the Writers' Union, one Walter von Molo, in addition to the recommendation by Schendell. Luckily for Lev, the *Legationsrat,* who was otherwise not friendly, happened to be in the writing trade himself. He did not wish to offend the young author's many powerful friends in German publishing. Why not simply remove the sections that had been criticized by Lieutenant-Colonel von Paraquin and the others? Lev agreed to consider it.

This was early in 1930, and Ziemke couldn't ban the book, because there was still freedom of the press in Germany. Three years later, no such freedom of the press—to say nothing of Jewish publishing figures—would exist. But for the moment, the foreign ministry let the matter of "Mr. Essad-Bey Leo Nussimbaum" drop.

While the Muslim nationalists and right-wing press attacked Lev's inauthentic "Orientalist" writings, some on the pro-communist left went after him for his unflattering depictions of the Soviets and the revolution. *Vorwärts! (Forward!),* the leading left publication, simply dismissed his *Stalin* and *OGPU,* saying that Essad Bey did not have "the necessary dialectical-materialist schooling" to understand events in Russia.

Attacks from the right and left made Lev a controversial figure in Germany, and his general response—to smile enigmatically and keep on writing more books—seemed to have the effect of keeping everyone guessing: What were his real politics? What was his racial background? What were the true motives of the "story swindler"? With his eclectic subject matter, odd clothes, sarcasm, and purposely Caucasian-accented German, Lev didn't fall into any of the generally accepted categories of the day. The venom spat out at him became so potently inchoate that a Prague paper would accuse him of pursuing "purely Bolshevist rather than Islamic interests," while in Warsaw he was denounced as "a Marxist werewolf." The Polish piece was written in 1938, and coauthored by a Prussian nobleman with two exiled Muslim nationalists, who may have been conflating the concepts of "Jew" and "Marxist"—not to mention "werewolf"—which had by that point become largely synonymous in many circles.

Lev never appeared to mind the controversy very much. It seems he only once took the time to respond to the flurry of accusations, when he let go with a brief, oblique piece entitled "Lies Forbidden!" In general, he gave the impression that, having survived a revolution, homelessness, escape, and exile, he wasn't going to let the hurly-burly of German factional feuding get to him. ("One doesn't get very far with politeness in Berlin, because such an audacious race of men lives there that one has to have a sharp tongue in order to keep oneself afloat," as Goethe once observed.)

The scandal certainly had a positive effect on book sales, and it made Lev (or rather, Essad) famous. For a young man who had recently been living with "a hundred kinds of hunger" and the prospect of life as a forsaken refugee, the idea of being the bête noire of a loose association of anti-Semites and Muslim nationalists probably did not seem that disturbing. The Nazis were scoring well in the elections by the early 1930s, but even this did not seem to worry Lev. He continued to write like a fiend, pouring out dozens of articles and working on many projects simultaneously. He wrote another book about the Caucasus, a biography of Lenin, a book on the history of oil exploration. He began gathering material for biographies of Ataturk, Reza Shah, and even former U.S. president Warren Harding (who interested him because of the Teapot Dome oil scandal). He remained one of the lead correspondents of *Die Literarische Welt,* and also took on big interviewing assignments for American magazines.

Except for von Paraquin, who had a particular sensitivity on account of the Armenian massacres, Lev's attackers were a venal and racist bunch. Many of the Muslim nationalists simply misread the humor in his book as an attack on Islam or Muslim independence movements in general, when Lev's writing was anything but that. But when it came to the accusations about his identity, the critics did have a point. "Essad" was not born in Kiev, as the attackers seemed to have convinced themselves, but otherwise, many of the facts they revealed were common knowledge among his circle: while never publicly deviating from his story that his father was a Muslim lord, Lev was sharing an apartment in Berlin with his father, who made no secret about being a Jewish businessman named Abraham Nussimbaum. Lev's public records and visa applications listed him as some awkward amalgam of Leo Nussimbaum and Essad or Asaj Bey.

But the latest accusation that the author of some of the most scathing exposés of Bolshevik terror was himself a "Marxist werewolf" suggest the extent to which Lev's mysterious persona had perplexed everyone. "Who is this Essad Bey?" Trotsky wrote from exile to his son in 1932. It was a question many people wanted answered, but was it clear that even Lev knew the answer by this point?

Lev preempted "unfriendly" and humorless critics in the lighthearted introduction to his second book, *Twelve Secrets of the Caucasus,* announcing that he was "aware from personal observation, that there are such things as hospitals and secondary schools for girls in the Caucasus." Indeed, coming from Baku, where many such innovations were first introduced to the Muslim world, he was more than aware of it. Readers of his articles would know that he held ambiguous views about Western "progress" in the East, not because he wished to insult the Orient but because he felt an overriding nostalgia and loss at the disappearing traditions he witnessed in the modernizing Baku of his youth.

Twelve Secrets of the Caucasus is a work dedicated to "a kind of curiosity shop of world history in its loyal preservation of all that is no more, all that is outlived and forgotten." As a leading exposer of the Communist onslaught in the Caucasus, Lev was keenly aware that modern innovations could bring much destruction, but in his works on the Muslim Orient, he chose a comic-romantic tone. This tone was invariably misunderstood by

Muslim expatriates as glibness about their situation, but his later personal correspondence, as well as a close reading of the books themselves, reveals that it was anything but that. Lev's attachment to the "Orient"—his view of himself as an "Oriental"—was perhaps more real than his understanding of himself as a European or as a Jew. Of course, he was all of these things.

"The many peoples that I have visited, the many events that I have seen, have made me into a complete cosmopolitan," he wrote in a 1931 newspaper, in one of many articles about "The Story of My Life." In 1931 in Germany this was tantamount to admitting one was a Jew, but Lev did not seem concerned. He looked to the Caucasus to protect his Jewish identity by absorbing it into its "racial curio shop," as he would adapt his phrase in an American anthropological magazine three years later.

Indeed, Lev's Orient was a different one from that of his detractors. One of the most striking chapters in *Twelve Secrets* describes a place Lev calls the "political Switzerland of the Caucasus," the Valley of the Khevsurs, or Khevsuria: "There a man could at last be safe." A reviewer for the *New York Herald Tribune* struggled to pinpoint Khevsuria on the map, with little help from Lev, who wrote:

> Khevsuria is quite near Tiflis, and yet the land is free, independent, and no policeman dares to follow his victim there. A gigantic wall of rock surrounds Khevsuria and separates it from the rest of the world. . . . From the cliff wall down into the void there hangs a long rope. Whoever has the courage can catch hold of the rope and let himself down to the Khevsurs. The police never follow. . . . Through it the first immigrants must have entered the land. Only the refugee dares use the rope, to be accepted if he is so inclined into the society of the Khevsurs and protected for ever from all dangers.

The *Tribune* critic concluded with annoyance that the author must provide more accurate information next time. Lev also published a longer article about Khevsuria in a geographical journal. The Khevsurs are Christians, he says, but Jesus is unknown to them; they keep kosher, practice polygamy, and worship beer. Out of respect for every religion, they keep the Sabbath on Friday, Saturday, and Sunday, but also on Monday—"to prove that the Khevsurs are different from all other people—a free people who can do as they please."

This is the Orient that Lev is from: a mountainous realm insulated from political and ethnic conflict, a refuge where no secret policeman can follow and where anyone with the courage to climb down a rope into the abyss is accepted—in short, the Orient of the imagination.

CHAPTER 11

Jewish Orientalism

I N HIS DEATHBED NOTEBOOKS, Lev includes dreamlike scenes in which he imagines himself a semi-comical figure of a learned professor, lost amid volumes of "hieroglyphics" and "holy inscriptions," whose fame rests on an Indiana Jones–like life of adventure in the desert. I was never able to find evidence of these journeys to places like Saudi Arabia and Libya, which Lev describes here and elsewhere with memorable intensity, but in this aspect of his self-invention, he would have been in good company. Weimar-era Berlin, I discovered, was a hotbed of Jewish Orientalists, some of whom were deeply involved with the vibrant Zionist movement, with its various arguing factions. But some of the most prominent, like Lev, were reviving an older tradition: an Orientalism that almost surreally linked Judaism and Islam, and East and West, in a common, harmonious past, and sought to conceive of a common, harmonious future. The Jewish Orientalists as a whole would largely be forgotten, so that well before Edward Said revived the popularity of the term "Orientalism" in his bestselling 1978 book, which depicted it exclusively through the insulting paradigms of the colonizing West, only the negative connotation remained.

This no doubt would have baffled Lev. He based his life and career on an urgent desire to explain the East to the West, all but rhapsodizing on the superiority of the former to the latter (while, to be sure, deploying the trademark satire that had angered the other exiles). He published *Twelve Secrets of the Caucasus* in Germany the year of the Nazis' "breakthrough" at the polls. Its pages offered the ultimate escape from the darkness settling around the regulars at the Café Megalomania. In the Caucasus Mountains, the descendants of crusader knights and Muslim warriors not only live in harmony with Jews but, in Lev's vision, almost merge with them as well.

While embracing a tradition of Jewish Orientalism stretching back to the nineteenth century—to Benjamin Disraeli and Arminius Vambery and William Gifford Palgrave ("Father Cohen")—Lev added a new element. For one thing, unlike these Victorian Jewish Orientalists, he actually was from the East. His father may not have been a Muslim or any kind of "mountain Jew," but Lev really could locate the Orient within himself. Of course, his friends in the Emigration were entirely of a Russian Jewish milieu, and his Muslim identity had been created, if not for their benefit, at least in part with that audience in mind. Vambery, Cohen, and Disraeli had "gone Oriental," in Muslim mufti, in order to enhance their status in a world where Jews like their fathers had assimilated too well.

Lev came of age when such assimilation was becoming an anachronism, and where revolution—whether of the Russian or the German kind, from the left or the right—was forcing people to choose sides. European Jews had been the greatest beneficiaries of liberalism, which had allowed them to live and prosper as individuals; the new tribalism was re-creating the ghetto walls. They were imperiled by the sudden collapse of the old imperial and monarchical regimes, even though this was what many of them had worked toward and wanted. The old empires and autocracies, even at their most oppressive, had provided space in which people could get on with their business. The totalizing, ideological systems of Lev's lifetime would not allow such space. The new map of Europe would be fraught with ubiquitous peril for liberals, for free thinkers, for misfits, and, above all, for Jews. The quest for a way out took on an undercurrent of desperation.

Lev was unique, but in Weimar Berlin he encountered a surprising number of other Jewish writers who sought refuge from the new political realities in esoteric vistas of sympathetic Orientalism, like Eugen Hoeflich, who wrote books calling for a merger of the Asiatic peoples of the world—Jews, Muslims, Buddhists, Confucians—into a united front against the forces of European mechanization and mass warfare. Hoeflich would applaud Lev's book about the Middle East, *Allah Is Great: The Decline and*

Rise of the Islamic World, which Lev wrote in collaboration with a leading Zionist, Wolfgang von Weisl. Von Weisl was Vladimir Jabotinsky's right-hand man and someone who also liked to go about the desert in Muslim garb, sometimes being mistaken for Lawrence of Arabia.

Like Lev, these Weimar figures—many from a wing of the Zionist movement that sought a pan-Asiatic merger with Muslims—found in the Orient a kind of escape hatch from the encroaching threats of brutal modernity. Over the course of the nineteenth century, as ideas of race and class struggle began to eclipse the faith in universal reason and progress, Europe's Jews had undergone both devastating rejections from without and identity crises from within: perhaps modern European ideals would not mean civic equality, or even tolerance, after all, but rather new and more fatal forms of exclusion.

But why had an increasingly prominent group of Jews chosen the Islamic world as the solution to their dilemma? They came to see themselves as being *of* the Orient—specifically, the Islamic Orient—in some very special and attractive way. Figures as diverse as Disraeli and the philosopher Martin Buber played a part in this relocation of the Jewish spirit to the realm of pan-Asia. They reinvented the historical Muslim Orient as a place free from clear ethnic and sectarian lines, and most especially free from anti-Semitism—no matter that the reality was more complex than that.

During the Enlightenment, Europeans had taken to depicting wise Jews and noble Oriental princes in the same garb, and in some senses, Jews and Muslims had begun to merge in the European mind. Voltaire characterized this common "Asian" quality in negative terms, as a sign of backward superstition. But many Jews of northern Europe saw in this redefinition of themselves as Asians an opportunity to escape their demeaning European image as insular, persecuted ghetto dwellers. It would be some time before they fully perceived the threat that hung behind the distinction: that perhaps they could not belong in Europe at all.

In the nineteenth century, Western European Jews adopted a vogue for the "Moorish style" in architecture that evoked the so-called Jewish-Muslim symbiosis of Andalusia and Granada, when the Muslim caliphates ruled in Spain and Jews rose to unprecedented status in society. Moorish-style office buildings, theaters, casinos, and, of course, synagogues sprang up all over Europe. (This was how Joseph Roth came to write his essay comparing the UFA Palace cinema in the Ku Damm to a mosque, though he meant to imply some other things as well.) In 1881, on the construction of the grand, Moorish-style "New Synagogue" in Berlin, the pride of German Jewry, a leading anti-Semitic pundit commented: "What is the sense of raising claims to be called an honorary German and yet building the holiest site that one possesses in Moorish style, so as to never ever let anyone forget that one is a Semite, an Asiatic, a foreigner?" Yet Jews persisted in the Moorish style, evoking a time when men such as Samuel ibn Nagrela lived a life Jews had never known in Christian Europe: while leading Muslim armies into battle and writing daring commentaries on the Koran, this eleventh-century Jewish poet who served as vizier of the kingdom of Granada, in Andalusia, also taught the Talmud and was a patron to Jewish artists, students, and scholars. In the twelfth century, Musa ibn Maymun, or Maimonides, became the most respected of all Jewish philosophers, writing almost all his works in Arabic while serving as court physician to Saladin. (The fact that Maimonides' family had fled to Saladin's Egypt because a fanatical Islamic theocracy had been imposed in his hometown of Córdoba is not usually mentioned.)

Given later events, what was most curious was that this fascination for Arab and Andalusian, or "Moorish," styles was strongest in the German-speaking countries, where the Jews were purely Ashkenazic, with no ties to Spain whatsoever. The Ashkenazim were proud of the Moorish tradition because it represented the most "at home" Jews had ever felt in Europe. Though it may have been a relatively brief and embattled flowering, it had made a deep impression. The synagogues were some of the first outward signs of the trend of Jewish Orientalism that was sweeping through the West, a trend that went far beyond synagogue and theater architecture. It caused the Jews of Europe to look back to Muslim Spain with a new admiration, and to see scholars such as Maimonides, a canonical part of the Orthodox Jewish tradition, for what they had been: reflections of a mixed Arab-Jewish culture that could not be separated easily into distinct parts. Maimonides and his fellow writers in Andalusian Spain had been experts on the cultures of the Orient—on Greek science and Arab mathematics and Persian poetry. From the beginning of the nineteenth century, the Jews of Europe began to take on the new role of interpreters of the East. In addition to their own search for identity in the Orient, they were encouraged by Europe's new openness to the East, now that the Muslims were in a state of decline and not threatening but rather were inviting targets for imperialism.

The most famous Orientalist when Lev was growing up was Arminius Vambery, an oddly romantic scholar-hero who not only reported on the East for a vast public in books and articles but also advised militaries and governments how they should proceed in the Islamic world. His travelogues of the Russian Caucasus and Central Asia surely sat on the shelf in the Nussimbaum library in Baku, where they would have been the closest thing to local guides available. Lev must also have read Vambery's famous autobiographies, vast Orientalist bildungsromanen of an Eastern European Orientalist's search for his own identity—as both a Hungarian and as a Jew—in the Muslim tribal lands of the Caucasus, Turkestan, Afghanistan, and Persia. Lev's own work not only refers to "the great Vambery" but also sometimes imitates his style.

Born Hermann Wamberger in 1831 or 1832 (he himself was never sure), the son of a Hungarian Talmudist, Vambery traveled to Constantinople as a young man, where he supported himself as a tutor and translator. Though he was often penniless, he soon became the invited guest of several pashas, who appreciated his knowledge of their elite culture. Vambery was brilliant at taking on the accents and tonal qualities of the natives, and the pashas remarked on his eloquence. He began using the honorifics "Reshid [the valiant one; the honest one] Effendi," a title bestowed on him for great linguistic ability.

Reshid Effendi dressed the part and did a perfect mimic of an upper-crust Turk. Immersed in the atmosphere of Stambul, he entered the service of the Ottoman government and earned the esteem of Sultan Abdul Hamid II, "Abdul the Red." But he left Turkey shortly thereafter, afraid that life in Constantinople court society was "emasculating" him. In 1863–64, Vambery traveled through Persia, the Caucasus, and Turkestan disguised as a dervish, following much the same route as Lev and Abraham would take some sixty years later, through the khanates of Khiva and Bukhara, to Samarkand, Tehran, and Trabzon, and finally, back to Constantinople. Noting the "primitiveness" of Persia compared to Turkey, Vambery was shocked that the Persians seemed to have no desire to follow the lead of the West. He traveled across the mountain steppes with several different caravans, some beggars, some robbers. He sometimes begged for food in nearby villages or simply ate what rotten spoils he could forage; he was infested with lice. He became more than ready to return to the comfort of the West.

Vambery's homecoming was tainted by a kind of culture shock in reverse. He found it hard to remove the "disguises" that had worn so deeply into his skin. He no longer felt he belonged anywhere. "In Asia they took me for a Turk, a Persian, or Central Asiatic, and very seldom for a European," he wrote. "Here in Europe they thought I was a disguised Persian or Osmanli, such is the curious sport of ethnical location!" He felt the sting of fin de siècle anti-Semitism, so strong in Budapest, and wrote that wherever he went, people said: "The Jew lies; he is a swindler, a boaster, like all his fellow believers."

Yet in 1864, when he published his first autobiographical account, titled *Travels in Central Asia,* it became a bestseller throughout Europe, especially in England, where it was read as a valuable military and political primer for playing the Great Game for dominance of Central Asia. Vambery made a triumphant tour of London and Paris that year, and the boy who had worked polishing shoes on the streets of Budapest until he was twelve became a personal friend of the prince of Wales, later King Edward VII, and a frequent guest at Windsor Castle. While visiting England, Vambery met three generations of British royalty: Queen Victoria, King Edward VII, and King George V.

Vambery's life was so colorful that it's no surprise that he wrote his autobiography a number of times. He befriended the Jewish Orientalist adventurer William Gifford Palgrave, and he met the explorer David Livingston, who apparently told him: "What a pity you did not make Africa the scene of your activity!" Perhaps his most interesting encounter, and one he loved to relate as an anecdote to friends, was the time he was questioned by then British prime minister Benjamin Disraeli on his ethnic origins—the communication of one proud, self-conscious "Jewish Oriental" with another.

Though Disraeli led Europe's most powerful Christian nation, he had made his mark years earlier by writing bestselling novels that preached the fundamental kinship of Jews and Muslims and the superiority of all Semites. His philosophy was a blithe mix of contemporary pseudoscientific views of race with the romanticism of Sir Walter Scott—a racial pride expressed in romantic musings about the creative power of his "Oriental" blood. (Bernard Lewis has aptly described Disraeli's worldview as "sentimental Semitism.") Disraeli idealized the desert and the Ottoman court. As a young man traveling across the Middle East, Disraeli had, like Lev, always identified with the Turks, and he felt proud to be mistaken for one: "I am quite a Turk," he wrote, "[I] wear a turban, smoke a pipe six feet long, and squat on a Divan." When he was prime minister, Disraeli's diplomacy and defense of the Ottoman Empire may well have extended its life by fifty years. His pan-Eastern ideology anticipated the complicated intersections of Jews, Muslims, anti-Semites, and Zionists that would crisscross over the next hundred years.

Disraeli died just as the shadow of anti-Semitism was falling over Europe, and in many ways his ideas of super-Jews and pure desert races presaged it, though in reverse. Attacked by an anti-Jewish Irish politician in Parliament in 1835, Disraeli replied: "Yes, I am a Jew, and when the ancestors of the right honorable gentleman were brutal savages in an unknown island, mine were priests in the temple of Solomon." Disraeli could be as racist as the worst anti-Semite. In some of his writings, he suggested that the liberal argument for the emancipation of the Jews was based on a false premise—it was not the universal rights of man that justified freeing the Jews from their ghettos but the superlative status of the Jews themselves, which made them better, not worse, than other men.

Benjamin was baptized on July 31, 1817, when he was barely twelve years old, and thus could not be accused of having abandoned his Judaism out of social calculation, or even voluntarily; it was his family's decision. This was an important distinction, for it armed him with the ability to enter English politics as a Christian, yet bearing the full pride of a Jew. His romantic notion of Jews as "Mosaic Arabs"—a term he used in his novel *Coningsby*—bore as much resemblance to the Jews Disraeli knew, and to his own family, as the knights of Walter Scott's *Ivanhoe* bore to nineteenth-century members of Parliament. But that was the point. He grew up in the age when Walter Scott was England's most admired novelist, indeed Europe's favorite writer, challenged on the continent by other romantic dreamers of heroic glory such as Alexandre Dumas. Scott was full of stereotypes of "racial nobility"—including positive portraits of Jewish nobility—and he influenced many of the racist thinkers of the nineteenth century.

Usually dismissed as mere curiosities in favor of his political biographies, his literary works weren't just the eccentricities of a fertile mind but the beginning of a century of imagined mergers between East and West that were supposed to resolve the coming crisis of the dominated Oriental peoples at the same time that they would save the Jews.

In the 1840s, Disraeli published his most important series of novels, the "Young England" trilogy, beginning with *Coningsby* and ending with *Tancred*. Despite the young Englishmen of the titles, the most important character in the novels is a mysterious old Sephardic millionaire named Sidonia. This aging genius, no less than a geriatric Jewish superman, was born in Aragon—that crusader kingdom in the Pyrenees—to a family of New Christians, or *morannos*, Jews forced to convert to Christianity by the Spanish Inquisition. He plays mentor and oracle for the young heroes of the trilogy, naïvely intelligent, handsome young Englishmen. (In his political career, soon to eclipse his writing, Disraeli was himself to become a kind of lone Jewish sage, passing out wisdom to generations of British politicians and to Queen Victoria herself.) Sidonia often explains the true "racial meaning" behind events to the younger protagonists: "All is race," he states definitively. "There is no other truth." The Nazis would later quote the line, with an ironic nod at its Jewish source. But in Sidonia's worldview, "Mosaic Arabs" and "Mohammedan Arabs"—that is, Jews and Muslims—are actually two strains of the same noble Semitic race. These long-lost brothers and their descendants need to come together to form the destiny of the modern world.

The final novel of the "Young England" series, *Tancred*, was also its most famous and the one most filled with Jewish Orientalist ideas. Tancred is a perfect aristocratic English boy—beloved by his family, honest, brave, intelligent, and religious. Tancred is slated for a "good marriage," a run in Parliament, and eventually the position of prime minister. But the naïve hero wants to follow in the footsteps of his ancestor Sir Tancred, who rode to the Holy Land in the First Crusade. Giving in to their headstrong son's wishes, the family asks Sidonia to help him in his quest. Tancred is dumbstruck by Sidonia's mysterious Eastern wisdom and power, and he takes Sidonia's guidance as he goes forth on his messianic imperial crusade into the Middle East. Though Zionism had not yet been articulated as a movement, Disraeli dreamed of the divine justice that would return Jews to the throne of Jerusalem.* The final message of *Tancred* is that England shall become the "supreme power" in the East, but it will never take the "throne of David." In this sense, it may be the first Zionist novel. As prime minister, Disraeli conceived of various schemes for a Jewish state in Palestine, under Britain's rule, an idea that was popular in Britain both because of the fascination of the upper classes with Judaism and also, almost unbelievably, because it was thought that a Jewish state would ensure stability in the region.

The idea of a modern incarnation of the ancient state of Israel in contemporary Palestine—the Zionist idea—got a great boost from the pro-Jewish climate of aristocratic England in the nineteenth century, as did Disraeli himself. But in the rest of Europe, things were growing darker. The development of the seemingly obscure academic discipline of comparative linguistics had divided the world into two broad camps of Semitic and Indo-Aryan language speakers: the Jews and Arabs spoke Semitic languages, while the ancient Indians, the Persians, and most Europeans spoke Indo-Aryan languages (now called Indo-European). Much as nineteenth-century racists misinterpreted Darwin's biological notions of competition and applied them to human history, they also misinterpreted the purely linguistic classifications of Semite and Aryan as racial terms. The most respected nineteenth-century scholars came to believe that the races had souls and particular characters. Semites, according to such thinking, had little or no creativity, while Aryans had an overabundance of it. (In the competition to see which race was more advanced, the new racial-linguistic terminology had given the Europeans a leg up, since "Aryan" means "noble" in Sanskrit.) The invention of comparative linguistics gave Jews another reason to identify with the East.

Jewish Orientalism took on both a more intense and a more tragic aspect in Germany than elsewhere. Cultured Jews, as one anti-Semitic tract put it, "may talk about Goethe, Schiller, and Schlegel all they please; they nonetheless remain an alien Oriental people." The charge of being European on the surface but Oriental at heart was leveled against assimilated German Jews throughout the nineteenth century. The very term "anti-

* Oddly enough, considering his admiration for all Semites and Turks, his weird merging of British and Jewish destiny forced Disraeli to defend the Crusades. There may also have been a fair dose of Walter Scott in this position.

Semitism" was coined in 1879 by Wilhelm Marr, a Hamburg pamphleteer, as a means of lumping Jews in with other Semites.

Many anti-Semites were equally if not more disgusted by the ultra-assimilated image of the Western Jew, and in the end, it was this argument—the *völkisch* objection to the Jews—that mattered most. It is hard to translate the term *völkisch* precisely: it is a concept of racial nationalism that sees the connection via blood to a tribe and its culture as romantic and creative, the root of everything worthwhile in life. This *völkisch* creativity is opposed to the "soullessness" and "rootlessness" of modern life, where people live in cities among strangers connected purely by commercial bonds.

The *völkisch* idea was both antimodern and anti-Semitic. It was racist romanticism, according to which all peoples were rooted to their national landscapes through a cultural-racial soul. The Jews, and perhaps the Gypsies, were the exception because they had no real land, much less a "landscape," with which to romantically connect. They were the only nonromantic people, according to the *Völkists*—the inherent transnational cosmopolitans whose soul was nourished by "stealing" and mimicking the creativity of other peoples. In this view the Jew sought to neuter world cultures by turning them into one transnational commercial culture.

For *völkisch* anti-Semites, it was the *emancipated* Jew—that creature of the nineteenth century—who most rankled, and not only because they resented Jewish competition. The development of this "international" Jew directly paralleled the rise of *völkisch* nationalism. "Rembrandt's Jews were real Jews, who wanted to be nothing but Jews, and they also had character. This is the exact opposite of today's Jews: they want to be Germans, Englishmen, Frenchmen, etc. and through this have become characterless." So wrote Julius Langbehn in the 1890s in his widely admired book *Rembrandt als Erzieher* (*Rembrandt as Teacher*).

Paradoxically, early Zionism drew much inspiration from inherently anti-Semitic German *völkisch* thought. This was in part because of their shared obsession: both needed to solve the "Jewish problem." Some Jews set out to prove that *völkisch* ideas could be adapted to their own lineage—by discovering true "rooted" and romantically primitive Jews to counter the stereotype of rootless internationalism. They searched for these *völkisch* Jews around the world: in the Caucasus mountains of Azerbaijan, among the Ethiopian Falashas, and even in the rural Jewish communities of Eastern Europe. In 1898, Max Grunwald, a young rabbi from Hamburg, established the Association for Jewish Folkloristics and began publishing articles dealing with the far-flung ethnic connections of Jewishness: Polish Hasidism, Caucasian mountain Jews, itinerant singers, *Wunderrebbes* ("wonder rabbis"), evil spirits, etc. Grunwald believed that the "ideal Jew" was the mystical cabalist or Hasidic dancer—the Jewish counterpart of the romanticized peasant, mountain climber, or forest woodcutter of the Aryan *Völkists*.

Much as Jews in Austro-Hungary in the 1890s became Europe's greatest fencers in order to defend challenges to their honor (only to have the anti-Semitic fencing fraternities declare that Jews had no honor to defend, sparing themselves the humiliation of having to fight superior Jewish opponents), Jews now tried to out-*völk* the *Völkists*. The Orientalist Jews embraced the Jewish Other to prove that it had an independent existence outside of Europe that connected Jews from ancient times with those of the nineteenth and twentieth centuries. Meanwhile, mainstream German Jews were still following Rathenau's tactic of total assimilation: in 1898, the same year Grunwald established his Association for Jewish Folkloristics, Rathenau published an essay ("Hear, O Israel!") advocating that Jews, especially all "Eastern" Jews, undergo a kind of voluntary genetic engineering whereby they would try to breed out over the course of a few generations the physical and ethnic traits that others found so odious.

Martin Buber called Judaism a "community of blood," and this very *völkisch* idea became increasingly accepted throughout the Zionist movement. The tragedy of the Western Jew, according to Buber, was the separation of his community of blood from the community of land and property he shared; a German *völkisch* anti-Semite could not have put it better. (Even Walther Rathenau began to speak of a Jewish *Stamm,* or "tribe"— but he was comparing the Jews to the Saxons and Bavarians and other German tribes in order to emphasize their essential Germanness and place in the landscape of the fatherland.) Such *völkisch* "blood," however, was essentially a spiritual substance.

But much as Zionists co-opted the anti-Semitic notion that Jews could never fit into other nations and turned it into the positive goal of modern Jewish statehood, German Jewish Orientalists took the anti-Semites' slur and turned it on its head. "Within the Jews lives the whole force of Asiatic genius: the unification of the soul," as Buber wrote, "the Asia of boundlessness and of sacred unity." Buber's Zionism was based on the idea that every Jew had an Oriental inside him that was his eternal and true self, and that this should be a source of pride rather than of embarrassment. Buber grouped Judaism with Chinese, Indian, Egyptian, and Persian cultures as part of the "Asian spirit." He linked the Jewish prophets to "the thinkers of the Upanishads, Zoroaster, and Lao-tse," and deliberately removed Jewish tradition from the realm of "Occidental" culture, especially German culture; it could not be judged by or absorb Western standards, Buber believed, for such westernization only sapped its strength.

The nineteenth century had seen the gradual effort among mainstream German Jews—copied by Jews in the United States—to "confessionalize" Judaism, redefining what had been an entire cultural framework for communal life as a private religious faith of individual citizens. Traditionalists contemptuously thought of such "reform" Judaism as more a branch of Protestantism than anything really Jewish. Buber and his followers also rejected the "confessionalization" of Judaism but were not in favor of a return to orthodoxy. They thought that this attempt at assimilation into the community of faiths—to turn Judaism into "merely" a religion—had weakened Jews and alienated them from their own culture. (The founder of Zionism, Theodor Herzl, himself represented this cultural danger in spades, for he had little familiarity with Jewish culture or religion. His Talmud was Wagnerian opera: he conceived his idea for a modern Jewish state while listening to *Tannhäuser*.)

Judaism was closer to Islam, in the conception of these Jewish Orientalists: a total worldview and framework for life. In 1901, at the Fifth Zionist Congress in Basel, Buber outlined the cultural Zionist program, calling for the promotion of Jewish art and publishing, the spread of Jewish culture in newspapers and journals, and the modernization of Jewish scholarship. In that same year, the cultural Zionist journal *Ost und West* was founded and quickly became the voice of what Buber called the "Jewish Renaissance" or "Renewal." This movement's first major venture contained the seeds of its later problems: a collection of poems and illustrations glorifying ancient Israel, titled *Juda*. The illustrations were done by Ephraim Moses Lilien, the man who was fast becoming the Dürer, or at least the Aubrey Beardsley, of the cultural Zionist movement. Lilien made a specialty of depicting sad-faced wandering Jews and biblical scenes in a highly symbolic style, which was like sublimated German neo-Romanticism with Jews and deserts replacing Rhinelanders and forests—Art Nouveau with *payos* and pyramids.

The poems to go along with these scenes were written by Börries von Münchhausen, a gentile aristocrat recently fascinated by Judaism and the Zionists. Theodor Herzl called Münchhausen the Byron of Zionism. But the aristocratic poet was upset by Lilien's next book of drawings, which depicted not the glorious ancient Israelite past but the current plebeian reality of Jewish life in Eastern Europe—the shtetl Jew. Münchhausen's aesthetic revulsion at such images grew into hatred: he began to see the Jews as a modern pestilence threatening more fortunate Europeans. Symbolic of the strange allies made and lost in the ideological wars of the early twentieth century, the Zionist movement's first true lyricist became an enthusiastic Nazi. In 1945 the Byron of Zionism committed suicide out of grief for the Third Reich's defeat.

The cultural Zionists "Orientalized" their names and sometimes their personalities as a way to experimentally return to their Middle Eastern roots. Asher Ginzberg, who called himself Ahad Ha'am, the leading cultural Zionist in Odessa, advocated a Jewish spiritual center in Palestine—though he didn't believe that most Jews actually needed to move there. Merely its existence, even in tiny and embryonic form, would be enough to spark renewal throughout Judaism. Buber was inspired by Ha'am's anticipation of a worldwide Jewish renewal. He felt that the Jewish spirit had been on the way to a kind of earthshaking breakthrough when it was crushed by the clash of Israel and Rome. He wrote in his seminal 1912 address, "On the Spirit of the Orient and Judaism," that the creative machinery of the Jewish race essentially shut down after the destruction of the Second Temple; two thousand years in the Diaspora represented a vast, unproductive holding pattern, a cultural coma. But Buber believed "the Jew's own soul" had survived intact: "despite all this, he has remained an Oriental."

By 1920 the image of the Jews' close bond to Muslims and their fellow Asians was embraced by almost all political sides in Germany and Austria, from the anti-Semitic right to the cultural Zionist left. A hundred years of Moorish synagogues and Orientalist writings left hardly anyone in doubt about the familial connection—it was only a matter of whether the relationship was cultural, religious, racial, or a psycho-historical mishmash of all of the above. A 1915 article in the *Jüdische Monatshefte*, a mainstream German Jewish monthly journal (edited by Rabbi Dr. P. Kohn), captures the degree to which the "Jewish Orientalist" viewpoint had become commonly received wisdom. The author, who signs himself only as R.B., is inspired by a new book called *The World of Islam,* which considers the Middle East through the lens of the new Teutonic-Turkish jihad against the West. The book's special significance is found in the satisfaction that German Jewish readers will feel upon knowing that "the world-mission of the German Reich is now more urgently and more hopefully directed toward the Orient than ever." And not merely "the Orient," but all of Islam, obviously so close to all German Jewish hearts:

> It is especially us, the German Jews, who follow this wonderful spectacle of how our Fatherland and the Islamic world are connected by political threads, with particular suspense. . . . Who is Ishmael to us? What does the Islamic world mean to us? The Muslim religious doctrine, customs and laws, the Muslim science and beautiful literature contain many golden seeds which seem borrowed from us and the Jewish hereditary stock and thus seem familiar and related.

Although Jewish Orientalism remained a subculture—defined largely by Buber, who edited a journal in the late teens and early twenties called *The Orient*—it was also embraced by many non-Zionist Jews as well, who advocated "the East" purely as an abstract means for assimilated Jews to achieve self-awareness and authenticity. A Jew did not need to leave Europe at all if he could only discover the Orient within himself. The writer Jacob Wassermann, then considered one of the greatest German men of letters, argued for such a non-Zionist Jewish Orientalism: "The Jew that I call the Oriental . . . cannot lose himself, since a noble consciousness, blood consciousness, links him to the past and commits him to an extraordinary responsibility to the future, and he cannot betray himself. . . . He is free, and the others are slaves. He is true and the others lie." For Wassermann, the "Oriental Jew" became a mystical construct that represented everything the German Jew was not. He could be a biblical warrior, a Talmudic sage—whatever he was, he basked in the virtue of being "authentic." Wassermann wrote that while the Western Jew represented "shame, misery, humbleness, darkness," the Asian Jew represented "power, honor, glory and great deeds."

One of the most interesting Jewish Orientalists, Eugen Hoeflich (who traveled in Lev's circle in Vienna), was a Zionist—and took on the name Moshe Yaacov Ben-Gavriel—but one whose personality and ideas defy every stereotype of Zionism. He was as concerned with bonding with the Arabs—as well as the Chinese and Indians—as with establishing a Jewish state. For him Zionism was a branch of pan-Asianism; it could not be a politically motivated, scientifically calculated endeavor, but rather must be driven by irrational, "eternal" ideas. There is an undertone of romantic racial "awareness" that seems derived from the *völkisch* thought, but Hoeflich sought to rise above the racial bonds among "Asians" to find the real meaning of the Jewish return to Palestine: "We want to return—but not as Europeans. . . . To safeguard the peoples of the East through thought and action . . . is our duty beyond the boundaries of our own people." (In 1937 he would favorably review Lev's *Allah Is Great,* praising its sympathetic and wide-ranging portrait of the Muslim world's resurgence and potential regeneration, complaining only that the book should have devoted more space to "the problems Jews face incorporating themselves into the Oriental World.")

Far from the image of Zionism as the last Western colonial project, the Orientalist Zionists wanted the return of the Jews to Israel to signal the rebirth of Asia and the end of colonialism. "The soul of Asia is being murdered," Buber wrote, decrying "the subjugation of India, the self-Europeanization of Japan, the debilitation of Persia, and lastly, the ravaging of China where the ancient Oriental spirit seemed to dwell in inviolable security." To Buber and Hoeflich and many others, the Zionist project was intended to stop this crisis—to be the catalyst for a rebirth of the Orient and the end of its subjugation to European colonial might. The difference between Lev and the other Jewish Orientalists was that while Buber, Hoeflich, Wassermann, and company offered the Jews as the mediators between East and West, Leo Mohammed Essad Bey Nussimbaum offered mainly himself.

CHAPTER 12

Backing into the Inferno

O NCE HIS ISLAMIC COLLEAGUES TURNED AGAINST HIM, Lev
seemed to shift his own personal definition of "East." He could
no longer participate in meetings of Islamia (though he may still
have attended a more liberal group called the Orient Bund, where he
likely met his future close friend Baron Omar-Rolf von Ehrenfels). Nor
did he focus his pieces for mainstream magazines on Islamic and Orientalist themes, as he had done up to this point. Instead, he began to direct
most of his attention to the Soviet Union and the plight of all the Russian
Empire's former subjects, rather than exclusively its Muslim minorities.
This would soon bring him into more controversial company than even
his fellow Jewish Orientalists would imagine.

In the summer of 1931, Lev began to dabble in a number of right-wing
anticommunist groups, including such obnoxious organizations as the
German-Russian League Against Bolshevism. This group of anti-Bolshevik
Russian émigrés was led by a German aristocrat named Alexander von
Melgunoff, and its members were mostly Nazis or future Nazis. When Lev
was "outed" in the racist press, association with them became impossible.
It is shocking that he would have wanted to join such a group at all, yet,
in the context of the times, not inconceivable, especially given his anti-
revolutionary obsessions.

I found a clue to Lev's developing political views in the conclusion of
his book *OGPU: The Plot Against the World,* which he was writing
throughout 1931 and published in 1932. After nearly three hundred pages

detailing the atrocities of the Cheka (which became the Soviet secret po-lice, known as the OGPU—precursor to the KGB), Lev introduces a wild, free-floating historical-philosophical argument that "Russia is America of the past and also, in a sense, America of the future!" The argument is based on a comparison of the countries in terms of their size and revolu-tionary heritage, and the relationship of each to its own "natives"—American Indians, on the one hand, Muslims and Tatars on the other. Then Lev comes to the real political point of the work, which he lays down matter-of-factly in a historical anecdote that would hardly occur to anyone else when considering Stalinist Russia.

Lev concludes his indictment of the Soviet secret police by recalling Edmund Burke's indictment, in Parliament, of Warren Hastings, the governor-general of India. Hastings had been impeached on a charge of oppressing the natives, and argued in his own defense that his actions could not be considered illegal because he had been granted arbitrary power in India. To this the British conservative and hater of revolutionary injustice—but also of all kinds of injustice, whether revolutionary or not—replied: "My lords, the East India Company have not arbitrary power to give him; the King has no arbitrary power to give him; your Lordships have not; nor the Commons; nor the whole legislature. We have no arbitrary power to give, because arbitrary power is a thing which nei-ther any man can hold nor any man can give. . . . Those who give and those who receive arbitrary power are alike criminal."

Unfortunately, there were not many political clubs or associations for followers of Edmund Burke in Berlin in 1932.

Far more common to "conservative" thinking in the late Weimar Re-public were the ideas espoused by the editorial staff of *Der Nahe Osten*, who had taken such a vigorous role in exposing "the whole grotesquerie" of the "Jewish dissident named Leo (Lob) Nussimbaum." The men be-hind this bimonthly journal belonged to a peculiar but highly influential intellectual coterie that called themselves Moellerians. As they announced in the first issue of *Der Nahe Osten*, in 1928, their specific goal was to "carry on the work left off by Arthur Moeller van den Bruck . . . particu-larly concerning the East."

Moeller van den Bruck—a Prussian philosopher and translator of Dos-toyevsky who committed suicide in 1925—had been obsessed with the coming triumph of "the East," from bolshevism to Islam over the bankrupt cultures of the West. In Germany the Occident is called *Abendland,* or "evening land," and Moeller—like his friend Oswald Spengler, author of *The Decline of the West*—thought that the sun was certainly setting on it. The rising sun was in the East, no matter how one defined it. Moeller thought that the right kind of collectivism, so manifestly "natural" among the Russians, offered an antidote to the anomie and selfishness of the Western societies.

Moellerians believed that the "German-Russian side of the world" was meant to do cosmic battle against the forces of Western bourgeois liberalism, with help from sundry other Eastern forces. They saw nations as either young or old. Germany was "young" because it was in an expansionary period, infused with a "leader-idea" (*Führergedanke*) and relying more on feelings than reason. Russia was in a similar phase, and the Bolshevik Revolution was a manifestation of it. Both Russia and Germany were searching, experimental nations, obsessed with their deep origins in barbarian conflict; therefore, the Soviet Union was a false enemy. The real enemies lay in the West: they were the victors of Versailles. The United States, however, would be welcome in the coming "Eastern" alliance because it had a youthful spirit, a farm culture, and a lively "inner barbarian." Moeller's ideas, at times difficult and fruitlessly obscure, would more than likely have sunk into obscurity after his death, eclipsed by the work of his more media-savvy and self-promoting friend Oswald Spengler.* But luckily for the Moellerians, their hero had written one final work before he killed himself and had given it, as an afterthought, a title that would resonate like no other. Moeller was going to call the little volume *The Third Force,*

---

* In fact, Moeller had originally helped Spengler to feel better about the "decline of the West" back in 1919. Spengler had gone into a funk when his book's publication had coincided with Germany's defeat in the First World War; though one might think the philosopher of decline and despair would feel vindicated, the decline he had been thinking about was supposed to result from Germany's *victory*—and the subsequent decline of its warrior fiber, as it grew fat and complacent—not from something as straightforward as an actual military defeat! Like most Germans, Spengler had not even considered that possibility. Moeller, apparently in a "high" period, convinced Spengler that by losing the war, Germany had *won,* because by facing the decline first, Germany could embrace its loss and form an "alternate West," with the "young nations" of the *East*—in order to deliver a coup de grâce to the *west* West, so that the *real* revolution—not the "bourgeois Marxist Revolution"—could succeed at last. . . . Whatever one thinks of the logic, it apparently cheered Spengler up. The two became fast friends.

but at the last minute he changed his mind and called it *The Third Reich*.

To the Moellerians, Lev did not have an inner barbarian worth bringing out. He masqueraded as a Muslim warrior—one of their potential earthy, "barbarian" Eastern allies—when he was merely a dissident café-house intellectual. The Moellerians were not strict racists, but the Jews had two big strikes against them: they were an "old" people and they were a "trading" people. For Moellerians, the world was made up of two basic types of nations—trader nations and hero nations. A member of a trader nation—a Jew or an Englishman—could never be a hero. It was that simple. For Lev to masquerade as a hero was a "grotesquerie."

Considering that the Moellerians were actually relatively moderate German conservatives for the time, the climate for a would-be Burkean conservative with a publicly exposed Jewish background was hardly propitious in Weimar Berlin. And Lev was not only conservative, he was a monarchist—as he announced in an article in *Die Literarische Welt* in 1931. "So why have I remained to this day a monarchist despite my having lived in a republic for years, and why am I becoming more monarchistic every day?" (The title of the piece is "Contemporary Résumé," as if to emphasize that Lev's views were somehow representative of the age.) His answer is simple and even rather sensible: "The world of today faces two great dangers: bolshevism and a nationalism that is overrunning everything. I know of only one means to stave off these two dangers: monarchy." To which he adds, it must be "true monarchy and not its constitutional, nationally limited, Wilhelmine version." The last point could have been pure Moeller, who thought one of the concepts the East could give back to the West was the idea of absolutism, simple, pure, self-sacrificing.

Lev's eclectic politics led him to ever weirder groups on the fringe of Weimar society. One such was the *Soziale Königspartei*—the "Social Monarchist party"—which ran against the spirit of the times in various conflicting ways: it was philo-Semitic and called for a restoration of the kaiser but also wanted to form a kind of "workers' state." The idea was to get the kaiser to return with the backing of the proletariat, thus ending the farce of competing extremisms and finger-pointing that parliamentary democracy had brought to Germany. The Social Monarchists attacked everything the Nazis stood for, and didn't find many allies anywhere else, so they were doomed from the start. It didn't help that their leaders were an obscure mixture of liberal but penniless nobles and "creative proletarians."

Lev's dabbling in such groups evokes something of the disorientation of the time. Many people in the 1920s looked back on the monarchies and could not fathom that it was all over. This was not ancient history—this was life the way it had always been throughout history, back to Charlemagne, Saladin, or King David, and up until last year, or the year before that. This was the world that Lev had over his shoulder. And it had been replaced by—what? Fiends on all sides, bloodthirsty, completely unrestrained by their fathers' and grandfathers' traditions of politics, society, and decency. All the groups Lev tried joining in these years would have in common the idea that the only way to avoid bolshevism or fascism was a revival of monarchism with the support of the "people," however defined. It was really a "happy valley" sort of politics that hoped to achieve something familiar from Robin Hood and King Arthur stories: the world righted by placing the "good" king back on the throne, his people content in their old time-tested traditions. But Lev's state of mind had something in common, too, with modern libertarianism and its suspicion of central authority (and with a lot more justification). As he commented, "The less a government tried to make me happy, all the better I felt."

His growing interest in monarchism reflected its increasing popularity among members of the Emigration throughout the 1920s and '30s. At the time of the February Revolution, in 1917, many nobles had been eager to reinvent themselves as democrats, supporting Alexandr Kerensky rather than the regent prince Lvov, and believing in some sort of republican government for Russia. But after the disaster of the October Bolshevik takeover, and the subsequent horrors of Bolshevik rule, émigrés of all stripes had grown more nostalgic for a czar. It is hard to even scratch the surface of the mass of fringe parties founded in the Russian Emigration to try to deal with the "new circumstances."

Leaving behind the vagaries of both ultra-liberal and ultra-reactionary anticommunist groups, for a time Lev joined up with one of the most interesting political entities to come out of the émigré period, the Young Russian movement. It was an émigré society led from Paris by the charismatic Alexander Kazem-Bek, which pushed a program that involved reconciling bolshevism with czarism, and was allied with the Eurasians, who argued that they alone understood the unique laws of Russia's authentic historical nature—its Mongol heritage. They rejected left-right distinctions as European concepts that did not apply to Russians and saw materialism in all its forms—whether capitalistic or Marxist—as a Western intrusion. Thus, the Communist victory in Russia was not the triumph of "Asiatic bolshevism"—as the pro-Nazi Russian Baltic émigrés saw it—but in fact the final "Europeanization" of Russia. The 1928 book *A New Party in Russia,* by P. Malevsky-Malevitch, one of the first and only books about Eurasianism written in English, points out that the Mongolian rule that brought Russia into contact with the East and Islam "taught us the art of government, thus creating a nation out of a multitude of petty principalities; it taught us tolerance and esteem for other civilizations and creeds." Most of the movement's appeal was to the youth of the Russian Emigration, who felt disillusioned by the backward-looking politics of their parents.

But not all the young intellectuals were converts. Writing in the Paris newspaper *Le Temps,* Vladimir Nabokov, Jr.—still writing as Sirin—took the position that Eurasianism was a kind of twentieth-century version of Slavophilism, only inverted. Just as the Slavophiles had long wanted to separate Russia from Europe, the Eurasians and their followers now wanted to do the same, but by cleaving to their Mongol or Tatar roots. Eurasianism petered out in the early 1930s, leaving behind only a string of fascinating monographs and manifestos, but its new "East-oriented" perspective continued to resonate with the youth of the Emigration, as it had with Lev.

Other pillars of the Young Russian movement proved more long-lasting. The Young Russians called for a "new man born of the mechanization of life . . . a man of a new style, a new morality and a new consciousness . . . a new romantic. The new man is a maximalist in all things." Alexander Kazem-Bek called himself Glava, for "leader," and by the late 1930s the Young Russians would be staging rallies in Paris and Prague, where they wore matching blue khaki shirts and listened, mesmerized, to the Glava's three-hour speeches, punctuating them with outstretched hands and cries of *"Glava! Glava!"* Kazem-Bek liked to say that liberalism represented "legalistic dysentery" that only weakened the body politic and left it open to extremists: constitutional democracy had ushered in leftist fanatics in Russia, and it was doing the same with rightist fanatics in Germany. Kazem-Bek wanted to find a radical new middle position, reconciling seemingly implacable foes: he planned to reinstate the Romanov heir, Grand Duke Cyril, on the throne of Russia, but with many of the new Soviet institutions kept in place. Grand Duke Cyril threw his support behind Young Russia for a time, so throughout the 1930s there was the odd spectacle of the main pretender to the absolute monarchy of Russia—a man who had financed Hitler in his early years—supporting the idea of a kinder, gentler czardom with full rights for the peasants and much of the Soviet collective apparatus left intact. Of course, it was easy to field such ideas from Cannes and Biarritz.

In 1929, Lev received a medal from Grand Duke Cyril—this was one of the main occupations of the pretender, handing out medals—and Lev would cherish it and talk about it until his dying day. In Vienna it would become part of his café attire, along with the Caucasian gear. For Lev, the monarch was an "entirely classless, nearly superhuman peak of the pyramid of humanity," but he did not entertain the fascist ideas of many of the Young Russians. He was not yet interested in a "Glava," führer, or duce, arguing that "dictatorship exhibits all the drawbacks of a monarchy and not a single one of its advantages."

Lev was never really a Young Russian, though he went to their meetings. The biggest problem he had with the group was simply the "young" part. He had had few friends growing up and had a precocious child's wariness of other children. Indeed, his passage praising absolute czardom begins with a short speech on why "I love old people, detest the youth"; the old are "calmer, cleverer, and more modest," and when the young turn their backs on them, as they inevitably do, they "must consequently fall into barbarism." But the great divide that opened up between Lev and the Young Russians concerned Kazem-Bek's most radical political innovation—the idea that bolshevism had some (limited) positive sides and that Stalin might as well. The idea of seeing anything good out of Soviet Russia was more than Lev could stomach.

The desire for an expedient rapprochement with communism—and Stalinism in particular—had disturbing analogs among the German rightists at the time. Long before the notorious Hitler-Stalin pact would seal the fate of Poland and begin the Second World War, the marriage of expediency between Nazis and Communists sealed the fate of Germany. The

unholy alliance between ultra-left and ultra-right had begun much earlier, even with the founding of the Nazi party and its National Bolshevik
wing, and it was one of the most confusing features of the end of Weimar
Berlin, something that Lev and his circle watched growing up all around
them. Lev's friend Alex Brailow remembered how confusing this alliance
was, writing of one of his intellectual friends: "With all his intelligence,
[he] did not see clearly through the deception and relied on the Communists to resist Hitler, by force if need be. My pointing out to him that the
Communists were actually helping Hitler to come to power did not have
any effect; he still believed that the Communists were enticing the Nazis
into the violent seizure of power which they could then resist, and crush
all their adversaries at once."

With the decline of the Berlin cabarets, practically the only political
satire being staged in the 1930s was the Communist agitprop that could be
found everywhere. Troupes such as the Red Revel Revue, Red Rockets, and
Red Megaphone conducted elaborate dance routines as part of specific
Communist campaigns. In 1928, for example, the Locarno Girls—a scant-
ily clad Communist girls' group whose moniker referred to the League of
Nations 1925 peace treaty, considered anti-Soviet—danced to songs such as
"Hands Off China!" and shook the slogans attached to their behinds for
male dancers dressed as imperialist generals and prime ministers.

Some performances were less lighthearted, for example, acting out the
bludgeoning with hammers and sickles of police, liberal government figures, and Nazis. In November 1930 the Red Torches presented a spectacle
in which the audience could choose how to punish the representatives of
bourgeois capitalism onstage—a policeman, a businessman, a priest, a
judge, and a Social Democratic politician—and the punishments were
quite enthusiastically applied. A journalist attended the performance of
the Red Pioneers dance troupe in March 1931, describing the "show": "Red
Pioneers attack armed policemen, beat them to the ground, and kick them
with mocking laughter while the audience applauds wildly." These attacks
were directed not mainly at Nazis but at figures of the democratic bourgeois establishment. (Ironically, most of the recordings of these agitprop
acts survive only because they were police evidence from surveillance operations during the late 1920s.)

Yet the KPD, or German Communist Party, which put on these performances, continued to maintain that "a 'sham battle' took place between

Nazis and Social Democrats," for in reality they were the same party—
that of bourgeois capitalism. If anything, the Social Democrats were more
devious; the Communists derided them as "Social Fascists." At least the
Nazis showed their hand. Some Communist agitprop actually depicted
Hitler admitting Jewish capitalists into his inner circle and then admon-
ishing his storm troopers for trying to throw them out: "Good Lord, you
don't have to take everything so literally!"

The Communists were not the only ones to write off Nazism during
the final years of Weimar. Many others took Nazism as a kind of joke.
Hitler, as an Austrian, could not even run for the Reichstag; he rarely set
foot in the building until coming to power in January 1933 (then in March
the building was burned down). Much of the American press dismissed
Hitler as passing Jazz Age looniness. He was the messiah of absurdity; a
German Rasputin; a "Mad Apostle." He was accused of being both a Bolshevik and a monarchist, neither of which he was. Few bothered to read
Mein Kampf or thought he had any of the potential of Mussolini. One of
the few who did was a peculiar man named George Sylvester Viereck, a
leading American columnist who interviewed Hitler in 1923, before almost any other foreign correspondent, and laid out a remarkably prescient
look at the nascent Nazi movement. Viereck quoted Hitler saying, "I shall
take Socialism away from the Socialists"; he debated with the would-be
führer about the contribution of Jews to German culture (Viereck defended their contribution), and he noted the vehemence with which
Hitler refused to be photographed, speculating on whether the attitude
was motivated by caution or by superstition or even as part of a "strategy
to be known only to his friends, so that in the hour of crisis, he can appear
here and there and everywhere without being recognized." Hitler was
so uninteresting to the American public that Viereck could not get the interview published in a national magazine or newspaper, though all his
interviews with now forgotten world leaders were widely syndicated at the
time. His 1923 interview had concluded: "If he lives, Hitler, for better or
for worse, is sure to make history."

More people agreed with Dorothy Thompson, who in 1932 went
to Berlin for *Cosmopolitan* magazine—back when it used to publish
Ernest Hemingway and Sinclair Lewis, Thompson's husband. She had a
private audience with Hitler, set up by Ernst "Putzi" Hanfstaengl, Hitler's
Harvard-educated press secretary. Thompson's conclusions—which, un-

like Viereck's, were published for more than a million readers—wildly misjudged the führer: "He is inconsequent and voluble, ill-poised, insecure. He is the very prototype of the Little Man. . . . When I finally walked into Adolf Hitler's salon in the Kaiserhof Hotel," she wrote, "I was convinced that I was meeting the future dictator of Germany. In something less than fifty seconds I was quite sure that I was not."

Nazism was a movement of the youth, and by the mid-1920s, the youth did not read books like *The Magic Mountain* or *Berlin Alexanderplatz*, which we associate with the Weimar period. They were far more likely to read bestsellers like Hans Grimm's deeply racist *Volk ohne Raum* (*People Without Space*), the classic argument for the Nazi invasion of Poland and one of Hitler's favorite books. *Volk ohne Raum* became a standard part of the high school curriculum in Berlin from 1927 onward, years before the country turned to Nazism. National Socialism triumphed in the school system before it triumphed at the ballot box: in fact, the political takeover might never have been possible if Nazism had not first been allowed to gain so many adherents and admirers in high schools and universities. Many students first became Communists, but, as Goebbels liked to say, the two were really not so far apart as they seemed: give me a young German Communist and I will show you the Nazi of the future, was his motto. In Berlin, Jewish students and teachers began to be roughed up, and students swelled courses on "racial science" and genetics.

The Nazis first achieved a sizable electoral showing in the Reichstag in the elections of September 1930. Conventional wisdom is that this was a reaction to the onset of the worldwide Depression. But the devastating effects of the crash did not really hit Germany until after the September elections. Some scholars of political demographics place a good deal of the blame on the rise to voting age of the hideous high school class of 1929, schooled to be Nazis before they ever saw a black or brown shirt or attended a political rally.

One of the first to suggest this "fatal student" theory was Peter Viereck, the son of George Sylvester Viereck, whom I went to see in South Hadley, Massachusetts, in a rambling Victorian house filled with books on Germany, Nazi politics, and poetry, overlooking the Mount Holyoke College soccer fields.

Viereck explained to me his theory that this "young generation" brought up by Nazi schoolteachers had voted in Hitler. "It's all there in my book *Metapolitics: From the Romantics to Hitler,*" explained the eighty-seven-year-old retired professor (the only man ever to win a Pulitzer Prize in both poetry and history). He had published the book in 1941, and it had been something of a sensation. "Nobody was talking about Wagner and Hitler then, not in this country. It was all about voguish Marxist arguments—Hitler was a representative of underlying structural economic forces and all that nonsense. Of course there were economic forces at work, but you can't explain racial nationalism that way. It's not caused by market forces. Now that's understood, and nobody ever refers to my book anymore, but when I first published it, I was in for a lot of criticism."

Actually, most of the criticism had to do with who Peter Viereck was rather than what he said. He was the son of George Sylvester Viereck, suspected at the time of being Nazi Germany's main "agent of influence" in the United States. I had come to see Viereck about his father because G.S.—or Sylvester, as everyone called him—had been a close friend of Lev's. The first I'd gotten wind of this was a mention of Viereck Sr. in a twenty-page Italian Fascist obituary of Essad Bey, which appeared in the journal *Oriente Moderno* in 1942. Then I'd scrounged old bookstores buying up copies of Viereck Sr.'s forgotten books. I discovered that he had once been one of America's best-loved lyric poets, a self-proclaimed soul mate of both Oscar Wilde and Kaiser Wilhelm II (see his 1915 poem "Love in a Zeppelin"), and one of the leading American writers on Jewish culture, producing bestselling novels such as *My First Two Thousand Years: The Autobiography of the Wandering Jew* (cowritten with his Jewish friend and partner Paul Eldridge). But he was also a fanatic Germanophile. As Hitler rose up, Viereck could not resist the Nazi appeal. Even as his Jewish friends, including Eldridge, denounced him, Viereck retained the support of international liberals such as George Bernard Shaw, and he found powerful allies in the U.S. Congress—until 1942, that is, when he was formally charged with being a Nazi agent, convicted, and sent to a federal penitentiary. He and Lev seem to have met on one of Viereck's many trips through Berlin.

At the end of Viereck's 1937 book, *The Kaiser on Trial,* I saw an acknowledgment: it said, "Thanks to Essad Bey."

"Sure my father knew Essad Bey," Peter Viereck had said in his booming voice, in some deliciously lost accent out of the early twentieth century, equal parts Brooklyn and old Harvard Square. "He admired him as a writer. I know they were good friends. But you might not be able to get a lot from me," Viereck said, as though letting me in on a secret. "You know my father and I didn't get along by that point. I tried to see him as little as possible during that period."

Viereck had gotten back to me with great excitement shortly after my first call to him: "I know this probably doesn't sound like much, but memory plays the strangest tricks on me at my age. I only realized just now that I'd read Essad Bey before my father ever mentioned him. Didn't he write a book called *Secrets of the Caucasus*? Well, that was one of the first books I ever reviewed. I wrote a review of it for the paper at Horace Mann School, in 1931—I liked it, as I recall." There was a pause. Then, "That's all for today," said the gravelly voice. I did some checking through Peter Viereck's work and found that it was no small thing for him, book reviewing. His 1985 essay on Ezra Pound in *The New York Times Book Review* may be one of the best pieces it ever published. The essay was about Pound's fascism and how it affected his art, which was something that Peter Viereck, son of America's leading Nazi-Freudian lyric poet, was in a unique position to judge.

"My father always admired Essad Bey, said he was one of the finest writers he knew." Viereck looked glassy-eyed and told me that my visit made him uncomfortable—that I reminded him of himself, during the war, when he'd been stationed with the O.S.S. in Italy and had to go on a strange little mission delivering messages between the philosopher George Santayana and the art critic Bernard Berenson. It was unclear whether he thought he was more like Berenson or Santayana or why exactly he had thought of the comparison. "You're this youthful figure, full of vigor and energy, confronting this tired old man, this lion who's now on his last legs, long at the tooth, you know, and you're thinking, well, I imagine you're thinking what I was thinking when I went to see Berenson." He proceeded to recall an anti-Semitic remark Santayana had made to him about Berenson, fifty-odd years before.

Peter Viereck had spent his life breaking with anti-Semitism because his father had brought it into the house. His father eventually returned home from prison after the war, and Peter took him in. "We didn't reconcile, exactly. My mother had left him during the scandal, my brother had died fighting the Nazis at Anzio. My father was all alone, everyone hated him by that point, so I felt sorry for him. He once told me I'd been right all along, but I don't believe he ever really reconciled his position—that he ever really regretted being a Nazi. He referred to it as his 'folly.' You don't refer to Nazism as a 'folly,' not if you understand it. My father never really understood it. But he was never an anti-Semite, of course, he had lots of Jewish friends—most of his friends were Jews, really—Einstein, Freud, well, Essad Bey, of course!"

A few weeks after I went to see him, Viereck called me to say he'd remembered another thing. In the late 1950s, he used to be friends with a White Russian professor who ran a literary review, Dmitri von Mohrenschildt—a Balt, in fact. This von Mohrenschildt had a very pretty wife named Erika; she was his third wife, Viereck believed. Sometimes he'd go over for dinner at the von Mohrenschildts, and Erika would get to talking about her first husband. "It only hit me after you came to visit me," said Viereck. "That's what I mean about being a feeble old lion—see, I'm so pathetic I forget the most obvious things. Mrs. von Mohrenschildt's first husband was Essad Bey! She seemed quite proud of the fact—always referred to him as her Arabian prince, said he had harems and such. She was the sort of gal—do you know the type?—who got a kick out of that, letting people know that her husband had had a harem. Anyway, that's all I remember about her. I think she wrote poetry as well. She was Essad Bey's wife, though; isn't memory the darnedest thing?"

In the fall of 1931, when Lev was twenty-six, a slim, attractive girl with bobbed hair had come to work as a volunteer at *Die Literarische Welt*. In his memoir, Lev calls her "Monika Brand"; he remembers registering at first only "dark smiling eyes" and beautiful hands with curiously dirty nails. She was a competent secretary, but there were things about her that soon caught Lev's attention.*

She had a vampish way of wearing men's suits. But most days, she wore

---

* German has far fewer words than English, and *Brand* is a very suggestive one, with many meanings: it means "fire" or "burning," but also has a stronger connotation, as in "inferno"; it can be a "mildew" that rots something; and in German scientific language, a *Brand* is a necrosis: the death of some or all of the cells in an organ or tissue, caused by disease, physical or chemical injury, or interference of the blood supply to that organ. It can hardly be a coincidence that Lev decided to give his ex-wife the name "Brand" at a time when he was dying of an agonizing necrosis caused by the lack of blood supply to his foot, a pain that he described as an inferno that was burning him alive.

tight-fitting skirts, with little bolero jackets and tiny hats at jaunty angles. Lev found her physical presence impossible to ignore. She sat there typing and licking stamps. "Her body was narrow and she had her legs crossed under the table. They were straight, slender legs in thin silk stockings." She said her name was Erika Loewendahl and that she was a poet. Her father was some kind of millionaire industrialist, which explained why she was driven to work every day by a uniformed chauffeur.

She was different from the girls Lev knew through the café scene. They were attractive, but they seemed interested mainly in a good time. "I can scarcely distinguish the individual faces. They flow together into a single happily smiling narrow delicate face with grey dreamy eyes," he wrote about the girls he took to films and cafés and wine gardens. He seems to have reacted with revulsion to his first sexual experiences—implying that things on the Green Island with the pedagogium girls hadn't gone much further than moonlight kisses. "I felt sullied and spit upon and yet somehow at the same time, happy and liberated. I hurried home, washed myself for hours." And the girls who invited him in for coffee after midnight became one more example of the rift between East and West. "So this was the love that influenced the lives of Europeans so powerfully," he writes with sarcasm—or bewilderment—of a one-night stand.

The scenes Lev must have caused with the gray-eyed girls—at first he most likely protected his *own* virginity—seem that much more ridiculous when one thinks of his public persona as the "man from the East," photographed in bandoliers and swords, with turbans and a straight dagger. The awkwardness, shyness—impotence?—he felt was so at odds with the image of the bedaggered sheik, the main sex symbol of the era, a virtual billboard for virility. Ever since Edith M. Hull's novel of that name had been turned into a 1921 film starring Rudolph Valentino, the image of the dark man sweeping a white European lady off on his horse was the decade's shorthand for sexual abandon. In America the word "sheik" got a new definition in Webster's in the 1920s: an "alluring man," which appeared somewhat incongruously beside more conventional definitions such as "Muslim religious official" or "leader of an Arab family, village or tribe." The word even inspired a line of condoms.

But the assistant with the slender legs was dark-eyed and distant, more like the girls back home. She was serious, and had had almost as strange and eclectic an education as Lev had. She left school at fourteen, she told him, and had been tutored at home by different specialists, learning a little of everything—her father's idea. She might have been a pampered Baku oil baron's daughter. But what was she doing at *Die Literarische Welt,* licking stamps?

She was there to gain experience, Erika said. She wanted to meet writers, famous writers. She thought she would make a good writer's wife. Lev later found out that she had planned to marry a writer since she was thirteen years old.

They went out together, and soon she was leaving with him instead of with the chauffeur.

On each of the six surviving notebooks that make up Lev's deathbed memoir, he scrawled the words, in his unmistakable microscopic print, "The Man Who Understood Nothing About Love." Though he ranges from his childhood in Baku to vividly captured moments in the present, of the strange circumstances he came to in Italy in 1942, the through-line of the narrative is the story of his love for Erika. This love would drive him crazy, literally (though his stay in the sanatorium would be brief), and it would bring no good to either of them.

Somehow, though, Erika made Lev forget his hesitancy. His writing about their flirtation and courtship has a sexual charge found nowhere else in his work. In the memoir, he often gives himself a stuffy professor persona, dazzled by the dark-haired girl; he overdoes his own creakiness (he was only twenty-six, after all) but otherwise captures the giddy helplessness he must have felt before true sex appeal. Like a creature trapped by a stronger predator, he gave up. "Now she laughed and I saw her teeth, and even these seemed soft and inviting to me," he wrote, "as if they were saying, 'Come, I'll bite you to pieces.'"

At home in the Fasanenstrasse, where he now shared a comfortable, if modest, sublet with his father, Lev had a small study with a wide comfortable couch. "When I was tired from sitting and writing, I would lie on the couch and read dictionaries, grammars, and scholarly magazines." Coming home one day, Lev lay down on the couch and told his father about the volunteer at the literary magazine, and how they had agreed that she might begin to do some typing and other work for Lev. "She will come every day and write down the things I dictate to her," he said. "My father looked at me, looked at the couch, and, shaking his head, said with all the experience of his age, 'Well, the couch is big enough for two. But be careful. A good woman is a man's most precious treasure, a bad woman is hell.' "

His father was proved right, on all counts.

Though Lev later liked to say that he had been married to an American Protestant, Erika was from a Jewish family and had been born in Leipzig in 1911. Her father, Walter Loewendahl, was a shoe wholesaler who built the Berlin franchise of the Czech shoe giant Bata into a multimillion-dollar business based on his own highly personal marketing strategy: "Daddy" Loewendahl, as everyone called him, put his face on shoe advertisements across the country; white tufts of hair flying out around his massive bald head, he smiled out of the pictures like Father Christmas. He became the Crazy Eddie of Weimar Berlin. By the late 1920s, Daddy Loewendahl was making trips to the United States for business and pleasure. Pictures from the era show the Berlin shoe king jaunting across New Mexico in a Ford Model T and a ten-gallon hat, his fashionably dressed wife by his side.

Daddy had moved the Loewendahls to Berlin in 1912. Erika had received an excellent education, thanks to the tutors, but she'd been bored. Then she'd discovered literature. Or rather, literary men. Before coming to the magazine, she'd tried working as a personal secretary for Stefan Lorant, a well-known author in Berlin, and after that didn't work out, she became "on good terms" with Peter Flamm, another well-known author. Erika liked authors, and she liked famous authors most of all. That she fell for a writer at *Die Literarische Welt* with possibly the most sensational name at the time—Bertolt Brecht was less attractive and unavailable—and who bore the closest resemblance to Rudolph Valentino may not have been a coincidence. Erika was enchanted by Lev's mysterious air. (As she would later complain to the tabloids during their divorce: "He told me he was of princely Arabian lineage. I learned after our marriage . . . that he was just plain Leo Nussinbaum! [*sic*]")

"What did I know of the effect of my name?" Lev wrote all those years later. "What did I know of the strange lust for fame, that many women hold for love? . . . She loved my face, because this face was often photographed."

Leo Nussimbaum and Erika Loewendahl—Essad Bey and Erika Renon (as the "poetess" would later start calling herself, in honor of the Italian mountain range where she fell in love with yet another writer, for whom she would soon leave Lev)—were married on March 7, 1932. For the time being, she became Erika Leo Essad Bey Nussimbaum, which was quite a thing to become in Berlin in 1932. The newlyweds moved into an apartment that Lev's friend Werner Schendell helped him secure in a nonprofit Housing Association "Artists' Colony." It was the first time Lev had lived in anything but a pension or a sublet. The apartment complex was actually known as the "Red block," because of its sponsorship by the union and a loose connection to socialist political parties, which was more than a little ironic considering Lev's politics and Erika's money. Daddy held his nose at their new digs and offered to put them up, but she was thrilled to be at the center of such a creative scene, sharing a block with a host of leftist artists and writers. And Lev had his pride. So instead of living off his nouveau riche father-in-law, Lev insisted that they allow his nouveau poor father to live with them. They set up homemaking with Abraham Nussimbaum in the background, quietly observing the whole mess.

Daddy Loewendahl, whom friends also called "the Consul" because he held some sort of honorary diplomatic position from the Czech government, did not particularly trust this Essad Bey. As a wealthy man, he naturally suspected anyone not wealthy of being a gold digger. This writer's strange dress and habits hardly dispelled the reservations, nor did his general reputation as a man with "controversial" rumors swirling about him. These last things did not necessarily bother the Consul, who as a businessman knew the value of publicity. He liked the idea of his daughter marrying a famous man. But he didn't trust this particular one. He hired a private detective to follow his new son-in-law around.

Lev didn't like his in-laws any better than they liked him. "The general consul had only three topics of conversation—shoes, money and pleasure," he wrote disdainfully.

Besides this, he only had a passion for spending as much money as possible, in as ostentatious a way as possible. His wife also had only three conversation topics—shoes, money and clothing. Besides this, she also had a passion—to save as much money as possible, in as ostentatious a way as possible. Despite this, the two seemed to be very happy with each other. . . . They had a 12-year-old son, but even the son only spoke of money and pleasure. The third topic of conversation, obviously, had to be found over a period of years.

Lev noticed that his vivacious wife was often quite silent when her father was around. "This was her way of being out of sorts," Lev concluded, and saw that Daddy's girl always got lots of concerned glances from the otherwise jovial, self-centered bald mountain.

As the Nussimbaum–Essad Beys were settling into homemaking in Berlin, the most important election year in the history of the German Republic was getting under way. There were four national elections in Germany in 1932—two rounds for the presidency and two for the Reichstag, the first coming up at the end of April—and all were crucial. Field Marshal Hindenburg, the block-faced eighty-three-year-old "war hero" (recall the slightly duller member of the dictatorial duo who, with Ludendorff, had led the German military to disaster in 1918) had been president of Germany since 1925. Germany's presidency had a seven-year term. Hindenburg's term was set to expire that year, unless he was reelected. He was planning on being reelected, but the word was out that an upstart Austrian—a corporal, no less—was gunning for the field marshal's job.

This enlisted man, this *foreigner,* who had dodged the draft in his own country, headed up the third-largest party in the Reichstag. Until a month before, the Austrian could not even legally run for parliament, much less Reichs president. On February 26, 1932, the man who in less than a year would be absolute ruler of Germany had finagled for himself a minor civil service post in the German province of Brunswick. The original scheme had apparently been for Hitler to be appointed adjunct professor of the arts in the Brunswick education department, but the Nazis decided that it might damage their führer's mystique to hear people shouting *"Heil Herr Professor!"* At any rate, the Austrian corporal could now legally run for president of Germany. Hindenburg, or rather the men who did the thinking for Hindenburg—for there had always been men who did the thinking for Hindenburg—had a plan.

This Hitler was said to rule through his voice, which had a mesmerizing effect on people and which he trained and guarded like an Italian tenor. Hindenburg, or rather his then chancellor Brüning, decided to ban this seductive voice from the radio. The logic the government employed was simple: Hitler was running against the government candidates—Hindenburg and his chancellor—in the elections. To run against the government was to oppose the state. The radio airwaves were state-owned.

Ergo, Hitler was banned from the radio. Though in retrospect any measure against Hitler's rise seems justified, at the time it was yet another reminder of what a bloody farce German democracy had turned out to be.

Hitler's press secretary and his entourage decided to arrange the fastest political tour in history, using trains, planes, and automobiles to shuttle the führer around the country so that he would reach as many listeners as if he'd been on the radio. The primary means of locomotion were a three-engine Lufthansa D 2001 and three long black Mercedes saloons. On the ground, the Mercedes cars raced together across Germany, with Hitler in the lead car, the top down, a leather flight helmet keeping his hair in place. In Nuremberg a bomb was thrown at the motorcade from a rooftop—unfortunately, it hit another car—and in Hamburg the cars had to dodge a crowd of angry Communists. The second Mercedes was filled with SA goons who'd get out and take to the crowd with truncheons. Hitler thrived on the crazy hours and the speed of it all. It was a political blitzkrieg.

But the real show was in the air, when the candidate would descend on German cities in his gleaming Lufthansa. The sympathetic German papers took to calling these the Freedom Flights, and they contributed mightily to the growing myth of Hitler as Germany's "dashing" savior—its redeeming angel from the skies, descending on all parts of the fatherland. Later, it was all famously rehashed for film, minus the electoral politics, by Leni Riefenstahl in *Triumph of the Will.* The lone foreign reporter who accompanied the entourage, the Englishman Sefton Delmer (who would later head British "Black Ops" during the Second World War but was at the time considered mildly sympathetic to Hitler), remembered the Nazis' 1932 political road tour as Hitler's Flying Circus. The reason there was a foreigner with the entourage at all was the work of the Nazis' able head of foreign press relations, Putzi Hanfstaengl. (Aside from the core group of Hanfstaengl, Goebbels, and of course Hitler, Sefton "Tom" Delmer was the only steady passenger on the Flying Circus. The rest were bodyguards and storm troopers.) Putzi had convinced Hitler to take up Roosevelt's habit of always having one member of the foreign press corps with him during a campaign as a way of seeming open and sophisticated.

Putzi was the Nazi movement's only Harvard man. Though a figure of fun among the more hard-core Nazis—Putzi played "Sam" to Hitler's Bogart, entertaining him at the end of the day with his piano playing—he was instrumental in making Nazism *salonfähig,* or "presentable to polite society," the upper classes who were a crucial source of funds for a party founded by a locksmith and led by a former army corporal. Hitler used Hanfstaengl's affable nature and white-shoe pedigree to forge many of his important links to German and American rich people. While the Baltic Germans provided access to the Russian aristocracy, Putzi was the connection to old American, British, and German families. His mother was a Sedgwick, from the old New England family. (Two of his grandfathers had been Civil War generals; one of them, a German immigrant 48er, was a pallbearer at Abraham Lincoln's funeral.) His full name was Ernst Sedgwick Hanfstaengl. The name Putzi, which means "little squirt" in the Bavarian dialect, was given to him by his wet nurse. His father was one of the most prominent men in Munich in the late nineteenth century, and the Hanfstaengls had visitors such as Mark Twain, Richard Strauss, and Fridtjof Nansen, the famous arctic explorer and passport inventor, to their lavish villa. How on earth had this white-shoe boy gotten involved with a bunch of lower class, anti-Semite beer-hall politicians?

In 1908 Putzi had taken part in an Orientalist cross-dressing show at Harvard's Hasty Pudding Club. For this show, called *Fate Fakir,* the WASP Harvard boys "cross-dressed" in two ways, some dressing up as girls and others as Hindu and Muslim fakirs. The hulking six-foot-five Ernst Sedgwick Hanfstaengl played a Dutch girl named Gretchen Spootsfeiffer. With him in the cast was a young man named Warren Robbins. Putzi and Warren went their separate ways after Harvard, one returning to Bavaria to serve in the Royal Bavarian Horse Guards and the other to join the American State Department. In 1922, when Robbins was working as a senior officer at the American embassy in Berlin, he called up his old chum "Gretchen" from the Pudding.

All the revolutionary nonsense down in Bavaria had the embassy concerned, Warren said, so they were sending down a young military attaché, Captain Truman-Smith, to have a look around. Would good old Gretchen mind taking care of the boy and introducing him to a few people in Munich? "He turned out to be a very pleasant young officer of about thirty, a Yale man, but in spite of that I was nice to him," Putzi wrote in his 1957 memoir, *Unheard Witness,* and recalled his fateful lunch with the Yalie on the last day of his visit to Bavaria. The American had been interviewing anyone who was anyone in Munich, but he told Putzi:

"I met the most remarkable fellow I've ever come across this morning."

"Really?" I replied. "What's his name?"

"Adolf Hitler."

"You must have the name wrong," I said. "Don't you mean Hilpert, the German nationalist fellow."

"No, no," Truman-Smith insisted. "Hitler. . . . They gave me a Press ticket for his meeting this evening, and now I shall not be able to go. Could you possibly have a look at him for me and let me know your impressions?"

Putzi took the ticket and went to hear Hitler speak at the Kindlkeller that night. He remembered Hitler talking a lot about Kemal Ataturk in Turkey and the example of Mussolini. Putzi described the speech to the Yale man, as he'd promised, and then he joined the movement himself.

An inventive cheerleader for the Harvard football team, Putzi transferred that position to Hitler's Nazi entourage. Among his many creative contributions to the early Nazi movement was turning the Harvard football song—"Fight Harvard! Fight! Fight! Fight!"—into the model for the chant *"Sieg Heil! Sieg Heil! Sieg Heil!"* of the Nazi mass meetings. According to Putzi's memoir, he and Hitler were together at the house of the Nazis' semiofficial photographer, Heinrich Hoffmann, in Munich at the time:

I started playing some of the football marches I had picked up at Harvard. I explained to Hitler all the business about cheerleaders and marches, counter-marches and deliberate whipping up of hysterical enthusiasm. I told him about the thousands of spectators being made to roar "Harvard, Harvard, Harvard, rah, rah, rah!" in unison and of the hypnotic effect of this sort of thing. I played him some of the Sousa marches and then my own *Falarah* [Putzi's contribution to the Harvard cheerleading repertoire], to show how it could be done by adapting German tunes, and gave them all that buoyant beat so characteristic of American brass-band music. I had Hitler fairly shouting with enthusiasm. "That is it, Hanfstaengl, that is what we need for the movement, marvelous," and he pranced up and down the room like a drum majorette. After that he had the S.A. band practicing the same thing. I even wrote a dozen marches or so myself over the course of the years, including the one that was played by the brown-shirt columns as they marched through the Brandenburger Tor on the day he took over power. Rah, rah, rah! became *Sieg Heil, Sieg Heil, Sieg Heil!* but that is the origin of it and I suppose I must take my share of the blame.

One of the many early Nazis who were slated to be done away with by Hitler's inner circle in the 1930s, Hanfstaengl escaped assassination by fleeing to Switzerland, then on to London and Washington, where he eventually went to work for the OSS—but only after proving he was not a homosexual by resisting the advances of Somerset Maugham's boyfriend, Gerald Haxton, who was apparently sent in by the Feds to see if Putzi could be seduced. When interviewed in the 1970s, Putzi rolled out all the piano tunes that Hitler had most enjoyed hearing him play—from the Harvard fight song to Wagner overtures—and complained how the Roosevelt administration had refused to take his advice on the invasion of Italy in 1943.

When the April and May 1932 election results were inconclusive, the gimmick of the speeding Mercedeses and the Freedom Flights was repeated. Hitler's Flying Circus took to Germany's skies again, gaining even more positive publicity. Hindenburg won, narrowly, but being forced from the airwaves that spring had immeasurably boosted Hitler's star.

That summer saw daily gun battles between Nazis and Communists on the streets of Berlin. Christopher Isherwood, living in Berlin at the time, thought there was something false and ritualistic about this street fighting, as though both parties were in it mainly for publicity purposes—"fifteen seconds, and then it was all over and dispersed," as Isherwood remembered it. There was no doubt that both sides, extreme left and extreme right, now had an interest in breaking down public order and scaring everyone away from the center parties.

In the midst of this "summer of hate," on July 31, 1932, a second round of national elections proved the extremists' violence-making strategies effective: both Nazis and Communists gained at the expense of moderate parties. The Nazis were now the largest party in the Reichstag.

At the Café Megalomania, words could not capture the disgust, yet still, almost no one thought the little corporal from Austria or Bavaria had a chance of replacing the solid field marshal as leader of the republic, let alone of ending the republic and becoming a Mussolini-style dictator, as he threatened to do when Hindenburg refused to appoint him to the cabinet in August 1932. One of the few who left the country was George Grosz, the satirical artist famous for his stiff-necked murderous Junkers, who took a fellowship in New York and did not return for twenty years. (He later said he'd had a premonition of national disaster in a nightmare that involved a wandering persecuted liberal, a Norwegian sailor, and a load of rotting fish.) Though badly beaten by storm troopers, the self-proclaimed "Wild Jew" Else Lasker-Schüler won the Kleist Prize that year, Germany's highest literary honor.

Lev was also enjoying his fame, despite the political situation, along with his beloved new bride, Erika. *Twelve Secrets of the Caucasus,* the biography of Muhammad, and *OGPU: The Plot Against the World,* as well as a number of more minor works, were all smashing successes. Lev finished the manuscripts for *Russia at the Crossroads* and the new Lenin biography. Lev and Erika could proudly count seventeen translations of his works in print.

On November 6, 1932, the gang at the Megalomania celebrated the best election news all year, though it was hardly real grounds for cheer. Nationwide, the Nazis lost ground, for Hitler had lost his alliance with the industrialist Hugenberg's nationalist party (and hence a good deal of his media support). But in Berlin the Nazis actually gained votes. And the Communists gained votes over the Social Democrats, for the first time becoming the majority left-wing party in the German capital. More than 70 percent of Berliners had voted for one extremist party or another.

In Berlin even the pretense of fighting between the Nazis and the Communists was dropped. It was time to deliver the coup de grâce to the bourgeois center—to German democracy. When the Berlin transport workers went on strike in late November, in an event that still seems almost too grotesque to fathom, even if it is logically understandable, Joseph Goebbels and Walter Ulbricht (the future Communist leader of East Germany) demonstrated together against the bourgeois municipal government; Communists and Nazis stood arm in arm, one shouting "Red Front," the other "*Heil* Hitler!" When Erika and Lev drove through the streets in her big American automobile—which was now a political statement that went along with their Jewish names and appearances—they saw rows of low-rent housing hung with alternating rows of fluttering swastika and hammer-and-sickle flags.

It was Lev's old nightmare—revolution—attacking from all sides. There was no benevolent monarch in sight.

With the Communists and Nazis rallying together in the streets of Berlin against the republic, General von Schleicher, the man in charge of the army's "political" unit, grew anxious. He knew that this gathering of extremists meant either Stalin or Hitler would soon be in power, with all signs pointing to the latter. This supreme backroom player, the lithe, bald-headed Prussian with the somewhat effeminate, aristocratic style, had told a friend earlier that year, "Either I will cut Hitler's balls off or he'll cut off mine." Now he was suddenly contemplating the latter possibility.

On Christmas Eve 1932, von Schleicher made a broadcast to the nation in which he laid out his bold plans for a socialist-nationalist coalition of all Germans. Lev must have listened dumbstruck, as did so many others. The republic was ending, turning into something else. Would it be rule by the army? Over the radio, von Schleicher's high-pitched, clipped Prussian voice—with none of Hitler's verbal virtuosity—announced plans to nationalize industries, to add new workers' insurance, to resettle thousands of the unemployed on 750,000 acres of "our thinly populated East."

That was it. The line about the resettlement in the East broke the back of von Schleicher's government. Soon the Nazis would enter with plans to resettle tens of millions "in the East," and no one would bat an eye. But they would resettle people on *foreign* land. Von Schleicher's Christmas Eve broadcast talked about German land: the Prussian plains, Junker land. The National Agrarian League, an organization of Junker landowners, denounced this planned "agrarian Bolshevism." None of the previous promises or alignments would matter anymore. Things would move fast and, unlike in Moscow in 1917, bloodlessly at first.

"The dead cold grips the town in utter silence, like the silence of intense midday summer heat," Isherwood wrote. "Outside, in the night, beyond the last new-built blocks of concrete flats, where the streets end in frozen allotment gardens, are the Prussian plains. You can feel them all around you, tonight, creeping in upon the city, like an immense waste of unhomely ocean." The captains of this ocean whisper in Hindenburg's ear that General von Schleicher is a Bolshevist, a degenerate, an agent of Moscow. A coup was being led from within Germany, and Hitler would be brought in to fight it. A deal must be struck with Hitler before the Russians broke down the Brandenburg Gate.

On December 31, 1932, the howling Prussian plains sent their winds whipping down the streets outside the Café Megalomania and the annual Ullstein Press Ball, the two places where all of Lev's Berlin were that night—two places that would no longer exist the following New Year's Eve. The revolution would finally finish in Germany, as it had in Russia— from 1905 to 1917, from 1919 to 1932: in each case the revolution had taken about twelve years to culminate—and now the revolution's government could at last take control. As January 1933 began, a swirl of new deals would be struck that would soon mean nothing, and the Communists would soon discover that Nazis were not in fact "the same" as Social Democrats.

The rest is the most familiar piece of European history ever written. The Weimar Republic ended in parades and bonfires. The field marshal's face remained on the stamps. Everything else changed.

In late November 1932, Lev went on a lecture tour to Turkey and Czechoslovakia. In Istanbul he spoke at the Center for Austrian Culture, and the Turkish press reported the event in glowing terms, emphasizing the German writer's excellent knowledge of Turkish. After that, he went to Prague, where he gave a lecture at the Urania Club on "The Spirit and Soul of Contemporary Russia" in German. The announcement for the lecture in the *Deutsche Zeitung Bohemia* indicated that "two suitcases and a portfolio" had been stolen from the presenter in Vienna and that the "documents and manuscript of the lecture" were inside the portfolio.

Lev may have gone back to look for them. In any event, he gave the same lecture at the Austrian Cultural Association in Vienna shortly thereafter. Then, with events taking an unusual turn in Germany in December 1932, he "simply stayed there," as an outraged official of the General Boards for Public Safety wrote in the margin of his surveillance file. Erika and her parents and brother got out, too, in early 1933. Lev traveled on a Nansen passport; his in-laws were still able to use their German papers. Abraham Nussimbaum was refused a visa by the Austrian authorities and was forced to stay in Berlin. He managed to join his son and new in-laws in Vienna, via Prague, a year later. Alice Schulte, Lev's old German governess from Baku, showed up, too, in early 1934; she had been in Berlin since 1922, though it's unclear if she was living with the Nussimbaums. In any case, when they had to leave, she left, too.

———

"There is even a chance that the vandals of the Third Reich will try to exploit such 'Aryan' writers of great renown as Thomas Mann and Gerhart Hauptmann (currently persecuted) for a while, in order to trick mankind into believing that National Socialism has some respect for the human spirit," wrote Joseph Roth in the spring of 1933, in an essay called "The *Auto-da-Fé* of the Mind."

> But we writers of Jewish descent are, thank God, safe from any temptation to take the side of the barbarians in any way. . . . Even if there were in our ranks a traitor, who, from personal ambition, stupidity, and blindness, wanted to conclude a shameful peace with the destroyers of Europe—he couldn't do it! That "Asiatic" and "Oriental" blood which the current wielders of power in the German Reich hold against us will quite certainly not permit us to desert from the noble ranks of the European army.

Things should have been that simple for Lev Nussimbaum in the spring of 1933—his particular brand of "Oriental" should have protected him from any association with the new barbarians in Berlin. But things were never simple for Lev.

In all the excitement of the new Thousand Year Reich, people still had time to remember old grudges. Kurt Ziemke, the officer at the German Foreign Ministry who had taken the initial complaint against Lev from the group of anti-Semites, Muslim Nationalists, and army officers, had not forgotten this Essad Bey. He had opened a dossier when the initial complaints came in, and had been following this suspicious character for the last three years, on a purely pro bono basis.

Now that a government that cared about secret Jews was in power, Ziemke took his case to Dr. Goebbels's new Ministry of Propaganda and appealed for it to do something to stop the "deceptive productions of this extremely businesslike Jew." He was particularly disturbed to see Leo Nussimbaum's books placed on the Third Reich Propaganda Ministry's recommended reading list of "excellent books for German minds."

Goebbels's ministry responded coolly with a letter supporting Essad Bey's work, especially his recent books, which exposed the evils of the Communist Empire. It had no evidence that Essad Bey was Jewish, so there was no cause to begin persecuting the author. In any case, it was "doubtful" that the author even belonged to the "Jewish *race.*"

Ziemke was furious. One could simply have looked in any "anti-Semitic lexicon" at any public library. This was a kind of dictionary-cum-encyclopedia published every year in Germany and Austria since the 1890s, purporting to list every single Jew in every possible walk of life, from farming to the film industry, with special sections devoted to Jewish influence in every sector of the economy, divided by geographic district and income level. In the 1931 *Sigilla Veri,* Philip Stauffer's Semi-Kürschnerr, 2nd edition, vol. 4, page 958, for example, they would have found Essad Bey cross-listed as "Nussenbaum (Nussimbaum, Noussim-baum) *Geschichtsschwindler*"—"story swindler."

But the new Nazi Propaganda Ministry did not, apparently, consult the standard anti-Semitic lexicon in Lev's case. Essad Bey soon received his new membership cards for the Reich Union of German Writers and the Reich Literary Chamber, which were necessary to publish books or articles in the Third Reich. It would take another two years before the Nazi bureaucracy assimilated the fact of his Jewishness.

PART 3

Berlin, 1933

CHAPTER 13

A Tough Morsel for the Melting Pot

Essad Bey is a hater of revolutions. One political upheaval after another has left him a man without a country, an exile from every land where he has attempted to make his home. Survivor of the Russian terror, he hates the Bolsheviks because they communized his father's oil fields and took over the family villa in Baku as headquarters for Stalin. Victim of the German terror, he hates the Nazis because they ruined his Berlin publisher and—adding insult to injury—burned his books about Russia without realizing that he had written against the Bolsheviks instead of for them.

Yet Mohammed Essad Bey, strangely enough, thrives on persecution.

SO BEGAN A PROFILE THAT RAN in the *New York Herald Tribune* on Sunday, December 16, 1934. In the center of the page was a large photograph of Lev, wearing the Caucasian mountaineer costume. He was a little fleshier than he had been in the Berlin pictures, as though living the high life with the Loewendahls had taken its toll. The reporter seemed struck by how "Oriental" Essad Bey looked, though he couldn't decide which part of the vast Orient he came from. "There is something almost Chinese about the way he drains his broad pale face of meaning and veils his yellow-brown eyes until they show only black shadows," the *Trib* man wrote, but at another point he was sure that Lev's "full, pallid face . . . might have peered for centuries from a Persian miniature." Lev was wearing a Persian wool hat in the newspaper's rakish picture of him. Beneath the photo a caption proclaimed:

ESSAD BEY—HE HATES TROUBLE, BUT HE'S READY FOR ANYTHING.

So Lev was now the Jimmy Cagney of the Orient. Apparently, he had been giving this reporter the full "Man from the East" razzle-dazzle for nearly a year and a half. The reporter said he'd first visited "the Essads" in Vienna in the spring of 1933, where they were living in a "white marble palace" whose façade reminded him of "an overornate wedding cake," while its interior was like "a medieval chateau with uneven stories, converging and diverging stairways, secret passages and hidden rooms. When you rang, doors opened in the walls and servants appeared from the least probable places to lead you up and down dark wells which gave steeply into unexpected apartments. Caucasian robbers would have loved the place."

The profile went on breathlessly about Lev's adventures, his collection of passports, and his many run-ins and near misses with the police—apparently most of this gleaned from the author over cocktails or coffee. "When he comes out of that Buddhistic dreaming which his wife calls laziness," the reporter wrote, he "moistens his lips, pushes back his chair and tells a story, he reveals himself as a true descendant of the race of Scheherazade." The remark "which his wife calls laziness" is the first sign in print of any tensions in the marriage—a small thing, to be sure, but in fact the first spit of a restless volcano.

The reporter portrayed Lev as an irreverent Muslim who "carries no prayer rug; he fails to salute Mecca when he prays . . . eats pigs and drinks wine; yet when he came to be married in Berlin he refused to abjure his creed." The result was that the German official marrying them told Erika:

"It is my duty to warn you that this man may enter Mohametan territory at any time and take three other wives."

"He has already boasted of that," answered Erica. "I'll take the risk."

But the *Tribune* painted the picture of a happy marriage, and it assured its readers that "Essad Bey is the most monogamous Moslem outside of

Kemal Pasha's New Turkey. He is as proud as any Occidental of his wife's tall, chic, slender figure." Indeed, Erika managed to bring up her figure a number of times in the interview, in which she backhandedly boasted about how slim she was in the context of "worrying" whether her Oriental husband wouldn't be too disappointed not to have a curvier harem girl.

In the spring of 1933, Lev and Erika took a trip to Rapallo, Italy, where he gave a reading to an audience that included Stefan Zweig and, as it turned out, Pima Andreae. Years later, Pima wrote that she remembered seeing him that night with his wife in Rapallo and recalled the strong feeling of *Zweieinsamkeit* she'd noted between them—a peculiar word that literally translates as "grace-filled dual solitude."

"Perpetual honeymoon Essad believes should be the writer's lot," noted the *Tribune* man cheerfully, and described how, during the last two years, presumably 1933 and 1934, Lev and Erika had honeymooned in Italy, Switzerland, Spain, Austria, and New York.

> The Essads quit Spain and went back to Vienna. Here they now share a house with an American couple, Binks and Jay Dratler. Any morning in their apartments is a better treat than a trip to the zoo. Nobody dresses til the day's chore is done. Erica types, Essad declaims, Binks paints and Jay reworks a novel. He and Essad spur each other on, each boasting of the work accomplished since breakfast.
>
> Erica's presence when he walks or when he works is necessary to her husband. Once she is near him, he works undisturbed, even when half a dozen guests talk with her in the same room.

The *Tribune* man dropped what for me was the most interesting news of the article at the end: Essad Bey "now, in his early thirties, plans to settle down to a humdrum life of letters and to apply for American citizenship. He will make a tough morsel for the melting pot, for he is as old as Asia in his prejudices. His voice strident and his wide, expressive black eyebrows contracted into furry knots, he once shouted at me: 'I am a Mohammedan, a monarchist and an Oriental!' "

Was Lev really planning to become an American citizen? That didn't fit with what I knew about him, though there were some reasons why he might have led the reporter in 1934 to believe he was considering it.

———

In early October 1933, Lev, Erika, Daddy Loewendahl, his wife, and Walter, Erika's thirteen-year-old brother, had boarded the liner *Vulcania* bound for New York City. Daddy had traveled to the United States throughout the late 1920s, and Erika and Walter had come along as well, with their governess, in 1929, the last golden spring before the Crash. But this was Lev's first trip to the United States.

In the box that Pima Andreae's grandson found at the family's old villa in Rapallo, sandwiched in among the hundreds of letters and manuscripts in Lev's microscopic hand, there was a menu for a shipboard dinner given "in honor of Mr. Mohamed Essad-Bey," Erika and her parents, on October 17, 1933. Along with the menu was a remarkable photograph showing many of the guests dressed in "Eastern garb"—Austrians, Germans, Hungarians, Italians, decked out in Turbans and veils, fezzes and fake swords. Among the Orientalized Europeans, Lev stood, slightly awkwardly, in white tie and tails. In the background, two wall-sized American flags hung incongruously, framing the gathering.

All noncitizens arriving in the United States by ship were required during those years to fill out a standard manifest, and a copy of every such manifest is stored in a small, fluorescently lit library in lower Manhattan called the National Archives and Records Administration office. NARA has one of the most obscure and multilayered cataloging systems I have ever encountered, in which a vague computer catalog from the 1970s directs you to an unspecified place in a numbered box of microforms on which are recorded a vast set of handwritten index cards from the 1950s. The Immigration Service stopped registering aliens in this way in the early 1950s, so the card catalog ends then, but that still means there is an index card for every foreigner who ever entered the United States through the port of New York before the fifties.

This is a staggering number of cards, and the computer system (which reminded me of one I once saw in East Germany) does not pinpoint anything more precise than the box containing names beginning with a certain combination of letters. I felt lucky that the names I was researching were fairly uncommon, until I realized that whoever was microforming the index cards did not do it in order, so that I needed to look at every single index card in the "La–Lo" box in order to find the Loewendahls. Once I finally found a relevant index card on microform, this yielded simply a name and a series of numbers; these in turn sent me to a special desk where rolls of microfilm contain images of every ship manifest ever filled out in New York Harbor. It's not surprising that most of the other people at the archives seemed to be retired and that I seemed to be the only person in the room not doing some sort of genealogical research on my own ancestors.*

The hidden benefit to not having all this information computerized is that it forces you to look at every aspect of the original documents. You cannot simply find information on a particular passenger on a manifest, for example, without scrolling through every page of names, comments, and bureaucratic notices. I was interested to note the instructions to the ship's officers on how to fill out the all-important column 10, "Race or People," which was sandwiched between column 9, "Nationality (Country of which citizen or subject)" and column 11, "Place of Birth." The Immigration Act of 1924 (partially passed in 1921) introduced a strict "national origins" system for the first time in America—a quota system designed to favor people of "Nordic" and Anglo-Saxon heritage and to limit all "darker" types, whether Slavic, Mediterranean, African, or Asian. The law was a consequence of the fear of revolution and the fear of "race degeneration" converging in the early 1920s to produce a uniquely harsh response. Every suspect people—from the Greeks to the Chinese—were kept out, and the law was particularly directed at keeping out Eastern Europeans and southern Italians.

But the law hurt one group out of all proportion to the others: it passed just in time to slam the escape hatch on Europe's Jewish population as the Nazis were rising to power. It lasted almost exactly as long as the period during which entry to the United States was a matter of life or death for the Jews (though it remained in effect until 1965, it was greatly mitigated by Truman after the war). Around the turn of the century, the pogroms in Russia had killed some thousands of Jews, yet some *millions* of Jews had

---

* However, this isn't entirely true, because I couldn't resist tracking down the manifest on which my mother arrived in the United States, traveling alone as a war orphan, in 1947. I was curious to see in the column for the name of "nearest relative or friend in country whence alien came" was written "Rabbi Kapel"; a little research revealed that this was probably Rabbi Samuel René Kapel, who had been "director of religious affairs" in the concentration camps of the Vichy French government. I gave a copy of the manifest to my mother, but while many first-generation Americans enjoy having a copy of their ship records, she understandably did not seem happy to be reminded of the trip.

immigrated to the United States as a result of them. In the 1930s and '40s, the situation was exactly reversed: millions of European Jews were murdered, while only thousands were allowed to immigrate to the United States.

So I had a special fascination in examining column 10 on these old manifests. It was the death column. If you had the wrong answer on column 10, you would not be allowed in. I had always wondered how the mechanics of the 1924 law had worked. Its intent had been racist, for Jews—along with certain other minorities—were considered both racially degenerating and politically revolutionary. But its directives buried this intent by expressing the racism in national terms, as country and region quotas. It was not blocking Jews or dark people, it was favoring the national groups that made up the "original" inhabitants of the United States—the English, Scottish, Dutch, Irish, and Germans—as well as those whom the eugenicists testifying before Congress claimed were "superior" and "assimilable." The instructions on the manifests were extremely explicit and seemed directed at ships' officers who might not be sufficiently racist in their perspective. Elaborate instructions were given as to how to distinguish between southern Italians and northern Italians, for example, and a general guideline cautioned officers insufficiently cognizant of good racial hygiene:

"Race or People" is to be determined by the stock from which aliens sprang and the language they speak. The original stock or blood shall be the basis of the classification, the mother tongue to be used only to assist in determining the original stock.

Beneath that there was a helpful list of forty-seven "Races or Peoples," from Bohemian and Dalmatian to Syrian and Welsh, and there, sandwiched in between Greek and Herzegovinian, was the word that symbolized the all-important political-racial decision of the era: "Hebrew." (No wonder Hitler directed the authors of the Nuremberg race laws to study local eugenics laws of the United States.)

The ships' officers must have gotten more "racially sensitive" with the times, for on the ship manifests that I found from the 1920s for the Loewendahl family, they are listed as "German" in both column 9, "Nationality," and column 10, "Race or People." In 1933 the entire party, including "Leo Essad Bey Nussinbaum" and "Erika Nussinbaum Essad Bey," are listed under column 10 as "Hebrew."

Under column 24, the question of whether they were seeking permanent residence, all of the travelers answered "Yes." Daddy Loewendahl had never had any doubts that he was making the trip for good. He was extremely canny in his assessments of the European situation, and did not have confidence in the stability of non-Nazi Europe—besides, he loved the United States, land of capitalism. And he was not bringing in a family of poor refugees. Under column 23, "Whether going to join a relative or friend; state name and complete address," all members of the Essad Bey–Nussimbaum–Loewendahl party had entered "Waldorf Astoria Hotel, Park Avenue, Manhattan."

After a few weeks, Daddy evidently purchased a large apartment on lower Fifth Avenue, and the Loewendahls set up lavish housekeeping there. Looking through the archives of correspondence with Lev's Italian publishers in Florence, I saw that he had American stationery printed up with the Fifth Avenue address as his own.

In a letter to Pima, Lev describes the absurdly luxurious life he lived at his in-laws' three-story penthouse and how utterly lousy it made him feel:

> I was offensively rich, $50,000 and still earning a thousand dollars a month [yet] I felt like a visitor in my own apartment. At seven in the evening came the black servant in his dress-coat and everything that goes with it and it was only that way that I found out that I had asked twelve people to dinner. . . . I hardly ever knew anything more than their names. And then, I was held to be exceedingly poor. Everyone believed in this so strongly, even Ery, that I believed in it myself, and had I dared forget about my great poverty, Ery would have immediately reminded me, what an honor it was for me to be married to her. And in fact I was the one who paid for the dinners, parties and the like.

The general atmosphere dovetails pretty closely with an unfinished novel of Lev's that I found among Pima's papers, set in Manhattan among a moneyed crowd, which Lev appears to have started in 1940. The story is narrated by a husband who increasingly feels sidelined by his heiress wife; he's a "wild Asian," Prince Ali Alaschidse, from Georgia, who has breeding and a ceremonial post in the army but lacks the $100 million inheritance of his spoiled wife. In the novel, the deathbed memoir, and the Pima letters, the high-flying social life and increasing snobbishness of the fashionable wife are all enough to cause the narrator to take up drinking. As Lev tells Pima, "I was a drunk for almost two years. I went quite overboard, even by American standards."

It's obvious in all of his writing that Lev didn't particularly like the United States and felt out of place in a land whose culture and people were bewitched by money. His American publishers treated him kindly, as did the press, but the lecture circuit grated on him. "The bad part is what comes after the lectures; they call it a 'reception' and . . . bucketfuls of human stupidity pour themselves over me."

But Lev liked some things about America: especially the vast air-conditioned movie houses and the courteousness of government officials. "Your officials are as courteous as European salesgirls," he told an interviewer, "and they act as if they had been warned: 'If you are not polite the customers will go across the way to your competitors!' "

And he was quite good on Manhattan of the 1930s—the "immense, straight gorge" of new Fifth Avenue skyscrapers, whose "lonely heights lead lives of their own. . . . They are inhabited every day by 50,000 people and visited by another 200,000. What would the mayor of an average European city do, if his city were to be visited daily by nearly one-quarter of a million people? He would lose his mind." In his description, New York sounds rather like Fritz Lang's *Metropolis,* a lonely, soaring place carved out of "cool American granite."

On the surface, he and Erika seemed to have had what might be called a "glittering social life," which on the evidence made Lev thoroughly miserable. The common theme is the wife's bustling social obligations, carried on without regard to the opinions of her husband, who is apt to do something like wear the wrong shoes with the wrong suit. "Once I put on dinner-jacket shoes with my evening-suit. My God, what a fuss my father-in-law made!"

In New York as in Vienna, Lev and Erika appear to have lived with her parents, and with her young brother, Walter. I discovered that Walter was still living in Manhattan, on the Upper East Side, and so I went to visit him to ask about his former brother-in-law.

Walter Loewendahl, now in his eighties, showed me into an elegant anteroom of his town house; there were photographs of opera singers on the walls, and, I believe, a picture of him with Pavarotti. He explained that his wife was a great patron of the opera and had gotten him interested, though he'd hated it before that. I didn't look around the room much, for Walter drew all my attention—not only because of the interview but because he'd just had an attack of low blood sugar and I was worried that he might collapse during our visit. He insisted on going through with it, though, and recovered his strength as he remembered the events of seventy years ago, traveling between Vienna and New York with his sister and her strange new husband.

"Essad Bey was my nemesis," Walter Jr. recalled, laughing. "I made his life miserable. Bad child!"

Walter said that he and Lev—whom he knew only as Essad Bey—had clashed from the start. "When I was an adolescent, oh, I really hated him, I took his manuscript and locked myself in the bathroom—this was in Vienna, when we were living in Vienna. And he went nuts—understandably; now I understand what that would mean to a writer."

Walter said that he pretended behind the door that he was ripping up the pages. "So it was quite a scene. . . . And they were pounding the doors, and screaming and yelling."

Of course, he said, he had no intention of tearing it up. "We had a sort of ongoing antagonism. Essad didn't care for me, and I didn't care for him."

Walter didn't seem to have thought about his old antagonist in about fifty years. He had been some sort of documentary filmmaker and had had a career in television advertising. He explained that his parents had both been against the marriage. He told me about his family in Germany, and informed me that his and Erika's grandmother had been no less than a Rothschild, and that another branch of the family descended from "some Danish king, Frederick the First, Second, Third, or something. He had an illegitimate son whose name was Loewendahl—who then developed into one of the great military minds and was fighting all the Napoleonic wars. He had a Danish army of mercenaries."

Walter had never figured out if Lev had been Muslim or Jewish or what, "it's all very, very confusing. . . . Well, he wore a fez, so he must have been Muslim."

I asked whether it had cut any ice with his rich and well-bred family that Lev's father was an oil millionaire from Baku. "A millionaire? Is that so?" he asked, raising an eyebrow. "I always thought he was just a poor old Jew."

Aside from living the high life and dealing with his in-laws, Lev spent his time in New York more in keeping with his avocations—writing and politics. To this end, he often saw George Sylvester Viereck, who lived on the Upper West Side and whom he would soon consider his best American friend.

Viereck admired Lev's anticommunist writing, and they would later collaborate on a book. But in the meantime, Viereck commissioned surely the strangest thing Lev ever wrote—an article for his newspaper, *German Outlook,* entitled "The Red Menace in the United States." The article essentially defended Nazism from a rush to judgment. The paper introduced Essad Bey as "the distinguished Russian publicist whose books . . . have challenged the attention of the civilized world. Like so many of his countrymen, Essad Bey looks upon Bolshevism as the enemy of all mankind and rejoices at the fact that National Socialism has doomed the Red Menace in Germany."

If Lev did not actually rejoice in National Socialism, he presented it in a different light from what one might expect. Writing that "for fourteen years, Germany stood at the brink of a red revolution," he continued, "Considering the present political and economic constellation, a successful communist revolution in Germany inevitably would have led to the spread of Bolshevism all over Europe and would have resulted in the destruction of traditional European culture as well as the spreading of the bolshevist wave to the United States." Hitler's government thus "acquires an historical importance. . . . Germany alone was able to erect the impenetrable wall of modern nationalism stopping the conspiracy against the world hatched by the red rulers of Russia, where within fifteen years ten million people have lost their lives through revolution, hunger, civil war and terror."

Lev excoriated Bolshevik crimes and did not even refer to Hitler, insisting that "it is impossible to pass final judgment on Germany without bearing in mind that the National Socialist revolution has saved Europe from a catastrophe."

Lev's opinions seem impossible to explain except by duplicity or mania—yet they were more in the mainstream than one might think. As with Mussolini and Stalin, observers at the time often saw what they wanted to see. Lev wrote his article at the end of 1933, Hitler's first year in power. A year later, *The New York Times* won a Pulitzer Prize for the work of Frederick T. Birchall, whose "unbiased reporting on Germany" had won him wide respect. Birchall was the chief of the *Times* Berlin bureau and covered the entire Nazi Revolution for the paper of record. In the spring of 1933, he described to *Times* readers the "boyish trick" of flying a swastika over a synagogue and actually made light of the book burnings around Germany. As late as 1936, Birchall found "not the slightest evidence of religious, political or racial prejudice" visible when he covered the Berlin Olympics, and wrote that the result of witnessing the Nazis' Olympic display "will surely be to send foreigners home with excellent opinions of the effects of dictatorship and wish that democracy might sometime show itself similarly showmanlike."*

The fact is that many papers across the United States took Lev's 1934 position—virtually up until the United States went to war, in 1941, which was long after they should have known better. Isolationist papers like the *Chicago Tribune* actively supported Hitler up until the Second World War as Europe's only defense against the "communist menace." Perhaps oddest of all, *The Christian Science Monitor* ran many explicitly pro-Nazi pieces in the 1930s. A 1933 two-part series entitled "A Traveler Visits Germany" described a contented nation where "traffic was well regulated. . . . I have so far found quietness, order and civility . . . not the slightest sign of anything unusual afoot." The *Monitor* reporter compared the brown shirts to "members of some student corps," and he wrote that the "harrowing stories" of Jews "deprived of their occupations . . . [applied] only to a small proportion of the members of this . . . community." Under the Nazis, the paper assured, the Jews in general are "not in any way molested." Even Walter Lippmann, probably the most influential Jewish writer in America

---

* To be fair to Birchall, he informed readers that the Nazis had made special efforts to remove all the anti-Semitic street signs and tone down the vitriol of anti-Semitic newspapers while the Olympics were in town. But Birchall was not critical of their duplicity: he complimented the Nazis on keeping "politics . . . out of a sphere in which they have no place. In the world of sport."

at the time, warned readers of his nationally syndicated column that to judge Nazi Germany by its concentration camps was to judge "Protestantism by the Ku Klux Klan or the Jews by their parvenus."

George Sylvester Viereck, who had presumably encouraged Lev to write his pro-Nazi article in the first place, was probably the most conflicted public figure with regard to issues of race and nation, identity and ideology, in the United States. But looking beyond his recklessness, experimentation, and habit of pushing all things to flamboyant extremes, George Sylvester Viereck represented, in extremis, America's entire confused relationship with fascist Europe in the 1930s. He would soon take his views a bit too far; or certainly further than friends like Sigmund Freud and Albert Einstein, or even his own family, wanted to follow him.

A June 15, 1940, *New Yorker* "Talk of the Town" story began,

George Sylvester Viereck is as staunch a partisan of Germany in this war as he was in the last, but is not an accredited German agent. We know this because our Fifth Column editor went up to his office-apartment on Riverside Drive and asked him. "I am a poet, a journalist, I have even mixed in politics in a small way, but I am not a propagandist," he told our man.

The New Yorker found Viereck to be slim, blond, and looking ten years younger than his age, which was fifty-six at the time; he was almost "oppressively neat in his dress; suit, shirt, tie, shoes, and pocket handkerchief were all in harmonizing shades of brown."

What really caught the reporter's eye were the pictures hanging on the walls of the study. It was the summer of 1940—after the Nazi invasion of France!—and the story described the following unique mélange: "Kaiser Wilhelm (in his Imperial days), other members of the Hohenzollern family, Hitler (in his Brown Shirt days), Dr. Goebbels . . . Sigmund Freud, and Albert Einstein."

"All these people I have known and admired," Viereck told *The New Yorker* without batting an eye.

"Some of them I have written about. The psychoanalyst, the scientist, and above all the dynamic force"—he waved his hand toward *der schöne*

Adolf—"all have been my friends. Of course I am no longer on speaking terms with some of them."

George Sylvester Viereck's father, Louis, was reputed to be the illegitimate son of His Imperial Majesty Wilhelm I, the grandfather of Kaiser Wilhelm II—*the* kaiser—which would make Willy and Sylvester, as young Viereck was called, cousins. Louis Viereck rebelled against his putative royal blood by becoming a socialist and corresponding with Marx and Engels, associations that forced him to flee Berlin for Munich. There, in 1881, he married his American cousin, Laura Viereck (Engels was a witness at the wedding), and on December 31 of that year, she brought Sylvester Viereck into the world. In the 1880s, Louis was in the German Parliament, but he also spent some time in prison for political "offenses," and in the 1890s, Laura convinced him to move the family to the United States. So Sylvester grew up an American from early childhood, but he never lost his nostalgia for those first six years.

Sylvester Viereck started writing poetry when he was eleven. He idolized Christ, Napoleon, and Oscar Wilde, wore velvet collars over his evening jackets, and wrote, "I identify with all things morbid and evil. I love the splendor of decay, the foul beauty of corruption." Such lines might have been written by any adolescent, but Sylvester was not any adolescent—by the time he graduated from City College of New York, he had published two volumes of poetry and a collection of plays, and *The Saturday Evening Post* had called him "the most widely-discussed young literary man in the United States today . . . unanimously accused of being a genius."

In August 1914—of all the months in all the years—the young man the *Atlantic Monthly* named "America's Oscar Wilde" cofounded *The Fatherland,* "a weekly devoted to Fair-Play for Germany and Austria-Hungary." Along with the paper, Viereck established the Fatherland Foundation, dedicated to making "German-Americans proud of the hyphen." Rumors started flying around that Viereck was receiving visits at his office from German agents, specifically by a shadowy fellow known as Dr. Albert. These rumors were cleared up, after a fashion, in July 1915, when Dr. Albert left his briefcase on the 6th Avenue El, which he was riding at the time with Viereck. The briefcase, snatched up by a trailing Secret Service agent, contained papers documenting "several wild and improbable schemes" causing papers across the country to scream: HUNS PAID $200,000 TO VIERECK . . . FOR PROPAGANDA SERVICES! Suddenly, he was nobody's favorite avant-garde poet. The Authors' League expelled him, his poems were expunged from anthologies, and his name was dropped from *Who's Who*. But in 1923, Viereck published a pop-science book, with heavy undertones of sex, called *Rejuvenation: How Steinach Makes People Young*—about a Viennese physician who used hormones to slow aging—and somehow Sigmund Freud got ahold of it. Freud wrote to Viereck asking if he might like to write a similar book on psychoanalysis.

"I have been compared to Columbus, Darwin, Kepler, and I have been denounced as a paralytic," Freud told Viereck, and Viereck snapped up the tagline, hailing his new hero "the Columbus of the Unconscious" and "the great Austrian explorer of the nether world of the soul." Viereck soon became one of the leading (at times misleading) popularizers of Freudianism in the United States. Freud helped launch Viereck on a career as America's number one interviewer. More fatefully, he introduced Viereck to the Jews.

Shortly after interviewing Freud in Vienna, Viereck flew to Munich and became the first American journalist to interview Hitler. When the would-be führer described the Jews as a "disturbing influence" and an "alien people in our midst," Viereck responded that Germany owed much to the Jews. They are guilty of "making a virtue of weakness," replied Hitler, causing Viereck to immediately pick up on Hitler's bowdlerized Nietzscheism. Germany has many productive, decent Jewish citizens, insisted Viereck, to which Hitler replied straightforwardly: "The fact that a man is decent is no reason why we should not eliminate him." While other interviews of the period wasted all their time on the Versailles Treaty or the situation with Austria, Viereck instantly slashed to Hitler's core— "The fact that a man is decent is no reason why we should not eliminate him." Viereck could not sell the interview with Hitler, then a nobody in America, and had to have it published by a vanity press.

In the mid-1920s, Viereck went on a series of whirlwind tours of Europe interviewing every imaginable public figure: Marshal Foch and Clemenceau . . . George Bernard Shaw and Oswald Spengler . . . Mussolini and Queen Elisabeth of the Belgians (a "modern queen . . . not content with wearing a crown, [she] is a champion of race hygiene") . . .

Henry Ford (who told Viereck that there was a "Master Mind" or "Brain of the Earth" transmitting thought waves to people) and Professor Albert Moll ("The Sherlock Holmes of Ghost Land," who devoted himself to exploring the supernatural with the new science of X rays) . . . and Dr. Magnus Hirschfeld ("The Einstein of Sex . . . Dr. Hirschfeld, chief of the Sex Science Institute in Berlin, espouses the theory of sex relativity. He is not the first to enunciate this doctrine, but he carries it to its logical conclusion").

Perhaps Viereck's most high-profile interview was with the real Einstein, and as with Freud, the topic quickly came around to Jews. They spoke about relativity, Zionism, religion, and nationalism:

> "We Jews," Einstein [said], "have been too adaptable. We have been too eager to sacrifice our idiosyncrasies for the sake of conformity. . . .
>
> The atmosphere of our infancy predetermines our idiosyncrasies and predilections. When I met you, I knew I could talk freely without the inhibitions which make the contact with others so difficult. I looked upon you not as a German nor as an American, but as a Jew."

Viereck protested that he wasn't Jewish. "My parents and my progenitors are Nordics from Protestant Germany," he said.

> "It is impossible," Professor Einstein observed, "for any individual to trace every drop of blood in his constitution. Ancestors multiply like the famous seed of corn on the chessboard, which embarrassed the Sultan. . . ."
>
> "So as far as I know," I replied, "we are Northerners, the Viereck family emigrated to Germany from Scandinavia. . . ."
>
> "Nevertheless," Einstein replied, "you have the psychic adaptability of the Jew. There is something in your psychology which makes it possible for me to talk to you without barrier."

In the late 1920s, Viereck embarked upon a fourth or perhaps fifth career with a vast intellectual novel, which he claimed was the first novel to apply Freud's theories to human history, beginning in ancient Babylonia. The story of *My First Two Thousand Years: The Autobiography of the Wandering Jew* is told by the eternal Jew of the title, who, while under hypnosis in the care of a psychoanalyst, relives the last past two thousand years of his travails. The book was an instant bestseller (500,000 hardcover printing) and went into twelve American editions and almost as many languages in short order. Critical success followed. Thomas Mann thought *The Autobiography* was "audacious and magnificent." *The New Republic* pronounced *My First Two Thousand Years* "saturated with the modern spirit," while the *Chicago Tribune* said it "approaches the beauty of the Greeks." When the book was censored in Ireland, the poet W. B. Yeats flew to the aid of his fellow poet Viereck. Viereck's reputation was suddenly resurrected. An article appearing in the newspaper *The World,* on April 13, 1930, titled "The Return of George S. Viereck," celebrated the lifting of the cloud over this great poet's reputation, and proclaimed that for "its enfranchisement in aesthetic freedom, American poetry has George Sylvester Viereck to thank more than anyone else, with the possible exception of Ezra Pound."

The comparison was prescient, for though they did not at the time know each other, Viereck and Pound would eventually cross paths later in life in more ways than one: both would support the Axis—though Pound's support for Mussolini, ironically, would be viciously anti-Semitic, while Viereck's support for Hitler would somehow attempt to stay perversely "pro-Jewish"; both would be denounced as traitors and imprisoned by the American government for their fascist sympathies, and both would try to help Essad Bey survive in fascist Europe during his final desperate days. But unlike Pound, a deep and native anti-Semite, Viereck prided himself on being mistaken for a Jew! "The quickness of the Jew, the restlessness of his mind," wrote Viereck in 1931, "his immediate response to nervous and cerebral stimuli, under the veil of Oriental languors, excites me. That is why I have become his chronicler."

But shortly after spending time with his friend Essad Bey in the fall of 1933 in New York, Viereck paid a visit to the man he once called "human dynamite," Adolf Hitler, now in power in Berlin. By the spring of 1934, when Viereck gave a speech at Madison Square Garden to more than twenty thousand "friends of the New Germany," the hall was hung with American flag shields, swastikas, and pictures of Washington and Hitler. Viereck stood in front of these tens of thousands of Nazi sympathizers and said passionately into the microphone, "I am not, and never will be, an anti-Semite. I am an admirer of Franklin D. Roosevelt!" He went on to compare Hitler and Roosevelt, saying they were both "trying their utmost to build a new world out of the wreck of the old." He concluded with the incredible suggestion that the audience should consider the possibility of sympathizing "with National Socialism without embracing anti-Semitism."

Viereck's Jewish friends—including his literary agent, Isaac Goldberg—published a series of denunciations of him in various papers, calling him "George Swastika Viereck." In June, Viereck met in Philadelphia with Putzi Hanfstaengl, who had taken a break from being the Third Reich's "Foreign Press Führer" to attend his thirtieth Harvard reunion. They both needed police protection from crowds of furious Jewish protesters. Yet Viereck claimed that he was not a Nazi. He clung to the hope that "Chancellor Hitler" would see the wisdom of Mussolini's system of fascistic monarchism and bring back the kaiser from his exile in Holland and serve under him as a kind of regent. Viereck had defended the kaiser throughout the First World War, and after His Imperial Majesty went into exile in 1918 in Holland, Viereck was the only journalist he allowed to visit him frequently in his exile.

Peter Viereck remembered running around the kaiser's vast house when he visited with his father. "It was a kind of sordid scene," he said. "Servants everywhere, but you felt like there was some sort of air of suspicion, with everyone very formal, like it was still at court, but somehow aware that it was all a farce. I remember that the Kaiser called my father *'mon cousin.'* But you know that was just a way that royalty talked to all other royalty, so I think he was paying my father a kind of compliment, maybe buttering him up a bit, but I don't think it meant he thought he was his cousin."

Around summer 1934, Viereck broached to Lev the idea of their collaborating on an unconventional biography of the ex-kaiser. In a letter to Pima, also Viereck's friend, in June 1941, Lev recalled how he had presented the project:

> If it were published under my name it would be a book like any other book, but under Viereck's name it would be a sensation, since for inexplicable reasons Viereck is regarded in America as an illegitimate cousin of the Kaiser. Since I am in no way a cousin of the Kaiser . . . the book was printed under Viereck's name, which is much better than if mine

were added. Both of us were satisfied and that is what one calls the business of literature.

Lev wrote the first draft during a sea voyage. "It wasn't difficult to write a book while traveling by boat," he told Pima, "since we would traverse the Atlantic in 30 days. I carried the material in my head. Every afternoon I would dictate ten pages to Ery. The book was finished in Venice." In fact, it took him longer than usual—six months' work—because of the amount of material to read through first. Lev also visited the kaiser at least once in exile ("He wasn't very young anymore, but he was mentally still very fit"), and from then on Lev sent the ex-emperor each of his books as they were published.

The Kaiser on Trial is a bizarre historical pastiche written in the form of courtroom testimony. It is ostensibly the trial of the kaiser for war crimes in front of a tribune of historical figures, both dead and living. It is also a reflection on the first years of the twentieth century and the events that ended the Europe's old empires in a vast spectacle of mass killing and destruction. George Bernard Shaw praised it as an effective "new method in the writing of history," providing "a mine of information . . . both dramatic and judicious." And something not exactly judicious—a kind of nationalistic, loopy mysticism, reimagining the old divide between East and West.

> Cradled in the East, Germany is "the face of the East turned towards the West." She is the Western outpost of Eurasian culture. England, France and the Mediterranean countries belong to the Atlantic sphere; this sphere, including the United States of America, is either "feminine" or "double-sexed."

And, of course, the Jews would come into it somewhere: "It is Disraeli, not Adolf Hitler or Henry Ford, who, in 'Coningsby,' sponsored the theory that two hundred members of an Inner Ring control the destiny of mankind."

Throughout the late 1930s, Viereck became increasingly isolated, and as a result of his pariah status, he became increasingly dependent on the Nazi government for work. He was eventually imprisoned in March 1942 for not revealing "aspects of his work" that were funded by the German Foreign Office; released a year later, he was picked up again for similar offenses in March 1943. His eldest son, George Sylvester, Jr., died fighting the Germans in January 1944, and his wife left him, apparently giving away most of his money to Jewish refugee committees and the Catholic charities. Upton Sinclair wrote to Viereck personally to say that "if there is a Benedict Arnold of this war, you are he."

Lev may have been Viereck's last Jewish friend in the world, indeed one of his last friends period, after Freud, Einstein, and all the rest—including his own family—had stopped speaking to him. Shortly before he died, Lev wrote sarcastically to Pima about Viereck: "Of course he is a spy, hangman, bandit, and above all every democratic journalist knows that Viereck sank the Lusitania in the World War. In reality he is a very nice man and was my only comfort in America."

Left: Lev Nussimbaum, about six years old, in fur hat and bandolier.

Below: Muslim-Jewish Christmas party, Baku, 1913. (Lev is in the third row, at far right, with the white collar and big ears.)

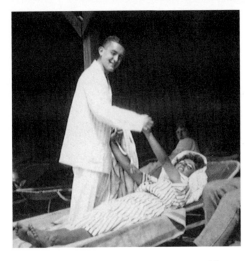

Above: Teenaged Lev in beach whites (possibly at the island sanatorium). *Above right:* Lev with the Voronov sisters, Tossia Peschkowsky, and a blond baby who may or may not be the future director Mike Nichols.

Far right: The cover of Lev's first book in American translation. *Right:* a passport-sized portrait from a Berlin department store, circa 1923 (Alexander Brailow, Lev's classmate, has penned in his aliases: Assad Bey and Kurban Said).

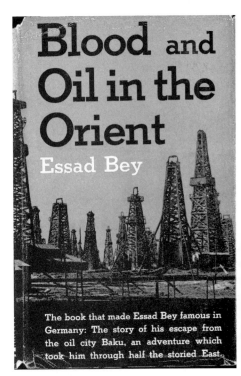

Blood and Oil in the Orient
Essad Bey

The book that made Essad Bey famous in Germany: The story of his escape from the oil city Baku, an adventure which took him through half the storied East.

Left: Lev surrounded by his fellow émigrés, Berlin Russian High School, circa 1922.

Above: Lev's class at the Russian High School, Berlin, 1922.
Right: Lev as a young writer.
Below: Lev's schoolboy nemesis, Georgie.

Lev in full café Orientalist outfit.

Erika, millionaire's daughter and Jazz Age poetess.

The Vienna gang, including (from left) Jay and Binks Dratler, Erika, Franzie (the starlet with the turtles, who would be the main witness against Lev at the trial), and an unidentified couple.

Lev as the Jimmy Cagney of the Orient, or, as the *New York Herald Tribune* captioned this photo: "Essad Bey—He Hates Trouble, but He's Ready for Anything."

Tabloid stories about the "Erika-Essad" divorce trial.

Scandale mondain en Autriche

Toute la société viennoise se passionne pour un procès sensationnel dont un biographe de Mussolini tient la vedette

Qui a raison, de la femme ou du mari ?

Mohammed Essad Bey and his wife Erika, dining in New York night club before the present unpleasantness.

Above: The New York *Daily News.*
Below: Sunday Mirror Magazine.

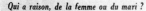

Mme Erika Essad Bey (à droite) et son témoin principal, Franzi Baumfeld.

Above: A French tabloid writes, "After the Scene of Seduction Came the Abduction," "World Scandal in Austria," and "All of Viennese Society is Obsessed with a Sensational Trial in Which a Biographer of Mussolini Takes the Starring Role." "Who is Right? The Wife or the Husband?"

Harem? Yes--But Scare 'Em? No!

The Broad-Minded Poetess Didn't Object to Her Mohammedan Husband's Having Multiple Wives---But When He Insisted on Reading Her His Horror-Stories, She Fled to America---and a Divorce

ALONE—AND LIKES IT
Madame Essad Bey, the Former Erica Lowendahl, Who Divorced Her Picturesque Husband So That She Could Have "Peace and Quiet to Write Poetry Again." She's Admittingly Holding a Sculpture-Portrait of Herself.

TAKE one fez-wearing Mohammedan—survivor of countless revolutionary and counter revolutionary perils, intimate of the murdered Czar Nicholas, author and adventurer of highly original ideas anent women and love—

And take one Czech poetess—dark, slim and lovely, with half a dozen volumes to her credit and a papa of unlimited means—

Also one fabulous, slightly mysterious Viennese literary gent, who wrote the sensational biography of one sinister Russian monk and was sued by another—

Stir well, allow to simmer a while, serve forth piping hot—and you get a three-decker emotional female that makes ordinary human relationships pallid indeed.

The spicy business was revealed when the exotic former Erica Lowendahl, daughter of Walter Lowendahl, ex-Czech diplomat and partner of Bata, the immensely wealthy Bohemian shoe king, zoomed into Bel Air, California, after starting divorce proceedings against her Mohammedan-Russian husband, Essad Bey.

There she became the close companion of the squeaky ex-nobility Dr. René Fülöp-Miller, who has just sold the biography of a Boston dentist to the films. Gossiperz gossiped, rumorers rumored, and pretty soon it was understood that as soon as the Viennese author was free of his first wife, he would wed Erica.

Hot upon this came whispers of Essad Bey, all full of hot Near East blood, storming up and down Europe, threatening to sue Dr. Fülöp-Miller as a love-thief. To which the latter replied that the Bey was a cad, and if he ever saw him again he would bat his ears down until he could hear naught but footprints.

Behind the spirited high-jinx lies a tale combining the gaudier elements of an Edgar Allan Poe creep-saga and the case-histories of Kraft-Ebing. Erica met her Oriental vagabond lover in the Berlin offices of a literary review, for which she was writing poetry and he articles. That was in 1932. He was 23, she 22.

Essad Bey—Essad meaning "lion" and Bey "prince"—was already an almost legendary figure. Author of works on Tsarist Russia—possessor of a Medieval house in Vienna which was said to be cluttered with subterranean passages and secret compartments—he had figured as the hero of innumerable melodramas, real and fictitious. Born in Caucasian Georgia, he had fled with his family from the Reds, crossing the Persian desert. The caravan was set upon by bandits. Many travelers were butchered, but, because Essad and his family were converted Mohammedans, the bandits had allowed them to escape with their lives.

Later, Erica gave a slightly different version of Essad's beginnings, saying that he was born plain Leo Nussimbaum; that his mother had committed suicide during the Red Revolution and he fled with Nussibaum, Sr., to Turkey, where both embraced Mohammedanism. "Bey," she said scornfully, was an hereditary title which Essad could not possibly claim.

However, Erica was completely captivated when she met him in 1932. She promptly offered to become his secretary because: "I wanted to get his mind on a better track and to help him with languages." Soon afterward they were married in Berlin and Papa Lowendahl furnished an apartment for them.

PAPA was soon to have a troubleau of his own. The pressure of Nazism drove him out of Europe and he settled in New York, with his millions more or less intact.

When the pretty poetess, whose works were all extremely gloomy, married Essad, she announced that even if he exercised the Mohammedan prerogative of taking several wives it would not interfere with their love. He might have a harem if he liked, she told the world. Other irregularities, however, she did not bargain for. A harem was one thing. But a gentleman of unruly and unusual disposition and temper, an Erica charges her husband was, was something else again! Harem, yes—scare 'em, no!

Shortly after the marriage, she alleged, strange things started to occur in the Essad Bey household. Erica's list of complaints reads like a compendium of Grand Guignol plots.

During fits of epilepsy, she averred, he would threaten to strangle or shoot her. He had a pretty trick of keeping her up all night, while he read passages from his unpublished works, which were so bloody horrible that no publisher would accept them.

Supposedly historical studies of the Russian Revolution, they were, says Erica, but actually fantasies of a diseased mind; and her greatest suffering, she claimed, was that she had the five

The Candid Camera Catches Essad Bey in One of His Most Turkish Moments, Telling One of the Too Perfectly Gruesome Yarns That Scared His Wife, She Says, Into Swing for Divorce.

down certain phony statements with which these masterpieces bristled. Under threats of death, she added, he made her listen over and over to his pet story about a man slashed to bits before the eyes of his enemy. If Erica came to confuse the Marquis de Sade with the Marquis d'Essad, it was no wonder, to hear her tell it.

Some very entertaining items in the scurrilous European press, involving herself as well as Fülöp-Miller, she ascribes to Essad's gift for publicity.

AND so Erica left her colorful husband forever. Arriving in New York harbor she was detained by Ellis Island officials on moral turpitude charges, freeing out of the European publicity. They released her within 12 hours, into the custody of her parents.

The Lowendahl fortune was placed behind Erica's efforts to procure a divorce. In this she was successful. Simultaneously, Fülöp-Miller announced his plan to marry Erica as soon as he himself was free. "I love her," he declared. "We have worked together and struggled together. We expect to find some happiness at the end of the road."

Baron "Omar" Rolf von Ehrenfels.

Baroness Elfriede von Ehrenfels, listed in the 1939 Nazi book registry as the author of *Ali and Nino*.

Baron Omar-Rolf, in pajamas, in a 1920s home movie about leaving Europe to find himself in "the East."

Left: Lev in the last year of his life—an old man at thirty-five—with Giamil Vacca-Mazzara (the mysterious Muslim paratrooper who was actually a drug and weapons smuggler).

Below: Lev's tombstone in the cliffside cemetery in Positano, with panoramic views of the Amalfi coast, and facing Mecca.

Left: The final page of Lev's deathbed manuscript, signed "Kurban Said."

CHAPTER 14

Mussolini and Mrs. Kurban Said

"HAREM? YES—BUT SCARE 'EM? NO!" proclaimed the *Sunday Mirror Magazine,* January 2, 1938:

The broad-minded poetess didn't object to her Mohammedan Husband's having multiple wives—but when he insisted on reading her his horror stories, she fled to America—and a divorce.

Next to an enormous portrait of a soulful Erika (and a much smaller one of Lev, grimacing), the story went on gleefully:

Take one fez-wearing Mohammedan—survivor of countless revolutionary and counter revolutionary perils, intimate of the murdered Czar Nicholas, author and adventurer of highly original ideas about women and love—

And take one Czech poetess—dark, slim and lovely, with half a dozen volumes to her credit and a papa of unlimited means—

Also one fabulous, slightly mysterious Viennese literary gent, who wrote the sensational biography of one sinister Russian monk and was sued by another—

Stir well, allow to simmer awhile, serve forth piping hot—and you get a three-decker emotional finale that makes ordinary human relationships pallid indeed.

Erika had "zoomed into Bel Air, California," as the papers put it, and was living with a glamorous lover—a Viennese writer named René Fülöp-Miller, who had just sold a script to Clark Gable. And she was "starting divorce proceedings against her Mohammedan-Russian husband, Essad-Bey."

The New York *Daily News* described the breakdown of "a romance which Mme. Essad Bey once said would survive even if her Moslem husband decided to set up a harem." But, as the *Sunday Mirror* article put it, Erika found that the "accounts of wild doings which had thrilled her in print, failed to have the same charm . . . when performed in real life," and it went on to quote her: "He would bounce into the bedroom when I was there disrobed . . . and would lock the door screaming, 'You will never leave this room alive!' "

She complained, "He told me he was of princely Arabian lineage. I learned after our marriage in Berlin on March 7, 1932, that he was just plain Leo Nussinbaum!"

The articles in American newspapers, uniformly unflattering to Lev, may have been planted by Daddy Loewendahl, who by this point was living in Bel Air and putting his shoe money to work in Hollywood. (One tip-off to his role was the excessively flattering portrait they tended to paint of him as having been "once high in the Czechoslovakian diplomatic service and a partner of Bata, the Bohemian shoe king.") Erika's "fez-wearing" spouse was invariably dragged through the mud, along with his work—"The great Disunion in Vienna began shortly after Essad Bey had published his 'Blood and Oil,' a gruesome bit of literature."

The other side of the story was to be found in the French and Austrian tabloids: "Essad Bey [is] in Vienna where he is daily delivering communiqués to the press, charging that his wife was stolen from him by René Fülöp-Miller, world famous writer of biographies." But the Viennese reporting was actually pretty balanced. In October 1937, the *Neues Wiener Journal* published a his-hers account of the drama:

> Frau Erika, who interestingly is filing her case in Los Angeles through the Viennese lawyer Dr. Eduard Firschauer, reports, that among other things, she suffered from her husband's outbreaks of rage. If that wasn't enough, the writer, according to his wife's reports, had another unusual

habit. He loved to tell his wife the most frightful horror stories about torture. He forced her to listen to these things about which he himself gladly fantasized. Later, so Erika claims, she experienced honest fear for her life, since she claims that her husband would take a revolver in his hand and wave it about when he would experience one of his rages. It was difficult to tear the weapon away from him, at which point, according to Erika's statement, the writer would threaten her life.

What Essad Bey Says:

In response to the statements of his spouse, the author, who is represented by Dr. Ernst Konstantin Wender, claims [that it] is altogether untrue that he tends to have fits of raving madness. And there were no threats to speak of. As far as the horror stories are concerned, he claimed that Frau Erika was his secretary a year before they were married and that at that time he dictated his cultural-historical study entitled, "G.P.U. The History of the Red Terror." Even after their marriage Erika continued to work as his secretary and participated in the revision of the manuscript. He did nothing besides dictate that book.

What had happened to the happy-go-lucky household of Erika and Essad and Binks and Jay—the world where "Erica types, Essad declaims, Binks paints and Jay reworks a novel"? Throughout 1934 and into the beginning of 1935, Lev had been living the high life in Vienna as well as jet-setting around Europe with his lovely new wife. By early 1935, their trips to the United States were announced respectfully in *The New York Times*—CZAR'S BIOGRAPHER HERE: ESSAD BEY DECLARES LEADER WAS NOT UNDERSTOOD—something that would never be possible again after these tabloid stories hit. In these years "the Essads" had prestigious addresses in Vienna's classy "1st district," near the Opera House, the Kaiser's Palace, and St. Stephan's Cathedral.* (Though Lev lived the high life, he liked to spread

* I hunted down one of these, a 1930s modern *Hochhaus,* or small skyscraper, in the Herrengasse, less than a couple of blocks from both the famous Café Central and the Café Herrenhof, the cafés that were, respectively, symbols of pre- and postwar intellectual life. Many of the apartments had been turned into offices: appropriately enough, the gleaming brass plate attached to the apartment where Lev had once lived now announced it as a detective agency.

his money around to friends who had less of it. Perhaps it was a little bit of his mother's socialist tendencies—or his father's seignorial ones. He would send money, for example, to his down-and-out writer friend Joe Lederer in Italy, and to his former editor, Arthur Rosen, from *Die Literarische Welt.*)

Returning from his trip to America in the spring of 1935—probably his apotheosis as a writer and international social figure, with a respectful write-up of his social schedule appearing, along with an article explaining his "Oriental" tastes in women, in *Vanity Fair*—Lev suffered two shocks from which he would never quite recover. He got a letter from the German Writers Union stating that he was being expelled and could no longer publish in the Third Reich. No specific reason was given, but none needed to be. And Erika disappeared. Lev soon received a letter from her asking for a separation. She had started an affair with Fülöp-Miller, Lev's friend and competitor, who also wrote books about the East (see *Rasputin: The Holy Devil* and *Lenin and Gandhi*). Though he was rather dumpy-looking and lacked Lev's sheik persona, in truth he was much more of a ladies' man. Erika traveled all around Europe that summer with René, making Lev feel even more of a fool, since before, they had spent a great deal of time together as a couple with René and his wife, Heddy, an opera singer. Both Heddy and Lev were left steaming in Vienna as their spouses went on a sort of illicit cuckolding honeymoon together.

I wondered how the dark Hungarian with the half-lidded eyes, Fülöp-Miller, had come into the bright world of Binks and Jay and Ess and Ery. The one person who seemed to connect the dots was Lev's New York publisher, the editor in chief of Viking, Ben Huebsch. Huebsch traveled to Europe frequently and always took his star author Essad Bey out to dinner. His date books, on file at the Library of Congress, show that he saw more of Lev than almost any of his other writers, though they record "tea with Rebecca West," "Zweig for lunch," "must call back Emil Jannings regarding his film idea for Joseph Roth," "Werfel fetched me . . . to dinner. W. read from his new biblical drama." Curiously, though, since Huebsch's correspondence with hundreds of authors is all there in the archive, there was no folder for Essad Bey. There are files for people who wrote Huebsch only a single query letter—I was surprised to find one from my grandfather Alfred, who had proposed in 1943 writing a book on how handwriting analysis could shore up "sound individualism" and help Americans resist "totalitarian regimentation."* But the only scrap of paper with Essad's signature on it that I found in the entire Huebsch archive, after going through dozens of overstuffed folders, was a postcard sent from Vienna in 1933. It was a group postcard, signed with greetings to their favorite American editor from, among others, Essad Bey, Erika Essad Bey, and René Fülöp-Miller.

Alice Schulte recorded the following description of this sad period in her hagiographic handwritten memoirs of Lev:

> Mid 1930s: Essad is inexplicably left by his wife for an older married man, even though she is pampered by her husband. Three times he is saved by his "foster mother" [that is, Alice herself] from suicide. He is sent to a sanatorium near Berlin; after a few months he returns home, without having recovered completely. He undergoes psychoanalysis; the therapy is unsuccessful.

With Erika gone and his ability to publish in the ever expanding Reich revoked, Lev remained firmly ensconced at his regular table in Vienna's Café Herrenhof, whose smoky rooms had become the unofficial capital of literary exile Europe. In the mid-1930s, Essad Bey shared the place with regulars such as Max Brod, Franz Werfel, and Egon Erwin Kisch, all recent arrivals from Prague, as well as his friend from Berlin, Walter Mehring. The Herrenhof was the most dynamic of what the writer Stefan Zweig called the city's "democratic clubs."

Trying to forget his troubles by his old method of super production, Lev sat in the café all day, writing in his unique microscopic style, fitting quadruple the normal number of words on a page, working simultaneously on biographies of Czar Nicholas II, under his own name, and the one of the kaiser, under his friend Viereck's. He wrote long articles for a Caucasian exile journal in Paris and short ones for the Viennese "boulevard" press, particularly for the *Neues Wiener Journal*, the highbrow gossip

---

* To make his way as a refugee in the U.S., my grandfather, a profoundly serious and modest man, tried many ways to market his doctorates from Heidelberg, which conferred on him a somewhat obscure combined expertise in the fields of psychology, graphology, and phrenology. A 1939 spread he did for *True Confessions* magazine comes to mind: "Let Dr. Reiss Help You Choose Your Mate by Head Size," copiously illustrated with the skulls of happily married world leaders and movie stars.

sheet that covered developments in his own "scandalous" divorce from Erika. He also began writing novellas that were, curiously, published only in Poland—*Manuela* and *Mitosc i nafta* (*Love and Petroleum*)—and began forging the relationships for what would become his two most fateful projects. Lev met with Schendell, his old business manager from *Blood and Oil* days, in Prague to discuss these new projects. And he kept up the friendship with Jay and Binks Dratler; Jay helped him place his work in England.

Around this time, he took on a new agent, Hertha Pauli, perhaps as much because they shared coffee together at the Café Herrenhof as for any concrete financial reason. The tradition of literary agenting in Europe was—and remains—much less developed than it is in the United States. Schendell was Lev's editor and had become his business manager by default when *Blood and Oil* became a sensation. Pauli was a writer herself, and an attractive young woman who had originally trained as an actress. She was from Vienna—a scientific family, in fact, for when trying to track her down, I found that her brother, Wolfgang Pauli, had won the Nobel Prize in physics in 1945—but had moved to Berlin in the Golden Twenties at the invitation of the great theater director Max Reinhardt. Pauli left Berlin in 1933, when everyone else did, and moved back to Vienna. Years later, after *Ali and Nino* was reprinted in the 1970s, she would be one of the first people to write in to *The New York Times* with a suggestion about the identity of Kurban Said. She remembered meeting Lev—he "looked somewhat like King Hussein without the mustache"—and being charmed by his uniquely forthright wit. She recalled how Lev joined a writers' cooperative that she organized for authors banned in the Third Reich. (Lev's influence on Pauli can be found in her 1941 book, *Alfred Nobel: Dynamite King, Architect of Peace,* which contains lengthy descriptions of Baku not found in other biographies of the great inventor.) "Essad Bey was soon contributing numerous articles about the history and customs of his Transcaucasian homeland." While she would describe its heroic anti-Nazi stance, the cooperative in fact placed all kinds of work. For Thomas Mann, Pauli managed to place some political pieces; for Lev her main work consisted in selling his adventure stories, as well as negotiating at least one of the Kurban Said contracts, for a second novel, *The Girl from the Golden Horn.*

Pauli wrote that Essad Bey "never made a secret of his ancestry," and that this was a key part of his charm: "he spoke of it openly in his usual amusing fashion. This may have been why he wasn't publicly attacked during those years of rising anti-Semitism in Vienna." She would remember everyone listening rapt to Lev's tales about Stalin the highwayman as they sat around the Herrenhof. When she read *Ali and Nino* all those years later, in English translation in New York, she suddenly heard "Essad talking again in his particularly witty way."

At the end of his *annus terribilis,* Lev would begin collaborating on a book that would rival his work with Viereck for sheer peculiarity, and reveal yet another side of his developing self-image. It was to be a survey of the political resurgence of the Muslim world called *Allah Is Great: The Decline and Rise of the Islamic World.* What was strange was not the subject matter but Lev's choice of coauthor: he would share billing with Dr. Wolfgang von Weisl, now closely associated with Vladimir Jabotinsky, head of the hard-boiled right wing of the Zionist movement.

When I tracked down von Weisl's granddaughter in Jerusalem, she told me that her family believed that von Weisl—"the Jewish Lawrence of Arabia"—had written the Arab sections of the book, while Lev had written the "German and Turkish" sections. Although it's unclear exactly how they divided the labor, Lev was almost certainly the main author. The book's ideas are a late-1930s Jewish Orientalist take on the Middle East. Lev and von Weisl pick and choose what they like in Islam and romanticize a good deal, while remaining in the realm of "realistic" political assessments. To them, Islam remains a vital force so long as it is simultaneously "true to reason" and a "rider in the desert." They also believe that the real leaders of Islam were never the diplomats or the intellectuals but the primitive Bedouins and tribal warriors. Islam was able to conquer Christian lands in the seventh century because of its youth and vitality, succeeding because it was primitive and barbaric in contrast to the "luxurious" Christian world. Significantly for this Zionist-Islamist author team, Muhammad's victories were not the result of religious fervor alone, since many of his soldiers were nonbelievers (they point out that Muslim armies often included nomadic mercenaries).

Allah Is Great, despite the title, sold to a more specifically Jewish market than any of Lev's other books, which could be accounted for both by its dual authorship with a leading Zionist and also because German-speaking Jews, desperate to escape Nazi Europe, were looking to learn everything they could about the Middle East. Indeed, *Allah Is Great* was widely and positively reviewed in the Zionist press. As Eugen Hoeflich, alias Moshe Yaacov Ben-Gavriel, put it in the Jewish periodical *Der Morgen* in 1937, the book should be "recommended to Jewish readers, despite the fact that only a few lines are included that deal with Palestine," because of its overview of the resurgent Islamic world. Hoeflich, somewhat bitter after twenty years of trying in vain to institute "pan-Asiatic Zionism" and "pan-Semitic" solutions in the Middle East, uses the book as an occasion to criticize the obtuseness of his fellow Zionists to the problem of militant Islam. He hopes *Allah Is Great* will inform the Jews in the Holy Land about the great sleeping dragon they are sitting atop. *Die Jüdische Rundschau* also thought the book illuminated a subject that was an enormous brewing problem that the West, so preoccupied with its own power struggles, ignored at its peril. Almost everywhere the authors look—Turkey, Iran, Afghanistan, Morocco, Tunis, Algeria, Syria, Iraq, Egypt, and Arabia itself—European influences "are being curbed or eliminated entirely." As this review notes, Lev and von Weisl conclude that the Oriental nations "will bring many surprises in the coming years. They predict the loss of European colonial empires in Asia and the corresponding fear of an alliance of Islam with the yellow and brown races."

Allah Is Great concludes with advice and warning: since Europe clearly does not want to ensure its hegemony through undisguised force, there is no alternative but to form a "community of interests with the Islamic world, in which surplus energy, and youthful drive to be active with the help of Europe, will be directed against the East. If this fails—then woe to Europe!"

Lev and von Weisl had a great deal in common. Both enjoyed dressing up as Arabs or Turks (and both claimed to have been arrested after being mistaken for the " 'notorious' Colonel Lawrence").* Though pessimistic

---

* In October 1930 the wire services quoted the office of the *Vossische Zeitung* in Teheran as saying that its Near East correspondent had been arrested by the Persian authorities and kept in custody for ten days because the Persians "mistook Herr von Weisl for the 'notorious' Colonel Lawrence." The dispatch went on that von Weisl had "followed for years the same paths as Colonel Lawrence. In his Arab dress, armed with his short sword, he has visited Ibn Saud, King Feisal, and all the Arab leaders. . . . Unfortunately, the Persian frontier guard had, it is stated, just received orders to keep a sharp look-out for Colonel Lawrence. . . . The description on the warrant seemed to fit Herr von Weisl."

about Muslim-Jewish relations, Dr. von Weisl spoke fluent Arabic and knew the Muslim countries extremely well. When he first arrived in the Middle East, his dream was to convert the Arabs to Zionism, and in the early 1920s, he started a paper in Cairo printed half in German, half in Arabic, which he called *The Nile and Palestine Gazette.* He convinced the German legation in Egypt to fund the venture, which folded after just a few issues for lack of interest.

Like Hoeflich, von Weisl had served with the Imperial Austrian Army during the First World War. But von Weisl was a hardier and less dreamy type, an artillery officer who was later trained as a physician. (After 1948 he would serve as commander of the Israeli artillery force in the Negev Desert.) Some of the best portraits of him are to be found in the first volume of Arthur Koestler's brilliant memoir, *Arrow in the Blue.* Koestler, who dabbled in Zionism, offers a rather bleak portrait of the early movement but a glowing, almost worshipful portrait of its "Jewish Lawrence." Koestler met von Weisl in 1924, when the ex-artillery man was working as the Middle East correspondent for Vienna's *Neue Freie Presse.* They were alumni of the same Jewish fencing fraternity, Unitas, and hence had both chosen to confront anti-Semitism by proving their fighting prowess—in some ways the perfect preparation for active Zionism.

Von Weisl's early journalism is full of prescient observations of the Middle East power struggle. His article called "Islam's Iconoclasts at Mekka's Gates," published in the fall of 1924, warned of the growing power of the Wahhabis in Arabia, and stated that "Hussein will have reason to regret that he refused to sign the Anglo-Hejaz Treaty, and to recognize the Jewish rights in Palestine. For Jews in Erez Israel—Israel—are far less dangerous enemies for him than are Wahhabis at the gates of Mekka." He also gives a good picture of the profound chaos unleashed in Muslim countries in 1924 by Ataturk's sudden abolition of the caliphate, an institution they had superficially not taken much notice of but which was central to a Muslim's whole identity.

If you look up the name "von Weisl" today in the *Dictionary of Austrian Literature in Exile,* you will find a staggering error, especially considering that lexicons and dictionaries are practically a high art form in German-speaking countries. The entry merges Essad Bey and Wolfgang von Weisl into one person. It explains that "Wolfgang (von) Weisl" also used the pseudonyms Leo Noussimbaum, Essad Bey, and Kurban Said—and hence the Austrian journalist, who otherwise had only a travel book and a book on Austrian artillery to his credit, suddenly was the prolific author of approximately twenty works of fiction and nonfiction prose. But even better, Lev Nussimbaum, alias Essad Bey/Kurban Said, suddenly becomes one of the founding leaders of the Zionist movement, and then an Israeli officer in the Negev Desert.

In the Austrian National Library sits the 1935 French edition of Lev's biography of Czar Nicholas II. It happens to be an inscribed copy. On the front flyleaf—in German and in *Hebrew*—Lev writes the following note to an unidentified person with whom he feels some sad affinity: "to my fellow sufferer / from Essad Bey / expelled / forsaken / betrayed / becoming mindless? E.B."

It was during this period of trying to emerge from his despair that Lev first got the idea of making himself into "Kurban Said"—"joyful sacrifice." This new pen name would allow Essad Bey, now banned in the Third Reich, to go on publishing there. But it would also be a liberation from Lev's persona as a nonfiction writer. In 1936 he began working for ten to twelve hours a day on a novel set in the Caucasus. He would later recall to Pima that there had been only two times "that I thought neither of the publishing company, nor of royalties, but just wrote happily away. These were the books *Stalin* and *Ali and Nino*."

Had he lived, "Kurban Said" might have produced many wonderful books, for Lev took intricate, good-humored delight in his new role as a novelist: "The heroes of the novel simply come to me demanding, 'Give us shape'—'we also possess certain characteristics that you've left out and we want to travel, among other things.'"

But there was the matter of Baroness Elfriede—or Baroness Kurban Said, as we might call her. Or, simply, Mrs. Kurban Said. I got my first introduction to Mrs. Kurban Said when I met the publisher who was trying to bring *Ali and Nino* back into print—Peter Mayer, of the Overlook Press—and wound up accompanying him to Vienna for his meeting with Dr. Heinz Barazon, the lawyer of Baroness Elfriede's heirs. We sat in the lawyer's book-lined apartment and looked at Nazi contracts together, trying to reenter the world of 1938 Vienna through the strange keyhole of this interracial love story and its elusive author. The gaunt and beautiful Leela von Ehrenfels lay on the couch, like a misplaced character from Proust, embellishing the lawyer's explanations in a faint voice that seemed about to disappear into the dusty air. (Whenever I think of Leela, I recall the little device she later described to me that she used to "whirl" her tap water at home—necessary because we were all being weakened by the effects of drinking water that was not in its natural, whirling state.)

With his client looking on, Dr. Barazon hefted down stuffed folders full of documents that backed up their case: legal papers and books-in-print lists from the late 1930s with Nazi eagles and swastikas stamped all over them. The family relations may have been complicated, but the story told by the names on the documents was simple. On page 1556 of the *Deutscher Gesamtkatalog* for the years 1935–39, the following two entries appeared:

Ehrenfels v. Bodmershof, Elfriede, Baronin [Baroness]—*Ali und Nino,* Roman [novel]. Von Kurban Said [d.i. Baronin Elfriede Ehrenfels v. Bodmershof].—Wien, Leipzig: Tal 1937.

Ehrenfels v. Bodmershof, Elfriede, Baronin [Baroness]—Kurban Said [d.i. Baroness Elfriede Ehrenfels v. Bodmershof]. *Das Mädchen vom Goldenen Horn.* Roman. [novel.]—Wien, Leipzig: Zinnen-Verlag 1938.

The latter entry referred to the second Kurban Said novel, *The Girl from the Golden Horn,* which Dr. Barazon said that he thought Elfriede had had an even greater hand in writing than *Ali and Nino.* He believed that while Kurban Said was listed as Elfriede's pen name, the name actually represented some sort of collaboration between the baroness and her friend and houseguest Essad Bey.

There was also a contract, dated April 20, 1937, between the publishing firm E. P. Tal & Co., Vienna, and Baroness Elfriede Ehrenfels von Bodmershof, Schloss Lichtenau, for a book called *Der Sterbende Orient—The Dying Orient.* Dr. Barazon explained that this had been the working title for *Ali and Nino.* Another document announced the sale of the Czech rights to the novel, now referred to as *Ali and Nino,* on June 7, 1938. While the first contract was signed by the company's owner in a loose, loopy hand—"Tal"—beneath the traditional salutation *hochachtungsvoll,* "with great respect," the second was signed by someone else, a certain Alfred Ibach, beneath the Nazi-era greeting *Mit deutschem Gruss,* a milder way of saying *Heil Hitler!* Dr. Barazon explained that this Alfred Ibach had been the "Aryanizer" of the Tal firm (much as Frau Theresa Mögle had "Aryanized" Lev's other Vienna publisher, the Passer firm).

I wondered aloud whether Elfriede couldn't have, in a sense, been the "Aryanizer" of Kurban Said, taking over responsibility for this pen name from Essad Bey because the latter was actually Lev Nussimbaum, a Jew. She could have been doing it as a favor to her friend, much as some non-writers "fronted" for writers with communist pasts in the McCarthy era. Leela seemed visibly distressed by the suggestion, and Dr. Barazon has-tened to point out that as the contracts were first signed in the spring of 1937, almost a full year before the Nazis marched into Austria, there could have been no reason to "Aryanize" Kurban Said. I tried testing further speculation about the collaboration between Elfriede and Essad Bey, but as Leela seemed on the verge of fainting, I let it drop.

I asked Leela about her father—in the mid-1920s, Dr. Barazon had ex-plained, Baron Rolf changed his name to Omar and converted to Islam—and about his friendship with Essad Bey. "I think you should speak with my mother; she knows much more about Essad Bey and my father and Aunt Elfriede than I do," Leela said. "But I should warn you, she's a slightly unusual person."

Leela's mother, the baron's third wife, lives in the Waldviertel, the "woods region" of Austria—an inhospitable little corner of the country near the Czech border. Leela had said that because her mother was quite reclusive and kept an odd schedule, one had to spend the night at her castle, Schloss Lichtenau, if one were really going to interview her. Besides, there were a great many documents up there that I might find of interest. I was late leaving Vienna, and the castle was lit by early moonlight when I drove up, making the high stone walls appear magical against the ice-blue twilight. I opened the gate and walked in. "Good evening!" I shouted a few times into the darkness, but when there was no reply, I went back down to the village to find a phone. The people in the inn I went to looked at me the way people drinking beer in the middle of absolute nowhere will, but someone dialed the number, and after a couple of rings, a bubbly French accent sang out, "But where are you? I have been *waaait*-ing for hours!"

Fifteen minutes later, the baroness, a robust woman with brown eyes and a mass of white hair, was showing me around the dank stone passageways of Castle Lichtenau. Through a heavy wooden door, we entered a room that was at least three centuries further along in cultural evolution than the hallways. It had Oriental carpets, a pianoforte, and a ceiling-high ceramic stove, not to mention a fax machine. The baroness offered me a bit of cheese, with many apologies that the lady who cooked for her had "not shown up in days," and escorted me to a small set of rooms done up like a cell in a very elegant Renaissance cloister. She asked me if I could "survive here" and excused herself in a flurry. It was 7 P.M., she said—long past her bedtime.

Five hours later, just past midnight, I was awakened by the tinny sounds of a rock opera echoing through the castle. The source of the sound was on the other side of the grand salon. I heard mild cursing and muttering in high-pitched French behind a door, along with what sounded like a Central European version of *Miss Saigon,* and then, "Aha? Ah-ha! Ahh-haaaa!"

I knocked.

The music suddenly stopped, and the French voice called for me to *entrez.* The baroness was sitting up on her bed surrounded by piles of sheet music. On a carved oak chest next to the bed sat a battered silver boom box. She looked up at me and said, "Do you know something about musicals?" I asked her what she meant. "Have you seen one?" I said of course I had seen one, but not in a long time. "I have never seen one," she said, full of genuine anguish. "But I am fascinated! Absolutely fascinated!" She explained that she was writing the French text for a rock musical being put on by an Israeli-German team from Frankfurt, some people she'd met during a trip with her son to sell Berber art; she had fallen in love with their work and insisted on becoming involved with the production. The problem, she said, was that she had never seen a musical in her life. "How could I? I never had time—I was either in India or fixing up the castle here."

At her request, I found myself singing bits of *On the Town, Singing in the Rain,* and *Camelot,* to give her some idea of what musicals sounded like.

The baroness explained that she always awoke and began her workday at midnight, and that usually she insisted on not being disturbed until well after 6 A.M., but since I had come all this way to find out about her husband and Elfriede and Essad Bey, she would talk with me about it at

4 A.M. Until then, however, she had to concentrate. So I left her with her music and went back to my cell.

The baroness came into my room sometime just before dawn, the peaked window by the desk still black except for the icicles. We had tea and cheese for breakfast, on the settee in the main salon, and she began to tell me about how her husband and his former wife, Elfriede, became absorbed in the East.

"They were called the Band of Four," she began, referring to her former husband, Baron Omar-Rolf; his sister, Imma; his second wife, Elfriede (aka Kurban Said); and Elfriede's brother, Willi. The relationships were hard to pin down, but basically, a brother and a sister born von Ehrenfels (Rolf and Imma) had married a brother and a sister von Bodmershof (Willi and Elfriede) so that Imma and Elfriede essentially exchanged last names. They'd all grown up together in neighboring ancestral castles in the Waldviertel and in Prague, when it was still a Hapsburg city. The two young men fought in the Great War, but only Willi saw a lot of action, on the eastern front, which may have been part of the reason he got so stuck on a German guru named Bo Yin Ra and then convinced the others to become acolytes as well.

It was the early 1920s, and they didn't know what to do with themselves. Imma actually wrote an open letter to Hermann Hesse in the *Prager Tagblatt* asking for advice: "I wanted to write you, dear Meister," she wrote, "for not only did I encounter in your 'book'—as we refer to it in this world of sign-language—many a dear old friend, but the two of us must have encountered one another as well. When in the deep solitude of the forest, with my philosopher/life-partner, who had become emotionally disturbed over the war, I was reading. . . . Was it not you who passed and gave the both of us a brief, warm handshake?" While other Austrians were finding their answers on the extreme left or right, this Band of Four in the Waldviertel looked to the Orient.

Rolf and Imma Ehrenfels' father, Christian von Ehrenfels, had been a prominent philosopher, a founder of the Gestalt theory of psychology, and a regular correspondent with Freud. But Rolf and Imma's parents had also been part of the anti-Semitic circle around Cosima Wagner in Bayreuth, and Grandpa Ehrenfels had developed some unique ideas about racial engineering. His pet peeve was that some of the best men in a race were its soldiers, hence the finest genetic stock was lost in battle. His solution was to propose that brave soldiers returning from the front have sexual access to as many women as possible. Largely because of such ideas, which he called "racial cosmogony," Christian von Ehrenfels never became the household name he should have been, but he was a beloved professor at the university in Prague. "Kafka wrote in one of his diaries that it was quite amusing to go to Ehrenfels's class with his wonderful bald head and his wonderful voice," recalled the baroness, "and Kafka said it was so amusing because on that morning, Ehrenfels said that one of the best things you can have in your blood is a few drops of Jewish blood." This had apparently been a great plus for the family's de-Nazification when they'd found mention of it in the writer's diaries. Old Christian von Ehrenfels may have been an insane racialist, but he hadn't been an anti-Semite.

Elfriede and Rolf married, the baroness thought, mostly in order to keep the Band of Four together, and by the late 1930s, the marriage broke apart. During the war, Omar-Rolf went to India, and Elfriede went to Greece, where she made her living reading horoscopes; she began studying ancient Greek and mathematics and developed an obsession with Plato. After the war, while Baron Omar was in India with his new wife (the current rock-opera-composing baroness), Elfriede lived in Lichtenau alone, reading Plato all day long. In the 1970s, when Omar-Rolf and the baroness returned from the East, they found the *Schloss* a ruin: the putative author of *Ali and Nino* had turned the part of the castle she occupied into a garbage dump of balled-up math equations, horoscope readings, notes on Plato, and household refuse. The baroness recalled trying to clean behind the settee we were now sitting on, but when she attempted to move it, Elfriede got very upset. "She said it has been thirty-five years that it has not been shifted, and it should not be shifted! Nevertheless, we moved it, and we got something like thirty or forty mice. Totally filled with them." Elfriede had made her kitchen off the main sitting room, where she kept a little stove and an old encyclopedia that she used as a cutting board. "At the end she cared only for her beloved Plato," the baroness said of the woman she maintained was the author of *Ali and Nino.* "Anything else was uninteresting."

It was sometime in the early 1970s that the baroness remembers getting the first inkling that Elfriede had once been Kurban Said. One day Baron Omar-Rolf's sister, Imma, by then quite a well-known haiku poet in Austria, told the baroness that she had "received a funny letter, some doctor wanted to know if I'd written a book call *Ali and Nino.*" She didn't know anything about it, but on the off chance, the baroness asked Elfriede about it, and Elfriede, pulling her head out of Plato for a moment, said, "Naturally, Immi does not need to know everything. Yes, I produced it."

"Then someone called Elfriede to ask her to rayad-it."

"To what? To read it?" I asked.

"To raaaay-yaaad it."

"To publish it?"

"No, to raaay-adit it."

"They wanted to re-edit it!"

"Exactly," said the baroness, smiling. But she recalled that Elfriede would have nothing to do with them, because she was terribly afraid of making any sort of money that might cause her to lose her state pension.

It was now late morning and the baroness was ready for a nap. Saying she would give me something to do while she was sleeping, she led me down a series of passageways that got more decrepit and freezing as we went, until we came to a battered old wooden door. She rammed her shoulder against it. Inside was what at first glance looked like the baggage room in an old train station—wall-to-wall boxes, trunks, suitcases, and bags, some in stacks reaching up to the ceiling, with two aisles cleared for walking.

"It is all here, all of the Ehrenfels family," she said, looking a bit sadly at the sea of containers. "But you can only look in here until the sun goes down, for there is not a light." So saying, she left me to roam in the baggage. It was not until I had poked around for almost an hour that I realized that seemingly every suitcase and steamer trunk was filled with some kind of paper. This medieval fortress, which had survived sieges by the Swedes and still had holes in its walls for pouring boiling oil, had been inhabited for at least the last two centuries by a family of intellectuals, poets, and bookworms.

I was trying to find anything relating to "Kurban Said," and hoped in such a setting that Nietzsche's dictum would apply—that the books I needed would jump off the shelves at me. Wherever I looked, though, I found mostly piles of documents relating to Rolf—Omar, after his conversion—and his strange forty-year ride through the Islamic world, beginning with some photographs taken of him at eleven or twelve in a turban twice the size of his head.

My "ticket" into this world was a telegram from December 21, 1932, that read, BARON OMAR ROLF EHRENFELS TAJMAHAL HOTEL BOMBAY= EIGHTY MILLION INDIAN MUSLIM BRETHREN WELCOME YOUR LORDSHIP= SECY SHUJAUDDIN MUSLIM LEAGUE PUNJAB. An article in *The Eastern Times* of Lahore a few days later described what must have been a truly bizarre reception:

> Omar Rolf Baron Ehrenfels, the Austrian convert to Islam, arrived here this morning by Frontier Mail. . . . The [train] platform was packed to its fullest capacity and it is estimated that there were not less than five thousand Muslims both inside and outside the station to pay their homage to their great Brother . . . [who] was taken out of the station amid lusty cheers of Allah-o-Akbar.

There were countless copies of magazines like *The Muslim Review* and *The Light,* to which Baron Omar-Rolf regularly contributed articles on prospects for world Islamic revival, the state of Muslim women, and interfaith healing between Muslims and Jews. While looking over them, I discovered a whole world of Orientalists and converts with names like Lord Headly al-Farooq, Major Abdullah Battersbey, and Her Highness the Dayang Muda of Sarawak, "the daughter of the late Sir Walter Palmer of Reading." There was Muhamud Gunnar Erikson from Sweden, Omar Mita from Japan, and Ismail Wieslaw Jazierski from Poland.

There was so much fascinating stuff to read about Baron Omar that it was a while before it dawned on me that the castle was yielding nothing at all about Kurban Said, whether Lev, Elfriede, or some combination of them both. According to the baroness, Essad Bey and her husband had corresponded frequently, as had Essad and Elfriede. But when I asked where this correspondence was, she pointed around the walls of the castle and said, "Who can tell? Perhaps it is here somewhere, but to find it!"

The only concrete connection between the von Ehrenfels family and Essad Bey that I found was the one thing I had brought with me: a Swiss edition of the second Kurban Said novel, *The Girl from the Golden Horn,* which had a brief introduction written by Baron Omar Ehrenfels: "As a young man I founded the 'Orient-Bund' for Afro-Asian students in Vienna and through it I became friends with the quietly observing Azerbaijani Kurban Said. . . . My way brought me shortly after that to India, from where I returned to Europe for the first time in 1954 and immediately went to visit the traditional Muslim grave of my then apparently forgotten friend which stood outside the wall of the cemetery in Positano."

I asked the baroness why Omar, at this late date, was referring to Kurban Said as an Azeri man who died in Italy rather than as his ex-wife, Elfriede. The baroness assured me that her late husband had simply never discussed the matter with Elfriede and therefore did not know of her great involvement. She repeated Dr. Barazon's theory that perhaps there had been a sexual relationship between Elfriede and Lev, but said "that's only his theory, we don't know a thing for sure."

A likely explanation for Elfriede's connection to Kurban Said first presented itself to me a few weeks after I visited the castle. I received an envelope from Dr. Barazon containing copies of four letters that he said the baroness had instructed him to forward to me. They were all addressed to Omar and signed in a small, looping hand, "Essad." They bore the return address "Casa Pattison, Positano"—the house where Essad Bey died in 1942. The first was dated July 21, 1938, and in it Lev is trying to entice Baron Omar-Rolf to come visit him, professing his loneliness and sense of disorientation. He then writes, "I had American Express Athens send 200 dollars from Yugoslavia in the name of Mrs. Kurban Said."

Mrs. Kurban Said. Of course, it had to be Elfriede.

In a letter dated September 8, Lev again refers to Kurban Said in the third person, and it sounds more and more like a cover name for transferring sums of money across international borders: "At the Publisher Gesa Kon, Belgrade. . . . An additional 150 dollars is being held there for Kurban Said. Can Kurban Said pick up this money on the way through? And how can one contact her? . . . Write me about this as soon as you can and have Kurban Said get in touch with the publisher." It is as though she were going to a publisher to pick up money she doesn't know anything about.

By September 21, 1940, Lev would write to Pima recommending she buy a copy of *Ali and Nino* herself, bragging that it was his favorite of his own books and explaining that it could still be published everywhere, since "according to the law on pseudonyms, K.S. is a woman! A young

Viennese baroness, who is even a member of the *Kulturkammer!*," the German Writers' Union from which Lev had been expelled.

The correspondence with Pima reveals Lev's relationship to "Mrs. Kurban Said" in great if oblique detail—as early as May 1940, Lev wrote of Elfriede that "the poor woman is an astrologer but she seems to have grown insane"—yet he depended on her for his livelihood. Well before I discovered the Essad-Pima correspondence, the few letters Lev wrote to Elfriede made it seem almost certain that Kurban Said was a cover for him so that he could continue to receive royalties from his work. Dr. Barazon had maintained that Elfriede would not have needed to provide an Aryan cover for the real author of *Ali and Nino,* because the book contract was signed in April 1937, almost a full year before the Nazi Anschluss of Austria. But in fact Jewish authors already had plenty of reasons to disguise their identity.

Dr. Murray Hall, an expert on publishing in the Nazi period, met me for coffee at the König von Ungarn Hotel, just off the Stefansplatz, where the largest spontaneous demonstration in Austrian history was held—to celebrate the Anschluss and Hitler's surprise tour of the city—in the spring of 1938. Dr. Hall was a Canadian with a peculiarly mild-mannered approach to unearthing some of the most disturbing moments in Austrian history. He had made a sort of subspecialty of studying intellectuals persecuted in the pre-Nazi era, and we discussed his fascinating work on the assassination of Hugo Bettauer, the writer and editor whose dystopian 1923 novel, *Die Stadt Ohne Juden* (*The City Without Jews*), remains one of the most uncanny predictions of a historic catastrophe ever written. The premise is that the Austrian anti-Semites unite into a single voting bloc, take power, and banish the Jews from Vienna. What the novel portrays is basically the reality of Vienna today: one of the world's great cities robbed of its lifeblood, reduced to a bland provincial capital filled with beautiful old buildings. At the novel's end, the anti-Semites are so bored by the city they create—the lack of culture or decent entertainment, for there is only so much *volks* dancing and lederhosen one can take, as well as the lack of anyone to blame for their problems—that they invite all the Jews back. That reality would turn out differently from the novel was foreshadowed by Bettauer's own fate shortly after he published it. In 1925 he was murdered by a Nazi fanatic who resented the message of feminism and sexual liberation promoted by a magazine he was editing at the time.

Dr. Hall explained to me the basics of getting published in Nazi Europe: Austrian publishers, the majority of whom were Jewish, had found themselves in a bind ever since Hitler came to power, in 1933. There were three markets for books published in the German language—Austria, Germany, and Switzerland—and Germany's was much larger than the other two markets combined (and remains so). It wasn't profitable to publish a book if you could not sell it in Germany, so Austrian publishers needed to get their books past the Nazi censors to reach the majority of the German-reading public. In order to confuse the censors, fake subsidiary houses were established in third countries like Holland or Sweden, and books were printed in one country, bound in the next, and then shipped across multiple borders before making it into the Reich. (Tal, the publisher of *Ali and Nino,* engaged in such subterfuge.) Another solution was to have authors use cover names.

In *The Lost Library,* Lev's friend Walter Mehring wrote, "The threat of the avalanche hung over Vienna and all the rest of Austria." In the novel, he imagines a metaphoric library, his father's, as a storehouse of all the culture that was destroyed by the Nazis and their totalitarian revolution:

> In front of the St. Stephan's Cathedral, where funeral bells and Bach's toccata and fugue on the organ called "dying Vienna" to the last midnight mass, some young ruffians shouted out anticapitalist, anticlerical and anti-Semitic obscenities—extracts from those trashy books and pamphlets which you, Father, had kept in the "poison cupboard" as cultural curiosities, and which I had read in secret.
>
> "Tomorrow," I heard one young fellow say, "we'll string them all up: the blacks and the reds and the Yids; we'll take care of the ones with a lot of books first."
>
> And I did not breathe easy until I had shut the door behind me, and saw my father's library before me again.

Lev's agent, Hertha Pauli, remembered the Anschluss through the professional lens of her trade—the week Hitler arrived in Austria was the same week Blanche Knopf had come scouting for new authors and books. Mrs. Knopf had been shown the new Kurban Said novel, *Ali and Nino,* but perhaps because of sudden distractions, she did not buy it. On Friday,

March 11, 1938, the day before the führer announced the formal annexation of Austria, Pauli remembered that "from the Hotel Bristol on the Ring, Vienna's grand boulevard, you normally get to the Herrenhof in ten minutes. Not on that eleventh of March, though. 'When the Ring is blocked, there's revolution,' the Viennese have been saying since 1918. This time the police barricade had gone up because young [Nazis] were demonstrating round the State Opera, bellowing, 'Heil Hitler.' . . . I managed to duck into a house, found another exit, and emerged across the street from the Herrenhof."

Mehring would meet Pauli in Paris, where they would both stay until they were trapped again by the Nazi invasion in the spring of 1940. Fleeing south after that, Pauli would eventually introduce Mehring, now her lover, to that lone hope of Europe's intellectual and artistic refugees, the young prep-school dropout Varian Fry. Fry had arrived in Marseilles in the summer of 1940 on a brilliant one-man mission to spirit Europe's refugee intellectuals and artists to safety by whatever means possible. He had no official sanction, merely $3,000 and a list of two hundred of Europe's greatest intellectuals and artists taped to his leg. The money and the list came from a group of concerned citizens in New Jersey, cobbled together after the fall of France, called the Emergency Rescue Committee.* Pauli would later recall the first time she visited the Hotel Splendide to see the man everyone in Marseilles simply called "the American": "Well, Miss Pauli," said Fry, "I've got you on my list. . . . Bring Mehring with you tomorrow. Au revoir."

* After he graduated from Harvard in the early 1930s, an assignment as a freelance journalist had taken Fry to Berlin, where he'd witnessed the persecution of the Jews and had a chilling chat with his fellow Crimson man, Ernst Hanfstaengel—the ubiquitous Putzi—who had tipped him off about rumors within the Nazi hierarchy for the mass murder of the Jews. Fry tried to publicize the Holocaust, but he was hindered at every step by the U.S. government. Fry personally escorted Franz Werfel, Alma Mahler, and Heinrich Mann over the Pyrenees, risking his own life at every turn. Almost two thousand refugees, including Hannah Arendt and Marc Chagall, owed their lives to him. He set up contacts with the French Resistance and the Corsican mob, hired forgers, and bribed border guards. My uncle Lolek's old friend Carel, who fled the Nazis by bicycling from occupied Paris to Marseilles, helped Fry run this underground railway. Growing up, I would play checkers at the headquarters of the International Rescue Committee, the successor of Fry's organization, where Carel continued to help refugees from around the world for five decades after the war.

When asked how he had escaped the Nazis, Mehring would later say, "I walked to the left when everyone else walked to the right and I kept on walking." In fact, he caused the greatest trouble to the implacable Fry: the American obtained forged papers for Mehring, but Lev's old friend got himself arrested while changing trains near the Spanish border; Fry then managed to get the Jewish cabaretist out of a concentration camp and the hands of the Vichy authorities by claiming that Eleanor Roosevelt was personally concerned for his safety. Eventually, Mehring would make it to Hollywood, where he would meet up with Lev and Erika's old Vienna roommates, Jay and Binks, who certainly got around. Jay was leveraging his Vienna connections into a successful Hollywood career, and he was happy to lend a hand to members of the old gang.*

Later that month, Lev would write to Baron Omar, who had made it to Greece. "Mimi Piekarski is in London, where much to the amazement of all who knew her she earns her own living," he managed to joke, and then informed Omar of a program a lady told him about whereby "some sort of committee . . . arranges [English visas] and one-year stays in English castles for Austrians. She unfortunately wasn't able to help me at all, since I'm not Austrian." But he advised Baron Omar to look into it. Lev bleakly contemplated the fate of his friends—the world of agents, editors, and writers whom he'd regaled at the Herrenhof with his tales and adventures—who were now "scattered throughout the whole world. . . . I do not know when or how I will ever see them again." His Viennese publishers were also gone. Lucy Tal escaped the day after the Anschluss, just beating the Gestapo agents to the train west (leaving her firm in the hands of Dr. Ibach). Rolf Passer, who had published *Allah Is Great* and Lev's biography of the shah, fled via Prague to London (leaving his company to Frau Mögle). "Zweig and Werfel are in London," Lev wrote to Omar. "Mehring, Pauli, Passer . . . in Paris." He asked if Omar had heard "anything about a man by the name of Alex Sacher-Masoch"—the son of the

---

* Recall that Jay and Lev used to race to see who could write the most words each morning. In the U.S., Jay turned out a string of novels while also writing such classic film noirs as *Laura, The Dark Corner,* and *Call Northside 777,* and working as a script doctor for Fritz Lang, Otto Preminger, and others. His first novel stateside, in 1940, was a roman à clef about "a young American's intrepid rescue of his best friend's sweetheart from the Nazi bloodhounds of Vienna" that is a dark fictionalization of what indeed happened to Lev, Hertha, Binks, and their whole circle. Unfortunately no genius for titles, Dratler called his novel *Ducks in Thunder.*

man for whom the term "masochism" was coined—"and his wife? And what has become of him?"

Every day, Jews jumped out of the windows of *hochhauses* like the one where Ery and Lev lived. Beyond his wildest imagination, Bettauer's satirical novel was coming true, but with brutality. Vienna was becoming *die Stadt Ohne Juden.*

One old Jew remained there: Abraham Nussimbaum, who had not been able to get out. Elfriede promised to go sit with him in his apartment when they had news that the Gestapo were making roundups, to offer whatever protection her Aryan status and noble title might afford. Lev himself seems to have left Vienna by this point, though it's unclear why he left his father behind. He would turn up next in Italy, in even more bizarre circumstances than usual, sometime in the spring of 1938.

In a seedy neighborhood in Los Angeles, in the back of a house stuffed with cats, snakes, gerbils, and every other living creature, I found an ancient woman named Franzie Baumfeld, who had once been a movie starlet, in the late 1930s ("Greta Garbo—Garbo!" she shouted in her Berlin accent. "That bitch took a great man away from me—he was a great lover, you understand, and she made him fall in love with her! Lost interest in me right away!") Franzie had been Erika's best friend, and the main witness in the trial against Essad. I flew out to Los Angeles to see her in the spring of 2001, but it was too late. Franzie was there, but she wasn't there. "Essad Bey! You want to know about that @#$@%(#$!*#?! I wouldn't talk about that (@*#)$(*@ if he was the last @###@*$)@*#! on this planet! What's a nice boy like you want to write about a @#($%*!@@! like him. We stuck it to him, we did, got him good, that @*(#$@!#@! He liked Mussolini, you know!" she shouted at me in the near-pitch darkness of her kitchen, where she sat on a stool surrounded by cats.

"What are you going to talk to a @#$*##@)! who likes Mussolini? Hey, watch out, are the turtles getting out!? Are all the doors closed? Because if the turtles get out, I'll never get them back again, you got it?!"

Franzie was incoherent, but she had a point about Mussolini.

In fact, the article that had made me aware of her role in the Essad-Erika mess appeared in the French newspaper *L'Intransigeant* (*"Le Journal de Paris"*), on November 3, 1937, and was titled: *"Scandale mondain en Autriche: Toute la societe viennoise se passionne pour un process sensationnel dont un biographe de Mussolini tient la vedette."* It posed the usual questions—*"Qui a raison, de la femme ou du mari?"*—but it was the ID in the title that grabbed me: "a biographer of Mussolini."

In 1937, after he'd completed his books with Viereck and von Weisl, and *Ali and Nino,* as well as penning another pair of books "for friends," Lev had managed to get himself invited as Mussolini's official biographer. His quest to acquire this commission had been obsessive and waged on numerous fronts, and it did not have a happy ending. Dozens of letters in archives in Florence and Rome tell the full story of his campaign.

In early 1936, from his bohemian base in Vienna, Lev began making trips to Fascist Italy, where he cultivated a circle of what might be called "liberal" Fascists who still held great sway around Mussolini.* Though Lev had once disdained dictatorship as exhibiting "all the drawbacks of a monarchy and not a single one of its advantages," by the mid-1930s he'd become more and more enamored of fascism. His early experience in Rome, watching the young Fascist marchers, had always stayed with him as a sign that Mussolini's movement could push back the specter of Stalin. Now, in the late 1930s, Mussolini and the Italian Fascists took on the bizarre role of defenders against Hitler and the Nazis as well—not only for Lev but for many Jews. Lev certainly heard something of this attitude from his friend von Weisl, who had been praising the Fascist Italian presence in the Middle East since the 1920s. For in the '20s and '30s, in the days before the fatal Pact of Steel alliance between Mussolini and Hitler, the Italian dictator promised the holy grail of a "Third Way" between the nightmares of Nazism and communism and the apparent weakness of the Western democracies. Many believed that Mussolini could moderate Nazism and use the alliance among Fascists to steer the Nazis away from the racial policies.

Lev's most important ally in gaining approval for the project was Gio-

---

* During this period Lev also traveled to the Italian colony of Libya, where his idol Italo Balbo, the barnstorming founder of the Italian Air Force, was busy creating a bizarre futurist experiment in the desert where race cars and antique cavalry processions shared the streets, and cooperation between Jews and Muslims was enforced in the name of Fascist brotherhood. The dashing rival to Mussolini would fall increasingly out of favor in the late 1930s, especially after he vehemently opposed the Duce's pact with Hitler and refused to implement the anti-Jewish measures in Libya. Balbo died in a mysterious plane crash in 1940, which many believed was murder.

vanni Gentile, the head of the Sansoni publishing house and a member of the Fascist Grand Council. The most prominent Italian intellectual to join with Mussolini, Gentile was one of his closest advisers and had been the architect of some of the most important Fascist laws. In June 1937, Gentile wrote requesting a personal audience with the Duce for Essad Bey and offering to vouch for him; Lev may have paid a visit to Mussolini's office, for in the files of the Ministry of Popular Culture in Rome I found a small notecard, dated July 3, 1937, written in Lev's distinctive schoolboy script:

His Excellency
Benito Mussolini
Chief of the Italian Government
with deepest respect
Essad-Bey

But only a day earlier, on July 2, Mussolini's secretary received a long letter from a man who claimed he had heard about the proposed project "from a friend" who had recently been introduced to Essad Bey at the Treves publishing house, and wrote "it is important that the *Duce* knows that this gentleman who makes people believe that he is of Azeri origin and the son of a Muslim, and of a Russian nihilist, but is nothing else but Leo Nussimbaum, son of Abraham." In the files of the Fascist Political Police in Rome, I found similar letters from an informant in Vienna, passing along the latest Gestapo revelations about the man "masquerading as Essad Bey."

These were the old denunciations, only in 1937 they carried far more impact than they had in 1929. And the letter went further than previous "outings," claiming that Lev's entire Oriental disguise was part of a grand Jewish conspiracy to present "a fantastic threatening Islamic world, which would be dangerous for Western civilization, for progress and all of Europe, with the evident goal, however well masked, to help his brothers in Palestine." The author concludes with a thin apology for bearing bad news but writes that since "it is about the *Duce,* whose person is sacred for every Italian, I hope that you will forgive me."

During most of its existence, Mussolini's regime had not been anti-Semitic, and early on, the Duce had explicitly criticized Hitler's racism—probably in part because Nazism did not include modern Italians in its pantheon of Aryan supermen. In fact, the regime had been notably *anti-anti-Semitic*. Mussolini called scientific racism and anti-Semitism "the German disease," a disparaging echo of the internationally used term "Prussian science" to describe eugenics, the study of racial selection. (Hitler responded by calling Mussolini's movement "Kosher fascism.") In 1920, while Hitler was drafting plans to revoke the citizenship of Jews and ban them from all walks of life, Mussolini wrote an article for his Fascist newspaper, *Il Popolo d'Italia,* stating that "in Italy we make absolutely no difference between Jews and non-Jews, in every field, religion, politics, the army, the economy. . . . Italian Jews have the new Zion right here, in our beautiful land, which many of them have defended heroically with their blood." Hundreds of Jews joined the fledgling Fascist Party, and during the first decade of fascism in Italy, there were Jewish generals, Jewish professors, and Jewish members of the Fascist Grand Council. Mussolini's mistress, a leading Fascist intellectual and theorist of the movement, was openly Jewish. Perhaps less well known is that the Israeli Navy was born out of a 1930s Fascist training program, and the Duce even endowed a Fascist chair at Hebrew University in Jerusalem.

All this would be eclipsed and forgotten by Mussolini's brief but disastrous alliance with Hitler. In September 1937, Mussolini went to Germany, where he watched the massive iron forges at Essen churn out munitions, and witnessed mock Luftwaffe bombing raids of fake Polish villages and Nazi troops participating in full-dress rehearsals for the coming blitzkrieg. The führer flattered him as the godfather of universal fascism, and a crowd of perhaps 250,000 spectators in Berlin cheered him. The following year, Mussolini introduced the Prussian goose step in the Italian army and insisted that Italians start saying *"Salute Il Duce!"* in imitation of the German *"Heil Hitler!"* Anti-Semitism became the new creed of Italy, though it contradicted almost everything that had come before.

By the summer of 1938, Italians from Milan to Naples had opened their newspapers to discover that they were all "pure Aryan Nordics" and that their Jewish colleagues were dangerous aliens. Jews, including die-hard Fascists, were dismissed from all military, university, and government posts. By that fall, Italian Jews were not allowed to have listed phone numbers, presumably because it corrupted the sea of pure Nordic names in the Italian telephone directory. A list of banned authors, with Essad Bey's name prominently included, was distributed to bookstores, schools, and police precincts.

For a writer whose real name was Nussimbaum to persist in a campaign to become Mussolini's official biographer in the spring and summer of 1938 took almost suicidal chutzpah. Of course, Lev didn't know that the Ministry of Popular Culture had already told Mussolini "that every support for Essad Bey has been withdrawn from our Ministry."

In March 1938—the month of the Anschluss—Lev wrote to Gentile begging him to help him arrange a visa to Italy so he could do research for the biography, although it had been clear for months that the project would not go forward. "It's so ridiculous that I can't enter a country in which I've published 20 books," he wrote, perhaps covering his desperation to escape Vienna.

A letter in the Italian secret police files dated September 5, 1938, states that "Leo Nussinbaum [*sic*]" did make his way to Rome and that the authorities were watching him and trying to determine his racial origins. The Italians were new at the game of racial typing, though, and the name was insufficient proof. In another move that the Gestapo would have scorned, the Italian police trailing Lev lost him in Rome, before picking up a vague lead that he had been seen in the coastal village of Positano, near Salerno, on the Amalfi coast. In the correspondence between the Ministry of Internal Affairs in Rome and the prefect in Salerno, I discovered that Lev had yet another identity switch up his sleeve: he was getting around Italy by posing as an American.

Lev used ship tickets and his expired U.S. entry permit to convince the Italian authorities that he was, in fact, an American citizen. The one concrete effect of the Italian racial laws and his inconclusive outing as a Jew there, however, was that his publishing contracts were forfeit. None of Lev's Italian publishers were willing to risk publishing him without approval from the Ministry of Popular Culture, which, in the new climate, would not make a move without the approval of its Nazi counterparts in Vienna and Berlin. (This is when he wrote the letters to Baron Omar-Rolf, requesting that "Mrs. Kurban Said" pick up royalty checks in various European capitals.) Lev also wrote increasingly frantic letters to his Italian publishers. In September 1938, near starving for lack of income in Positano, he made a bizarre and desperate appeal to his benefactor in Florence, Giovanni Gentile:

The documentary airtight evidence of Aryan background back to the third generation in my family is extremely difficult to obtain, as all the relevant papers are in the hands of the Bolsheviks. [However] . . . Aryan background must not only be provable on paper but also through pure scientific examination. Could you please recommend to me in either Rome or Florence a competent anthropologist, who after appropriate examination can produce a definitive verdict as to my racial composition. It must of course be done by a scholar who has the trust of the official authorities. I think that in this way the problem could most simply be solved and we could finally have peace. . . . As soon as I get money from you, I will go to Florence and I hope that by then you will have found an anthropologist who is prepared to prove, scientifically, to which race I now actually belong.

There is no record of a reply to this suggestion. The next letter in the archives of the Ministry of Internal Affairs in Rome is from a surgeon named Dr. Vito Fiorentino, who informs Gentile that "Essad Bey is very sick and is afflicted by Raynaud's disease, for which at the moment science does not have a cure." Raynaud's syndrome is an extremely rare blood disease that produces the effects of accelerated leprosy and gangrene. In early 1939, Lev was taken to a hospital in Naples, where they began treatment by amputating a number of toes on his left foot—apparently where the myth about stabbing himself in the foot originated. The Italian police, far from arresting him, did everything they could to raise money for his medical care. When the town of Positano ran out of money, a request was forwarded to Salerno, and from there to the Ministry of Internal Affairs, which handed the matter over to the Foreign Ministry, which in turn made a request to the American embassy on Lev's behalf. The Italian authorities were told that he had never been a citizen of the United States.

CHAPTER 15

Positano

P OSITANO, I DISCOVERED, is the kind of resort town that used to
be famous as the haunt of Italian film figures such as Vittorio De
Sica in the 1950s and is now host to less famous but richer fashion
and film people. When a deep-throated local count promised me "possibly vital" information about Essad Bey—or "the Muslim," as he is still
known in the town—our meeting turned out to involve drinks with a
vaguely familiar actor, whom I finally recognized as the star of *RoboCop*,
and a dimly recalled anecdote about a White Russian princess at a beach
party in the 1960s. But as is so often the case with such towns, there was
an entirely different place just beneath the veneer, a harder place hiding in
the memories of the old people who live above the four-star hotels, in the
honeycomb of little pastel houses that rise up over the cliff.

Physically, the war left the town untouched. When you compare photographs of the Amalfi coastline in this spot from the summer of 1942 to
the coastline now, it's hard to notice any difference. There is one: since the
town's founding, two great rocks—nicknamed *Mamma e Figlio*—had jut-
ted high out of the water next to a medieval tower, creating a natural barrier from the open sea. *Mamma* was blown away entirely by British
torpedoes aimed at cargo ships in February 1943, and only a bit of *Figlio*
survived; this gave locals the pleasant story that "*Mamma* had sacrificed
her life for her son." Other than that, the town was spared.

Indeed, one reason Neapolitan nobles sent their children to Positano
during the war was that it was considered safe from aerial bombardment:

its steep hillsides made it an extremely difficult target. But for the exile community in Positano, refuge was less certain. In those days, before the Americans and the film stars and the money, the foreigners were all poor and came to escape the persecutions of the more Fascist north and the Nazi nightmare beyond it. They had various reasons for taking a permanent vacation in a small Italian fishing village: they were left-wing writers, pacifist poets, and modernist artists—members of the Bauhaus, painters engaged in radical color experiments, composers, dancers—and Jews.

However, the experience for the Jews and the non-Jews was entirely different. For the cultural dissidents, they soon found that the Amalfi coast in Fascist Italy was still the Amalfi coast. They spent their days working, learning Italian, hiking to nearby Monte Pertuso, and enjoying sun-drenched picnics on the rocks, and at night they gathered at the *Buca di Bacco*—"Bacchus's Cave," a converted wine cellar where German and Russian were now the *lingue franche*—and drank until the owners kicked them out. The relaxed atmosphere held, at least in part, because the cultural exiles were not in any particular danger. In contrast to other fascist regimes, Italian fascism had never been very serious about eliminating cultural dissent, at least when it did not threaten the state. With typical Italian tolerance, the censor looked the other way for things that would have landed any German in a concentration camp.

For the Jews, it was another matter. They came with the same expectation of refuge as the others—indeed, many had left Nazi Europe for artistic and political reasons—but from 1938 onward, when the Italian racial laws were passed, their position became markedly different. For them, the apparently idyllic existence in the tolerant enclave on the Amalfi coast could end at any time.

I went to see a gentle, sad-eyed woman named Nicoletta Rispoli, whose mother, Dorothea Flatow, known as Dojo, had been a Jewish owner of a pension largely frequented by refugee Jews during the 1930s and early 1940s. I had been told that Dojo walked across town to the apartment where Lev stayed to bring him plates of pasta, and that her generosity may at times have kept him from starving. Her family had come from Germany in the mid-1930s and started the pension; in Berlin they had owned a sanatorium, and they found that the skills needed for running a small hotel were similar. The Pensione San Matteo became the most popular guesthouse for German refugee artists and intellectuals in Positano. The hotel ceased to exist many years ago, but Nicoletta still had its guest book, a collage of paintings, cartoons, photos, and illustrated stories by grateful guests. We found two lines in a poem about how "the Muslim" owed everyone money, but nothing else about him.

The townspeople are filled with jaunty memories of Positano during the war: one elegant gentleman, who as a child had been sent here during the bombing of Naples, recalled with delight riding go-carts down the plunging streets to the beach. Speaking to me alternately in German-laced Italian and Italian-laced German, Nicoletta said she wanted me to know that the town's memories of surviving the war concealed another past. "It was not always the way they like to remember it."

She showed me newspaper clippings she had saved for sixty years, including a letter to the local paper from a "decent citizen," demanding to know when the "Jewish filth from all across Europe" would be cleaned out of Nicoletta's parents' hotel. Of course, this would have included her and her mother, so she still remembers the shock of reading the letter. Not to worry, the editors had responded, the authorities were aware of the matter, and it would be taken care of soon. Their hotel was indeed closed down, but Nicoletta and her mother were spared deportation because her mother had married a local Italian; they were allowed to remain in Naples for the rest of the war.

Lev, as Essad Bey, had arrived in Positano in April or May 1938. Hitler's Anschluss with Austria had kept the hotels overflowing that spring, and the Jewish population and German-speaking population of the town had grown exponentially. Lev had many contacts among the exiles, but he remained largely aloof from them. The authorities would later have his typewriter sealed and his radio confiscated, and some thought he was a spy—but for whom?

"He was a secretive man," recalled a German exile, Elisabeth Castonier, in her memoirs. She had passed through Positano in 1939. "[His] only form of identification was a ship ticket from the North German Lloyd, which the gendarmes regarded with awe as a diplomat's passport." She also recalled with amusement that "the Muslim" had had his *frak,* his black tie and tails, specially shipped from Vienna.

Lev evidently regarded his new beach town, with "the hysterical faces of the bathers," as a prison. In those first couple of years, he received visits from his well-connected American friend George Sylvester Viereck, soon to be jailed as a Nazi agent, and from the poet Gerhart Hauptmann, who had brought Lev's plight to the attention of Frau Pima Andreae, in Rapallo. But aside from Alice Schulte, the "disheveled Russian" woman who had arrived once again to take care of him, Lev's main contacts with the outside world were through the mail.

In 1938 and 1939 he wrote dozens of letters, primarily to Baron Omar in India; to "Frau Said," Baroness Elfriede, who was in Greece; and, beginning in March 1939, to Pima. Lev's friendship with Pima began when she introduced herself through the mail and sent him money, and continued— with many frustrating interruptions from censors and from the war— until he died. It was among the few bright spots in these last years. Pima had close friendships with a number of writers—Pound, Yeats, Gerhart Hauptmann—but apparently none so close as her epistolary romance with the young man half her age, whom she would never meet, dying in Positano. Pima would be the last person who really got to know Lev Nussimbaum, though perhaps it is more correct to say she was the first person who really got to know Kurban Said.

Certain themes remain the same in all Lev's letters. Always he is desperately in need of money and trying one scheme after another to either earn some or get access to his royalties and bank accounts. And he thinks obsessively of Erika.* In 1940 he began the notebooks that he titled "The Man Who Knew Nothing About Love"—the memoir-cum-novel-cum-diary that his former publisher, Frau Mögle, would take away with her and stash in her closet for the next sixty years.

For two years Lev wrote obsessively in the notebooks, in an almost indecipherable scrawl; a servant in the house where he was living would remember Lev writing "sometimes, into the night, into the morning—I would leave and come back and find him sitting the next day with his

---

* Just before he died, Lev would even instruct that the final edition of *Ali and Nino*, published a few months after his death, substitute the name "Erika" for "Nino" wherever it appeared in the text. So if you were to pick up the 1943 Italian Fascist paperback edition of his most famous work—which few people have because it was a very small edition, though copies of it are still floating around Italy in used bookshops—you would find that the magical love story set on the eve of the Russian Revolution in Baku is actually the story of Ali and Erika. It is also not by "Kurban Said" but by "Essad Bey," a first posthumous restoration of Lev's authorship of the novel.

head tilted the same way, writing." In microscopic blue script he told the story of his life, interrupted by scenes of his present pain. In rapidly unfolding scenes he meets Arab paratroopers, king's emissaries, blond girls, tuxedoed millionaires, ragged gurus, until, alone, naked in a hotel room, washing the desert off his body, he notices a black spot growing on his foot. He takes morphine while writing some sections, smokes hashish while writing others, but the most surreal prose comes when he's taking only pain, trying to adjust to a stark reality that cannot be mediated by language or culture or learning or attitude.

His illness had appeared suddenly in 1939—starting in his left foot, then spreading to both of his legs. He was hospitalized that year in Naples for four or five months (according to police surveillance files), but there was no cure for his condition, so he was sent back to his room in Positano, where he had to buy or beg the morphine from the local pharmacist.

"All in all the future lies in God's hand, but one can feel this hand more and more distinctly," he wrote Baroness Elfriede in September 1939. "Life sometimes appears somewhat strange to me. I've finished my book and actually I don't have anything left to do." This, as much as the lack of food and money and medicine, was the really unbearable thing. So he started *The Man Who Knew Nothing About Love.*

"The Muslim was a dignified man who never went out without being perfectly dressed and carrying his walking stick," Genario Passerotti, who had once been Positano's version of a mayor, told me. "He was *molto elegante.* His best friend was the priest, Don Serviglio Cinque, with whom he used to spend long hours walking and talking." Actually, Passerotti—universally known as "old Passerotti"—didn't tell me much himself, since he was escorted by four generations of women, from his granddaughter to his mother, who chaperoned every word out of his mouth. "Did you ever discuss . . . ?" I'd ask. To which he'd respond, "Oh, of course, I'd sometimes discuss with him . . ." before the ladies would give him a pinch or a sharp tug on his suspenders and say, "What Grandpa means is . . ." To which old Passerotti would reply with resignation: "Yes, exactly so, exactly so."

Contessa Raimonda Gaetani-Pattison, who designs cinema and opera costumes for a living, accompanied me on the interview. She lives in the house where Lev died, and she was eager to help me solve the mystery of her family's most mysterious guest. On the way up the dozen flights of cliff-rock staircases separating the levels of the Passerotti compound—the family had been buying up property for generations—we were escorted by the old man's daughter, whose head was wrapped in a hot-pink scarf. She brought us to a tiny, dark room at the top of the compound, where the censored interview proceeded at an excruciating pace. But it did become clear why Don Serviglio Cinque had gotten along famously with "the Muslim": they were both men of culture who spoke many languages and knew the world firsthand. And both had spent time in America, so they could converse in Italian and English.

Was it true that the priest had been a devoted Fascist? I asked. Could political affinity have been a source of their relationship?

"Oh, yes," began old Passerotti, "Don Serviglio was a *big* Fascist, and he . . ."

"Old Passerotti doesn't know about the Don's politics—he was a man of the cloth!" barked his daughter, the duce of the household, adjusting her hot-pink turban.

I didn't mean anything by it, of course, I explained. Presumably many people were nominally Fascist in those days, especially in civil administration.

"Well, of course, in those days . . ." began the old man.

"He had *nothing* to do with politics!" said the turbaned face, her eyes boring into me. "Nobody had anything to do with politics that he remembers!"

"Yes, exactly so!" said old Passerotti. "Neither the Don nor I were ever political."

When the contessa and I left and returned to her palazzo, she said, "Weren't they fantastic! Fantastic! Sixty years later and they were completely spooked about mentioning fascism. Like they think somehow their position could be jeopardized because someone finds out that there were Fascists here in 1942—in the middle of Fascist Italy!—what a shock!" Yes, perhaps the family wasn't all Social Democrats. "But that they think anyone would care now, especially since these are not secrets, everyone knows the priest was a big Fascist, and he is dead for thirty years! And what about our Muslim—was he a Fascist, too? An Islamist? A Nazi? Why had he really come to Positano, can you find that out? These people here know nothing, even if they knew him when he was here, like old Passerotti. I don't think he ever showed himself to any of them. When he was in Positano, he was just biding his time, I don't think he ever revealed himself to the people here."

Lev was staying in a small apartment attached to the contessa's family's house, a seventeenth-century palazzo with a cheerful yellow façade and a series of ivy-columned terraces facing the sea. The palazzo had been purchased by her father, Alfred Pattison—Giovanni Alfredo Pattison—around 1908. Captain Pattison, whose Naples shipyards built much of the Italian Navy, was one of many enterprising Englishmen who moved to Naples in the nineteenth century to make their fortune. The transfer of British know-how and industriousness to the area had begun after the Napoleonic wars, and had left behind a small, elite hybrid culture marked by names such as Gaetani-Pattison, Giovanni Smith, and Carlo Knight. The "English Neapolitans" had continued to do well right through the first decade of fascism, in the years when Scotland Yard still helped Mussolini round up anti-Fascists and the wives of British ministers pinned Fascist badges on their evening dresses.

Captain Alfredo Pattison had married a German woman named Luisa Straub, and the contessa suspected it was her grandmother Straub, the family intellectual and salon hostess, who had invited the Muslim to live there. It was unlike her stiff-necked grandfather to have brought a shadowy fugitive, no matter how great a writer he was, into the household. The English shipbuilder and the German bohemian had a child, Nora Pattison, a spoiled tomboy who spent the 1930s having affairs with handsome fishermen and driving race cars through the hills to Naples. The carefree German-English-Neapolitan girl helped her family's position by marrying Count Gaetani, a sour-faced man from one of the oldest families in Italy and an early member of the Fascist party. (I found his 1925 membership card beneath a stack of vacation photographs in the palazzo.) The offspring of this marriage was the current contessa Gaetani-Pattison.

The boisterous contessa had given me the run of the house and told me to stay as long as I needed. I would have slept in the apartment where Lev had stayed, but an ascot-wearing yacht builder from South Africa was now renting it. Instead, I was in the very back of the main palazzo, down a cavernous hallway lined with ancient chests and terraced rooms.

It was an irresistible if daunting task. Each room had a window that opened onto a balcony with a view of the sea, bombarded with Mediterranean sunlight, but the interesting things were all in the dark. I must have spent more time in a cavelike darkness than any visitor to Positano had since the Muslim himself—rarely going out even onto the terraces for fear of missing one more box, one more shelf, one more stack of letters. There were chests bursting with love letters in German, English, and Italian, postcards from holidays spent in the Third Reich, and correspondence with American friends after war was declared. None of it had anything to do with Lev.

Leafing through the enormous leather guest book of the palazzo, I noted that the names of the visitors told the history of the period: from the 1920s until the late 1930s, the guests were from all over Europe, leaning toward English aristocrats and American plutocrats, accompanied by insouciant descriptions of things Italian and rhapsodies to the classical heritage of the coast; from 1938, the year Mussolini introduced the race laws, the names became entirely Italian; and from 1944 on, the arrival of the Allies was told in an endless stream of American officers and British soldiers of all ranks and origins. The Casa Pattison must have seemed like a little bit of England to these conquerors far from home.

Still, from 1938 to 1942, at a time when their guest book was purged of foreign names, to have rented to a foreigner with shadowy political connections and no money who was being pursued by the secret police? It only added to the puzzle.

"My mother, she was a teenager then but very impolite and cheeky," said the contessa, pointing to photos of her sporty half-English mother, who was wearing a long flowing white scarf. "Mama would sneak next door when Dr. Fiorentino would come to attend my grandmother's guest, Essad Bey, to treat the gangrene in his leg—some said he had a bullet wound untreated there; others said he had stabbed himself during a suicide attempt in Switzerland."

The gangrene would be from Raynaud's syndrome, in which the oxygen-starved tissue of the limbs starts to die. Without proper drugs and treatment, it can produce an excruciating condition, like some kind of medieval torture. Toward the end of Lev's life, his feet looked pitch black, as though someone had held them in a fire or scorched them with a blowtorch.

"My mother and her friends would watch as he screamed in pain," said the contessa, somewhat guiltily, "and then come running down the street shouting: 'They cut off a piece of the Muslim! They cut off a piece of the Muslim!' "

"He would howl like an animal when the pain came, other times he was very quiet and contemplative. You could never forget his eyes, big black eyes, Oriental you know, burning brighter even as his body decayed." The cheerful, wiry eighty-six-year-old adjusted his backward New York Yankees cap, took a pull on his Coke, and leaned back terrifyingly in his chair. We were in a makeshift café whose tables were poised between the road and a cliff with a six-hundred-meter drop, and waiters dodged traffic as Fioravante Rispoli recalled how he had once worked as the Muslim's manservant. He had been employed at the big house, serving the contessa's grandfather, the capitano Pattison—who always needed everything *"Preciso! Preciso!* If lunch was a minute late or early, he would shout like thunder and make you feel *this* big!"—and was ordered to run errands for their boarder. When I asked him if he'd ever served the Muslim lunch in the big house, with the captain and his family, he laughed.

"That man was not their type! He had a dubious background! He was poor! But even though he couldn't pay me nothing, he always treated me very politely, saying, 'Giovanni, would you mind going to the *farmacia* to try to get me some morphine?' Even though it was clear he was in fantastic pain, he found strength to say, 'Would you mind'! And you know what the pharmacist said? I still remember sixty years later because it was so cold, like ice he was: 'It would be better if that guy would just kick the bucket—I'm sick of giving him drugs he can't afford. That one would be better dead.' " Lev had arrived in Positano a handsome young man in his early thirties. Four years later, he resembled a man twice that age and was addicted to opiates.

I asked Rispoli if he knew that the Muslim had once been a famous man, a writer. He said he hadn't known but that it wouldn't surprise him. When he was not in pain, he explained, the man was either looking out at the sea or writing. "He wrote ten, fifteen hours a day, sometimes." When the town watchman came to confiscate his typewriter—the authorities in Rome sent word that the Muslim could not have either a typewriter or a radio, as he might use them for espionage—he continued to write in long-hand, and when he could no longer afford paper and notebooks, he wrote on the margins of old books and scraps of cigarette paper. One German visitor reported in his memoirs after seeing Lev in the summer of 1941 that although entering his apartment was "like entering a Persian opium den . . . his political senses were as sharp as ever."

Though the old servant recalled many of these foreign visitors to the Muslim, the one that stuck out in his mind was a strapping young Middle Easterner in a military officer's uniform. Rispoli couldn't recall his name. He remembered the man only because of his uniform and because it was the first and only time he ever heard the Muslim speak Arabic, rather than Italian or German.

"They all called him a Muslim," said the servant, leaning forward and adjusting his cap like an eighty-five-year-old playground snitch. "I personally think he was a Jew."

Why did he think the Muslim was a Jew?

"I don't know—he kept a Koran by his bed, and everyone called him the Muslim. His friend seemed like a Muslim Fascist. I just felt he was more like a Jew." The old ex-servant cackled and ordered another Coke. "But I would have kept working for the Muslim, if he hadn't died. He was not rich and fine, but he always acted like a gentleman."

Romolo Ercolino, the watchman's son, pointed up past the cliff houses to a spot at the highest edge of the town. I looked but could make out only a deep patch of green and what looked like a tiny chapel hanging, as if in midflight, against the deep blue sky.

"My father knew they were going to come for him sometime. There was an SS camp not far away in Salerno, something like the SS, our Italian version. It was the end of August 1942. Two big black sedans pulled up in front of the house, the long kind that only the secret police drove, and men with hats—they always wore the big hats, fedoras—got out. They went into the house and said to my father, 'Where is he? Where is the Muslim?'

" 'You're too late,' said my father. 'He's gone. Up there.' My father was pointing to the cemetery."

Romolo Ercolino (aka Romulus Hercules) wore a dark jacket and tie, even in the blazing sun. His father, Luigi, the equivalent of the town's sheriff, had been the last person to see Lev alive.

At the top of the town, reached via nearly vertical staircases carved into the rock, Romolo led me through the cemetery, past graves piled one on top of another like miniature tenements for the dead. From up here you could survey the entire coast overlooking the Tyrrhenian Sea. On a jutting piece of land sat the medieval tower, which had been erected to warn of approaching Saracen raiders.

"Eccola," said Hercules in a gentle singsongy voice. We stood before a narrow white tombstone with a turban on top. "It is the Turkish style," he said. "A man came after the war, Dr. Giamil Mazzara, an Algerian, and made the plans and donated the money for the gravestone." The name read MOHAMMED ESSAD BEY.

Mazzara was the man in an officer's uniform whom Rispoli remembered, whom Lev spoke Arabic with. I had read letters by the Algerian in Essad Bey's police file. His full name was Dr. Ahmed Giamil Vacca-Mazzara, and his letterhead said *journaliste*. I had had trouble finding a straight paper trail on this man, but what I pieced together from various sources—UN documents from the late 1940s, letters in the Ehrenfels castle from the 1970s, an angry ex-wife living in Rome who was the daughter of a high Fascist senator—revealed that the "Algerian" had been a most unusual person in his own right: an Islamic Fascist parachute officer and a journalist with access to a string of expensive cars and villas, and a shadowy series of missions that took him between Italian-controlled Libya and French Algeria, apparently smuggling information and other things. The letters were written in a florid hand, and were the only handwritten letters in a file stuffed with typed memoranda, surveillance reports, and official telegrams. They were stamped "Anno XIX and XX"—the nineteenth and twentieth years of the Fascist era (in the style of the Jacobins, Mussolini had restarted the Italian calendar with the year of his march on Rome, 1922).

Had Ercolino ever met the Algerian himself? "Dr. Giamil never returned to Positano during my father's lifetime. But I was fortunate to meet him once, in the 1970s, when he came to look at the grave. He was very pleased with it." Did he know anything about him? "He was a very rich and powerful man, with much property in Algeria and Turkey. He told me that the one who was buried here was the greatest man he had ever known. I told him that we had always felt the same way, that he had been like family to us. That must have been 1975. Dr. Giamil said he would return, but he never did."

Baron Omar had made a pilgrimage here on his return from India in 1954 and noted with displeasure that Essad Bey's grave was just outside the holy ground, presumably because he had not been a Catholic. I asked the cemetery keeper about this, and he said he thought the sanctified ground went up all the way to the edge of the cliff. Unfortunately, he was a young man, and his father, who had kept the cemetery before him, was long dead. He could not tell me much. But did I know that the Muslim had once been dug up and moved? I asked if his father had told him about this. When he said he knew it from the great novelist John Steinbeck, my heart sank a little, but I listened anyhow as he told the story.

Sooner or later, everyone in Positano wanted to tell me about digging up the Muslim. In 1953, John Steinbeck had published a travel article about Positano in *Harper's Bazaar,* and the tourist office still reprinted it in elegant little bound editions on watermarked cream paper, available in six languages. So many Positanesi knew of it that Steinbeck's version had become the basis of what most of them "remembered" about Essad Bey.

About ten years ago a Moslem came to Positano, liked it and settled. For a time he was self-supporting, but gradually he ran out of assets and still he stayed. The town supported him and took care of him. Just as the mayor was their only Communist, this was their only Moslem. They felt that he belonged to them. Finally he died, and his only request was that he might be buried with his feet towards Mecca. And this, so Positano thought, was done. Four years later some curious meddler made a discovery. The Moslem had been buried by dead reckoning and either the compass was off or the map was faulty. He had been buried 28 degrees off course. This was outrageous to a seafaring town. The whole population gathered, dug the Moslem up, put him on course and covered him up again.

There is no evidence that this actually happened, but in any case perhaps the most jarring thing about the passage is that Steinbeck clearly has no idea that the man who occupies his amusing anecdote had been a famous writer only a decade before. They had been successful contemporaries in the 1930s, yet Steinbeck had survived to continue writing both great books and fluff like this, while Lev/Essad had fallen into an abyss. To all but a handful of devoted followers—and the secret-police forces of

Nazi Germany and Fascist Italy—in the last years of his life, he had become simply "the Muslim" of Positano.

When I told Romolo Ercolino what Rispoli had said, about the Muslim really being a Jew, he vehemently objected. There was the gravestone with the turban and the Arabic inscription. Everyone called him "the Muslim." He had read the Koran and asked to be buried with his feet facing Mecca. *"Eccola,"* he said finally, pointing to a passage in a document I had showed him. It was a footnote in Dr. Giamil's long obituary of Essad Bey in a fascist journal called *Oriente Moderno,* from 1942:

> That Essad Bey was not a Jew we can conclude from the fact that in the pre-bolshevist Caucasus it was for Jews absolutely forbidden to have property in oil, be it of single persons or for firms, in the Caucasus, as in White Russia, there was never a Jewish Nobility, the Imperial Gymnasium in Baku was a priori closed to Jewish children, and it was strictly forbidden for them to live in the city. The Anthropological Institute in New York noted "Leo Mohammed Essad Bey, son of Ibrahim Arslan-Oglu, born in Baku on the 20th October 1905, religion Mohammedan." The following notes on race say: "50% Russian, 24% Turkoman, 24% Iranian."

The essay was a monument in print to complement the monument in marble that Giamil created in the cemetery—part eulogy, part literary tribute, part racist apologia. In 1941, while Lev was still alive, Italian reviews of his reprinted books on Stalin and the G.P.U. had begun referring to him as a "Jewish author," a turn of fate that soon could have been deadly, had not Lev already been in the grip of death for other reasons. After 1942, as Giamil undertook the posthumous translation of the Kurban Said novels and tried to establish an Essad Bey Foundation "for the children of refugees," it was crucial to him to restore his hero to pure Aryan status. (He even invented an elaborate story whereby one of the Slutzki sisters—whom Giamil described as wealthy White Russian princesses—had married a "Mr. Nessim-baum [Israelite], thus becoming E.B.'s 'uncle Nessim.' ")

I became fairly obsessed with tracking this multitalented Algerian, and I dug fruitlessly through every conceivable Italian government ministry. When I kept coming up blank, I began to wonder if his files could have been deliberately purged or stolen by someone. Though I found the letters from him in Lev's government files, it was inconceivable that he did not have a significant paper trail of his own in a Fascist police state, a paper trail too big for even the Italians to entirely misplace. But finally, it became clear why Dr. Giamil Vacca-Mazzara had been so hard to locate in the bureaucratic record: he had had an "identity crisis" of his own.

A jovial Orientalist at an institute in Rome named Professore Castro said that he remembered hearing rumors about Dr. Giamil—specifically that he was not to be trusted or given valuable materials—when Castro first arrived at his post in the early 1950s. Dr. Giamil was quite notorious, Castro remembered, but the people who would know *why* were all dead. He referred me to another professor, in Pisa, a woman named Anna Baldinetti, who was the world's expert on Italian colonial records in Libya, who traveled often to North African archives and might be able to help tame my wild goose chase. After what seemed like another dead end, Professoressa Baldinetti recalled something—it was just a piece of paper in the midst of thousands of pieces of paper she'd gone through in the Italian Foreign Ministry archives, but because it dealt with student agitation in North Africa during the fascist period, one of her specializations, she'd copied it. She vaguely remembered that it had a name something like Giamil Mazzara on it. She promised to look for it, and what passed through my fax machine a few days later was a memo from the general director of political affairs in the Resident Department of African Italy, dated March 1938, reporting that "(alias) Giamil Ibn Ysuf Mazara, Italian citizen," was actually a native of Tripoli named Bello Vacca. An "ex-reserve officer in the Italian army" and recent convert to Islam, he

> lived in Cairo from the second half of the previous year up until February of this current year, [at which time] the Egyptian government determined him to be undesirable on account of drug trafficking and because explosives and propaganda documents were found in his possession, and consequently expelled him from the country.

The report concluded that "Bello Vacca posed as a defender of the rights of Libyan Muslims" but was in fact involved in various plots and schemes for his own purposes.

All this would tend to explain why Giamil does not exactly come off as the earnest follower one expects in Lev's notebooks. Instead, he's a strangely lurking figure whose appearances in the text are, perhaps not coincidentally, often followed by opium-like clouds of eerie prose:

> Djamil remains with me. He gives a satisfied smile. I reach out my hand to him. "Hashish, Djamil, give me hashish." . . . He sighs and hands me the package. . . .
>
> I lay stretched out in the shade on the terrace. The pain in my foot slowly fades. I stare dully into space and see the pain wandering down the stairs. The pain wears a red velvet coat and carries a straight sword. It is small of stature and wears a hat with a feather and a broad brim. Only I see it and only I feel it. The little grains of hashish are powerful. They drive away the dwarf in the red coat. The terrace is empty. Somewhere behind me I hear Djamil's quiet whispering. I no longer understand him. I see the sky and the smooth, still water. Slowly, very slowly, the water rises up out of the sea. It covers the sky. A bluish-gray color spreads out in front of me. The color covers everything—the terrace, the sea, the sky, even me. Nothing in the world exists except for this color—no deserts, no universities, no books, no pain, no kings. The bluish-gray color moves, as though it were being moved by an invisible hand. Soon it will come, very soon. I am completely calm, the little grains never fail.

There is one last burst of hope, in the spring of 1942. Pima had written to the Duce, and money was starting to come in to Lev, and the cordon around him to loosen. Lev got his radio back, and he sold a few articles for the Fascist cause. Pima established a connection between Lev and her friend "Herr Ezra"—Ezra Pound—who, of course, had many contacts in Italian radio. In a letter to Pima in December 1941, about Pound's efforts to get him radio work, Lev sounds quite confused: "For God's sake who is Herr Ezra[?] . . . I am dying for work, but Ezra is a biblical prophet. There is the 'Book of Ezra.' I know the Bible in three languages." Lev was aware he was having trouble keeping things straight, and he informed Pima drolly: "Don't be frightened—but I regret to tell you with all formality that I have lost my mind."

The fall and winter of 1941 had been particularly rough. A fellow Orientalist, a German exile living in Positano named Armin Wegner, technically a competitor of Lev's and no great friend, described him in his day-books from the period: "A thin specter . . . [who] hobbles around in his room"; Lev's "nanny," he added, had "a face like a caricature by Daumier, stupid, malicious, rustically sly, greedy, always stuffing something into herself." Wegner's rather callous assessments of Lev in his diary in September 1942, days after he died—"a typical literary swindler," "a Jewish-Viennese journalist"—reveal that the German Orientalist knew his secret all along. There is a spiteful undercurrent to the entry (Lev's books sold better than Wegner's), but also a penetrating offhand analysis of his colleague's life: "the horrifying fairy tale of a young, unhappy, apostate Jew!"—"one [trying to] make a fairy tale out of his life in order to escape sad reality." Hearing of Giamil's elaborate tombstone for "the Muslim," Wegner comments acerbically that Lev "kept up the comedy until the last moment."

If Ezra Pound had known about "the comedy"—that the Muslim was really a Jew—he surely would not have tried to help. But he did not know, and he did try, and it did help. In June 1942, Essad Bey was invited to record propaganda speeches in Persian for a radio broadcast on the Fascist Colonial Service. He was to be accompanied to Rome on September 1. That was the long black sedan that drove up, a week after he died, to take him away with the men in fedoras. They weren't coming to take him to a concentration camp. They were taking him to a recording studio.

"Looking back now, what is important is the realization that fate meant well for me. Twice it stretched its hand out to rescue me, and twice I pushed this hand away—for my fate was Monica." In his strange, swirling manuscript, Lev calls his wife "Monica" and himself "Ali," and the more I read the obsessive, haunting account, the more it made sense to me that he could not let go of her. It was not jealousy—it went way beyond that. In one of his bitter digressions within the narrative, Lev creates the idea that it was Erika who refused to move to the United States when they could still get out of Europe. In fact, it was Lev who had doubts about moving, and it likely accelerated their breakup. The man Erika left him for, René Fülöp-Miller, had written a book about Hollywood and was itching to move to the States. In the letters to Pima, there are hints of what was really going on.

Lev had written to her about his adventures in Asia and the Weimar Republic, in Chicago and Calcutta, about Erika and Ataturk—about love and politics and war and publishing and movies and money. He regaled her as if he were Scheherazade, as if his life depended on it, and it did. He dared not reveal the whole truth about himself to Pima, for even if this friend of high Fascists understood, the censor would not have; for the latter's benefit, they often spoke in a kind of jovial code.

A central theme of the letters is the fate of the correspondent, whether he will survive to continue the correspondence, but this, too, is handled in code. He has been curious about the fate of "our mutual friend Kurban Said," Lev writes in a letter of November 21, 1940,

> I therefore wrote to his other friends. . . . Writing and telegraphing all and sundry (one is allowed to send telegraphs) may have cost a lot of money, but now I can at least give you more specific information on Said. . . . This is what happened: our friend was denounced by his own wife! Yes, such things happen. The denunciation didn't contain anything the officials didn't already know—that Said, with the best of intentions, is not able to produce the birth certificates of his grandparents. For his grandparents were born 80–100 years ago, and birth certificates were introduced in his wild and faraway country of birth only 50 years ago. It is clear that he cannot possess papers that never existed. The officials knew this and therefore let it pass without pressing the matter. Now there is a denunciation by his wife, however, signed with date and place.

The suspicion that Erika had denounced him as a Jew was more psychically than literally true. In his letters, Lev tells the story of a Mr. Percy, a hard-boiled detective-lawyer for his ex-wife, who he supposedly believes is traveling all over fascist Europe to expose him and put his life in danger. Whenever Lev hits a patch of despair, he brings up this bloodhound on his trail. "Percy? Yeah, I'm always forgetting about him," he writes in the middle of a dejected rant, on January 15, 1942. "Of course he can harm me, that is why he's there! But a Jew—that's unreasonable!! I can easily prove the opposite." It is almost inconceivable that Erika would have sent someone to Europe to denounce Lev as a Jew—and anyway, by 1942 there was no need for an American gumshoe to accomplish that. The accusation appears on nearly every communication about him from Nazi Germany to Mussolini's Italy from 1939 onward, and it seems likely that Lev understands this. Knowing that he gave up his last chance to escape, and that he must survive in Fascist Europe with the help of the Fascists, adds to Lev's game of blaming everything on his ex-wife and the Americans.

There are also psychological reasons why he would associate the marital and "racial" disasters in his mind, for it was in the spring of 1935 that he received, within a month of each other, the two pieces of news that devastated his life: the German Writers' Union had banned his works in Germany, and Erika had been sleeping with another man. Erika's public statements ("I learned that he was just plain Leo Nussinbaum") had the sound of a joke in the American press, and the real punch lines were about his supposed "Muslim side": how he had threatened to keep a harem, told her ghastly stories, attempted to strangle her but then collapsed on the floor. But Erika could hardly have been unaware that for Lev, who lived in the middle of fascist Europe, such statements reverberated across the seas with very different effects. They went into dossiers, police files, and publishers' notes. Of course, none of it was really a secret—for that matter, how could Erika claim that she had no idea about Lev's background at the time of their marriage in 1932? She was his secretary, after all, during a time when a scandal still simmered about his Jewish identity.

But Lev thrived on hiding in plain sight. The whole point of his secret was that it wasn't really a secret. It was a rumor, a part of his underground cachet, and his friends and colleagues supported him in the charade. It was about toughing it out, smiling enigmatically in the face of insults. It was a sort of defiance that had something insane about it, yet it was the baldness of it that kept Lev going. In this sense, Wegner was right—Lev *was* trying to turn "sad reality" into a fairy tale—perhaps the Muslim identity was merely a form of assimilation. Or perhaps it was something more profound. Lev's way of telling the world—and himself—that it could not put him in the cage of its latest modern barbarity. It couldn't so long as he imagined it couldn't.

The power of Erika's denunciations in the press was that they ripped off all the masks at once: Lev was not only not a Muslim and not a prince (though he never said he was, the word "princeling" must have stung), he was not the great sheik lover he dressed up to be, and he was not her lover at all anymore. There was no mystery left to her ex-husband when she got through with him. In America, Essad Bey's magical tale, which had previously been written up in the pages of respectable papers, was now smeared in the tabloids, and after the reporters repeated the exotic exploits, they would now add, as the *Sunday Mirror Magazine* did in January 1938, "Erica gave a slightly different version of Essad's beginnings, saying that he was born plain Leo Nussinbaum; that his mother had committed suicide during the Red Revolution and he fled with Nussimbaum, Sr., to Turkey, where both embraced Mohammedanism. 'Bey,' she said scornfully, was an hereditary title which Essad could not possibly claim." Born plain old Leo Nussimbaum. And the press knew the secret about his mother, too—the one that no one in his family would even mention and that he'd told his wife only in confidence. It was no wonder that he confused his Nazi persecutors with his ex-wife, for in the depths of their vicious divorce, she had unmasked him as no Gestapo agent had ever quite managed to do.

Alice had nursed him back to health after the bout in the sanatorium, and he'd written his book with von Weisl and then the Kurban Said novels as a kind of therapy. He'd ensconced himself in his new café-and-castle culture, shuttling between Schloss Ehrenfels and the Herrenhof, and managed to feel better about things. But now he was facing the illness and the poverty and the race laws in Italy and Mr. Percy and the news of his father.

"Don't be frightened—but I regret to tell you with all formality that I have lost my mind."

In the end, both Lev and his father were trapped. The notebooks in part record his attempt to understand how it all happened, how his fate brought him to this place. He thought back again and again on the "chance" he'd had to stay in America—the offers from his millionaire father-in-law, from Viereck, from an Oriental Institute:

One thought kept bothering me: Why in the world hadn't I accepted [the] proposal? . . . I didn't know; I just couldn't understand it. It was as though an invisible power had me under its spell. Better conditions were not to be had, nor better work. And yet an incomprehensible horror crept over me at the thought of going to America forever. There was no rational explanation, it was an irrational feeling that drove me to the edge of the abyss, one of those few moments in which a person makes by himself a decision that affects the course of his life. It was fate.

Anything would have been possible for Lev in 1934 or 1935. He was an internationally famous writer with friends in high places. It had all been possible, even throwing in the towel and going to America, "to settle down to a humdrum life of letters and to apply for American citizenship," as the *Herald Tribune* reporter had said. But he wasn't any Jewish refugee writer. He was Essad Bey. ("He hates trouble, but he's ready for anything.") Lev didn't finally blame his ex-wife, much as he couldn't stop thinking about her. He knew that the source of his troubles went deeper.

In a stray bit of text near the end of the manuscript, he wrote: "The author of this book is dead. He was the victim of an airplane crash that occurred when he wanted to cross the short stretch that separates southern Europe from Asia." Then he struck the text out.

When I met her in Vienna, Frau Mögle had told me that after Lev left Austria she had seen Abraham Nussimbaum several times and had tried to help him.

"The old Nussimbaum, yes, Essad's father; when he saw me, he said I was a Nazi, you see I had such white-blond hair, platinum-blond, you know, but Camilla, that was my secretary, she said, 'She's here to help you,' but still the old Nussimbaum was scared of me."

She said that Abraham had spoken to her of funding Stalin's early career with bribes and of the millions he had in Baku, and she described how he still dressed perfectly in expensive suits and how he hired servants to polish his shoes up until the very end, when he ran out of everything and they finally came for him. "Camilla went up to see him—I was waiting downstairs in the car—and she came back and said Nussimbaum has been transported away to Modliborzyce, but where is that? How could I know where that was?" (According to Viennese Jewish community records, Abraham was put on a transport to Poland on March 5, 1941, and most likely murdered in Treblinka shortly after.) "We never got a letter, nothing."

She said that before Abraham disappeared, he had begged her to go down to Positano to see Lev. She showed me four separate passports—all apparently legal and all containing her Aryan certification—that she'd needed to get around Europe in those days, and said, "It was very difficult to go to Positano then, it was the war, but when I give my word, that's it, so I went." She'd spent two weeks with Lev. "He didn't scream," Frau Mögle said. "He howled like an animal—*howled,* a noise you cannot imagine."

After she gave me his notebooks to read, I spent weeks deciphering their tiny pain-filled lines. As they progressed, both Lev's scrawl and his stories became more densely packed; I found myself slipping into the role of the obtuse reviewer of *Twelve Secrets of the Caucasus,* long ago, trying to find Khevsuria on the map. The author's descent and the destruction were almost as fantastic as his ascent had been, and I realized what it was that was so compelling about Lev: he believed he could invent his way in and out of anything—even confined in a tiny room watching his own body disintegrate, he still fights to enclose one more persona inside another, like living Chinese boxes. In the final notebook, he creates a foreword to the work, in which he constructs a framing fiction for its composition—a mysterious scholar whose name he prefers not to disclose. He describes his meeting and subsequent friendship with this cosmopolitan young Dr. X, of whom every trace, after some years, suddenly vanishes.

"His postcards stopped coming, and the scholarly journals published no new works of his. He seemed to be lost; indeed to have disappeared. . . . How great then was my astonishment when a few months ago I received in the mail a thick notebook that contained the account that follows here." But he adds, reflecting upon Dr. X's sad story, "I had the immediate impression that the true cause of all of these derailments and misfortunes remained a mystery not only to me, but to the author himself as well, and that this cause was to be sought somewhere outside the events here."

Indeed, for Lev, the cause was outside the events of the tale. At moments in the notebooks, he becomes frantic that his father's letters have stopped coming, but he always refrains from confronting why this would be. The manuscript closes with a final letter from Dr. X, return address Mecca, in which he describes his new life in an Arabian kingdom that accepts him as the real thing, the Orient's Orientalist, and establishes him in an intellectual palace surrounded by harmony and brotherly love. But in the notebook's last sentence, Lev Nussimbaum returns to his deepest disguise in a world that has left him without an audience for the most disturbing of his stories:

I feel I have nothing to add to these lines.

—KURBAN SAID

Notes

INTRODUCTION: *On the Trail of Kurban Said*

xi "If Kurban Said can't push Erich Segal": Kurban Said, *Ali and Nino* (New York, 1972, Pocket Books edition).

xi "buried treasure": Christopher Lehmann-Haupt, "A Passage to the Caucasus," *The New York Times,* April 28, 1971.

xi 'Ali Khan, you are stupid': Kurban Said, *Ali and Nino* (New York, 2000 Anchor Books edition), p. 6.

xii Baku as center of burgeoning oil industry: Robert W. Tolf, *The Russian Rockefellers: The Saga of the Nobel Family and the Russian Oil Industry* (Stanford, 1976); Charles van der Leeuw, *Oil and Gas in the Caucasus & Caspian* (Surrey, 2000).

xii Mir Babayev, a popular singer: Interview with Fuad Akhundov, Baku, May 1998.

xii Haji Zeynalabdin Taghiyev: van der Leeuw, *Oil and Gas,* p. 54.

xii Hitler wanted Baku's oil so badly: Daniel Yergin, *The Prize: The Epic Quest for Oil, Money, and Power* (New York, 2003), pp. 334–40.

xii the führer cutting himself the piece with BAKU: Fuad Akhundov's collection of historic film outtakes and photographs of Baku.

xiii "I entered these edifices": Interview with Fuad Akhundov, Baku, May 1998.

xv endless stream of documentation: Interview with Orhan Veziroff, Baku, May 2000.

xv " 'Kurban Said' is a pen-name": John Wain, Introduction to Kurban Said, *Ali and Nino* (New York, 1996 Overlook Press edition), p. 5.

xvi "Essad-Bey, the narrator of the tales": Morteza Negahi, Foreward to Essad Bey, *Blood and Oil in the Orient: Petroleum Industry and Trade in Azerbaijan* (Baku, 1997), pp. iii–iv.

xvi odd similarities: Compare Said, *Ali and Nino* (2000), pp. 40–47, with Essad Bey, *Blood and Oil in the Orient* (London, 1931), pp. 291–97.

xvii "My father often had to work": Interview with Miriam and Sara Ashurbekov, Baku, May 1998.

xviii *Times* story on Essad: "Czar's Biographer Here: Essad Bey Declares Ruler Was Not Understood," *The New York Times,* March 11, 1935, p. 19.

xix "Who is this Essad Bey?": Lev Trotsky, Letter to Lev Sedov, September 13, 1931.

xix "everything in a foreign language": Interview with the Potts family, Los Angeles, June 2001.

xix Kipling on the floor: Letter from Essad Bey to Pima Andreae, September 22, 1941.

xix quest for Oriental authenticity: William Gifford Palgrave, *Travels in Central and Eastern Arabia* (London, 1871). Also see Benjamin Braude, " 'Jew' and Jesuit at the Origins of Arabism: William Gifford Palgrave," in Martin Kramer, ed., *The Jewish Discovery of Islam: Studies in Honor of Bernard Lewis* (Tel Aviv, 1999).

xx Jews on horseback: Earl of Beaconsfield, K. G. (Benjamin Disraeli), *Tancred or The New Crusade* (London, 1877), p. 233.

xx attempted to explain Semitic culture: Bernard Lewis, "The Pro-Islamic Jews," in Bernard Lewis, *Islam in History: Ideas, People, and Events in the Middle East* (Chicago, 1993).

xxiv "intellectual love affair": Pima Andreae, "Denkmal and Essad Bey" (Foreword to unpublished collection of letters between Essad Bey and Pima Andreae), p. 2.

xxiv "And the state has suddenly remembered me": Letter from Essad Bey to Pima Andreae, June 22, 1942.

xxv the first American ever to interview Hitler: George Sylvester Viereck, "Hitler the German Explosive," *American Monthly* 15, no. 10 (1923).

xxvi "left without saying a word": Interview with Therese Mögle, Vienna, February 1999.

xxvi "Pain is stronger than life": Kurban Said, *Der Mann, der Nichts von der Liebe Verstand* (unpublished manuscript), I, 3A–3B.

PART 1

CHAPTER 1: *Revolution*

3 1905 revolution in Baku: Robert Tucker, *Stalin as Revolutionary 1879–1929: A Study in History and Personality* (New York, 1973), p. 101.

3　"a raging madness": Kurban Said, *Der Mann, der Nichts von der Liebe Verstand* (unpublished manuscript), I, 20A–21B.

4　"Born in . . . ?": Essad Bey, "Lebensläufe von heute: Die Geschichte meines Lebens," *Die Literarische Welt* 7, no. 5 (1931), p. 3.

5　"an oriental sheepskin cap": Essad Bey, *Blood and Oil in the Orient* (London, 1931), pp. 10–11.

6　FN—dismemberment of Poland: W. Bruce Lincoln, *The Romanovs: Autocrats of all the Russias* (New York, 1981), pp. 344–50.

6　Russian Empire and the Jews: David Vital, *A People Apart: The Jews in Europe, 1789–1939* (Oxford, 1999), p. 82.

6　"Old Believers": James H. Billington, *The Icon and the Axe: An Interpretive History of Russian Culture* (New York, 1970), p. 138.

6　Old Believers . . . staged vast rebellions: Abraham Ascher, *Russia: A Short History* (Oxford, 2002), pp. 54–55; Billington, *The Icon and the Axe*, pp. 40, 62, 138.

6　the Judaizers: George Vernadsky, *A History of Russia* (New Haven, 1969), pp. 106–10; H. H. Ben-Sasson, ed., *A History of the Jewish People* (Cambridge, Mass., 1976), p. 814.

7　Like Freemasonry . . . Judaism: Billington, *The Icon and the Axe,* p. 288.

7　Society of Israelite Christians: Ben-Sasson, ed., *A History of the Jewish People,* pp. 813–14.

7　a wandering "fool-in-Christ": Robert C. Williams, *Ruling Russian Eurasia: Khans, Clans and Tsars* (Malabar, 2000), p. 64.

7　Count Pestel . . . suggested giving the Jews: David Vital, *A People Apart,* pp. 208–9.

7　the "Jewish problem" should be solved by thirds: Flora Solomon and Barnet Litvinoff, *Baku to Baker Street: The Memoirs of Flora Solomon* (London, 1984), p. 17.

8　"he had his sights on faraway Caucasus": Solomon and Litvinoff, *Baku to Baker Street,* p. 20.

8　"just as all was ready, our butler": Ibid., pp. 42–43.

9　"fat, bearded brunettes": Banine, *Jours Caucasiens* (Paris, 1945), p. 39.

10　"Gambling is forbidden in the Koran": Ibid., pp. 91–92.

10　background on Baku oil: Daniel Yergin, *The Prize: The Epic Quest for Oil, Money and Power* (New York, 2003), pp. 25–32, 57–58.

10　"I have memories of the flaming waves": Solomon and Litvinoff, *Baku to Baker Street,* p. 21.

10　previous uses of oil: Yergin, *The Prize,* pp. 20, 24.

10　Alexandre Dumas marveled: Alexandre Dumas, *Adventures in Caucasia* (Westport, 1975), p. 141.

10　The Baku gushers: Robert W. Tolf, *The Russian Rockefellers: The Saga of the Nobel Family and the Russian Oil Industry* (Stanford, 1976), pp. 47–48.

11 naming their first tanker *Zoroaster:* Ibid., p. 56.

12 fin de siècle Baku: Audrey Altstadt-Mirhadi, "Baku: Transformation of Muslim Town," in Michael F. Hamm, ed., *The City in Late Imperial Russia* (Bloomington, Ind., 1986), p. 284.

12 A British visitor: E. A. Brayley Hodgetts, *Round About Armenia: The Record of a Journey Across the Balkans, Through Turkey, the Caucasus and Persia* (London, 1916), p. 155.

12 czar's advisers had dreamed up the 1904–5 Russo-Japanese War: Orlando Figes, *A People's Tragedy: The Russian Revolution 1891–1924* (New York, 1996), p. 168; Ascher, *Russia,* pp. 136–37.

12 "little, short-tailed monkeys": Quoted in W. Bruce Lincoln, *In War's Dark Shadow: The Russians Before the Great War* (New York, 1983), p. 236.

13 FN—lessons of the Russo-Japanese War: John Ellis, *The Social History of the Machine Gun* (New York, 1975), pp. 65–68.

13 thirty-six hundred government officials: Anna Geifman, *Thou Shalt Kill: Revolutionary Terrorism in Russia, 1894–1917* (Princeton, 1993), p. 21.

13 Nearly seven hundred pogroms: Figes, *A People's Tragedy,* p. 197.

13 uprisings in Baku: Altstadt-Mirhadi, "Baku," pp. 303–11.

14 "blood flowed": Said, *Der Mann,* I, 7B.

14 "Thousands of dead": Armen Ohanian, "The Dancer of Shamakha," *Asia* 22, no. 5 (May 1922), pp. 343–44, 396.

15 "The Sluzki lineage": Giamil Vacca-Mazzara, "Mohammed Es'ad-Bey: *Scrittore Musalmano dell'Azerbaigian Caucasico*" (Obituary of Essad Bey), *Oriente Moderno* 22 , no. 10 (1942), p. 434.

16 "airtight documentation of Aryan ancestry": Letter from Essad Bey to Giovanni Gentile, September 1938.

16 "My mother brought me into the world": Said, *Der Mann,* III, 4B.

17 "All Caucasian peoples without exception": Essad Bey, *The Twelve Secrets of the Caucasus,* p. 196.

18 "Yes, there is a reason": Letter from Essad Bey to Pima Andreae, February 7, 1942.

18 "Believe me—it's better": Letter from Essad Bey to Pima Andreae, June 16, 1941.

18 Lev "never smiled": Interview with Noam Hermont, Paris, July 2003.

19 "very revolutionary letters": Letter from Essad Bey to Pima Andreae, October 26, 1940.

19 Berta had killed herself by drinking acid: Interview with Noam Hermont, Paris, July 2003.

19 "She was right back then": Letter from Essad Bey to Pima Andreae, June 16, 1941.

19 a quarter of the city's population: Tucker, *Stalin as Revolutionary*, p. 105.

20 Stalin's violent "expropriations": Geifman, *Thou Shalt Kill*, pp. 112–15.

20 Stalin told Lev about Lev's mother: Letter from Essad Bey to Pima Andreae, October 26, 1940.

20 young Stalin as mafioso radical : Edward Ellis Smith, *The Young Stalin: The Early Years of an Elusive Revolutionary* (New York, 1967), p. 58; Alex de Jonge, *Stalin and the Shaping of the Soviet Union* (New York, 1986), p. 67.

21 "My mother, along with Krasin": Essad Bey, "Essad Bey: Oel und Blut im Orient," *Das Tagebuch* 11, no. 5 (1930), p. 195.

21 "a perfect specimen of the double life": Alan Moorehead, *The Russian Revolution* (New York, 1958), p. 79.

21 "immaculately groomed": Timothy Edward O'Connor, *The Engineer of Revolution: L.B. Krasin and the Bolsheviks, 1870–1926* (Boulder, Colo., 1992), p. 46.

21 Krasin's double life: Ibid., p. 71.

21 "She suffered horribly": Interview with Noam Hermont, Paris, July 2003.

21 Lev's mother's "crime": Letter from Essad Bey to Pima Andreae, June 16, 1941.

21 "poisoned my father's life": Letter from Essad Bey to Pima Andreae, May 18, 1941.

21 "He took my homeland": Letter from Essad Bey to Pima Andreae, June 24, 1941.

22 many women joined movements: Geifman, *Thou Shalt Kill*, pp. 12–13.

22 Their paragon was Vera Zasulich: Edward Crankshaw, *The Shadow of the Winter Palace: Russia's Drift to Revolution, 1825–1917* (New York, 1976), pp. 252–55.

23 "[Their] obstinacy put me into such a rage": Quoted in Crankshaw, *The Shadow of the Winter Palace*, p. 167.

23 serfs more and more like slaves: Richard Pipes, *Russia Under the Old Regime* (New York, 1974), p. 150; Geoffrey Hosking, *Russia: People and Empire* (Cambridge, Mass., 1997), pp. 198–200.

24 Alexander II had resolved to modernize: W. Bruce Lincoln, *The Romanovs: Autocrats of all the Russias* (New York, 1981), pp. 575–80; Ascher, *Russia*, pp. 110–16.

24 improved conditions for Russia's Jews: Ben-Sasson, ed., *A History of the Jewish People*, p. 820.

24 "liberated sixty million peasants": Pauline Wengeroff, "Memoirs of a Grandmother," *The Golden Tradition: Jewish Life and Thought in Eastern Europe*, Lucy Dawidowicz, ed. (New York, 1967), p. 163.

25 To the People: Figes, *A People's Tragedy*, pp. 136–37.

25 the students dressed like peasants: Hosking, *Russia,* pp. 349–56. For a more detailed discussion, see Franco Venturi, *Roots of Revolution: A History of the Populist and Socialist Movements in Nineteenth Century Russia,* trans. Francis Haskell (Chicago, 1983), pp. 469–506.

25 "The ideal of the French Revolution": Essad Bey, *Nicholas II: Prisoner of the Purple* (New York, 1937), p. 54.

25 People's Will terrorist organization: See George Vernadsky et al., eds., *Source Book for Russian History from Early Times to 1917,* vol. 3 (New Haven, 1972), p. 664.

25 Sofya Perovskaya: Lincoln, *The Romanovs,* p. 445; Crankshaw, *The Shadow of the Winter Palace,* pp. 263, 266, 269.

26 FN—Lenin's background was faked: Essad Bey, *Lenin* (Italy, 1937), p. 1. Dmitri Volkogonov, *Lenin: A New Biography* (New York, 1994), pp. 8–9.

26 Sofya hated the whole ruling establishment: Lincoln, *The Romanovs,* p. 443.

26 Sofya led group of terrorists: The following account of March 1, 1881, is described in ibid., pp. 443–46; Venturi, *Roots of Revolution,* pp. 709–20; Crankshaw, *The Shadow of the Winter Palace,* pp. 270–71.

27 Alexander III reversed his father's reforms: Lincoln, *The Romanovs,* pp. 446–47; Crankshaw, *The Shadow of the Winter Palace,* pp. 270–71.

27 "revolt that was as demonical as": Essad Bey, *Nicholas II,* p. 53.

28 "the frail boy . . . with beautifully shaped eyes": Ibid., p. 5.

28 "the imperial family had come to suspect": Ibid., p. 9.

28 "Because of the staggering event": Ibid., p. 44.

28 "the Czar and I, we have": Letter from Essad Bey to Pima Andreae, March 3, 1940.

CHAPTER 2: *Wild Jews*

31 threat of kidnapping and extortion: Anna Geifman, "The Anarchists and the 'Obscure Extremists,' " in Anna Geifman, ed., *Russia Under the Last Tsar: Opposition and Subversion 1894–1917* (Oxford, 1999), pp. 94–110.

31 FN—Stalin and protection money: Alice Schulte, *Biographie Essad-Bey* (unpublished manuscript), p. 1.

32 terrorists assassinated fifty local businessmen: Anna Geifman, *Thou Shalt Kill: Revolutionary Terrorism in Russia, 1894–1917* (Princeton, 1993), pp. 22–23.

32 Terror of the City: Ibid., p. 145.

32 "My father was a millionaire": Kurban Said, *Der Mann, der Nichts von der Liebe Verstand* (unpublished manuscript), I, 9A.

32 Banine's grandfather was seized: Banine, *Jours Caucasiens* (Paris, 1945), pp. 93–97.

32 "peculiar manner": Said, *Der Mann,* I, 8B.

32 "I see them again": Ibid., I, 1B–2A.

33 "Surrounded by teachers": Ibid., I, 2A.

33 "Not a single person": Letter from Essad Bey to Pima Andreae, May 8, 1941.

33 "For days and days": Said, *Der Mann,* I, 18A.

33 "his favorite walks": Alice Schulte, *Biographie Essad-Bey,* p. 1.

33 "My love for the old": Essad Bey, "Lebensläufe von heute: Die Geschichte meines Lebens," *Die Literarische Welt* 7, no. 5 (1931), p. 3.

34 "Things I had read": Said, *Der Mann,* I, 16A.

34 "To this day": Ibid., I, 15B.

34 "Liova was fascinated": Interview with Zuleika Asadullayeva, Baku, June 2000.

36 "The wall": Said, *Der Mann,* I, 18A.

36 the "Jassaians": Essad Bey, *Blood and Oil in the Orient* (London, 1931), pp. 48–50.

36 the Khevsurs: Essad Bey, *Twelve Secrets of the Caucasus* (New York, 1931), pp. 118–26.

37 the Aisors: Essad Bey, *Blood and Oil,* p. 53.

37 the so-called Kipta: Essad Bey, *Der Kaukasus: Seine Berge, Völke und Geschichte* (Berlin, 1931), p. 105.

37 tribal Jews wore daggers, boots: Valery Dymshits, "Jews of the Caucasus: Mountain Jews," in Exhibition Catalogue, *Facing West: Oriental Jews of Central Asia and the Caucasus* (Zwolle, 1999), p. 108.

37 remarkable appearance of local Jews: Valery Dymshits, "The Eastern Jewish Communities of the Former USSR," in *Facing West,* p. 11.

37 "in their Oriental dress": Flora Solomon and Barnet Litvinoff, *Baku to Baker Street: The Memoirs of Flora Solomon* (London, 1984), p. 26.

38 "proud families of princes": Essad Bey, *Blood and Oil,* pp. 101–2.

38 "a Jewish emperor once ruled": Essad Bey, *Twelve Secrets of the Caucasus,* p. 192.

38 "through some error; the name Kipta": Essad Bey, *Blood and Oil,* p. 105.

38 earliest record of Khazars: Kevin Alan Brook, *The Jews of Khazaria* (Northvale, N.J., 1999), p. 13. See also Ken Blady, *Jewish Communities in Exotic Places* (Northvale, N.J., 2000), p. 117.

39 the Arab-Khazar wars: Brook, *The Jews of Khazaria,* pp. 157–62.

39 Kagan Bulan's conversion: Ken Blady, *Jewish Communities in Exotic Places* (Northvale, N.J., 2000), pp. 116–17. Also Brook, pp. 124–25.

39 Khazaria provided a sanctuary: Brook, *The Jews of Khazaria,* pp. 117–18. Also Blady, *Jewish Communities,* p. 117.

39 tolerant and welcoming toward all outsiders: Blady, *Jewish Communities,*

pp. 116–17. See also Simon Dubnow, *History of the Jews in Russia and Poland from the Earliest Times Until the Present Day* (Philadelphia, 1916), p. 22.

39 Khazars established a supreme court: Brook, *The Jews of Khazaria,* p. 64.

39 the Subbotniks: James H. Billington, *The Icon and the Axe: An Interpretive History of Russian Culture* (New York, 1966), p. 288. See also Dubnow, *History of the Jews in Russia and Poland,* pp. 401–3.

40 "Entire settlements were laid waste": Dubnow, *History of the Jews in Russia and Poland,* p. 403.

40 Cossacks who turned Subbotnik: Yo'av Karny, *Highlanders: A Journey to the Caucasus in Search of Memory* (New York, 2000), pp. 340–44.

40 FN—the Subbotniks and Vichy, France: Richard H. Weisberg, *Vichy Law and the Holocaust in France* (New York, 1996) pp. 214–28.

40 native Jews hostile to "foreign Jews": Essad Bey, *Blood and Oil,* p. 104.

41 "savage, brutal warriors, knights": Essad Bey, *Twelve Secrets of the Caucasus,* p. 196.

41 FN—*The Exiled and the Redeemed:* Itzhak Ben-Zvi, *The Exiled and the Redeemed* (Philadelphia, 1957), p 257.

41 insurrection of the Kipta: Essad Bey, *Blood and Oil,* p. 106.

41 "As incomprehensible as my love": Said, *Der Mann,* I, 20B.

41 Peter Stolypin returned order: W. Bruce Lincoln, *In War's Dark Shadow: The Russians Before the Great War* (New York, 1983), pp. 340–48.

41–42 decadent prosperity and futurist poetry nights: Harold B. Segel, *Turn-of-the-Century Cabaret: Paris, Barcelona, Berlin, Munich, Vienna, Cracow, Moscow, St. Petersburg, Zurich* (New York, 1987), pp. 303–20.

42 economist Edmond Terry's verdict: quoted in Edvard Radzinsky, *The Last Tsar: The Life and Death of Nicholas II* (New York, 1993), p. 119.

42 frequently withdrawing Lev from school: Alice Schulte, *Biographie Essad-Bey,* p. 1.

42 Bolsheviks harnessed terror: Richard Pipes, *The Russian Revolution* (New York, 1990), pp. 533–55, 822–25; Orlando Figes, *A People's Tragedy: The Russian Revolution 1891–1924* (New York, 1996), pp. 520–25, 627–49.

42–43 Lenin's newfound respect for Stalin: Simon Sebag Montefiore, *Stalin: The Court of the Red Tsar* (New York, 2004), p. 30.

43 "Declaration of the Rights of the Peoples of Russia": reprinted in Robert V. Daniels, ed., *A Documentary History of Communism,* vol. 1 (New York, 1960), p. 125.

43 Lev heard machine guns from basement: Essad Bey, *Blood and Oil,* pp. 92–111; Kurban Said, *Der Mann,* I, 22A.

43 hiding in the cellar seemed a game: Kurban Said, *Der Mann,* I, 22B–24A.

44 "Local carts were squeaking": Ibid., I, 23B–24A.

CHAPTER 3: *The Way East*

47 "Truth can only be obtained": Kurban Said, *Der Mann, der Nichts von der Liebe Verstand* (unpublished manuscript), I, 5B.

48 Lev cast himself as Essad Bey: Essad Bey, *Blood and Oil in the Orient* (London, 1931), pp. 12–13.

49 Abraham on list of "bloodsuckers": Ibid., p. 112.

50 armies converged on Turkestan: John Keegan, *The First World War* (New York, 1999), pp. 383–85.

50 Russia absorbed fifty square miles a day: David Fromkin, *A Peace to End All Peace: Creating the Modern Middle East 1914–1922* (New York, 1989), p. 475.

50 Nikolai Danilevski on Turkestan: Ivar Spector, *The Soviet Union and the Muslim World 1917–1958* (Seattle and London, 1959), p. 17.

50 Russia's treaties with local khans: Ibid., p. 35.

51 soviet in Samarkand: Ibid., p. 36.

51 *Izvestia*'s complaint about Turkestan: Ibid., p. 103.

51 An American journalist: Edward Ross, *Russia in Upheaval* (New York, 1918), p. 70.

52 heroes' welcome in Kizel-Su: Essad Bey, *Blood and Oil*, pp. 118–19.

52 "I could not become accustomed": Ibid., p. 119.

52 moved to Kizel-Su cinema: Ibid., p. 119.

53 Baron von Osten-Sacken: Ibid., pp. 122–23.

54 Lenin's views on Muslim independence: Fromkin, *A Peace to End All Peace*, pp. 475–77.

54 murder of the twenty-six Baku commissars: For a general overview, see Tadeusz Swietochowski and Brian C. Collins, *Historical Dictionary of Azerbaijan* (Lanham, 1999), p. 33.

54–55 two of twenty-six were friends of Lenin: Peter Hopkirk, Introduction to *The Spy Who Disappeared: Diary of a Secret Mission to Russian Central Asia in 1918,* by Reginald Teague-Jones (London, 1991), p. 9.

54 "make themselves secure": Essad Bey, *Blood and Oil*, p. 128.

55 "The entire dialectic of Marxism": Ibid., p. 129.

55 "Do you know who is on": Ibid., p. 130.

55 the commissars in shackles: Ibid., p. 131.

56 "Most of them were pale": Said, *Der Mann*, I, 26B.

56 Trotsky wrote a book about the twenty-six: Hopkirk, Epilogue to *The Spy Who Disappeared*, pp. 205–6.

56–57 the story of Teague-Jones: Hopkirk, Introduction to *The Spy Who Disappeared*, pp. 9–13.

57 "prisoners had been quietly shot": Teague-Jones, *The Spy Who Disappeared*, p. 121.

57 Lev and Abraham continued toward Bukhara: Essad Bey, *Blood and Oil,* pp. 136–39.

58 salted fish as fuel: Ibid., pp. 139–40.

58 "To get lost in the desert": Ibid., p. 143.

58 the ways of the *chalwadar*: Ibid., pp. 145–46.

59 "tediousness, melancholy, and suffering": Ibid., p. 141.

59 the ways of the hakim: Ibid., p. 157.

59 "I had an insane fear of *pindinka*": Ibid., p. 157.

60 the emir survived by ruthlessness: Fromkin, *A Peace to End All Peace,* p. 486.

60 the emir was up to his ears in debt: Essad Bey, *Blood and Oil,* pp. 183–85.

60 "kill all these foreigners": Kurban Said, *Ali and Nino* (New York, 2000), pp. 140–41.

60 "with the help of a few hundred Soviet": Essad Bey, *Blood and Oil,* p. 188.

61 these princes and ministers in Berlin: Ibid., p. 176.

61 Winston Churchill's calls: Fromkin, *A Peace to End All Peace,* pp. 473, 488.

61 lieutenant colonel's description: Dudley Carleton, "The Fate of the Turkomans," *Blackwood's Magazine* 207, no. 1,251 (January 1920), pp. 87–88.

62 forty thousand half-starving POWs: Peter Hopkirk, *Setting the East Ablaze: Lenin's Dream of an Empire in Asia* (New York, 1984), pp. 13–14, 19, 24–26, 32–33, 37–38, 53.

62 "the desert fell beneath the power": Essad Bey, *Blood and Oil,* p. 174.

63 Nussimbaums joined a caravan: Ibid., p. 190.

63 "I had forgotten [reflects Ali]": Said, *Ali and Nino,* pp. 213–14.

64 "Nothing is alive in Persia": Essad Bey, *Blood and Oil,* pp. 190–91.

64 "In Persia religion alone is alive": Ibid., p. 191.

64 Lev encountered Ismailis, devil worshippers, etc.: Ibid., p. 191–97.

64 FN—anti-Semitism was uncommon in Persia: Roy Mottahedeh, *The Mantle of the Prophet: Religion and Politics in Iran* (New York, 1985), 238–40, 388–89.

65 Muharram passion festival: Essad Bey, *Blood and Oil,* pp. 200–4.

66 "merchants, warriors, princes": Ibid., p. 195.

67 "Of what use is your money": Ibid., p. 215.

67 "For this reason he wished to kill us": Ibid., p. 215.

67 the court of the Jafar Khan: Ibid., pp. 216–22.

68 "For example . . . 'Pillar of Justice' ": Ibid., p. 208.

68 antique sexual ambiguities: Ibid., pp. 219–22.

68 "since our interests lay on another plane": Ibid., p. 221.

70 the Jangalis: Ibid., 222–24.

70 Iranian Constitutional Revolution: Ira M. Lapidus, *A History of Islamic Societies* (Cambridge, 1988), pp. 578–79.

70 Unity of Islam party: See Mottahedeh, *The Mantle of the Prophet,* pp. 56–57, 219.

70 "let their hair and nails grow": Ibid., p. 224.

70 "Unbelievers, step to the side": Ibid., p. 226.

71 Committee of Iron: Essad Bey, *Blood and Oil,* p. 230.

71 "That is the head of the villain": Ibid., p. 230.

72 This group would sail back across the Caspian: Ibid., pp. 231–41.

72 "At last the four captains": Ibid., p. 232.

74 "The ship was like an insane asylum": Said, *Der Mann,* I, 26B.

74 Their rescue: Essad Bey, *Blood and Oil,* pp. 239–41.

74 "The birds in the forest sing": Ibid., p. 241.

CHAPTER 4: *Escape*

75 FN—bizarre British–Cossack–Social Revolutionary coalition: David Fromkin, *A Peace to End All Peace: Creating the Modern Middle East 1914–1922* (New York, 1989), pp. 355, 359–60.

75 "political activity": Essad Bey, *Blood and Oil in the Orient* (London, 1931), p. 242.

76 "Hanged for theft": Ibid., p. 249.

76 "One of the first who appeared": Essad Bey, *Blood and Oil,* p. 251.

76 "According to the general view": Ibid., p. 251.

76 British were downright contemptuous: Tadeusz Swietochowski, *Russian Azerbaijan: 1905–1920* (Cambridge, England, 1985), p. 141.

77 democracy in Azerbaijan: See Charles van der Leeuw, *Azerbaijan: A Quest for Identity* (New York, 2000), pp. 117–18.

77 "very dignified and interesting gentleman": Mark Elliott, *Azerbaijan with Georgia* (West Sussex, England, 1999), p. 43.

77 "violated the principles of civilization": Essad Bey, *Blood and Oil,* p. 254.

77 "For the oil lords": Ibid., p. 256.

77 "We were all proud": Interview with Zuleika Asadullayeva, Baku, June 2000.

78 treaties and an oil deal: van der Leeuw, *Azerbaijan,* pp. 117–18.

78 improbably apt coincidences: Essad Bey, *Blood and Oil,* pp. 261–63.

79 the Cheka: Ronald Hingley, *The Russian Secret Police: Muscovite, Imperial Russian, and Soviet Political Security Operations* (New York, 1970), pp. 118–26.

79 "If under the Czar's regime": Vladimir Korolenko, "Guilty!," *The Atlantic Monthly* 129, no. 6 (June 1922), p. 817.

79 Azeri government's capitulation: Swietochowski, *Russian Azerbaijan,* p. 182.

79 "expressly bound themselves not to persecute": Essad Bey, *Blood and Oil,* p. 262.

79 Cheka carried out "liquidations": Swietochowski, *Russian Azerbaijan,* p. 185.

79 Lev saw victims of the purge: Essad Bey, *Blood and Oil,* p. 263.

80 murders increased: van der Leeuw, *Azerbaijan,* p. 125.

80 The head of the Baku Cheka: Essad Bey, *Blood and Oil,* p. 264.

80 prisoners taken to Nargen: van der Leeuw, *Azerbaijan,* p. 125.

80 but prisoners often simply shot: Essad Bey, *Blood and Oil,* p. 264.

80 "were thrown on a huge pyre": Ibid., pp. 265–66.

80 Bolsheviks filmed these exhibitions: Ibid., p. 266.

80 Gestapo took Cheka as model: See Edward Crankshaw, *Gestapo, Instrument of Tyranny* (London, 1956).

80 Abraham . . . "as an 'old bandit, bloodsucker' ": Essad Bey, *Blood and Oil,* p. 265.

81 Stalin came to stay: Letter from Essad Bey to Pima Andreae, May 3, 1940.

81 Lev told a journalist about Stalin's stay: William Leon Smyser, "He Has Lived His Stories," *New York Herald Tribune,* December 16, 1934.

81 "I often sat opposite him": Letter from Essad Bey to Pima Andreae, December 15, 1941.

81 " 'My God' ": Ibid.

81 "Only when the *Pockennarbige*": Letter from Essad Bey to Pima Andreae, October 26, 1940.

81 "We spoke almost all night": Letter from Essad Bey to Pima Andreae, June 16, 1941.

81 "She was right back then": Letter from Essad Bey to Pima Andreae, June 16, 1941.

81 "week of plundering": Essad Bey, *Blood and Oil,* p. 267.

82 silk sheets and pillow covers: Ibid., p. 267.

82 "The Proletariat can stand no dirt!": Ibid., p. 268.

84 Lev claimed to man machine-gun posts: Ibid., p. 273.

85 Bolsheviks gradually drew the circle tighter: Compare to Tadeusz Swietochowski and Brian C. Collins, *Historical Dictionary of Azerbaijan* (Lanham, 1999), pp. 56–57; van der Leeuw, *Azerbaijan,* p. 125.

85 "the bullets gliding through [his] hands": Kurban Said, *Ali and Nino* (New York, 2000), p. 274.

86 "The court procedure was as simple": Essad Bey, *Blood and Oil,* p. 275.

86 "When I was arrested": Kurban Said, *Der Mann, der Nichts von der Liebe Verstand* (unpublished manuscript), I, 29A–30B.

87 "Comrade, please make out a permit": Essad Bey, *Blood and Oil,* pp. 275–76.

87 "The Cheka of Ganja": Essad Bey, *Blood and Oil*, p. 277.

88 "Defense-guard . . . of Helenendorf": Ibid., p. 277.

88 replica of a Black Forest community: Ibid., pp. 278–82.

88 Swabians settled parcels of land: Elliott, *Azerbaijan with Georgia*, p. 191.

88 "a land of freedom and happiness": H. H. Schweinitz, *Helenendorf: eine deutsche Kolonie im Kaukasus* (Berlin, 1910), p. 3.

89 the inhabitants of Helenendorf: Essad Bey, *Blood and Oil*, p. 281.

90 "The German colonists": Ibid., p. 282.

90 German colonists deported by Stalin: Elliott, *Azerbaijan with Georgia*, p. 191.

91 Lev and the Armenian made a plan: Essad Bey, *Blood and Oil*, pp. 282–83.

92 Cheka's attempt to bolshevize the village: Ibid., p. 283.

93 "the guests who did not rob": Ibid., p. 287.

94 "If a guest enters your house": Said, *Ali and Nino*, p. 253.

94 campfire feasts and the knife dance: Essad Bey, *Blood and Oil*, p. 287.

94 wandering poets compete: Ibid., pp. 291–96.

95 "Your clothes stink of dung": Said, *Ali and Nino*, pp. 45–47.

96 "remnants of feudalism": Essad Bey, *Blood and Oil*, p. 291.

96 "devil worshippers," or Jezids: Ibid., pp. 298–300.

97 rumored sexual perversions drew contempt: Ibid., p. 300.

98 stopped by anti-Bolshevik militia: Ibid., pp. 301–2.

99 "Armenian peddlers, Kurdish fortune-tellers": Said, *Ali and Nino*, p. 130.

99 "Here they drank wine, danced": Ibid., p. 119.

100 "the sad gaze of refugees": Said, *Der Mann*, I, 32A–33A.

100 "I can remember only one dream": Ibid., I, 35A–35B.

101 "an inordinate number of beautiful women": Said, *Der Mann*, I, 33A.

101 Lev half believed a tale: Essad Bey, *Blood and Oil*, p. 310.

101 Lermontov's "Tamara": Susan Layton, *Russian Literature and Empire: Conquest of the Caucasus from Pushkin to Tolstoy* (Cambridge, England, 1994), pp. 200–201.

101 Georgian woman as a hellion: Ibid., p. 210.

101 "still see the delicate faces": Said, *Der Mann*, I, 34A.

102 "an angelic being walked in": Ibid.

102 "whether the Bolsheviks would fall": Ibid.

102 " 'I provoke you' ": Ibid.

103 Lev gave the Russian a gash: Ibid.

103 "Strange, how seldom a person knows": Said, *Der Mann*, I, 36A.

104 "somehow become a Dutch consul": Essad Bey, *Blood and Oil*, p. 316.

104 "as though in a dream": Said, *Der Mann*, I, 36A.

CHAPTER 5: *Constantinople, 1921*

105 Lev and father steamed toward capital: Essad Bey, *Blood and Oil in the Orient* (London, 1931), pp. 316–17.

106 Constantinople divided into zones: Mansel, *Constantinople*, p. 381.

106 Young Turks spoke of universal rights: Howard M. Sachar, *Emergence of the Middle East: 1914–1924* (New York, 1969), p. 12.

106 "Whether one goes to a synagogue": Essad Bey and Wolfgang von Weisl, *Allah ist gross: Niedergang und Aufstieg der islamischen Welt* (Leipzig-Vienna, 1936), p. 68.

107 FN—Constantinople as Czargrad vs. pan-Turanian principle: Ibid., pp. 7–8, 47, 153–57.

107 Enver Pasha clinched Turkish-German axis: Ibid., pp. 26–27.

107 *"Deutschland über Allah"*: Ibid., p. 34.

107 Enver turned over command: Ibid., pp. 14–26.

107 Turkish deaths fighting Russia: Ibid., p. 182.

108 deportation of Armenians: Norman M. Naimark, *Fires of Hatred: Ethnic Cleansing in Twentieth-Century Europe* (Cambridge, Mass., 2002), pp. 22–35.

108 Armenian massacre figures: Ibid., pp. 40–41.

109 Armenian separatist movement: Efraim Karsh and Inari Karsh, *Empires of the Sand: The Struggle for Mastery in the Middle East, 1789–1923* (Cambridge, Mass., 1999), p. 153.

109 Young Turk leaders escaped to Berlin: Sachar, *Emergence of the Middle East*, p. 249.

109 Curzon's Hagia Sofia campaign: Philip Mansel, *Constantinople: City of the World's Desire* (New York, 1996), p. 383.

109 Vatican wanted in on: Ibid., p. 384.

109–10 FN—Ottomans didn't sack St. Sofia, the crusaders did: "The Byzantine Monuments: Hagia Sofia," Ecumenical Patriarchate of Constantinople (www.patriarchate.org).

110 "Suffering Armenia": Sachar, *Emergence of the Middle East*, pp. 340–46.

110 the Ottoman government at Versailles: Justin McCarthy, *The Ottoman Peoples and the End of Empire* (London, 2002), pp. 120–21.

110 rise of Mustafa Kemal (Ataturk): Ibid., p. 388.

111 inspections along strict class lines: Essad Bey, *Blood and Oil*, pp. 316–17.

111 British-backed "Army of the Caliphate": Mansel, *Constantinople*, pp. 391–93.

112 Wrangel's exiles in 126 ships: Ibid., p. 398.

112 headquarters of "Russia abroad": W. Chapin Huntington, *The Homesick Million: Russia-out-of-Russia*, p. 13.

113 "strange businesses": Essad Bey, *Das weisse Russland, Menschen ohne Heimat* (Leipzig, 1932), p. 64.

113 Russians ran theaters and nightclubs: Mansel, *Constantinople*, p. 399.

113 "One of the great attractions": Banine, *Jours Caucasiens* (Paris, 1945), p. 274.

113 Turkish wives' and widows' association petitioned: Mansel, *Constantinople*, p. 400.

114 a black American entrepreneur: Ibid., pp. 399–400.

114 Lev at the center of everything: Kurban Said, *Der Mann, der Nichts von der Liebe Verstand* (unpublished manuscript), I, 36B.

114 Khilafat resentment against the West: Mansel, *Constantinople*, p. 391.

115 Ataturk's reasons for disbanding caliphate : Ibid., p. 413.

115 "What is the Afghan kingdom?": Interview with Ertugrul and Zeynap Osman, New York, 2000.

116 "My grandfather very politely said": Ibid.

117 Constantinople resurrected tradition of tolerance: Mansel, *Constantinople*, pp. 400–1, 413.

117 the caliph "read a great deal": Constantine Brown, "The Tragicomic Exit of the Osman Dynasty," *Asia* 24, no. 6 (June 1924), p. 449.

118 "the Caliph should be treated": Ibid., p. 450.

118 "His Majesty was reading Montaigne's *Essays*": Ibid., p. 451.

119 "I wasn't too much affected": Interview with Ertugrul and Zeynap Osman, New York, 2001.

119 "Oh, it wasn't only aristocrats": Ibid.

120 "Monarchy is dead": Ibid.

120 "It is a shame": Ibid.

120 Lev discovered meaning of his life: Said, *Der Mann*, I, 37A.

120 "I think I went mad for days": Ibid., I, 36B–37A.

CHAPTER 6: *Minarets and Silk Stockings*

123 FN—French were largest investors in czarist Russia: Gordon Wright, *France in Modern Times* (New York, 1995), p. 306.

123 Banine locked herself in train compartment: Banine, *Jours Caucasiens* (Paris, 1945), pp. 80–83.

124 Nussimbaums boarded ship for Adriatic coast: Kurban Said, *Der Mann, der Nichts von der Liebe Verstand* (unpublished manuscript), I, 40A–40B.

125 national "self-determination": Margaret Macmillan, *Paris 1919: Six Months That Changed the World* (New York, 2002), pp. 10–14.

125 Jews mourned the lost emperors: Stanford J. Shaw, *The Jews of the Ottoman Empire and the Turkish Republic* (New York, 1991), pp. 169, 176, 207–8.

125 "From the day of the abdication": Essad Bey, "Lebensläufe von heute," p. 3.

126 "To understand my cousin's attitude": Interview with Noam Hermont, Paris, July 2003.

126 "Ah, you've seen our Communist Bastille": Said, *Der Mann*, I, 40A–40B.

127 "Europeans sat in bistros": Ibid., I, 38B–39A.

127 "without seeing any street battles": Ibid., I, 40B.

127 " 'Where to?' ": Ibid., I, 41A–42A.

128 origins of the word "fascist": Robert O. Paxton, "The Five Stages of Fascism," *The Journal of Modern History* 70 (March 1998), pp. 1–23.

128 "Down, down, down!": Said, *Der Mann*, I, 42B.

129 *Times* compared Mussolini with Caesar: P. W. Wilson, "Mussolini Dreams of a Spiritual Empire," *The New York Times*, December 27, 1925.

129 Littlefield was decorated by Mussolini government: John P. Diggins, *Mussolini and Fascism: The View from America* (Princeton, N.J., 1972), p. 25.

129 American support for Mussolini: Ibid., pp. 146–56.

129 Mussolini compared to Teddy Roosevelt: Ibid., p. 61.

129 "Dictator government is the greatest": Ibid., p. 27.

129 Coolidge's ambassador ghostwrote "autobiography": Ibid., pp. 27–28.

129 Mussolini's "admirable social experiment": Ibid., p. 27.

130 "dead souls": Said, *Der Mann*, I, 43B.

132 "there are people who ride second": Ibid., I, 43A.

132 émigré figures: Marc Raeff, *Russia Abroad: A Cultural History of the Russian Emigration, 1919–1939* (New York, 1990), p. 24.

133 the ritual of leaving bags: Said, *Der Mann*, I, 43A.

134 "Around Cannes there were many Cossacks": Michael Glenny and Norman Stone, *The Other Russia: The Experience of Exile* (New York, 1990), p. 270.

134 FN—Cossacks in Paraguay: Robert Johnston, *"New Mecca, New Babylon": Paris and the Russian Exiles, 1920–1945* (Kingston, 1988), p. 81.

134 an acute labor shortage: Ibid., pp. 73–80.

135 "The Russian dustmen of Cannes": Glenny and Stone, *The Other Russia*, p. 269.

135 French identity card: Johnston, *"New Mecca, New Babylon,"* p. 75.

136 "Sometimes I took a taxi": Letter from Essad Bey to Pima Andreae, February 5, 1942.

136 "A person who is born": Letter from Essad Bey to Pima Andreae, April 28, 1941.

136 "I don't know why": Said, *Der Mann*, I, 43B.

136 Lev regarded as rather an idiot: Ibid., I, 44B.

136 "Once I spent an entire hour": Ibid., I, 45A–45B.

137 "among the dozens of relatives": Letter from Essad Bey to Pima Andreae, April 28, 1941.

138 "Mr. Nussimbaum could offer shelter": Interview with Noam Hermont, Paris, July 2003.

138 "a bit romantic": Ibid.

139 "The four princes": Letter from Essad Bey to Pima Andreae, June 16, 1941.

139 "English education had to be good": Said, *Der Mann,* II, 1A.

139 "sixteen-year-old boy from Baku": Ibid., II, 1A.

139 "The general curiosity was great": Ibid., II, 2A.

140 "While Jusef or Joe was very modest": Ibid., II, 2A–2B.

140 Abraham entranced by uncle's education: Ibid., II, 3A.

141 money . . . "was becoming tighter": Ibid.

141 "I was convinced . . . a monocle was as necessary": Ibid., II, 5A.

PART 2

CHAPTER 7: *The German Revolution*

145 Lev crossed into Germany in 1921: Gerhard Höpp, "Mohammed Essad Bey oder Die Welten des Lev Abramovič Nussenbaum," Afterword to Essad Bey, *Allah ist gross: Niedergang und Aufstieg der islamischen Welt* (Munich, 2002), p. 387

145 "It wasn't my revolution": Kurban Said, *Der Mann, der Nichts von der Liebe Verstand* (unpublished manuscript), II, 4A.

146 Lev's thoughts stayed dark: Ibid., II, 4B–5A.

147 the Spartacists: Adam B. Ulam, *The Bolsheviks: The Intellectual and Political Triumph of Communism in Russia* (New York, 1968), p. 330.

147 FN—Spartacus in Germany: Richard M. Watt, *The Kings Depart: The Tragedy of Germany: Versailles and the German Revolution* (New York, 1968), p. 129.

148 Ludendorff's dreams for "living space": Gordon A. Craig, *Germany, 1866–1945* (New York, 1978), pp. 373–93; Norman Cohn, *Warrant for Genocide: The Myth of the Jewish World Conspiracy and the Protocols of the Elders of Zion* (London, 2001), p. 149.

148 A.J.P. Taylor's estimate: A.J.P. Taylor, *The Course of German History* (London and New York, 1988), p. 208.

148 FN—Ludendorff's philo-Semitic "drive east": Steven E. Aschheim, "Strange Encounter: Germany, World War I and the Osjuden," in *Brothers and Strangers: The East European Jew in German and German Jewish Consciousness 1800–1923* (Madison, Wisc., 1982), pp. 139–84.

149 kaiser and Ludendorff hastily endorsed the Zionist plan: Howard M. Sachar, *Dreamland: Europeans and Jews in the Aftermath of the Great War* (New York, 2002), p. 222.

149 Ludendorff instituted negotiations: Craig, *Germany*, p. 397.

150 "That Sunday I heard shots": Sebastian Haffner, *Defying Hitler: A Memoir* (New York, 2002), p. 24.

150 "On November 9 and 10 army bulletins": Haffner, *Defying Hitler*, pp. 25–27.

151 "All moral restraint seems to have": George Grosz, *George Grosz: An Autobiography* (Berkeley, 1997), p. 119.

152 "Inhabitants, half-crazed": Ibid., p. 119.

152 The influenza pandemic: Alexandra Richie, *Faust's Metropolis: A History of Berlin* (New York, 1998), pp. 295–96.

152 "You could buy guns": Grosz, *George Grosz*, p. 119.

152 the Freikorps: Richie, *Faust's Metropolis*, p. 305.

152 Blood-red recruiting posters screamed: Sefton Delmer, *Weimar Germany: Democracy on Trial* (London, 1972), pp. 57–65.

153 volunteer Freikorps sprang up: Dave Hollins and William Younghusband, *Austrian Auxiliary Troops 1792–1816 (Men-At-Arms, No. 299)* (Oxford, 1996), pp. 19–21; Vejas Gabriel Liulevicius, *War Land on the Eastern Front: Culture, National Identity, and German Occupation in World War I* (New York, 2000), p. 234.

153 the Freikorps in Baltics: Vejas Gabriel Liulevicius, *War Land on the Eastern Front: Culture, National Identity, and German Occupation in World War I* (New York, 2000), pp. 234–36.

153 "worthy of the battles": Quoted in Ibid., p. 235.

153 "I had to think of the past": Ibid.

154 Ernst von Salomon: Quoted in Ibid., p. 234.

154 "Were they surprised": Quoted in Ibid., p. 235.

154 men ordered to don Russian caps: Ibid., p. 232.

154 "This morning Christmas Eve began": Charles Kessler, ed. and trans., *Berlin in Lights: The Diaries of Count Harry Kessler (1918–1937)* (New York, 1999), pp. 40–41.

155 "The machine-gun on top of the Brandenburger Tor": Ibid., pp. 54–55.

155 Freikorps attacked the revolutionary neighborhoods: George L. Mosse, *Fallen Soldiers: Reshaping the Memory of the World Wars* (New York, 1990), pp. 168–71.

156 FN—sex murder in postwar Berlin: Beth Irwin Lewis, "Lustmord," in *Berlin: Culture and Metropolis* (Minneapolis, 1990), pp. 123–36.

156 "Allegedly she was killed": Kessler, ed., *Berlin in Lights*, p. 58.

156 hundreds dying in Berlin street battles: Ibid., pp. 82–83.

156 "Germany is having a nervous breakdown": Ben Hecht, *A Child of the Century* (New York, 1954), p. 283.

157 "Units of twenty-five men": Ibid., p. 291.

157 Ernst Jünger hailed this "New Man": Ernst Jünger, "Fire," reprinted in

Anton Kaes et al., eds., *The Weimar Republic Sourcebook* (Berkeley, 1994), p. 19.

157   supreme court defined "supra-legal" emergency: Mosse, *Fallen Soldiers,* p. 171.

158   theater critic Kurt Eisner: Sachar, *Dreamland,* pp. 230–35.

158   "believing that at last": Ernst Toller, *I Was a German: The Autobiography of a Revolutionary* (New York, 1991), p. 161.

159   The Freikorps attacked Munich: Ibid., pp. 237–40.

159   The Ehrhardt Brigade: Richie, *Faust's Metropolis,* pp. 319–20.

159   FN—Hitler flew to Berlin for the putsch: Sefton Delmer, *Weimar Germany: Democracy on Trial* (New York, 1972), p. 64.

159   Spartacists raised a new armed force: Craig, *Germany,* p. 431.

160   Lev crossed the border: Said, *Der Mann,* II, 4A.

160   "The usual image of a train station": Ibid., II, 5A.

161   "that there was no shooting": Ibid., II, 6B.

161   Lev as an "amphibian": Ibid., II, 7A.

162   "I regarded the listeners as fools": Ibid., II, 12B.

162   "Splendid chap": Ibid., II, 13A.

162   "the best face of Europe": Ibid., II, 7B.

163   "as good as veiled": Ibid., II, 8B.

163   women were "like beautiful pictures": Ibid., II, 8B–9A.

164   Lev watched the blond couples kissing: Ibid., II, 9B–11A.

164   "I was a strange creature": Ibid., II, 9A.

164   "Chaotic visions tormented me": Ibid., II, 10B.

164   "She resisted in jest and with a smile": Ibid., II, 11A.

165   "the horror of . . . craving eyes": Ibid., II, 12A.

166   "everything changed completely": Ibid., II, 11, 14A.

167   "I saw now what was more": Ibid., II, 15B.

CHAPTER 8: *The Berlin Wall*

169   postwar hopelessness: Alexandra Richie, *Faust's Metropolis: A History of Berlin* (New York, 1998), p. 321.

169   The Nussimbaums were broke: Kurban Said, *Der Mann, der Nichts von der Liebe Verstand* (unpublished manuscript), II, 16A.

169   the second capital of Russia: Robert C. Williams, *Culture in Exile: Russian Émigrés in Germany, 1881–1941* (Ithaca, N.Y., and London, 1972), p. 114.

169   Charlottengrad: Andrei Belyi, "Wie schön es in Berlin ist," quoted in Fritz Mierau, ed., *Russen in Berlin. Literatur, Malerei, Theater, Film 1918–1933* (Leipzig, 1987), p. 56.

170   tram drivers yelled "Russia!" at Bülowstrasse: Richie, *Faust's Metropolis,* p. 287.

170 "At every step, you could hear Russian": Quoted in Otto Friedrich, *Before the Deluge: A Portrait of Berlin in the 1920s* (New York, 1972), p. 82.

170 "If one were to hear German": Belyi, "Wie schön es in Berlin ist," p. 59.

171 The city's population: Heidrun Suhr, *"Fremde in Berlin: The Outsiders' View from the Inside,"* in Charles W. Haxthausen and Heidrun Suhr, ed., *Berlin: Culture and Metropolis* (Minneapolis and Oxford, 1990), p. 222.

171 "a stone coffin": Ibid., p. 222.

171 "It seemed as though everything was bound to collapse": Quoted in Friedrich, *Before the Deluge*, p. 82.

172 FN—Red Cross worker in Berlin: Conrad Hoffmann, *In the Prison Camps of Germany* (New York, 1920), p. 222.

172 the landlord seemed to be pimping: Said, *Der Mann*, II, 17A.

172 finally found a school: Said, *Der Mann*, II, 16A.

172 the Russian gymnasium: Bettina Dodenhoeft, *"Lasst mich nach Russland heim": Russische Emigranten in Deutschland von 1918 bis 1945* (Frankfurt am Main, 1993), pp. 114–16; Gerhard Höpp, "Mohammed Essad Bey oder Die Welten des Lev Abramovič Nussenbaum," Afterword to Essad Bey, *Allah ist gross: Niedergang und Aufstieg der islamischen Welt* (Munich, 2002), p. 388.

173 The émigré community: Marc Raeff, *Russia Abroad: A Cultural History of the Russian Emigration, 1919–1939* (New York, 1990), pp. 48–57.

173 "Perhaps it was the wall": Said, *Der Mann*, II, 16B.

174 "the few friends I still have": Ibid., II, 16B.

174 Boris Alekin would die in Nazi uniform: Höpp, "Mohammed Essad Bey," p. 388.

174 Myron Isacharowitsch also joined nationalists: Alex Brailow, *Survivor's Tale* (unpublished manuscript), II, pp. 88–89.

174 Lev's classmates and friends: Alexander Brailow, Introduction to *The Oriental Tales of Essad-Bey* (unpublished manuscript).

174 "a 'blood and milk' complexion": Brailow, *Survivor's Tale*, II, p. 56.

175 Vladimir Nabokov, Sr.: Williams, *Culture in Exile*, pp. 182–83.

175 *Rul (The Rudder)* and the Emigration: Ibid., pp. 183–86. Also see Mark R. Hatlie, "Die Zeitung als Zentrum der Emigrations-Öffentlichkeit: Das Beispiel der Zeitung *Rul*" ("The Newspaper as Center of the Emigrant Community: The Case of the Newspaper *Rul*"), *Russische Emigration in Deutschland 1918 bis 1941*, Karl Schlögel, ed. (Berlin, 1995), pp. 153–63.

176 Nabokov shot: See Norman Cohn, *Warrant for Genocide: The Myth of the Jewish World Conspiracy and the Protocols of the Elders of Zion* (London, 2001), p. 156.

176 "Jewish story swindler": entry for "Nussenbaum (Noussimbaum)" in *Sigilla veri (Philip Stauff's Semi-Kürschner) Lexikon der Juden, -Genossen und -Gegner aller Zeiten und Zonen, insbesondere Deutschlands, der Lehren,*

Gebräuche, Kunstgriffe und Statistiken der Juden sowie ihrer Gauner-sprache, Trugnamen, Geheimbünde, usw., 20th ed., vol. 4 (Erfurt, Germany, 1931), p. 958.

176 *The Protocols of the Learned Elders of Zion:* Cohn, *Warrant for Genocide,* pp. 72–73.

177 the czarina and the *Protocols:* Ibid., p. 127.

177 "What are these Protocols?": Quoted in Ibid., p. 168.

178 FN—*Times* reversed itself, exposed the *Protocols* as forgery: Ibid., pp. 78–83.

178 Vinberg's "documentary proof": See Ibid., p. 138.

179 murder attempt planned by Vinberg: Williams, *Culture in Exile,* pp. 208–9.

180 376 political assassinations: Howard M. Sachar, *Dreamland: Europeans and Jews in the Aftermath of the Great War* (New York, 2002), p. 247.

182 "My religion [is] that Germanic faith": Quoted in Ibid., p. 254.

182 FN—Cohen sees Jew's duty to spread German supremacy: Hermann Cohen, *Deutschtum und Judentum* (Giessen, 1915); Sachar, *Dreamland,* p. 243.

182 "a guide for the redistribution": Quoted in Hecht, *A Child of the Century* (New York, 1954), p. 304.

183 "Why have you done this to me?": Quoted in Sachar, *Dreamland,* p. 249.

183 "play the Russian card": Ibid., p. 250.

183 Rapallo Treaty's secret codicils: Richie, *Faust's Metropolis,* p. 328.

184 "his own countrymen's vindictive hostility": Charles Kessler, ed. and trans., *Berlin in Lights: The Diaries of Count Harry Kessler (1918–1937)* (New York, 1999), p. 155.

184 word of an assassination plot: Sachar, *Dreamland,* p. 251.

184 "What motive shall I give": Quoted in Friedrich, *Before the Deluge,* p. 107.

184 the driver's convincing testimony: Cohn, *Warrant for Genocide,* pp. 160–61.

185 Martha Dodd gushed: Martha Dodd, *Through Embassy Eyes: My Years in Germany* (New York, 1939), p. 84.

185 FN—*Liana, the Jungle Goddess:* Michael J. Weldon, *The Psychotronic Video Guide* (New York, 1996), p. 331.

186 "It is as if all the life": Quoted in Peter Viereck, *Meta-politics: The Roots of the Nazi Mind* (New York, 1941), pp. 270–71.

CHAPTER 9: *A Hundred Kinds of Hunger*

187 "Some of my friends and I": Alexander Brailow, *Survivor's Tale* (unpublished manuscript), II, p. 113.

188 Georgian monarchists in Berlin: Robert C. Williams, *Culture in Exile: Russian Émigrés in Germany 1881–1941* (Ithaca, N.Y., 1972), pp. 61, 151.

189 "the petty officials": Brailow, *Survivor's Tale,* II, p. 46.

364 Notes for Chapter 9: A Hundred Kinds of Hunger

189 who was "the wife of a German officer": Letter from Essad Bey to Pima Andreae, January 28, 1942.

189 "I was walking": Ibid.

189 representative of the High Commissariats: Karl Hoffmann, "Essad Bey, *Oel und Blut im Orient*," *Deutsche Rundschau* 57 (1930), p. 80.

190 "There are a hundred different kinds": Kurban Said, *Der Mann, der Nichts von der Liebe Verstand* (unpublished manuscript), V, 12B–13A, II, 17A.

191 "I would lie down in bed": Ibid., II, 17A.

191 "How obsequious, how submissive": Ibid., II, 17B.

191 Germans had built five hundred cinemas: John Baxter, *The Hollywood Exiles* (New York, 1976), p. 20.

192 "I had long ago set aside": Joseph Roth, *What I Saw: Reports from Berlin 1920–1933* (New York, 2003), p. 167.

193 "In Berlin I learned that everything": Said, *Der Mann*, II, 18B.

193 "There was no holding me back": Ibid., II, 18B–19A.

193 his new name on application: Gerhard Höpp, "Mohammed Essad Bey: Nur Orient für Europäer?," *Asien Afrika Lateinamerika* 25 (1997), p. 78.

193 "the professors spoke about their subject": *Der Mann*, II, 19A.

194 "While the teacher was explaining": Ibid.

194 "I almost always went on foot": Ibid., II, 19B.

194 "Most likely I would have perished": Ibid., II, 19B.

195 "with excessively broad a's": Alexander Brailow, Introduction to *Oriental Tales of Essad Bey* (unpublished manuscript), p. 5.

196 "romantic immersion in Islam": Ibid.

196 "forget his origins": Brailow, *Survivor's Tale*, II, p. 64.

196 "Essad, besides being a nervous type": Ibid., p. 53.

196 Zhenia "hardly read anything": Ibid., p. 81.

197 "tenderly beautiful profile": Brailow, Introduction to *Oriental Tales*, p. 4.

197 "fat, urbane, very intelligent": Ibid., p. 4.

197 "The whole love affair": Ibid.

197 "usually pink-cheeked": Ibid., p. 5.

197 "18-year-old girls and boys": *Der Mann*, II, 16B.

198 "in his melancholy aristocratic": Ibid., II, 22A.

198 "Tell us something about the dominion": Ibid., II, 22B.

198 "I saw before us the wide": Ibid., II, 22B–23A.

199 "What made Essad a temporary center": Brailow, Introduction to *Oriental Tales*, p. 6.

199 Lev converted to Islam: Höpp, "Mohammed Essad Bey: Nur Orient für Europäer?," p. 77.

199 FN—Lev's first attempt to convert: Brailow, Introduction to *Oriental Tales*, p. 2.

200 "the world of native servants": Ibid., p. 1.

200 founding member of Islamic groups: Höpp, "Mohammed Essad Bey: Nur Orient für Europäer?," p. 77.

201 "In a dark, smoky pub": Essad Bey, "Lebensläufe von heute: Die Geschichte meines Lebens," *Die Literarische Welt* 7 (1931), p. 3.

201 Abdel Jabbar Kheiri, the "Indian eunuch": Höpp, "Mohammed Essad Bey: Nur Orient für Europäer?," pp. 77–78.

CHAPTER 10: *Weimar Media Star*

203 "the texture of this fine book": P. W. Wilson, "A Mohammedan Interpretation of Mohammed's Life," *The New York Times,* October 11, 1936, p. 9.

204 BOOK SEES RUSSIA: "Book Sees Russia in Grip of Cruelty," *The New York Times,* August 21, 1933, p. 11.

204 Drinking, writing, and publishing: Robert C. Williams, *Culture in Exile: Russian Émigrés in Germany, 1881–1941* (Ithaca, N.Y., 1972), pp. 132–33.

205 "In the Attic": Gerhard Höpp, "Mohammed Essad Bey oder Die Welten von Lev Abramovič Nussenbaum," Afterword to Essad Bey, *Allah ist gross: Niedergang und Aufstieg der islamischen Welt* (Munich, 2002), pp. 391–92.

205 Germany had been the world's: Williams, *Culture in Exile,* p. 133.

206 From then on, Paris: Marc Raeff, *Russia Abroad: A Cultural History of the Russian Emigration, 1919–1939* (New York, 1990), p. 77.

206 "Having discovered the dynamite": Walter Benjamin, "A Discussion of Russian Filmic Art and Collectivist Art in General," reprinted in Anton Kaes et al., eds., *The Weimar Republic Sourcebook* (Berkeley, 1994), p. 626.

207 Lev's first article: Essad-Bey, "Aus dem Osten," *Die Literarische Welt* (*DLW*) 2, no. 23 (1926).

207 range of Lev's contributions: Essad-Bey, "Tschingis-Chan, der Dichter. Zu seinem 700. Todestag," *DLW* 3, no. 47 (1927), p. 7; Essad-Bey, "Das Prestige der weissen Rasse und der Film," *DLW* 5, no. 3 (1929), p. 7.

207 And he wrote a positive review: Essad-Bey, "Buch-Chronik der Woche. Dagobert von Mikusch: Gasi Mustafa Kemal," *DLW* 5, no. 45 (1929), p. 5.

207 "Buchara at the Hotel Adlon": Essad-Bey, "An Asiens Fürstenhöfen. Buchara im Hotel Adlon—Der letzte Emir—Märchen aus Tausendundeiner Nacht im 20. Jahrhundert," *Dresdner Neueste Nachrichten,* November 15, 1929.

207 Lev's articles on Afghan king: Essad-Bey, "Chefredakteur S. M. Amanullah," *DLW* 4, no. 10 (1928), p. 3. See also "Die Europa-Reisen islamischer Herrscher und die islamische Welt," in *Die islamische Gegenwart* 2, nos. 4/5 (1928).

208 "America is our friend": Essad-Bey, "Chefredakteur," *DLW* 10, (1928).

208   "more books, and often greater ones": Walter Mehring, *The Lost Library: The Autobiography of a Culture* (Indianapolis and New York, 1951), p. 136.

208   "red-haired, hunchbacked" waiter: Ibid., pp. 141–43.

209   Else Lasker-Schüler: Frederic V. Grunfeld, *Prophets Without Honor: A Background to Freud, Kafka, Einstein and Their World* (New York, 1979), pp. 96–145.

209   "glowed with the fire of Oriental fantasy": Quoted in Ibid., p. 97.

209   "I have been trying to avoid": Harry Kessler, *Berlin in Lights: The Diaries of Count Harry Kessler (1918–1937)* (New York, 1999), p. 114.

209   "indiscriminate spasms of the brain": Quoted in Grunfeld, *Prophets Without Honor,* p. 97.

209   "archangel and fishwife": Quoted in Ibid., p. 96.

209   FN—"Even King David would have moved on": Ibid., p. 143.

209   "harem pants, a turban": Oskar Kokoschka, *Mein Leben* (Munich, 1971), p. 10.

209   Lasker-Schüler gave her friends silly nicknames: Grunfeld, *Prophets Without Honor,* p. 106.

210   THE WORLD WITHOUT VEILS: Peter Jelavich, *Berlin Cabaret* (Cambridge, Mass., 1993), pp. 175–76.

211   FN—Jewish jokes and cabaret stars: Ibid., pp. 79–80, 258–82.

211   "The Book of Exodus accompanied": Mehring, *The Lost Library,* p. 13.

211   "there is no longer an Orient": Essad-Bey, "Walter Mehring: Algier oder die 13 Oasenwunder," *DLW* 3, no. 22 (1927), p. 6.

212   Schendell begged his client: Quoted in Gerhard Höpp, "Mohammed Essad Bey: Nur Orient für Europäer?," *Asien Afrika Lateinamerika* 25 (1997), p. 86.

212   "We know Essad-Bey": G.M., "Essad-Bey. Oel und Blut im Orient," *DLW* (date unknown), 1929, p. 5.

213   FN—"It is apparently difficult, particularly difficult": Kurban Said, *Der Mann, der Nichts von der Liebe Verstand* (unpublished manuscript), I, 4A–5B.

213   "a djin, an immortal ghost": Essad-Bey, "Der orientalische Lenin-Mythos," *DLW* 4, no. 49 (1928), pp. 5–6.

213   "suggestive of the life": Editorial blurb in *Outlook,* April 1932, p. 233.

213   Essad failed "in persuading us": "A Study of Stalin," *Times Literary Supplement,* June 2, 1932, p. 398.

214   There were favorable German reactions: Quoted in Höpp, "Mohammed Essad Bey: Nur Orient für Europäer?," p. 81; Karl Hoffmann, "Erdölsensationen," *Deutsche Rundschau* 225 (October 1930), p. 80.

214   "a really capable and likable storyteller": Quoted in Höpp, "Mohammed Essad Bey: Nur Orient für Europäer?," p. 81.

215 "This book is one of the most": "Buchbesprechungen: Essad Bey, 'Oel und blut im Orient,' " *Der Nahe Osten* 11, no. 1 (1930), p. 16.

215 "too Asiatic": Quoted in Höpp, "Mohammed Essad Bey: Nur Orient für Europäer?," p. 81.

216 publisher Schendell blamed by critics: Quoted in Ibid., p. 80.

216 "unprecedented slander against Germany": Review, "Essad Bey, Oel und Blut im Orient," *Der Nahe Osten* 11, no. 1 (1930), p. 16.

216 "The entire contents of this 'memoir' ": "Protest," *Berliner Tribüne*, February 22, 1930.

216 Islam Institute joined campaign against Lev: Quoted in Höpp, "Mohammed Essad Bey: Nur Orient für Europäer?," p. 80.

217 "a pornographic tableau": Quoted in Ibid., p. 80.

217 The leading point man: Hilal Munschi, *Die Republik Aserbeidschan. Eine geschichtliche und politische Skizze* (Berlin, 1930), p. 5. Also see Munschi's contributions in *Berliner Tribüne*, May 24 and June 14, 1930, and in *Der Tag*, January 31, 1931.

218 Islamic nationalists contacted right wing: Höpp, "Mohammed Essad Bey: Nur Orient für Europäer?," p. 80.

218 von Paraquin: Essad Bey, *Oel und Blut im Orient* (Stuttgart, 1929), pp. 231–38.

219 "Everyone knows how Germans": D. E. Paraquin, " 'Oel und Blut im Orient,' " *Berliner Börsen-Courier*, December 17, 1929, p. 1. The article also appeared in the *Hamburger Nachrichten*, December 28, 1929, and in the *Münchner Neueste Nachrichten*, January 1, 1930.

219 FN—von Paraquin, Germany, and Turkey: Ibid., p. 2.

219 "this Jewish falsifier of history": Quoted in Höpp, "Mohammed Essad Bey oder Die Welten von Lev Abramovič Nussenbaum," p. 394.

220 Union of German Writers put out: Höpp, "Mohammed Essad Bey: Nur Orient für Europäer?," p. 80.

220 "Since its publication, it has been claimed": Karl Hoffmann, "Erdölsensationen," *Deutsche Rundschau* 57 (1930), p. 80.

221 "to damage the reputation of Germany": Quoted in Höpp, "Mohammed Essad Bey: Nur Orient für Europäer?," p. 80.

221 Lev was summoned: Ibid.

221 "the necessary dialectical-materialist schooling": *Vorwärts!*, October 9, 1931.

222 "purely Bolshevist rather than Islamic interests": Quoted in Höpp, "Mohammed Essad Bey. Nur Orient für Europäer?," p. 82.

222 "Lies Forbidden!": Essad-Bey, "Lügen verboten!," *DLW* 6, no. 9 (1930), p. 1.

222 "One doesn't get very far": Alexandra Richie, *Faust's Metropolis: A History of Berlin* (New York, 1998), p. xv.

223 "aware from personal observation": Essad-Bey, *Twelve Secrets of the Caucasus* (New York, 1931), pp. ix–x.

223 "a kind of curiosity shop": Ibid., p. vii.

224 "The many peoples that I have visited": Essad Bey, "Lebensläufe von heute. Die Geschichte meines Lebens," *DLW* 7, no. 5 (1931), p. 4.

224 "racial curio shop": Essad Bey, "The Caucasus—A Racial Curio Shop," *Asia* 34, no. 4 (1934), pp. 201–3.

224 "Khevsuria is quite near Tiflis": Essad-Bey, *Twelve Secrets of the Caucasus,* pp. 116–17.

224 The *Tribune* critic concluded: Charles J. Finger, "Where Lies This Country?," *New York Herald-Tribune,* October 11, 1931, pp. 3–4.

224–25 "to prove that the Khevsurs": Essad Bey, "The Fabulous Khevsurs," *Asia* 34 (May 1934), p. 286.

CHAPTER 11: *Jewish Orientalism*

227 lost amid volumes of "hieroglyphics": Kurban Said, *Der Mann, der Nichts von der Liebe Verstand* (unpublished manuscript), III, 18B–19A.

227 Edward Said revived term: Edward Said, *Orientalism* (New York, 1978).

230 anti-Semitic pundit on "New Synagogue": Ivan Davidson Kalmar, "Moorish Style: Orientalism, the Jews, and Synagogue Architecture," *Jewish Social Studies* 7, no. 3 (2001), p. 89.

230 Jewish philosopher Maimonides: Abraham Leon Sachar, *A History of the Jews* (New York, 1968), pp. 178–81. Also see Paul Johnson, *A History of the Jews* (New York, 1987), pp. 177–93.

231 Vambery began using honorifics: Arminius Vambery, *The Story of My Struggles* (London, 1904), p. 123.

231 court society "emasculating" him: Ibid., p. 154.

231 shocked by lack of Western influence in Persia: Ibid., p. 182.

232 "In Asia they took me": Ibid., p. 229.

232 "The Jew lies; he is a swindler": Ibid., p. 263.

232 Vambery's triumphant book tour: Lory Alder and Richard Dalby, *The Dervish of Windsor Castle: The Life of Arminius Vambery* (London, 1979), pp. 371–84.

232 "What a pity you did not": Quoted in Ibid., p. 232.

232 Vambery questioned by Disraeli: Ibid., p. 250.

232 Disraeli's novels preached kinship: Bernard Lewis, "The Pro-Islamic Jews," in Bernard Lewis, *Islam in History: Ideas, People, and Events in the Middle East* (Chicago, 1993), pp. 140–41.

233 "I am quite a Turk": Quoted in Patrick Brantlinger, "Disraeli and Orientalism," in *The Self-fashioning of Disraeli: 1818–1851,* Charles Richmond and Paul Smith, eds. (Cambridge, England, 1998), p. 96.

233 "Yes, I am a Jew": Quoted in Ivan Kalmar, "Jewish Orientalism," in Judit Targarona Borrás and Angel Sáenz-Badillos, eds., *Jewish Studies at the Turn of the Twentieth Century: Proceedings of the 6th EAJS Congress, Toledo, July 1998*, vol. 2, Judaism from the Renaissance to Modern Times (Leiden and Boston, 1999), p. 308.

234 "All is race": Benjamin Disraeli, *Tancred, or the New Crusade* (Westport, Conn.: 1970), p. 149.

235 As prime minister, Disraeli: Minna Rozen, "Pedigree Remembered, Reconstructed, Invented: Benjamin Disraeli Between East and West," in Martin Kramer, ed., *The Jewish Discovery of Islam: Studies in Honor of Bernard Lewis* (Tel Aviv, 1999), pp. 65–67.

235 comparative linguistics had divided the world: Lawrence I. Conrad, "Ignaz Goldziher on Ernst Renan: From Orientalist Philology to the Study of Islam," in Kramer, ed., *The Jewish Discovery of Islam*, pp. 138–42.

236 "Rembrandt's Jews were real Jews": Quoted in Michael Brenner, *The Renaissance of Jewish Culture in Weimar Germany* (New Haven, Conn., 1996), p. 30.

237 Association for Jewish Folkloristics: Brenner, *The Renaissance of Jewish Culture*, pp. 29–30.

237 Rathenau published an essay: Discussed in Amos Elon, *The Pity of It All: A History of Jews in Germany, 1743–1933* (New York, 2002), pp. 232–33.

237 a Jewish *Stamm:* Brenner, *The Renaissance of Jewish Culture*, pp. 36–37.

238 "Within the Jews lives": Martin Buber, "Das Judentum und die Menschheit," in *Der Jude und sein Judentum: Gesammelte Aufsätze und Reden* (Gerlingen, 1993), p. 23.

238 Buber grouped Judaism with Chinese: Martin Buber, "The Spirit of the Orient and Judaism," in Buber, *On Judaism*, Nahum N. Glatzer, ed., pp. 56–78.

238 Herzl's Talmud was Wagnerian opera: Carl E. Schorske, *Fin-de-Siècle Vienna: Politics and Culture* (New York, 1980), p. 163.

238 *Juda,* the movement's first venture: Brenner, *The Renaissance of Jewish Culture*, pp. 25–28.

238 Ephraim Moses Lilien: Michael Stanislawski, *Zionism and the Fin de Siècle: Cosmopolitanism and Nationalism from Nordau to Jabotinsky* (Berkeley, Calif., 2001), pp. 98–115.

239 Byron of Zionism committed suicide: Quoted in Brenner, *The Renaissance of Jewish Culture*, p. 26.

239 "the Jew's own soul": Reprinted under the title "The Spirit of the Orient and Judaism," in Buber, *On Judaism*, pp. 74–75.

240 "the world-mission of the German Reich": R.B., "Die Welt des Islam," *Jüdische Monatshefte* 2, no. 12 (1915), p. 389.

240   "The Jew that I call the Oriental": Jacob Wassermann, "Der Jude als Orientale," in Verein Jüdischer Hochschüler Bar Kochba, ed., *Vom Judentum. Ein Sammelbuch* (Leipzig, 1914), p. 7.

240–41 Wassermann and Western vs. Asian Jews: Quoted in Brenner, *The Renaissance of Jewish Culture*, pp. 135–36.

241   Viennese journalist Eugen Hoeflich: Josef Schmidt, *Der Unterhaltungsschriftsteller Mosche Ya-akov Ben-gavriel* (Bonn, 1979), pp. 9–10.

241   "We want to return": Eugen Hoeflich (M. Y. Ben Gavriël), *Die Pforte des Osten (Das arabisch-jüdische Palaestina vom panasiatischen Standpunkt aus)* (Berlin and Vienna, 1923), pp. 99–100.

241   "problems Jews face incorporating themselves": M. Y. Ben-Gavriël, review of Essad Bey and Wolfgang von Weisl, *Allah ist gross: Niedergang und Aufstieg der islamischen Welt* (Leipzig, 1936) in *Der Morgen* 13, no. 1 (1937), pp. 45–46.

241   "The soul of Asia is being murdured": Buber, "The Spirit of the Orient and Judaism," p. 77.

CHAPTER 12: *Backing into the Inferno*

243   German-Russian League Against Bolshevism: Gerhard Höpp, "Mohammed Essad Bey oder Die Welten des Lev Abramovič Nussenbaum," Afterword to Essad Bey, *Allah ist gross: Niedergang und Aufstieg der islamischen Welt* (Munich, 2002), p. 393.

244   "Russia is America of the past": Essad Bey, *OGPU: The Plot Against the World* (New York, 1933), p. 290.

244   "My lords, the East India Company": Quoted in Essad Bey, *OGPU*, p. 287.

244   Moellerians: Otto-Ernst Schuddekopf, *Linke Leute von rechts* (Stuttgart, 1960), pp. 80–83.

244   "carry on the work": Quoted in Fritz Stern, *The Politics of Cultural Despair: A Study in the Rise of the Germanic Ideology* (Berkeley, Calif., 1961), p. 263.

246   "So why have I remained": Essad-Bey, "Lebensläufe von heute. Die Geschichte meines Lebens," *Die Literarische Welt* 7, no. 5 (1931), pp. 3–4.

247   "The less a government tried": Essad-Bey, "Lebensläufe von heute," p. 4.

247   the Eurasians: Robert H. Johnston, *"New Mecca, New Babylon": Paris and the Russian Exiles, 1920–1945* (Montreal and Kingston, Ont., 1988), pp. 91–92.

248   "taught us the art of government": P. Malevsky-Malevitch, *A New Party in Russia* (London, 1928), p. 24.

248   Nabokov's position on Eurasianism: Johnston, *"New Mecca, New Babylon,"* pp. 92–93.

248   "new man born of the mechanization": Quoted in Nicholas Hayes, "Kazem-

Bek and the Young Russians' Revolution," *Slavic Review* 39, no. 2 (1980), p. 264.

248 Alexander Kazem-Bek: Ibid., pp. 258–64.

248 "legalistic dysentery": Ibid., p. 261.

249 "entirely classless, nearly superhuman peak": Essad-Bey, "Lebensläufe von heute," p. 4.

249 "I love old people": Ibid., p. 3.

250 "With all his intelligence": Alexander Brailow, *Survivor's Tale* (unpublished manuscript), II, pp. 205–6.

250 the Locarno Girls: Peter Jelavich, *Berlin Cabaret* (Cambridge, Mass., 1993), pp. 212–17.

250 "Red Pioneers attack armed policemen": Ibid., p. 221.

250–51 German Communist Party and "sham battle": Ibid., p. 226.

251 "Good Lord, you don't have to": Ibid., p. 227.

251 Hitler as "Mad Apostle": Philip Metcalfe, *1933* (Sag Harbor, N.Y., 1988), pp. 51–52.

251 "I shall take Socialism away": Excerpt from interview reprinted in Niel M. Johnson, *George Sylvester Viereck, German-American Propagandist* (Urbana, 1972), p. 118.

251 "If he lives, Hitler": Quoted in Ibid., p. 117.

252 "He is inconsequent": Quoted in Philip Metcalfe, *1933*, pp. 56–57.

252–53 "It's all there in my book *Metapolitics*": Interview with Peter Viereck, South Hadley, Mass., October 2001.

253 "Thanks to Essad Bey": George Sylvester Viereck, *The Kaiser on Trial* (New York, 1937), p. 500.

253 "Sure my father knew Essad Bey": Interview with Peter Viereck, October 2001.

254 Viereck's essay on Ezra Pound: Peter Viereck, "Pound at 100: Weighing the Art and the Evil," *The New York Times Book Review*, December 29, 1985, p. 3.

254 "My father always admired Essad Bey": Interview with Peter Viereck, October 2001.

255 Lev meets "Monika Brand": Kurban Said, *Der Mann, der Nichts von der Liebe Verstand* (unpublished manuscript), III, 16A.

256 "Her body was narrow": Ibid., III, 18B.

256 "I can scarcely distinguish": Ibid., III, 9A–10A.

256 "So this was the love": Ibid., III, 12B.

256 definition of "sheik":

257 Erika wanted to marry a writer since thirteen: Erika Essad Bey Nussimbaum Loewendahl von Mohrenshield Fülöp-Miller, *Personal History* (unpublished manuscript), p. 17.

257 "Now she laughed and I saw her teeth": *Der Mann,* III, 19A.

257 "When I was tired from sitting": Ibid., III, 39A.

257 "She will come every day": Ibid., III, 39B.

258 "He told me he was of princely": George Dixon, "Poetess Freed of Moslem Mate by 'Remote Control,' " New York *Daily News,* November 28, 1937, p. 20.

258 "What did I know of": *Der Mann,* IV, 7B.

259 "The general consul had only three": *Der Mann,* IV, 10A.

260 Adjunct Professor Hitler: Ernst Hanfstaengl, *Hitler: The Missing Years* (New York, 1994), p. 176.

260 Hindenburg banned Hitler's seductive voice: Sefton Delmer, *Trail Sinister: An Autobiography* (London, 1961), p. 142.

261 In Nuremberg a bomb was thrown: Hanfstaengl, *Hitler,* p. 177; Metcalfe, *1933,* p. 58.

261 Hitler's Flying Circus: Delmer, *Trail Sinister,* pp. 141–58.

262 Robbins called "Gretchen" from the Pudding: Hanfstaengl, *Hitler,* p. 31.

263 "I met the most remarkable fellow": Ibid., pp. 31–32.

263 "I started playing some . . . football marches": Ibid., p. 51.

264 Hanfstaengl escaped assassination and fled: Ibid., pp. 276–84.

264 "fifteen seconds, and then it was all over": Quoted in Alexandra Richie, *Faust's Metropolis: A History of Berlin* (New York, 1998), p. 403.

265 Grosz's premonition of a national disaster: George Grosz, *A Little Yes and a Big No: The Autobiography of George Grosz* (New York, 1946), pp. 253–59.

265 best election news all year: Richie, *Faust's Metropolis,* p. 405.

265 Goebbels and Ulbricht demonstrated together: Ibid., p. 404.

266 "Either I will cut Hitler's balls off": Quoted in Otto Friedrich, *Before the Deluge: A Portrait of Berlin in the 1920s* (New York, 1972), p. 352.

266 von Schleicher announced plans on radio: Ibid., p. 379.

266 "The dead cold grips the town": Christopher Isherwood, *The Berlin Stories* (New York, 1945), p. 186.

267 Lev's lecture tour: Gerhard Höpp, "Mohammed Essad Bey: Nur Orient für Europäer?," *Asien Afrika Lateinamerika* 25 (1997), p. 95, FN 110.

267 Lev stayed in Vienna: Gerhard Höpp, "Mohammed Essad Bey oder Die Welten des Lev Abramovič Nussenbaum," p. 396.

268 "There is even a chance that the vandals": Joseph Roth, "The *Auto-da-Fé* of the Mind," in *What I Saw: Reports from Berlin 1920–1933* (New York, 2003), p. 208.

268 Ziemke went to Goebbels's Ministry of Propaganda: Höpp, "Mohammed Essad Bey: Nur Orient für Europäer?," p. 85.

PART 3

CHAPTER 13: *A Tough Morsel for the Melting Pot*

273 "Essad Bey is a hater of revolutions": William Leon Smyser, "He Has Lived His Stories," *New York Herald Tribune,* December 16, 1934, p. 7.

273 "There is something almost Chinese": Ibid., p. 20.

275 Pima recalled "grace-filled dual solitude": See letter from Essad Bey to Pima Andreae, March 20, 1940.

275 "Perpetual honeymoon Essad": Ibid., p. 20.

275 "The Essads quit Spain": Ibid.

275 "now, in his early thirties": Ibid., p. 7.

276 menu for a dinner: Papers of Pima Andreae, courtesy of her grandson Alessandro Andreae.

277 Immigration Act of 1924: Richard Easterlin et al., *Immigration* (Cambridge, Mass., 1982), pp. 94–103.

277–78 Jewish immigration figures: Raul Hilberg, *Perpetrators Victims Bystanders: The Jewish Catastrophe, 1933–1945* (New York, 1992), p. 228.

278 act favored "original" inhabitants: Easterlin et al., *Immigration,* pp. 94–103.

278 " 'Race or People' ": Affidavit of Surgeon, U.S. Department of Labor Immigration Service form (1933), National Archives and Records Administration.

278 Hitler directed authors of race laws: Stefan Kühl, *The Nazi Connection: Eugenics, American Racism, and German National Socialism* (New York, 1994), pp. 98–99.

279 Daddy Loewendahl had never had any doubts: Interview with Walter Loewendahl, New York, 2001.

279 "Waldorf Astoria Hotel": "List or Manifest of Alien Passengers to the United States," S.S. *Vulcania,* Sailing from Port of Trieste, October 4, 1933, arriving in port of New York, October 19, 1933 (column 23).

279 "I was offensively rich": Letter from Essad Bey to Pima Andreae, December 15, 1941.

280 "I was a drunk": Letter from Essad Bey to Pima Andreae, January 18, 1941.

280 "The bad part": Kurban Said, *Der Mann, der Nichts von der Liebe Verstand* (unpublished manuscript), V, 4A.

280 "Your officials are as courteous": Smyser, "He Has Lived His Stories," *New York Herald Tribune,* December 16, 1934, p. 7.

280 "immense, straight gorge": Essad Bey, unfinished New York novel manuscript, p. 6.

280 "Once I put on dinner-jacket shoes": Letter from Essad Bey to Pima Andreae, December 15, 1941.

281 "Essad Bey was my nemesis": Interview with Walter Loewendahl, New York, 2001.

281 "some Danish king": Ibid.

281 "it's all very, very confusing": Ibid.

282 Viereck commissioned article: Essad Bey, "The Red Menace in the United States," *German Outlook,* January 27, 1934.

282 "the distinguished Russian publicist": Ibid., editorial note.

282 "for fourteen years, Germany stood": Ibid.

282 "it is impossible to pass final judgment": Ibid.

283 "unbiased reporting on Germany": "Our Company: Pulitzer Prizes, *New York Times,*" The New York Times Company website (www.nytco.com).

283 "boyish trick": Frederick T. Birchall, "Nazi Bands Stir Up Strife in Germany," *The New York Times,* March 9, 1933, pp. 1, 10; Frederick T. Birchall, "Nazi Book Burning Fails to Stir Berlin," *The New York Times,* May 11, 1933, pp. 1, 12.

283 "not the slightest evidence": Frederick T. Birchall, "Olympics Begin Today in Germany; 80,000 to Witness Winter Sports," *The New York Times,* February 6, 1936, p. 1. Also see Frederick T. Birchall, "Torch to Be Lit at Olympia Today," *The New York Times,* July 20, 1936, p. 1.

283 FN—Birchall and the Olympics: Ibid.

283 "communist menace": Deborah E. Lipstadt, *Beyond Belief: The American Press and the Coming of the Holocaust* (New York, 1986), pp. 27–28.

283 "A Traveler Visits Germany": "A Traveler Visits Germany" Part I, *Christian Science Monitor,* August 2, 1933, editorial page; "A Traveler Visits Germany" Part II, *Christian Science Monitor,* August 9, 1933, editorial page.

284 "Protestantism by the Ku Klux Klan": Lipstadt, *Beyond Belief,* p. 45.

284 "George Sylvester Viereck is as staunch": "Viereck," *The New Yorker,* June 15, 1940, p. 15.

284 "oppressively neat in his dress": Ibid., p. 16.

284 "Kaiser Wilhelm (in his Imperial days)": Ibid., p. 16.

284 "All these people I have known": Ibid., p. 16.

285 George Sylvester Viereck's background: Niel M. Johnson, *George Sylvester Viereck: German-American Propagandist* (Urbana, Ill., 1972), pp. 8–9; Elmer Gertz, *Odyssey of a Barbarian: The Biography of George Sylvester Viereck* (Buffalo, N.Y., 1978), pp. 12–26; George Sylvester Viereck, *My Flesh and Blood* (New York, 1931), pp. 236–40.

285 idolized Christ, Napoleon, and Oscar Wilde: "Viereck," *The New Yorker,* June 15, 1940, p. 16.

285 "I identify with all things morbid": Phyllis Keller, *States of Belonging: German American Intellectuals and the First World War* (Cambridge, Mass., 1979), p. 130.

285 "the most widely-discussed": Gertz, *Odyssey of a Barbarian,* p. 75.

285 "a weekly devoted to Fair-Play": Ibid., p. 123.

285 Viereck established the Fatherland Foundation: Johnson, *George Sylvester Viereck*, p. 66.

286 "HUNS PAID $200,000": Gertz, *Odyssey of a Barbarian*, p. 151.

286 Authors' League expelled him: Johnson, *George Sylvester Viereck*, p. 137–38; Gertz, *Odyssey of a Barbarian*, pp. 26–37.

286 his poems were expunged: Gertz, *Odyssey of a Barbarian*, p. 151.

286 *Rejuvenation:* Ibid., p. 185.

286 "I have been compared to Columbus": George Viereck, *Glimpses of the Great* (New York, 1930), p. 23.

286 "disturbing influence": Johnson, *George Sylvester Viereck*, pp. 235–38.

286 "modern queen": Viereck, *Glimpses of the Great*, p. 237.

287 "Master Mind" or "Brain of the Earth": Ibid., p. 416.

287 "The Sherlock Homes of Ghost Land": Ibid., p. 323.

287 "The Einstein of Sex": Ibid., p. 285.

287 "We Jews": Ibid., pp. 449–51.

288 Thomas Mann's review: Jacket copy of *Salome: The Wandering Jewess: My First Two Thousand Years of Love* (New York, 1930), by George Sylvester Viereck and Paul Eldridge.

288 "saturated with the modern spirit": Jacket copy of *Glimpses of the Great*.

288 "approaches the beauty": Ibid.

288 Yeats promised to come to aid: Ibid.

288 "The Return of George S. Viereck": Quoted in Johnson, *George Sylvester Viereck*, p. 117. For direct citation, see Shaemas O'Sheel, "The Return of George S. Viereck," *The World*, April 13, 1930.

288 "The quickness of the Jew": Viereck, *My Flesh and Blood*, p. 145.

288 Viereck met Hitler again: Johnson, *George Sylvester Viereck*, pp. 174–75.

288 "I am not . . . an anti-Semite": "Address by George Sylvester Viereck at Madison Square Garden, May 17, 1934," George Sylvester Viereck scrapbook, New York Public Library.

289 "It was a kind of sordid scene": Interview with Peter Viereck, South Hadley, Mass., October 2001.

289 "If it were published under my name": Letter from Essad Bey to Pima Andreae, June 23, 1941.

290 "It wasn't difficult to write a book": Ibid.

290 "He wasn't very young": Ibid.

290 "new method": George Bernard Shaw to George Sylvester Viereck, January 27, 1938.

290 "Cradled in the East": George Sylvester Viereck, *The Kaiser on Trial* (New York, 1937), p. 241.

290 "It is Disraeli, not Adolf Hitler": Ibid., p. 408.

290 Viereck was eventually imprisoned: Johnson, *George Sylvester Viereck,* pp. 238, 251; Gertz, *Odyssey of a Barbarian,* pp. 272–73.

291 "Of course he is a spy": Letter from Essad Bey to Pima Andreae, June 5, 1941.

CHAPTER 14: *Mussolini and Mrs. Kurban Said*

293 "The broad-minded poetess": "Harem? Yes—But Scare 'Em? No!," *Sunday Mirror Magazine,* January 2, 1938, p. 10.

294 "zoomed into Bel Air": Ibid.

294 "a romance which Mme. Essad Bey": George Dixon, "Poetess Freed of Moslem Mate," New York *Daily News,* November 28, 1937, p. 3.

294 "accounts of wild doings": "Harem? Yes—But Scare 'Em? No!," *Sunday Mirror Magazine,* p. 10.

294 "He told me . . . princely Arabian lineage": Dixon, "Poetess Freed of Moslem Mate," New York *Daily News,* p. 3.

294 "once high in the Czechoslovakian": Ibid., p. 20.

294 Erika's "fez-wearing" spouse: Ibid., p. 20.

294 "Essad Bey [is] in Vienna": Ibid., p. 3.

294 "Frau Erika, who interestingly is filing": "Gerichtssaal: Scheidungsprozess gegen den Schriftsteller Essad Bey," *Neues Wiener Journal,* no. 15, October 31, 1937, p. 33.

295 "CZAR'S BIOGRAPHER HERE": "Czar's Biographer Here: Essad Bey Declares Leader Was Not Understood," *The New York Times,* March 11, 1935, p. 13.

296 respectful write-up: Editor's note to "Wives, Odalisques, and Sighs," by Mohammed Essad-Bey, *Vanity Fair,* September, 1935, p. 16.

296 no longer publish in the Third Reich: Gerhard Höpp, "Mohammed Essad Bey oder Die Welten des Lev Abramovič Nussenbaum," Essad Bey, Afterword to *Allah ist gross: Niedergang und Aufstieg der islamischen Welt* (Munich, 2002), p. 398.

296 letter asking for separation: Kurban Said, *Der Mann, der Nichts von der Liebe Verstand* (unpublished manuscript), VI, 38B.

296 Huebsch's date books: Papers of Benjamin W. Huebsch, Library of Congress Manuscript Division.

296 one from my grandfather: Letter from Alfred Reiss to Benjamin Huebsch, December 8, 1943, Papers of Benjamin W. Huebsch.

297 group postcard sent from Vienna: Essad Bey, Erika Essad Bey, et al., to Benjamin Huebsch, September 1933, Papers of Benjamin W. Huebsch.

297 Alice Schulte recorded sad period: Alice Schulte, *Biographie Essad-Bey* (unpublished manuscript), Rascher Publishers Archive, Zurich Public Library.

297 Essad Bey shared the place with regulars: Paul Hofmann, *The Viennese: Splendor, Twilight and Exile* (New York, 1988), pp. 177–78.

297   "democratic clubs": Ibid., pp. 177–78. See also Stefan Zweig, *The World of Yesterday* (New York, 1943), p. 39.

297   working simultaneously on biographies: Höpp, Afterword to *Allah ist gross,* p. 397.

298   began writing novellas: Ibid., p. 397–98.

298   a new agent, Hertha Pauli: Ibid., p. 396.

298   "looked somewhat like King Hussein": Hertha Pauli, Letter to the Editor, *The New York Times,* August 8, 1971.

298   Lev joined a writers' cooperative: Ibid.

298   Pauli placed pieces for Thomas Mann: Hertha Pauli, *Break in Time* (New York, 1972), p. 8.

298   selling Lev's adventure stories: Höpp, Afterword to *Allah ist gross,* p. 396.

298   "never made a secret of his ancestry": Hertha Pauli, Letter to the Editor, *The New York Times,* August 8, 1971.

299   "Essad talking again": Ibid.

299   "true to reason": Essad Bey and Wolfgang von Weisl, *Allah ist gross* (Vienna, 1936), p. 23.

299   real leaders of Islam were never diplomats: Ibid., p. 146.

299   Islam was able to conquer Christian lands: Ibid., p. 21.

299   Muhammad's victories: Ibid.

300   "recommended to Jewish readers": M. Y. Ben-Gavriel, "Essad Bey und Wolfgang von Weisl, *Allah ist gross,*" *Der Morgen,* April 1937, p. 45.

300   European influences "are being curbed": Dr. N., "Die islamische Welt: Essad Bey und Wolfgang von Weisl, 'Allah ist gross,' " *Die Jüdische Rundschau,* February 5, 1937.

300   "community of interests with the Islamic world": Ibid.

300   FN—von Weisl mistaken for " 'notorious' Colonel Lawrence": "The 'Lawrence Legend': German Journalist's Misadventure," *The Times* of London, October 2, 1930, p. 12, col. 4.

301   Dr. von Weisl started a paper: Arthur Koestler, *Arrow in the Blue* (London, 1952), pp. 155–56.

301   Koestler's portraits of von Weisl: Ibid., pp. 107–8, 155–56.

301   "Hussein will have reason": Dr. Wolfgang von Weisl, "Islam's Iconoclasts at Mekka's Gates," *The Living Age,* October–December 1924, p. 321.

301   picture of chaos unleashed by Ataturk: Dr. Wolfgang Weisl, quoted in *The Living Age,* April–June 1924, pp. 122–23.

301   If you look up the name "von Weisl": Höpp, Afterword to *Allah ist gross,* p. 385.

302   "to my fellow sufferer / from Essad Bey": Ibid., p. 399.

302   there had been only two times: Letter from Essad Bey to Pima Andreae, June 11, 1942.

303   "Ehrenfels v. Bodmershof, Elfriede, Baronin": *Deutscher Gesamtkatalog; Neue Titel, 1935–1939* (Berlin, 1940), p. 1556.

306   "They were called the Band of Four": Interview with Baroness Mireille Ehrenfels-Abeille, the Waldviertel, Austria, July 1999.

306   open letter to Hermann Hesse: Emma v. Ehrenfels, "Brief an Hermann Hesse," *Neue Freie Presse,* no. 24921, January 30, 1934.

306   Rolf and Imma Ehrenfels' father: Interview with Baroness Ehrenfels-Abeille, July 1999.

307   "Kafka wrote in one of his diaries": Ibid.

307   "She said it has been thirty-five years": Ibid.

308   "It is all here": Ibid.

309   telegram from December 21, 1932: Ehrenfels Castle Archive.

309   An article in *The Eastern Times:* "Omar R. Baron's Reception at Lahore," *The Eastern Times,* December 25, 1932.

309   Her Highness the Dayang Muda: Advertising insert for *Relations and Complications* by H. H. the Dayang Muda of Sarawak, from *Muslim Review* 19, no. 1, July 1936.

309   "Who can tell?": Interview with Baroness Ehrenfels-Abeille, July 1999.

309–10 "As a young man I founded": Omar-Rolf von Ehrenfels, Foreword to Kurban Said, *Das Mädchen vom goldenen Horn* (Basel, 1973), pp. 6–7.

310   "that's only his theory": Interview with Baroness Ehrenfels-Abeille, July 1999.

310   "I had American Express Athens send": Letter from Essad Bey to Omar Ehrenfels, July 21, 1938.

310   "At the Publisher Gesa Kon": Letter from Essad Bey to Omar Ehrenfels, September 8, 1938.

310   Lev recommended that Pima buy *Ali and Nino:* Letter from Essad Bey to Pima Andreae, September 21, 1940.

311   "the poor woman is an astrologer": Letter from Essad Bey to Pima Andreae, May 15, 1940.

311   Hugo Bettauer's dystopian novel: Hugo Bettauer, *The City Without Jews. A Novel of our Time* (New York, 1991).

311   Bettauer murdered: See Murray G. Hall, *Der Fall Bettauer* (Vienna, 1978); Hofmann, *The Viennese* (New York, 1988), pp. 41–42.

312   getting published in Nazi Europe: Interview with Murray G. Hall, Vienna, February 1999.

312   "The threat of the avalanche": Thomas Mehring, *The Lost Library: The Autobiography of a Culture* (New York, 1951), p. 199.

312   "In front of the St. Stephan's Cathedral": Ibid., pp. 199–201.

312   Hertha Pauli, remembered the Anschluss: Pauli, *Break in Time,* p. 2.

313   Mehring would meet Pauli in Paris: Ibid., pp. 191, 198–217. Also see Sheila Isenberg, *A Hero of Our Own: The Story of Varian Fry* (New York, 2001).

313 FN—Fry rescued refugees: See Isenberg, *A Hero of Our Own.*

314 "I walked to the left": Anthony Heilbut, *Exiled in Paradise: German Refugee Artists and Intellectuals in America from the 1930s to the Present* (New York, 1983), p. 27.

314 Fry claimed Eleanor Roosevelt's concern for Mehring: Isenberg, *A Hero of Our Own,* pp. 79–83.

314 "Mimi Piekarski is in London": Letter from Essad Bey to Omar Ehrenfels, September 8, 1938.

314 "scattered throughout the whole world": Letter from Essad Bey to Omar Ehrenfels, July 21, 1938.

314 "Zweig and Werfel are in London": Letter from Essad Bey to Omar Ehrenfels, September 8, 1938.

315 "Greta Garbo—Garbo!": Interview with Franzie Baumfeld, Los Angeles, May 2001.

315 *"Scandale mondain en Autriche":* R. E. Singer, "Scandale mondain en Autriche," *L'Intransigeant,* November 3, 1937.

316 "all the drawbacks of a monarchy": Essad Bey, "Lebensläufe von heute: Die Geschichte meines Lebens," *Die Literarische Welt* 7 (1931), p. 3.

317 "His Excellency": Letter from Essad Bey to Benito Mussolini, July 3, 1937.

317 "it is important that the *Duce* knows": Enrico Insabato to Dr. Osvaldo Sebastiani, private secretary to His Excellency the Head of State, July 2, 1937.

317 Mussolini explicitly criticized Hitler's racism: Renzo De Felice, *The Jews of Fascist Italy: A History* (New York, 2001), p. 111. Also see Howard M. Sachar, *Farewell España: The World of the Sephardim Remembered* (New York, 1994), p. 240.

318 "we make absolutely no difference": Ibid., p. 62.

318 Hundreds of Jews joined the fledgling Fascist party: Susan Zuccotti, *The Italians and the Holocaust: Persecution, Rescue and Survival* (Lincoln, 1996), p. 24.

318 there were Jewish generals, Jewish professors: Ibid., pp. 17–18, 25–26.

318 Israeli Navy from Fascist training program: Sachar, *Farewell España,* pp. 239–40. Also see Zucotti, *The Italians and the Holocaust,* p. 32.

318 Mussolini's trip to Germany: Piers Brendon, *The Dark Valley* (New York, 2000), pp. 564–66. Also see Joachim Fest, *Hitler* (New York, 1974), pp. 523–25; Denis Mack Smith, *Modern Italy* (Ann Arbor, 1959), pp. 393, 396; Denis Mack Smith, *Mussolini's Roman Empire* (New York, 1976), p. 97.

318 Italians opened their newspapers: Smith, *Modern Italy,* p. 396.

319 support for Essad Bey withdrawn: Letter from the Cabinet of the Ministry of Culture to Lieutenant Colonel Modest Mileti, private secretary to His Excellency the Head of State, Rome, July 7, 1937.

319 "It's so ridiculous that I can't enter": Letter from Essad Bey to Giovanni Gentile, Sensoni Archive, Florence, March 28, 1938.

319 "Leo Nussinbaum [*sic*]" . . . did make his way to Rome: Letter from Ministry of Internal Affairs, Department of Public Safety, Division of General and Private Affairs, Section I to Section III, September 5, 1938.

319 Italian police trailing Lev lost him: Letter from chief of police to Ministry of Internal Affairs, Department of Public Safety, Division of General and Private Affairs, Section III, Rome, October 28, 1938; prefect of Salerno to Ministry of Internal Affairs, Department of Public Safety, November 24, 1938.

320 "The documentary airtight evidence": Letter from Essad Bey to Giovanni Gentile, G. C. Sensoni Archive, Florence, September 12, 1938.

320 Italian police raised money for him: Letters from the prefect of Salerno, Division of Public Safety, to Ministry of Internal Affairs, General Department of Public Safety, Division of General and Private Affairs, Section III, Rome, October 30, 1939; Ministry of Internal Affairs, Division of General and Private Affairs, Section III, to Ministry of External Affairs, Rome, November 7, 1939; Ministry of External Affairs, A.G. IV, to Ministry of Internal Affairs, General Department of Public Safety, Division of General and Private Affairs, Section III, Rome, January 9, 1940.

CHAPTER 15: *Positano*

322 left-wing writers, pacifist poets: For an intimate portrait of this period, including photographs of a number of the artists, see Giulio Rispoli, *Positano: Luoghi e Persone, "Ieri e Oggi"* (Positano, Italy, 1989).

322 For the Jews, it was another matter: For a discussion of the racial laws and their impact, see Susan Zuccotti, *The Italians and the Holocaust: Persecution, Rescue and Survival* (Lincoln, Neb., 1996), pp. 28–51.

323 "It was not always": Interview with Nicoletta Rispoli, Positano, May 2000.

323 "Jewish filth" newspaper clippings: Ibid.

323 typewriter and radio confiscated: Carlo Knight, "Essad Bey a Positano," *Posidonia,* Estratto dal no. 6 (December 1993), p. 138.

323 some thought Essad was a spy: For example, see letter from prefect of Salerno to Ministry of Internal Affairs, General Division of Public Safety, Rome, "Subject: Essad Bey Leo of Ibrahim—stateless, resident of Positano," March 20, 1941, and letter from Ministry of Internal Affairs to prefect of Salerno, "Subject: Essad Bey Leo of Ibrahim—stateless," April 3, 1941.

323 "He was a secretive man": Elisabeth Castonier, *Stürmisch bis heiter: Memoiren einer Aussenseiterin* (München, 1964), pp. 304, 307.

324 the "disheveled Russian" woman: Ibid., p. 303.

324 "sometimes, into the night": Interview with Fioravante Rispoli, Positano, May 2000.

325 hospitalized that year in Naples: Letter from prefect of Salerno, Department of Health, to police chief of Salerno, "Subject: Inspection of Stateless Essad Bey of Ibrahim," March 15, 1941.

325 "All in all": Letter from Essad Bey to Elfriede Ehrenfels, September 14, 1939.

325 "The Muslim was a dignified man": Interview with Genario Passerotti, Positano, May 2000.

326 "Don Serviglio was a *big* Fascist": Ibid.

326 "Weren't they fantastic!": Interview with Contessa Raimonda Gaetani-Pattison, Positano, May 2000.

327 when Scotland Yard still helped Mussolini: Denis Mack Smith, *Mussolini's Roman Empire* (New York, 1976), pp. 13–14.

327 Captain Alfredo Pattison: Interview with Contessa Raimonda Gaetani-Pattison, Positano, February 1998.

328 "My mother, she was a teenager": Ibid.

328 "My mother and her friends": Ibid.

329 "He would howl": Interview with Fioravante Rispoli, May 2000.

329 "That man was not their type!": Ibid.

329 "He wrote ten, fifteen hours a day": Ibid.

329–30 he continued to write on scraps: Knight, "Essad Bey a Positano," p. 138.

330 "like entering a Persian opium den": Quoted in Gerhard Höpp, "Mohammed Essad Bey: Nur Orient für Europäer?," *Asien Afrika Lateinamerika* 25 (1997), p. 89.

330 "They all called him a Muslim": Interview with Fioravante Rispoli, Positano, May 2000.

330 "My father knew": Interview with Romolo Ercolino, Positano, February 1998.

331 "It is the Turkish style": Ibid.

331 "Dr. Giamil never returned": Ibid.

332 Baron Omar's pilgrimage: Omar-Rolf von Ehrenfels, Foreword to Kurban Said, *Das Mädchen der goldenen Horn* (Basel, 1973), p. 6.

332 John Steinbeck's article: John Steinbeck, "Positano," *Harper's Bazaar,* no. 2898 (May 1953), p. 188.

333 "That Essad Bey was not a Jew": Giamil Vacca-Mazzara, "Mohammed Essad-Bey: Scrittore Musalmano dell'azerbaigian Caucasico" (obituary of Essad Bey), *Oriente Moderno* (1942), pp. 434–43.

333 "Jewish author": Gerhard Höpp, "Mohammed Essad Bey oder Die Welten des Lev Abramovic Nussenbaum," Afterword to Essad Bey, *Allah ist gross* (Munich, 2002), p. 407.

333 Giamil tried to start an Essad Bey Foundation: Letter from Gjamil-Mazhara to Omar Ehrenfels, Algiers, June 20, 1975.

333   He even invented an elaborate story: Vacca-Mazzara "Mohammed Essad-Bey: Scrittore Musalmano dell'azerbaigian Caucasico," pp. 434–43.

334   "(alias) Giamil Ibn Ysuf Mazara": Nota Codesto R. Ministero no. 100285, March 8, 1938, R. Ministero dell'Africa Italiana.

335   "Djamil remains with me": Kurban Said, *Der Mann, der Nichts von der Liebe Verstand* (unpublished manuscript), V, 12B–13A.

335   "For God's sake who is Herr Ezra[?]": Letter from Essad Bey to Pima Andreae, December 11, 1942.

336   "A thin specter": Quoted in Höpp, "Mohammed Essad Beg Nur Orient für Europäer?," p. 89.

336   Lev's "nanny" had "a face like a caricature": Ibid.

336   "a typical literary swindler": Ibid., p. 90.

336   "the horrifying fairy tale": Ibid.

336   "kept up the comedy": Ibid.

336   Essad Bey was invited to record propaganda: Letter from Salvator Aponte, head of the First Division, inspectorate of Radio Broadcast and Television, Ministry of Popular Culture, to Dr. Essad Bey, June 23, 1942.

336   was to be accompanied to Rome: Letter from prefect of Salerno to Ministry of Internal Affairs, General Division of Public Safety, Rome, "Subject: Essad Bey Leo of Ibrahim—Stateless," August 26, 1942.

336   "Looking back now, what is important": Said, *Der Mann,* VI, 12B.

337   "our mutual friend Kurban Said": Letter from Essad Bey to Pima Andreae, November 21, 1940.

337   "Percy? Yeah": Letter from Essad Bey to Pima Andreae, January 15, 1942.

338   how he had threatened to keep a harem: Ibid.

339   "Erica gave a slightly different version": "Harem? Yes—But Scare 'Em? No!," *Sunday Mirror Magazine,* January 2, 1938, p. 10.

339   "One thought kept bothering me": Said, *Der Mann,* V, 21B.

340   "to settle down to a humdrum life": William Leon Smyser, "He Has Lived His Stories," *New York Herald Tribune,* December 16, 1934, p. 7.

340   "He hates trouble": Ibid., photo caption.

340   "The author of this book is dead": Said, *Der Mann,* VI, 52B.

340   "The old Nussimbaum, yes": Interview with Therese Kirschner-Mögle, Vienna, February 1999.

340   "Camilla went up to see him": Ibid.

340   Abraham was put on a transport: Dokumentationsarchiv des Österreichischen Widerstandes, record showing Abraham Nussimbaum was deported from Vienna to Modliborzyce on March 5, 1941.

340   "We never got a letter": Interview with Therese Kirschner-Mögle, Vienna, February 1999.

340 "It was very difficult to go": Ibid.

341 he creates a foreword: Said, *Der Mann*, VI, 53A–55B.

341 "His postcards stopped": Ibid., VI, 53B–54A.

341 manuscript closes with final letter: Ibid., VI, 54A–55B.

341 "I feel I have nothing": Ibid., VI, 55B.

Selected Bibliography

WORKS BY LEV NUSSIMBAUM

Nonfiction

The majority of Lev Nussimbaum's nonfiction work first appeared in German under the name Essad Bey. (Later in his career, since this Turkish alias was, in the old Ottoman style, without a first name, he added "Mohammed.") His books were translated into many languages and published around the world; in the United States, his main publisher was Viking. In the selected list below, where English-language editions are not available, entries are listed in the language in which they first appeared, with an English translation of the title.

Allah ist Gross: Niedergang und Aufstieg der Islamischen Welt (Allah Is Great: The Decline and Rise of the Islamic World). Essad Bey and Wolfgang von Weisl. Vienna: Verlag Dr. Rolf Passer, 1936.

Blood and Oil in the Orient. Trans. Elsa Talmey. London: Nash & Grayson Ltd., 1931. (Original German language edition: *Oel und Blut im Orient.* Stuttgart: Deutsche Verlags-Anstalt, 1929.)

Das weisse Russland: Menschen ohne Heimat (White Russia: People Without a Homeland). Leipzig: Gustav Kiepenheuer Verlag, 1932.

Flüssiges Gold: ein Kampf um die Macht (Liquid Gold: A Fight for Power). Berlin: E. C. Etthofen-Verlag, 1933.

Giustizia Rossa: I Processi Politici nell' U.R.S.S. (Red Justice: Political Processes in the U.S.S.R.). Trans. Mario Bacchelli. Florence: Sansoni, 1938. (Published only in Italian.)

Der Kaukasus: Seine Berge, Völker und Geschichte (The Caucasus: Its Mountains, People, and History). Berlin: Verlag Dt. Buch-Gemeinschaft, 1931.

Lenin. Italy: Garzanti, 1937. (Published only in Italian.)

Mohammed: A Biography. Trans. Helmut L. Ripperger. New York: Longmans, Green and Co., 1936. (Original German language edition: *Mohammed.* Berlin: Gustav Kiepenheuer Verlag, 1932.)

Nicholas II: Prisoner of the Purple. Trans. Paul Maerker Branden and Elsa Branden. New York and London: Funk & Wagnalls Company, 1937. (Original German-language edition: *Nikolaus II: Glanz Und Untergang Des Letzten Zaren.* Berlin: Holle & Co. Verlag, 1935.)

OGPU: The Plot Against the World. Trans. Huntley Paterson. New York: Viking Press, 1933. (Original German-language edition: *OGPU: Die Verschwörung gegen die Welt.* Berlin: E. C. Etthofen Verlag, 1932.)

Reza Shah. Trans. Paul Maerker Branden and Elsa Branden. London: Hutchinson & Co., 1938. (Original German-language edition: *Resa Shah: Feldherr, Kaiser, Reformator.* Vienna: R. Passer Verlag, 1936.)

Russland am Scheideweg. (Russia at the Crossroads) Berlin: E. C. Etthofen, 1933.

Stalin: The Career of a Fanatic. Trans. Huntley Paterson. New York: Viking Press, 1932. (Original German-language edition: *Stalin.* Berlin: G. Kiepenheuer, 1931.)

Twelve Secrets of the Caucasus. Trans. G. Chychele Waterston. New York: Viking Press, 1931. (Original German-language edition: *Zwölf Geheimnisse im Kaukasus.* Berlin: Deutsch-Schweizerische Verlagsanstalt, 1930.)

Selected Articles

The following is a selected list of Lev's articles, signed Essad Bey. Except in the case of various American publications (*The Saturday Review of Literature, Asia,* or *Vanity Fair*), his journalism was in German; I have translated the titles. He was a prolific correspondent for *Die Literarische Welt* (a sort of Weimar-era equivalent of *The New York Review of Books*), which launched his career. Another prolific correspondent at the time was Walter Benjamin (though Lev published more articles than Benjamin did), and almost all important European writers from Thomas Mann to Romain Rolland contributed. Lev became a protégé of the paper's influential editor, Willy Haas, his "expert on everything to do with the East," and when he was only twenty-one, Lev's caricature appeared on the front page, next to those of established luminaries.

"Alja Rachmanowa: Students, Love, Cheka, and Death." *Die Literarische Welt* (*DLW*) 50 (1931).

"American History in Five Hundred Words." *DLW* 25 (1930).

"The Caucasus—a Racial Curio Shop." *Asia* (1934).

"A Disagreement Between Poets." *DLW* 2 (1929).

"Egypt and the Arabic Freedom Movement." *Germania* (1928).

"The Fabulous Khevsurs." *Asia* (1934).

"Film and the Prestige of the White Race." *DLW* (1929).

"From the East." *DLW* 23 (1926).

"Genghis Khan, the Poet." *DLW* 47 (1927).

"His Majesty, the King of Buchara." *Das Tagebuch* (1929).

"How Are Things in Soviet Russia? An Alternative." *DLW* 32 (1929).

"Ibn Saud and the Wahhabites." *Die Propyläen* (1934).

"Ichbal—the Poet of Modern India." *DLW* 33 (1926).

"In Defense of Tungusians." *DLW* 35 (1930).

"Ivan Bunin." *Saturday Review of Literature* (1933).

"The Last Poetry Competition." *DLW* 29 (1929).

"Lieutenant Dostoyevsky." *DLW* 33 (1929).

"The Literary Figure as Assassin of the President." *DLW* 21 (1932).

"Modern Criminal Studies in the Service of Literary History." *DLW* 1 (1928).

"Mohammed's Miracle." *DLW* 26 (1932).

"The Monarchist Index." *DLW* 33/34 (1930).

"Selbstanzeigen" (autobiographical sketch). *Das Tagebuch* (1930).

"The Oriental Lenin Myth." *DLW* 49 (1928).

"Poets on the Front!" *DLW* 28 (1930).

"The Press in the Wild West." *DLW* 18 (1931).

"Red Menace in the United States." *German Outlook* (1934).

"The Republic of Azerbaijan." *Der Deutschen Spiegel* (1928).

"Stalin at Home." *The Living Age* (1931).

"The Story of My Life." *DLW* 5 (1931).

"Theodor Dreiser: Soviet Russia." *DLW* 3 (1929).

"To the Royal Courts in Asia: Buchara at the Hotel Adlon, the Last Emir, Fairytales from 1,001 Nights in the 20th Century." *Dresdener Neueste Nachrichten* (1929).

"Tradition in the Orient." *DLW* 35/36 (1931).

"Walter Mehring, Algeria or the Three Miracles of the Oasis." *DLW* 22 (1927).

"Was Tolstoy Epileptic?" *DLW* 3 (1930).

"Wives, Odalisques, and Sighs: Discussion of Women and Marriage." *Vanity Fair* (1935).

Fiction

Lev's fiction was published under the pseudonym Kurban Said and written in German. Current translations are in print in seventeen different languages.

Kurban Said. *Ali and Nino.* Trans. Jenia Graman. New York: Random House, 2000.

———. *Ali und Nino.* Vienna: E. P. Tal, 1937 (first edition).

———. *Ali and Nino.* Trans. Jenia Graman. New York: Random House, 1970. This was the novel's first translation into English—more than twenty years after Jenia Graman, née Almuth Gitterman, first discovered Lev's novel in a bookstall in Berlin in the late 1940s.

———. *Ali i Nino.* Baku: Literaturni Azerbaycan, 1994. This edition could not be published before 1991, because it was banned in the Soviet Union. In the introduction to the Turkish edition published in the early 1970s, it was claimed that Kurban Said had written the novel originally in Azeri; in reality, *Ali and Nino* was first translated into Azeri only in the late 1970s, for broadcast into Azerbaijan by the Voice of America as anti-Soviet propaganda.

———. *Das Mädchen vom goldenen Horn.* Basel: Desch, 1973. Originally published as *Die Prinzessin vom goldenen Horn.* Vienna: Zinnen, 1938.

———. *The Girl from the Golden Horn.* Trans. Jenia Graman. New York: Overlook Press, 2001.

Mohammed Essad Bey. *Alì Khàn.* Rome: Editoriale I.T.L.O., 1944. An Italian translation of *Ali and Nino* published two years after Lev's death, with significant changes to the original text and without the pseudonym Kurban Said.

Unpublished Materials

A very partial list. I collected documents from Azerbaijan, England, France, Germany, Holland, Italy, Sweden, Turkey, the United States, and other countries. The two most important sources were Lev's deathbed memoir-cum-novel, in six leather notebooks, which he called *The Man Who Knew Nothing About Love,* and the roughly three hundred letters between "Essad Bey" and Pima Andreae, a patron of the arts in Rapallo, Italy, from 1939 to 1942. Other sources include:

By Lev Nussimbaum

Unfinished manuscript for a novel about New York City, found along with his correspondence with Pima Andreae in Rapallo, Italy. (Original is German handwritten manuscript.)

Manuscript for a book entitled *The March on Rome,* supposedly blocked from publication by Italian Fascist officials.

Another manuscript on the history of the Caucasus.

Collection of fairy tales, "Oriental" satiric tales, and poems, read or recited by Lev during gatherings with Pasternaks, Nabokovs, and other Russian émigrés in Berlin in the 1920s. (His classmate Alexander Brailow transcribed these at the time in Russian, and fifty years later, he and Jenia Graman translated them into English and German.)

Correspondence with Senator Giovanni Gentile, Lev's most prominent Fascist patron, who also owned one of Italy's largest publishing companies, Sansoni (Archives of Sansoni Publishing Company, Florence).

"Last Will and Literary Testament of Essad Bey" (Zurich Public Library, Rascher Archive).

By Other Authors

Baumfeld, Franzie. Correspondence with Erika Nussimbaum (Loewendahl/ Fülop-Miller), photos, court proceedings, clippings.

Beveridge, Ray. Correspondence (Zurich Public Library, Rascher Archive).

Brailow, Alexander. Correspondence with Charlotte Mayerson (1970 Random House editor of *Ali and Nino*), Christopher Lehmann-Haupt at *The New York Times,* and Jenia Graman; memoirs, written in the 1990s; essay introducing Lev's "Oriental Tales," written in the 1970s.

Guest books for Casa Pattison (the house of Lev's landlord), Margherita Hotel, and Pensione San Matteo in Positano, Italy.

Ehrenfels, Elfriede. Correspondence with Essad Bey, 1940. Novels and stories published as Ottmar Steinmetz, apparently written with her brother Omar Ehrenfels. Analyses of Plato's works with mathematical and philosophical calculations in ancient Greek. Horoscope and tarot readings (Ehrenfels Castle Archive).

Ehrenfels, Mireille. Correspondence with Giamil Vacca-Mazzara, 1975–76. Correspondence with Jenia Graman, 1976–99 (Ehrenfels Castle Archive).

Ehrenfels, Omar. Correspondence with Christian von Ehrenfels (1930), Max Brod (1939–40, 1960–65), Essad Bey (1938–40); extensive newspaper reports from India of his travels and his contributions to Western Islamic journals of the 1930s and '40s; childhood writings; stories and articles published in the *Prager Tageblatt* in the 1920s and '30s under the pen name Ottmar Steinmetz, apparently shared with his sister Elfriede (Ehrenfels Castle Archive).

Pauli, Hertha. Correspondence with Charlotte Mayerson, 1971.

Fülop-Miller, René. Personal papers, articles, and documents of Lev's "arch-rival," a writer who allegedly "stole" his wife, Erika (Deutches Exilarchiv, Frankfurt, Germany).

Fülop-Miller, Erika Essad Bey Nussimbaum Loewendahl von Mohrenschildt. Personal papers, poems, memoirs, and documents of Lev's ex-wife.

Graman, Jenia. Correspondence with Giamil Vacca-Mazzara, 1975.

Haleen, Cerle. Correspondence with Jenia Graman, 1975.

Huebsch, Benjamin. Archive of the founder and editor in chief of Viking, Lev's main American publisher and a friend during the 1930s (Library of Congress).

Ibragimov, Mirza. Correspondence with Charlotte Mayerson, 1971.

Pound, Ezra. Correspondence (Yale University).

Schulte, Alice. *Biographie Essad-Bey.* Handwritten, unpublished biographical sketch she was preparing for Lev's Swiss publisher (Zurich Public Library, Rascher Publishers Archive); death certificate (Town Hall, Meran, Italy).

Vacca-Mazzara, Giamil. Correspondence with Lev's doctor (1943), Hutchinson Press (1975), and Omar Ehrenfels (1975).

Viereck, George Sylvester. Freedom of Information Act file (FBI, Washington, D.C.); scrapbook (New York Public Library archives).

Official Documents

Random House file on *Ali and Nino* publication dispute, 1970–77.

Documents detailing the surveillance of Lev by the Italian government, discussions between officials regarding his interment in Positano, publications and racial status; petitions on his behalf to Mussolini (Archivio del Ministero dell'Interno, Rome).

Discussions of illegal activities and false identities of both Lev and Giamil Vacca-Mazzara, né Bello Vacca. (Archivio Storico-diplomatico del Ministero degli Affari Esteri, Rome; Archivio Storico-diplomatico del Ministero dell'Africa Italiana, Rome).

Files of the Positano police and mayor's office.

Ship manifests for Essad Bey, Erika Nussimbaum, and the Loewendahls, documenting their arrival in the United States (National Records Archive, Manhattan).

INTERVIEWS

Abutalybov, Ramiz, 2000

Akhundov, Fuad, 1998 and 2000

Andreae, Alessandro, 2002–03

Ashurbekov, Miriam and Sara, 1998

Asadullayeva Weber, Zuleika, 2000, 2001

Barazon, Heinz, 1998

Brailow, Norma, 1998–2000

Baumfeld, Franzie, 2001

Ehrenfels, Leela, 1998–2001

Ehrenfels, Lou Lou, 2001
Ehrenfels-Abeille, Mireille, 1998–2001
Ercolino, Romolo, 1999
Fabre, Giorgio, 1999
Flatow-Rispoli, Nicoletta and Massimo, 2000
Fülöp-Miller, Ingrid, 2001
Gaetani-Pattison, Raimonda, 1998 and 2000
Graman, Jenia, 1998 and 1999
Gurbanly, Cherkez, 2000
Halielov, Panach, 2000
Hermont, Noam, 2003
Höpp, Gerhard, 1998, 2000, and 2001
Honigsberg, Peggy, 2001
Huseinov, Baylar, 2000
Huseinov, Rafael, 2000
Huseynoglu, Tofiq, 2000
Ibragimbekov, Rustam, 2000
Kerimov, Pasha, 2000
Kirschner-Mögle, Therese, 1998
Knight, Carlo, 2000
Loewendahl, Walter, 2001
Miller, Irene, 2001
Osman, Ertugrul, 2000–01
Rispoli, Fiorvante, 2000
Rispoli, Giovanni, 2000
Rispoli family, 1999
Rondeli, Alex, 2000
Sersale, Franco, Anna, and Julia, 1998 and 2000
Sheppard, Brian, 1998 and 2000
Spalek, John, 2001
Streena family, 2000
Veziroff brothers, 2000
Viereck, Peter, 2001

ARTICLES, CONFERENCE PROCEEDINGS, ETC.

Anonymous. "Faschismus Und Judentum (Fascism and Judaism)." *Jüdischer Rundschau* 16 (1937), p. 3.
R.B. "Die Welt Des Islams." *Jüdische Monatshefte* 2.12 (1915), pp. 389–96.
Ben-Gavriel, M. Y. "Blick Nach Mecca." *Jüdische Rundschau* 16 (1937), p. 11.

————. "Oestliche Impressionen." *Der Morgen* 11 (1935/6), pp. 307–9.

Carleton, Lieut.-Col. The Hon. Dudley. "The Fate of the Turkomans." *Blackwood's Magazine* 207, no. 1251 (January 1920), pp. 83–91.

Ercolino, Romolo. "Mohammed Essad Bey: Il Musalmano di Positano" (pamphlet).

F.F. "Lossage Vom Orient." *Der Morgen* 13.3 (1937), pp. 128–29.

Groseclose, Elgin E. "The Prisons of Despair: An Experience in the Russian Cheka." *The Atlantic Monthly* 132 (December 1922), pp. 833–44.

Hassan, Mohammed. "Das Islam-Institut in Berlin." *Minerva-Zeitschrift* 4.5/6, pp. 124–27.

Höpp, Gerhard. "Mohammed Essad Bey: Nur Orient Für Europäer?" *Asien Afrika Lateinamerika* 25 (1997), pp. 75–97.

Husseinov, Rafael. "About Essad Bey." Baku, Azerbaijan: Aran Press.

Kalmar, Ivan Davidson. "Moorish Style: Orientalism, the Jews, and Synagogue Architecture." *Jewish Social Studies,* vol. 7, no. 3, Spring/Summer 2001.

Korolenko, Vladimir. "Guilty!" *The Atlantic Monthly* 129 (June 1922).

Miliukov, Paul. "Eurasianism and Europeanism in Russian History." *Festschrift Th.G. Masaryk zum 80. Geburtstage* 1 (1930), pp. 225–36.

Ohanian, Armen. "The Dancer of Shamakha." *Asia: The American Magazine on the Orient* 22, no. 5 (May 1922), pp. 339–44.

Paxton, Robert O. "The Five Stages of Fascism." *The Journal of Modern History* 70 (March 1998), pp. 1–23.

Smyser, William Leon. "He Has Lived His Stories." *New York Herald Tribune* (1934).

Steinbeck, John. "Positano." *Harper's Bazaar* 86.2898 (1953), pp. 158ff.

Vacca-Mazzara, Giamil. "Mohammed Essad-Bey: Scrittore Musalmano dell'-Azerbaigian Caucasico" (obituary of Essad Bey). *Oriente Moderno* (1942), pp. 434–43.

Tabloid Articles, Court Proceedings

Below are some of the tabloid features about the "Erika-Essad-René-Heddy" divorce/annulment fights, from American, French, Italian, and Austrian newspapers. I also refer to official American court transcripts of the "annulment," from Los Angeles County Court, November 18, 1937, as well as some later transcripts from Maryland.

Hilal Munschi, et al. "Protest," *Berliner Tribüne,* May 24, 1930.

"Scheidungsprozess gegen den Schriftsteller Essad Bey. Eine aufsehenerregende Eheaffäre." *Neues Wiener Journal,* October 31, 1937.

"Scandale mondain en Autriche." *Le Journal de Paris,* November 3, 1937.

"Annulment Case Proceeds in Suing Wife's Absence." *Los Angeles Times,* November 19, 1937.

"Poetess Freed of Moslem Mate by Remote Control." New York *Daily News,* November 28, 1937.

"Harem? Yes—But Scare 'Em? No!" *Sunday Mirror Magazine,* January 2, 1938.

"Film Writer Sued by Wife, Tells of Destitution in Vienna." *Los Angeles Times,* January 20, 1939.

"Diva Sues Mate's Friend for $200,000 Heart Balm." *Los Angeles Times,* January 21, 1939.

SECONDARY SOURCES

Ackroyd, Peter. *Ezra Pound and His World.* London: Thames and Hudson, 1980.

Alder, Lory, and Richard Dalby. *The Dervish of Windsor Castle: The Life of Arminius Vambery.* London: Bachman and Turner, 1979.

Alter, Peter, ed. *Nationalismus: Dokumente zur Geschichte.* Munich: Piper GmbH., 1994.

Altstadt, Audrey L. *The Azerbaijani Turks: Power and Identity Under Russian Rule.* Stanford, Calif.: Hoover Institution Press, 1992.

Hamm, Michael F., ed. *The City in Late Imperial Russia.* Bloomington: Indiana University Press, 1986.

Anderson, Lisa, et al., eds. *The Origins of Arab Nationalism.* New York: Columbia University Press, 1991.

Andres, Stefan. *Positano.* Munich: R. Piper and Co., 1957.

Antonov-Ovseyenko, Anton. *The Time of Stalin.* New York: Harper & Row, 1970.

Arendt, Hannah. *Jew as Pariah: Jewish Identity and Politics in the Modern Age.* Ed./intro. Ron H. Feldman. New York: Grove Press, 1978.

Arnold, Sir Thomas Walker. *Legacy of Islam.* Ed. Sir Thomas Arnold and Alfred Guillaume. London: Oxford University Press, 1931.

Ascher, Abraham. *The Revolution of 1905: Authority Restored.* Stanford, Calif.: Stanford University Press, 1992.

Aschheim, Steven E. *Brothers and Strangers: The Eastern European Jew in German and German Jewish Consciousness, 1800–1923.* Madison: University of Wisconsin, 1982.

———. *Culture and Catastrophe: German and Jewish Confrontations with National Socialism and Other Crises.* New York: New York University Press, 1996.

Baird, Jay W. *To Die for Germany: Heroes in the Nazi Pantheon.* Bloomington and Indianapolis: Indiana University Press, 1990.

Balbo, Italo. *Stormi d'Italia sul Mondo.* Milano: A. Mondatori, 1934.

Bamberger, Bernard J. *The Story of Judaism.* New York: Schocken Books, 1957.

Banine. *Jours Caucasiens.* Paris: Julliard, 1945.

———. *Jours Parisiens.* Paris: Julliard, 1947.

Baxter, John. *The Hollywood Exiles.* New York: Taplinger Publishing, 1976.

Beller, Steven. *Vienna and the Jews.* Cambridge, England: Cambridge University Press, 1989.

Belloc, Hilaire. *The Crisis of Civilization.* New York: Fordham University Press, 1937.

———. *The Jews.* London: Constable and Company, 1922.

Ben-Ghiat, Ruth. *Fascist Modernities: Italy 1922–1945.* Berkeley: University of California Press, 2001.

Ben-Sasson, H. H., ed. *A History of the Jewish People.* Trans. George Weidenfeld and Nicolson Ltd. Tel Aviv: Dvir Publishing House, 1969.

Ben-Zvi, Itzhak. *The Exiled and the Redeemed.* Philadelphia: Jewish Publication Society, 1957.

Berkowitz, Michael. *Zionist Culture.* Chapel Hill: University of North Carolina, 1996.

Berman, Nina. *Orientalismus, Kolonialismus und Moderne. Zum Bild des Orients in der deutschsprachigen Kultur um 1900.* Stuttgart: M & P Verlag, 1997.

Bettauer, Hugo. *The City Without Jews: A Novel of Our Time.* Trans. Salomea Neumark Brainin. New York: Bloch Publishing Company, 1991.

Beveridge, Ray. *Mein Leben für euch! Erinnerungen an glanzvolle und bewegte Jahre. Mit 39 Abbildungen.* Berlin: Ullstein, 1937.

Biagini, Furio. *Mussolini e il Sionismo.* Milano: M & B Publishing, 1998.

Billington, James H. *The Icon and the Axe: An Interpretive History of Russian Culture.* New York: Alfred A. Knopf, 1966.

Bilski, Emily D. *Berlin Metropolis: Jews and the New Culture 1890–1918.* Berkeley: University of California Press, 1999.

Black, Antony. *The History of Islamic Political Thought.* New York: Routledge, 2001.

Blady, Ken. *Jewish Communities in Exotic Places.* Northvale: Jason Aronson Inc., 2000.

Blake, Robert. *Disraeli's Grand Tour.* New York: Oxford University, 1982.

Böss, Otto. *Die Lehre der Eurasier. Ein Beitrag zur russischen Ideengeschichte des 20. Jahrhunderts.* Wiesbaden: Otto Harrossowitz, 1961.

Boveri, Margret. *Minaret and Pipe-Line.* London: Oxford University Press, 1939.

Brantlinger, Patrick. *The Self-Fashioning of Disraeli.* Cambridge, England: Cambridge University Press, 1999.

Brechtefeld, Jörg. *Mitteleuropa and German Politics: 1848 to the Present.* New York: St. Martin's Press, 1996.

Brendon, Piers. *The Dark Valley: A Panorama of the 1930s.* New York: Alfred A. Knopf, 2000.

Brenner, Michael. *The Renaissance of Jewish Culture in Weimar Germany.* New Haven, Conn.: Yale University Press, 1996.

Broido, Vera. *Apostles into Terrorists.* New York: Viking, 1977.

Brook, Kevin Alan. *The Jews of Khazaria.* Northvale: Jason Aronson, 1999.

Brower, Daniel R., and Edward J. Lazzerini. *Russia's Orient: Imperial Borderlands and Peoples 1700–1917.* Bloomington: Indiana University Press, 1997.

Blair Brysac, Shareen. *Resisting Hitler: Mildred Harnack and the Red Orchestra.* New York: Oxford University Press, 2000.

Buber, Martin. *On Zion.* London: Horovitz, 1952.

Buchan, John. *Greenmantle.* New York: Pocket Books, 1941.

Bullock, Alan. *Hitler and Stalin: Parallel Lives.* New York: Alfred A. Knopf, 1991.

Bunin, Ivan. *Cursed Days: A Diary of Revolution.* Trans. Thomas Gaiton Marullo. Chicago: Ivan R. Dee, 1998.

Burchard, Amory, et al., eds. *Das russische Berlin.* Berlin: Die Ausländerbeauftragte des Senats, 1994.

Burleigh, Michael. *The Third Reich: A New History.* New York: Hill and Wang, 2000.

Burleigh, Michael, and Wolfgang Wipperman. *The Racial State: Germany 1933–1945.* Cambridge, England: Cambridge University Press, 1991.

Burnaby, Frederick. *On Horseback Through Asia Minor.* Oxford, England: Oxford University Press, 1898.

Burt, N. C., and D. D. *The Far East.* Cincinnati: Robert Clarke, 1869.

Byron, Robert. *The Road to Oxiana.* Oxford, England: Oxford University Press, 1937.

Castonier, Elisabeth. *Stürmisch bis heiter: Memoiren einer Aussenseiterin.* Munich: Nymphenburger Verlagshandlung, 1964.

Chaliand, Gerard, and Jean-Pierre Rageau. *The Penguin Atlas of Diasporas.* New York: Penguin, 1991.

Chamberlain, Houston Stewart. *Foundations of the Nineteenth Century.* Trans. John Lees. New York: John Lane Company, 1912.

Chubarov, Alexander. *The Fragile Empire: A History of Imperial Russia.* New York: Continuum, 2001.

Clark, Alan. *Suicide of the Empires: the Battles on the Eastern Front, 1914–1918.* New York: American Heritage, 1971.

Clarke, Sir Edward. *Benjamin Disraeli: Romance of a Great Career.* New York: Macmillan & Co., 1926.

Cohen, Arthur A., ed. *Jew, Essays from Martin Buber's Journal* Der Jude, *1916–1928.* Trans. Joachim Neugroschel. University: University of Alabama Press, 1980.

Cohn, Norman. *Warrant for Genocide: The Myth of the Jewish World Conspiracy and the Protocols of the Elders of Zion.* London: Serif, 1967.

Notestein, Wallace. *Conquest and Kultur: Aims of the Germans in Their Own Words.* Washington, D.C.: Committee on Public Information, 1918

Conrad, Joseph. *Under Western Eyes.* New York: Modern Library, 2001.

———. *Notes on Life and Letters.* London and Toronto: J. M. Dent & Sons Ltd., 1921.

Craig, Gordon A. *Germany, 1866–1945.* New York: Oxford University Press, 1978.

Crankshaw, Edward. *Gestapo: Instrument of Tyranny.* London: Putnam, 1956.

———. *The Shadow of the Winter Palace: Russia's Drift to Revolution, 1825–1917.* New York: Viking, 1976.

Cunsolo, Ronald. *Italian Nationalism: From Its Origins to World War II.* Malabar, Fla.: Robert E. Krieger Publishing Company, 1990.

Curtis, William Eleroy. *Around the Black Sea.* New York: Hodder & Stoughton, George H. Doran Company, 1911.

Daniel, Mooshie G. *Modern Persia.* Toronto: Henderson & Company, 1898.

Daniels, Robert V., ed. *A Documentary History of Communism, Volume I.* New York: Vintage Books, 1960.

D'Annunzio, Gabriele. *Teneo te Africa.* Milan: Il Vittoriale Degli Italiani, 1939.

David, Itzhac. *Istoriia evreev na Kavkaze* (*History of the Caucasian Jews in Palestine*). Tel Aviv: Kavkasioni, c. 1989.

Dawidowicz, Lucy, ed. *The Golden Tradition: Jewish Life and Thought in Eastern Europe.* New York: Holt, Rinehart and Winston, 1967.

Delmer, Sefton. *Trail Sinister: Top Newsman Remembers Europe.* London: Secker & Warburg, 1961.

———. *Weimar Germany: Democracy on Trial.* New York: American Heritage, 1972.

Diggins, John. *Mussolini and Fascism: The View from America.* Princeton, N.J.: Princeton University Press, 1972.

Disraeli, Benjamin. *Coningsby, or the New Generation.* Boston: L. C. Page & Co., 1844.

———. *Tancred, or the New Crusade.* Westport, Conn.: Greenwood Press, 1970.

———. *Contarini Fleming: A Psychological Romance.* New York: AMS Press, 1976.

Dubrovic, Milan. *Veruntreute Geschichte: Die Wiener Salons und Literatencafes.* Vienna: Paul Zsolnay Verlages, 1985.

Dodd, Martha. *Through Embassy Eyes: My Years in Germany.* New York, Harcourt, Brace and Company, 1939.

Dumas, Alexandre. *Adventures in Caucasia.* Trans. A. E. Murch. Westport, Conn.: Greenwood Press, 1975.

Dymshits, Valery. "The Eastern Jewish Communities of the Former USSR." In

Facing West: Oriental Jews of Central Asia and the Caucasus. Amsterdam: Joods Historisch Museum, 1996.

Ehrenburg, Ilya. *Memoirs (1921–1941).* New York: Grosset and Dunlap, 1963.

Ehrenfels, Christian von. *Leben und Werk.* Amsterdam: Rodopi, 1986.

Eickelman, Dale F., ed. *Russia's Muslim Frontiers.* Indianapolis: Indiana University Press, 1993.

Elliott, Mark. *Azerbaijan with Georgia.* West Sussex, England: Trailblazer, 1999.

Ellis, John. *The Social History of the Machine Gun.* New York: Random House, 1975.

Elon, Amos. *The Pity of It All: A History of the Jews in Germany, 1743–1933.* New York: Metropolitan Books, 2002.

Endelman, Todd M., ed. *Jewish Apostasy in the Modern World.* New York: Holmes & Meier, 1987.

Fabre, Giorgio. *L'Elenco.* Torino: Silvio Zamorani, 1998.

Felice, Renzo De. *Fascismo e l'Oriente: arabi, ebrei e indiani nella politica di Mussolini.* Bologna: Società editrice il Mulino, 1988.

———. *Jews in an Arab Land: Libya, 1835–1970,* Trans. Judith Roumani. Austin: University of Texas Press, 1985.

———. *Jews in Fascist Italy.* Trans. Robert Miller. New York: Enigma Books, 2001.

Ferguson, Niall. *The House of Rothschild.* New York: Viking, 1999.

Fermi, Laura. *Mussolini.* Chicago: University of Chicago Press, 1961.

———. *Illustrious Immigrants: The Intellectual Migration from Europe, 1930–41.* Chicago: University of Chicago Press, 1968.

Fest, Joachim. *Hitler.* Trans. Richard and Clara Winston. New York: Harcourt Brace Jovanovich, Inc., 1974.

Fichtner, Paula Sutter. *Habsburg Empire: From Dynasticism to Multinationalism.* Malabar, Fla.: Krieger Publishing Company, 1997.

Floyd, David. *Russia in Revolt, 1905: The First Crack in Tsarist Power.* New York: American Heritage, 1969.

Ford, Franklin L. *Political Murder.* Cambridge, Mass.: Harvard University Press, 1985.

Friedländer, Saul. *Nazi Germany and the Jews: The Years of Persecution, 1933–1939,* vol. 1. New York: HarperCollins, 1997.

Friedrich, Otto. *Before the Deluge: A Portrait of Berlin in the 1920s.* New York: HarperPerennial, 1972.

———. *City of Nets: A Portrait of Hollywood in the 1940s.* New York: Harper & Row, 1986.

Fromkin, David. *A Peace to End All Peace.* New York: Henry Holt, 1989.

Fromm, Bella. *Blood and Banquets: A Berlin Social Diary.* London: Geoffrey Bles, 1943.

Fülöp-Miller, René. *Leaders, Dreamers and Rebels: An Account of the Great Mass-Movements of History and the Wish-Dreams That Inspired Them.* New York: Viking, 1935.

———. *Lenin and Gandhi.* New York: G. P. Putnam's Sons, 1927.

Fussell, Paul. *Abroad: British Literary Traveling Between the Wars.* New York: Oxford University Press, 1980.

Geifman, Anna, ed. *Russia Under the Last Tsar: Opposition and Subversion 1894–1917.* Oxford, England: Blackwell Publishers, 1999.

———. *Thou Shalt Kill: Revolutionary Terrorism in Russia 1894–1917.* Princeton, N.J.: Princeton University Press, 1993.

Gertz, Elmer. *Odyssey of a Barbarian: The Biography of George Sylvester Viereck.* Buffalo, N.Y.: Prometheus Books, 1978.

Gillette, Aaron. *Racial Theories in Fascist Italy.* London: Routledge, 2002.

Glenny, Michael, and Norman Stone, eds. *The Other Russia: The Experience of Exile.* New York: Viking, 1991.

Goodwin, Jason. *Lords of the Horizons: A History of the Ottoman Empire.* New York: Henry Holt, 1998.

Graham, Stephen. *A Vagabond in the Caucasus.* London: John Lane, 1911.

Goitein, S. D. *Jews and Arabs: Their Contacts Through the Ages.* New York: Schocken, 1974.

Goldstone, Jack A., ed. *The Encyclopedia of Political Revolutions.* Washington, D.C.: Congressional Quarterly, 1998.

Grey, Ian. *Stalin: Man of History.* Garden City: Doubleday, 1979.

Grosz, George. *George Grosz: An Autobiography.* Trans. Nora Hughes. New York: Macmillan, 1983.

Grunfeld, Frederic V. *Prophets Without Honor: A Background to Freud, Kafka, Einstein, and Their World.* New York: Holt, Rinehart and Winston, 1979.

Gubbay, Lucien. *Sunlight and Shadow: The Jewish Experience of Islam.* New York: Other Press, 1999.

Haffner, Sebastian. *Defying Hitler: A Memoir.* Trans. Oliver Pretzel. New York: Farrar, Straus and Giroux, 2002.

———. *The Meaning of Hitler.* Trans. Ewald Osers. Cambridge, Mass.: Harvard University Press, 1983.

Haimson, Leopold. *The Russian Marxists and the Origins of Bolshevism.* Boston: Beacon Press, 1955.

Hall, Murray. *Der Fall Bettauer.* Vienna: Loecker Verlag, 1978.

Hanfstaengl, Ernst. *Hitler: The Missing Years.* New York: Arcade Publishing, 1994.

Harcave, Sidney, ed. *The Memoirs of Count Witte.* Armonk, M. E. Sharpe, Inc., 1990.

Harlow, Barbara, and Mia Carter, eds. *Imperialism and Orientalism: A Documentary Sourcebook.* Malden, Mass.: Blackwell, 1999.

Hauptmann, Gerhart. *Sämtliche Werke.* Berlin: Propyläen Verlag, 1974.

Haxthausen, Charles W., and Heidrun Suhr, eds. *Berlin: Culture and Metropolis.* Minneapolis: University of Minnesota, 1990.

Hecht, Ben. *A Guide for the Bedevilled.* New York: Scribner and Sons, 1944.

———. *A Child of the Century.* New York: Simon & Schuster, 1954.

Hedgepeth, Sonja, and Ernst Schurer. *Else Lasker-Schüler: Ansichten und Perspektiven.* Tübingen, Germany: Francke, 1999.

Heering, Kurt Jürgen, ed. *Das Wiener Kaffeehaus.* Frankfurt am Main: Insel Verlag, 1993.

Heiber, Helmut. *The Weimar Republic.* Trans. W. E. Yuill. Oxford, England: Blackwell Publishers, 1993.

Heiden, Konrad. *The Führer.* Trans. Ralph Manheim. Edison, N.J.: Castle Books, 2002.

Heilbut, Anthony. *Exiled in Paradise: German Refugee Artists and Intellectuals in America from the 1930s to the Present.* New York: Viking, 1983.

Heizer, Donna K. *Jewish-German Identity in the Orientalist Literature of Else Lasker-Schüler, Friedrich Wolf, and Franz Werfel.* Columbia, S.C.: Camden House, 1996.

Henri, Ernst. *Hitler over Europe?* New York: Simon & Schuster, 1934.

Herber, Agnes. *Casuals in the Caucasus: The Diary of a Sporting Holiday.* London: John Lane Company, 1912.

Herman, Arthur. *The Idea of Decline in Western History.* New York: Free Press, 1997.

Hermand, Jost. *Old Dreams of a New Reich: Volkish Utopias and National Socialism.* Bloomington: Indiana University Press, 1992.

Hess, Moses. *Rome and Jerusalem: A Study in Jewish Nationalism.* New York: Bloch, 1918.

Hilberg, Raul, ed. *Documents of Destruction: Germany and Jewry, 1933–1945.* Chicago: Quadrangle Books, 1971.

Hindenburg, Paul von. "The Stab in the Back." In Anton Kaes et al., eds. *The Weimar Republic Sourcebook.* Berkeley: University of California Press, 1994.

Hingley, Ronald. *The Russian Secret Police: Muscovite, Imperial Russian, and Soviet Political Security Operations.* New York: Simon & Schuster, 1970.

Hirschfeld, Magnus. *The Sexual History of the World War.* New York: The Panurge Press, 1934.

Hodgetts, E. A. Braylet. *Round About Armenia: The Record of a Journey Across the Balkans, Through Turkey, the Caucasus and Persia.* London: Sampson Low, Marston and Company, 1916.

Hoeflich, Eugen. *Die Pforte des Ostens: Das Arabish-Jüdische Palästina vom panasiatischen Standpunkt aus.* Berlin and Vienna: Benjamin Harz Verlag, 1923.

Höpp, Gerhard. *Fremde Erfahrungen: Asiaten und Afrikaner in Deutschland, Österreich und in der Schweiz bis 1945.* Berlin: Klaus-Schwarz-Verlag, 1996.

————. *Muslime in der Mark: als Kriegsgefangene und Internierte in Wünsdorf und Zossen, 1914–1924.* Berlin: Klaus-Schwarz-Verlag, 1997.

Hoffmann, Conrad. *In the Prison Camps of Germany, a Narrative of "Y" Service Among Prisoners of War.* New York: Association Press, 1920.

Hofmann, Paul. *The Viennese: Splendor, Twilight and Exile.* New York: Anchor Press, 1988.

Hollins, Dave. *Austrian Auxiliary Troops 1792–1816.* Oxford, England: Osprey Publishing Co., 1996.

Hook, Sidney. *Marx and the Marxists: The Ambiguous Legacy.* Malabar, Fla.: Robert E. Krieger Publishing Co., 1982.

Hopkirk, Peter. *Like Hidden Fire: The Plot to Bring Down the British Empire.* New York: Kodansha, 1994.

————. *Setting the East Ablaze.* New York: Kodansha, 1984.

Hosking, Geoffrey. *Russia: People and Empire.* Cambridge, Mass.: Harvard University Press, 1997.

Hourani, Albert. *A History of the Arab Peoples.* New York: MJF Books, 1991.

Hull, E. M. *The Sheik.* New York: Dell, 1921.

Huntington, W. Chapin. *The Homesick Million: Russia-out-of-Russia.* Boston: Stratford Co., 1933.

Hynes, Samuel, et al., eds. *Reporting World War II,* 2 vols. New York: Library of America, 1995.

Isenberg, Sheila. *A Hero of Our Own: The Story of Varian Fry.* New York: Random House, 2001.

Isherwood, Christopher. *The Berlin Stories.* New York: New Directions, 1945.

Jelavich, Peter. *Berlin Cabaret.* Cambridge, Mass.: Harvard University Press, 1993.

Johann, A. E. *Das Land ohne Herz: eine Reise ins unbekannte Amerika.* Berlin: Deutscher Verlag, 1942.

Johnson, Niel M. *George Sylvester Viereck: German-American Propagandist.* Urbana: University of Illinois Press, 1972.

Johnson, Paul. *A History of the Jews.* New York: Harper & Row, 1987.

Johnston, Robert. *"New Mecca, New Babylon": Paris and the Russian Exiles, 1920–1945.* Kingston: McGill–Queen's University Press, 1988.

Joll, James. *The Anarchists.* Cambridge, Mass.: Harvard University Press, 1964.

Joly, Maurice. *The Dialogue in Hell Between Machiavelli and Montesquieu: Humanitarian Despotism and the Conditions of Modern Tyranny.* Trans. John S. Waggoner. Lanham: Lexington Books, 2002.

Jonge, Alex de. *Stalin and the Shaping of the Soviet Union.* New York, 1986.

Kaes, Anton, et al., eds. *The Weimar Republic Sourcebook.* Berkeley: University of California Press, 1994.

Kann, Robert A. *A History of the Habsburg Empire, 1526–1918.* Berkeley: University of California Press, 1974.

Kappeler, Andreas. *The Russian Empire: A Multiethnic History.* Trans. Alfred Clayton. New York: Longman, 2001.

Karny, Yo'av. *Highlanders: A Journey to the Caucasus in Search of Memory.* New York: Farrar, Straus and Giroux, 2000.

Karsh, Efraim, and Inari Karsh, *Empires of the Sand: The Struggle for Mastery in the Middle East, 1789–1923.* Cambridge, Mass.: Harvard University Press, 1999.

Katkov, George, and Harold Shukman. *Lenin's Path to Power: Bolshevism and the Destiny of Russia.* New York: American Heritage Press, 1971.

Katz, Jacob. *From Prejudice to Destruction: Anti-Semitism 1700–1933.* Cambridge, Mass.: Harvard University Press, 1982.

Kaufmann, Walter. *Monarchism in the Weimar Republic.* New York: Bookman, 1953.

Keegan, John. *The First World War.* New York: Alfred A. Knopf, 1999.

Keller, Phyllis. *States of Belonging: German American Intellectuals and the First World War.* Cambridge, Mass.: Harvard University Press, 1979.

Kershaw, Ian. *Hitler 1889–1936: Hubris.* New York: W. W. Norton, 1998.

Kessler, Harry. *Berlin in Lights: The Diaries of Count Harry Kessler.* Trans. Charles Kessler. New York: Grove, 2000.

Keyserling, Hermann. *Travel Diary of a Philosopher.* Trans. J. Holroyd Reece. New York: Harcourt, Brace and Company, 1925.

Klemperer, Victor. *The Language of the Third Reich: LTI—Lingua Tertii Imperii: A Philologist's Notebook.* New York: Continuum, 2002.

Knight, Carlo. *La Torre Di Clavel: Un Romanzo.* Capri: La Conchiglia, 1999.

Kohn, Hans. *Die Europaisierung des Orients.* Berlin: Schocken, 1934.

———. *Nationalism and Imperialism in the Hither East.* London: G. Routledge and Sons, 1932.

Kolnai, Aurel. *The War Against the West.* New York: Viking, 1938.

Koestler, Arthur. *The Thirteenth Tribe.* New York: Random House, 1976.

———. *The Yogi and the Commissar.* New York: Macmillan Company, 1945.

———. *Arrow in the Blue.* London: Collins, 1952.

Kracauer, Siegfried. *From Caligari to Hitler: A Psychological History of the German Film.* Princeton, N.J.: Princeton University Press, 1947.

Kramer, Martin, ed. *The Jewish Discovery of Islam: Studies in Honor of Bernard Lewis.* Tel Aviv: The Moshe Dayan Center for Middle Eastern and African Studies, 1999.

Kreimeier, Klaus. *The Ufa Story: A History of Germany's Greatest Film Company, 1918–1945.* London: University of California Press, 1999.

Kropotkin, Peter. *Memoirs of a Revolutionist.* New York: Dover Publications, 1899.

Kühl, Stefan. *The Nazi Connection: Eugenics, American Racism, and German National Socialism.* New York: Oxford University Press, 1994.

Kuen, Odette. *In the Land of the Golden Fleece, Through Independent Menchevist Georgia.* Trans. Helen Jessiman. London: John Lane, 1924.

Kurzman, Charles. *Modernist Islam 1840–1940: A Sourcebook.* Oxford, England: Oxford University Press, 2002.

Lamb, Richard. *Mussolini as Diplomat: Il Duce's Italy on the World Stage.* New York: Fromm International, 1999.

Lane, Barbara Miller, and Leila J. Rupp, eds. *Nazi Ideology Before 1933: A Documentation.* Austin: University of Texas Press, 1978.

Lapidus, Ira M. *A History of Islamic Societies.* Cambridge, England: Cambridge University Press, 1988.

Laqueur, Walter, ed. "The Origins of Modern Terrorism." In *The Terrorism Reader: An Historical Anthology, Part II.* Philadelphia: Temple University Press, 1978, pp. 47–114.

———. *Russia and Germany: A Century of Conflict.* Boston: Little, Brown and Co., 1965.

Lasker-Schüler, Else. *Konzert.* Berlin: Rowohlt, 1932.

———. *Hebrew Ballads and Other Poems.* Philadelphia: Jewish Publication Society of America, 1980.

Lawrence, T. E. *Seven Pillars of Wisdom: A Triumph.* New York: Anchor Books, 1991.

Layton, Susan. *Russian Literature and Empire: Conquest of the Caucasus from Pushkin to Tolstoy.* New York: Cambridge University Press, 1994.

Leeuw, Charles van der. *Azerbaijan: A Quest for Identity.* New York: St. Martin's Press, 2000.

Levine, Don Isaac. *Stalin.* New York: Cosmopolitan Book Corporation, 1931.

Levy, Avigdor, ed. *The Jews of the Ottoman Empire.* Princeton, N.J.: Darwin Press, 1994.

Bernard Lewis, *The Jews of Islam.* Princeton, N.J.: Princeton University Press, 1984.

———. *Islam in History: Ideas, People, and Events in the Middle East.* Chicago: Open Court, 1993.

Liberman, Simon. *Building Lenin's Russia.* Chicago: University of Chicago Press, 1945.

Lichtheim, George. *Marxism: An Historical and Critical Study.* New York: Columbia University Press, 1982.

Lieven, D.C.B. *Empire: The Russian Empire and Its Rivals.* London: John Murray, 2000.

———. *Russia's Rulers Under the Old Regime.* New Haven, Conn.: Yale University Press, 1989.

Lilla, Mark. *The Reckless Mind: Intellectuals in Politics.* New York: New York Review Books, 2001.

Lilli, Virgilio. *Racconti di una Guerra.* Milan: Bompiani, 1943.

Lincoln, W. Bruce. *In War's Dark Shadow: The Russians Before the Great War.* New York: Dial Press, 1983.

—. *The Romanovs: Autocrats of All the Russias.* New York: Dial Press, 1981.

Linse, Ulrich. *Barfüssige Propheten. Erlöser der zwangziger Jahre.* Berlin: Siedler, 1983.

Lipstadt, Deborah E. *Beyond Belief: The American Press and the Coming of the Holocaust.* New York: Free Press, 1986.

Liulevicius, Vejas Gabriel. *War Land on the Eastern Front: Culture, National Identity and German Occupation in World War I.* Cambridge, England: Cambridge University Press, 2000.

Lukacs, John. *The Hitler of History.* New York: Alfred A. Knopf, 1997.

Luke, Harry Charles. *Anatolica.* London: Macmillan, 1924.

Lyons, Eugene. *Stalin: Czar of All the Russias.* Philadelphia: J. B. Lippincott Company, 1940.

Macfie, A. L., ed. *Orientalism: A Reader.* New York: New York University Press, 2000.

—. *Orientalism.* London: Longman, 2002.

Maclean, Fitzroy. *All the Russians: The End of an Empire.* New York: Smithmark, 1992.

—. *To Caucasus, the End of All the Earth: An Illustrated Companion to the Caucasus and Transcaucasia.* London: J. Cape, 1976.

Macmillan, Margaret. *Paris: 1919.* New York: Random House, 2001.

Malevsky-Malevich, P. *A New Party in Russia.* London: George Routledge & Sons, 1928.

Malia, Martin. *Russia Under Western Eyes: From the Bronze Horseman to the Lenin Mausoleum.* Cambridge, Mass.: Harvard University Press, 1999.

Mamedov, Farid. *Azerbaijan: Fortresses, Castles.* Trans. Shaik Djabiroglu. Baku: Interturan, Inc., 1994.

Mansel, Philip. *Constantinople: City of the World's Desire.* New York: St. Martin's Press, 1996.

Mansfield, Peter. *A History of the Middle East.* New York: Viking, 1991.

—. *The Ottoman Empire and Its Successors.* New York: St. Martin's Press, 1973.

Marcus, Jacob R. *The Rise and Destiny of the German Jew.* Cincinnati: Union of American Hebrew Congregations, 1934.

Massing, Paul. *Rehearsal for Destruction: A Study of Political Anti-Semitism in Imperial Germany.* New York: Harper, 1949.

Mazower, Mark. *Dark Continent: Europe's Twentieth Century.* New York: Alfred A. Knopf, 1999.

McCarthy, Justin. *The Ottoman Peoples and the End of Empire.* London: Arnold, 2002.

Mehring, Walter. *Staatenlos im Nirgendwo. Die Gedichte, Lieder und Chansons 1933–1974.* Düsseldorf, Germany: Claasen Verlag, 1981.

———. *The Lost Library.* Trans. Richard and Clara Winston. New York: Bobbs-Merrill Co., 1951.

Mendes-Flohr, Paul R. *Divided Passions: Jewish Intellectuals and the Experience of Modernity.* Detroit: Wayne State University Press, 1991.

Metcalfe, Philip. *1933.* Sag Harbor, N.Y.: Permanent Press, 1988.

Meyer, Karl E., and Shareen Blair Brysac. *Tournament of Shadows: The Race for Empire in Central Asia.* Washington, D.C.: Counterpoint, 1999.

Michaelis, Meir. *Mussolini and the Jews: German-Italian Relations and the Jewish Question in Italy 1922–1945.* Oxford, England: Clarendon Press, 1978.

Montefiore, Simon Sebag. *Stalin: The Court of the Red Tsar.* New York: Alfred A. Knopf, 2004.

Moore, Joseph, Jr., *Outlying Europe and the Nearer Orient.* Philadelphia: J. B. Lippincott, 1880.

Moorehead, Alan. *The Russian Revolution.* New York: Harper & Row, 1958.

Mosse, George L. *Fallen Soldiers: Reshaping the Memory of the World Wars.* Oxford, England: Oxford University Press, 1900.

———. *The Nationalization of the Masses: Political Symbolism and Mass Movements in Germany from the Napoleonic Wars Through the Third Reich.* Ithaca, N.Y.: Cornell University Press, 1975.

Mottahedeh, Roy. *The Mantle of the Prophet: Religion and Politics in Iran.* New York: Pantheon, 1985.

Munschi, Hilal. *Die Republik Aserbeidschan. Eine geschictliche und politische Skizze.* Berlin: Neudt Verlag, 1930.

Naimark, Norman M. *Terrorists and Social Democrats: The Russian Revolutionary Movement Under Alexander III.* Cambridge, Mass.: Harvard University Press, 1983.

———. *Fires of Hatred: Ethnic Cleansing in Twentieth-Century Europe.* Cambridge, Mass.: Harvard University Press, 2001.

Nasmyth, Peter. *Georgia: In the Mountains of Poetry.* New York: St. Martin's Press, 1998.

Nawrath, Alfred. *Im Reiche der Medea. Kaukasische Fahrten und Abenteur.* Leipzig, Germany: F. U. Brockhaus, 1924.

Neaman, Elliot Yale. *A Dubious Past: Ernst Jünger and the Politics of Literature After Nazism.* Berkeley: University of California Press, 1999.

O'Brien, Conor Cruise. *The Siege.* New York: Simon & Schuster, 1986.

O'Connor, Timothy Edward. *The Engineer of Revolution: L. B. Krasin and the Bolsheviks, 1870–1926.* Boulder, Colo.: Westview Press, 1992.

O'Connor, Richard. *The German Americans: An Informal History.* Boston: Little, Brown and Company, 1968.

Palgrave, William Gifford. *Travels in Central and Eastern Arabia.* London: Macmillan, 1871.

Patai, Raphael. *Apprentice in Budapest: Memories of a World That Is No More.* Salt Lake City: University of Utah Press, 1988.

———. *The Seed of Abraham: Jews and Arabs in Contact and Conflict.* New York: Scribner, 1986.

Pauli, Herta E. *Alfred Nobel: Dynamite King, Architect of Peace.* New York: L. B. Fischer, 1942.

———. *Break in Time.* New York: Hawthorne Books, 1972.

Paxton, Robert O. *The Anatomy of Fascism.* New York: Alfred A. Knopf, 2004.

Peukert, Detlev. *The Weimar Republic: The Crisis of Classical Modernity.* New York: Hill and Wang, 1987.

Pfanner, Helmut F. *Exile in New York: German and Austrian Writers After 1933.* Detroit: Wayne State University Press, 1983.

Phillips, Henry Albert. *Germany Today and Tomorrow.* New York: Dodd, Mean and Company, Inc., 1935.

Poliakov, Leon. *The History of Anti-Semitism: From the Time of Christ to the Court Jews.* Trans. Richard Howard. New York: Schocken Books, 1965.

Poliakov, Leon, and Jacques Sabille. *Jews Under the Italian Occupation.* Paris: Editions du Centre, 1955.

Powell, E. Alexander. *By Camel and Car to the Peacock Throne.* Garden City, N.Y.: Garden City Publishing Co., 1923.

Pulzer, Peter G. J. *The Rise of Political Anti-Semitism in Germany and Austria.* New York: John Wiley & Sons, 1964.

Radzinsky, Edvard. *The Last Tsar: The Life and Death of Nicholas II.* New York: Doubleday, 1993.

Ra, Bo Yin (J. A. Schneiderfranken). *The Wisdom of St. John.* Berkeley, Calif.: Kober Press, 1924.

Rabinbach, Anson. *In the Shadow of Catastrophe: German Intellectuals Between Apocalypse and Enlightenment.* Berkeley: University of California Press, 1997.

Raeff, Marc. *Russia Abroad: A Cultural History of the Russian Emigration 1919–1939.* New York: Oxford University Press, 1990.

Raisin, Jacob S. *Gentile Reactions to Jewish Ideals: With Special Reference to Proselytes.* New York: Philosophical Library, 1953.

Raswan, Carl R. *Black Tents of Arabia: My Life Among the Bedouins.* London: Hutchinson and Co., 1935.

Rauschning, Hermann. *The Revolution of Nihilism: Warning to the West!* New York: Alliance Book Corporation, 1939.

Rawlinson, A. *Adventures in the Near East 1918–1922.* New York: Dodd, Mead and Co., 1925.

Redman, Tim. *Ezra Pound and Italian Fascism.* Cambridge, England: Cambridge University Press, 1991.

Reitlinger, Gerald. *The SS: Alibi of a Nation 1922–1945.* New York: Viking, 1957.

Remnick, David. *Lenin's Tomb: The Last Days of the Soviet Empire.* New York: Random House, 1993.

Richie, Alexandra. *Faust's Metropolis: A History of Berlin.* New York: Carroll & Graf, 1998.

Rigge, Simon. *War in the Outposts.* Alexandria, Va.: Time-Life Books, 1980.

Rispoli, Giulio. *Positano, Luoghi e Persone, "Ieri e Oggi."* Verona, 1989.

Robertson, Esmonde M. *Mussolini as Empire-Builder: Europe and Africa, 1932–36.* London: Macmillan Press, 1977.

Robertson, Ritchie, ed. *The German-Jewish Dialogue: An Anthology of Literary Texts, 1749–1993.* New York: Oxford University Press, 1999.

Robinson, Paul. *The White Russian Army in Exile, 1920–1941.* New York: Oxford University Press, 2002.

Rosenbaum, Alan S., ed. *Is the Holocaust Unique? Perspectives on Comparative Genocide.* Boulder, Colo.: Westview, 1998.

Rosenbaum, Ron. *Explaining Hitler: The Search for the Origins of His Evil.* New York: HarperPerennial, 1998.

Rosenbloom, Joseph R. *Conversion to Judaism: From the Biblical Period to the Present.* Cincinnati: Hebrew Union College Press, 1978.

Roshwald, Aviel. *Ethnic Nationalism and the Fall of Empires: Central Europe, Russia and the Middle East, 1914–1923.* London: Routledge, 2001.

Ross, Edward. *Russia in Upheaval.* The Century Company: New York, 1918.

Roth, Joseph. *Juden auf Wanderschaft.* Berlin: Die Schmiede, 1927.

———. *What I Saw: Reports from Berlin, 1920–1933.* Trans. Michael Hofmann. New York: W. W. Norton, 2003.

Sachar, Abram Leon. *A History of the Jews.* New York: Alfred A. Knopf, 1968.

Sachar, Howard M. *Emergence of the Middle East.* New York: Alfred A. Knopf, 1969.

———. *Dreamland: Europeans and Jews in the Aftermath of the Great War.* New York: Alfred A. Knopf, 2002.

Said, Edward. *Orientalism.* New York: Vintage, 1978.

Salomon, Ernst von. *The Answers of Ernst von Salomon to the 131 Questions in the Allied Military Government "Frageboge."* Trans. Constantine Fitzgibbon. London: Putnam, 1954.

Sarti, Roland. *The Ax Within: Italian Fascism in Action.* New York: Franklin Watts, Inc., 1974.

Saunders, Thomas J. *Hollywood in Berlin: American Cinema and Weimar Germany.* Berkeley: University of California Press, 1994.

Schechtman, Joseph. *Fighter and Prophet: The Vladimir Jabotinsky Story, the Last Years.* New York: Thomas Yoseloff, 1961.

Schewertfeger, Ruth. *Else Lasker-Schüler: Inside This Deathly Solitude.* Oxford, England: Berg, 1991.

Schmidt, Josef. *Der Unterhaltungsschriftsteller Mosche Ya-Akov Ben-Gavriel: Bio-Bibliographie und literaturkritische Bestimmung.* Bonn: Bouvier Verlag Herbert Grundmann, 1979.

Schnapp, Jeffrey T., ed. *A Primer of Italian Fascism.* Lincoln and London: University of Nebraska Press, 2000.

Schnauber, Cornelius. *Hollywood Haven.* Riverside, Calif.: Ariadne, 1997.

Scholem, Gershom. *On Jews and Judaism in Crisis.* Trans. Werner Dannhauser. New York: Schocken Books, 1976.

Schmitz, David F. *United States and Fascist Italy: 1922–1940.* Chapel Hill: University of North Carolina, 1988.

Schorsch, Ismar. *Jewish Reactions to German Anti-Semitism, 1870–1914.* New York: Columbia University Press, 1972.

Schorske, Carl E. *German Social Democracy, 1905–1917: The Development of the Great Schism.* Cambridge, Mass. : Harvard University Press, 1983.

———. *Fin-de-Siècle Vienna: Politics and Culture.* New York: Alfred A. Knopf, 1980.

Schueddekopf, Otto-Ernst. *Linke Leute von Rechts: die nationalrevolutionären Minderheiten und der Kommunismus in der Weimarer Republik.* Stuttgart, Germany: W. Kohlhammer Verlag, 1960.

Schweinitz, H. H., *Helenendorf: eine deutsche Kolonie im Kaukasus.* Berlin: Vossische Verlag, 1910.

Segel, Binjamin W. *A Lie and a Libel: A History of the Protocols of the Elders of Zion.* Trans. and ed. Richard S. Levy Lincoln, Nebraska: University of Nebraska Press, 1995.

Seton-Watson, R. W. *Disraeli, Gladstone, and the Eastern Question.* New York: Norton Library, 1972.

Shaw, Roger. *Handbook of Revolutions.* New York: Stratford Press, 1934.

Shaw, Stanford. *The Jews of the Ottoman Empire and the Turkish Republic.* New York: New York University Press, 1991.

Shavit, Yaacov. *Jabotinsky and the Revisionist Movement 1925–1948.* Totowa, N.J.: Frank Cass, 1988.

Sheean, Vincent. *The New Persia.* New York: Century Co., 1927.

Shirer, William L. *Berlin Diary.* New York: Alfred A. Knopf, 1941.

———. *Rise and Fall of the Third Reich.* New York: Simon & Schuster, 1981.

Shoskes, Henry. *Your World and Mine.* New York: Lipton, 1952.

Sinor, Denis, ed. *Orientalism and History.* Cambridge, England: W. Heffer, 1954.

S.K. *Agent in Italy.* New York: Doubleday, Doran, and Co., 1942.

Smith, Denis Mack. *Modern Italy.* Ann Arbor: University of Michigan Press, 1959.

———. *Mussolini's Roman Empire.* New York: Viking, 1976.

Smith, Edward Ellis. *The Young Stalin: The Early Years of an Elusive Revolutionary.* New York: Farrar, Straus and Giroux, 1967.

Solomon, Flora, and Barnet Litvinoff. *Baku to Baker Street.* London: Collins, 1984.

"Spartacus Manifesto" (1918). In Anton Kaes et al., eds. *The Weimar Republic Sourcebook.* Berkeley: University of California Press, 1994.

Spector, Ivar. *The Soviet Union and the Muslim World 1917–1958.* Seattle and London: University of Washington Press, 1959.

Stephan, John J. *The Russian Fascists: Tragedy and Farce in Exile, 1925–1945.* New York: Harper & Row, 1978.

Stove, Robert J. *The Unsleeping Eye: Secret Police and Their Victims.* San Francisco: Encounter Books, 2003.

Stern, Fritz. *Dreams and Delusions.* New York: Vintage, 1987.

Stillman, Norman. *The Jews of Arab Lands.* Philadelphia: Jewish Publication Society, 1979.

Stoddard, Lothrop. *The New World of Islam.* New York: Charles Scribner, 1921.

———. *The Rising Tide of Color.* New York: Charles Scribner, 1920.

Sulzberger, C. L. *The Fall of Eagles: The Death of the Great European Dynasties.* New York: Crown, 1977.

Suny, Ronald Grigor, and Terry Martin. *A State of Nations: Empire and Nation-Making in the Age of Lenin and Stalin.* Oxford, England: Oxford University Press, 2001.

Swietochowski, Tadeusz. *Russian Azerbaijan: 1905–1920.* Cambridge, England: Cambridge University Press, 1985.

Swietochowski, Tadeusz, and Brian C. Collins. *Historical Dictionary of Azerbaijan.* Lanham: Scarecrow, 1999.

Taylor, A.J.P. *The Course of German History.* New York: Routledge, 2001.

Teague-Jones, Reginald. *The Spy Who Disappeared.* London: Victor Gollancz, 1991.

Toland, John. *Adolf Hitler.* New York: Doubleday & Company, Inc., 1976.

Tolf, Robert. *The Russian Rockefellers: The Saga of the Nobel Family and the Russian Oil Industry.* Stanford, Calif.: Hoover Institution Press, 1976.

Toller, Ernst. *I Was a German: The Autobiography of a Revolutionary.* Trans. Edward Crankshaw. New York: Paragon House, 1991.

Tolzmann, Don, ed. *German-Americans in the World Wars: The Anti-German Hysteria of World War One.* Munich: K. G. Saur, 1995.

Torberg, Friedrich. *Kaffeehaus war überall.* Munich: Deutscher Taschenbuch, 1982.

Tuchman, Barbara W. *Bible and Sword: England and Palestine from the Bronze Age to Balfour.* New York: New York University Press, 1956.

———. *Proud Tower: A Portrait of the World Before the War, 1890–1914.* New York: Macmillan, 1966.

Tucker, Robert. *Stalin as Revolutionary 1879–1929: A Study in History and Personality.* New York: W. W. Norton, 1973.

Tutuncu, Mehmet, ed. *Turkish-Jewish Encounters: Studies on Turkish-Jewish Relations Through the Ages.* Haarlem, Netherlands: Stichting SOTA, 2001.

Ulam, Adam B. *The Bolsheviks: The Intellectual, Personal and Political Triumph of Communism in Russia.* New York: Collier Books/Macmillan, 1968.

———. *Stalin: The Man and His Era.* Boston: Beacon Press, 1987.

Vacca-Mazzara, Giamil. *Asiadeh,* Preface. Rome: Instituto Traduzioni Letterarie Orientali, 1943.

Vambery, Arminius. *Story of My Struggles.* London: T. F. Unwin, 1904.

———. *Western Culture in Eastern Lands: A Comparison of the Methods Adopted by England and Russia in the Middle East.* London: John Murray, 1906.

Vassilyev, T., and René Fülöp-Miller. *The Ochrana: The Russian Secret Police.* Philadelphia: J. B. Lipincott, 1930.

Venturi, Franco. *Roots of Revolution: A History of the Populist and Socialist Movements in Nineteenth Century Russia.* Trans. Francis Haskell. Chicago: University of Chicago Press, 1983.

Verein Jüdischer Hochschüler Bar Kochba in Prag, ed. *Vom Judentum, ein Sammelbuch.* Leipzig, Germany: K. Wolff, 1914.

Viereck, George. *Confessions of a Barbarian.* New York: Moffat, Yard & Co., 1910.

———. *Songs of Armageddon and Other Poems.* New York: Mitchell Kennerley, 1916.

———. *Glimpses of the Great.* New York: Macaulay, 1930.

———. *My Flesh and Blood.* New York: Horace Liveright, 1931.

———. *The Kaiser on Trial.* New York: Greystone Press, 1937.

Viereck, George, and Paul Eldridge. *My First Two Thousand Years.* New York: Gold Label Books, 1942.

Viereck, Peter. *Metapolitics: From the Romantics to Hitler.* New York: Alfred A. Knopf, 1941.

Vital, David. *A People Apart.* New York: Oxford University Press, 1999.

Volkogonov, Dmitri. *Stalin: Triumph and Tragedy.* London: Weidenfeld & Nicolson, 1991.

————. *Lenin: A New Biography.* New York: Free Press, 1994.

Wasserman, Jacob. *Mein Weg als Deutscher und Jude.* Berlin: S. Fischer Verlag, 1921.

Wasserstein, Bernard. *The Secret Lives of Trebitsch Lincoln.* New Haven, Conn.: Yale University, 1988.

Watt, Richard M. *The Kings Depart: The Tragedy of Germany: Versailles and the German Revolution.* New York: Barnes & Noble, 1968.

Weber, Eugen, ed. *Paths to the Present.* New York: Dodd, Mead and Co., 1962.

————. *Varieties of Fascism.* Malabar, Fla.: Robert E. Krieger, 1964.

Weisberg, Richard H. *Vichy Law and the Holocaust in France.* New York: New York University Press, 1996.

Weldon, Michael J. *The Psychotronic Video Guide to Film.* New York: St. Martin's Press, 1996.

Wengeroff, Pauline. *Rememberings: The World of a Russian-Jewish Woman in the Nineteenth Century.* Bethesda: University Press of Maryland, 2000.

Werfel, Franz. *The Forty Days of Musa Dagh.* New York: Carroll & Graf, 1933.

Wheatcroft, Andrew. *The World Atlas of Revolutions. The Antecedents, Character, and History of the Revolutions of the Modern Age—from the American Revolution to the Revolutionary Violence of the 1980s.* New York: Simon & Schuster, 1983.

Wheatcroft, Geoffrey. *The Controversy of Zion.* New York: Addison-Wesley, 1996.

White, Alma. *My Trip to the Orient.* Bound Brook: Pentecostal Union, 1911.

Williams, Robert C. *Culture in Exile: Russian Émigrés in Germany 1881–1941.* Ithaca, N.Y.: Cornell University Press, 1972.

————. *Ruling Russian Eurasia: Khans, Clans and Tsars.* Malabar, Fla.: Krieger Publishing Company, 2000.

Wilson, Edmund. *To the Finland Station.* London: Macmillan, 1940.

Wilson, Neil, et al. *Georgia, Armenia and Azerbaijan.* Melbourne, Oakland, London, Paris: Lonely Planet, 2000.

Windhager, Günther. *Leopold Weiss Alias Muhammad Asad: Von Galizien nach Arabien 1900–1927.* Vienna: Boehlau Verlag, 2003.

Winter, Nevin O. *The Russian Empire of Today and Yesterday.* Boston: L. C. Page & Company, 1913.

Wolfradt, Willi. "The Stab in the Back Legend?" In Anton Kaes et al., eds. *The Weimar Republic Sourcebook.* Berkeley: University of California Press, 1994, pp. 16–18.

Yagan, Murat. *I Come from Behind Kaf Mountain.* Putney, Vt.: Threshold, 1984.

Yarmolinsky, Avrahm. *Road to Revolution: A Century of Russian Radicalism.* New York: Collier Books, 1962.

Ypsilon (pseud.). *Pattern for World Revolution.* New York: Ziff-Davis Publishing Co., 1947.

Zagoruiko, Ivan Giovanni. *I Pittori Russi a Positano.* Ravello, Italy: Il Punto, 1995.

Zuccotti, Susan. *The Italians and the Holocaust.* New York: Basic Books, 1987.

Zunz, Leopold. "On Rabbinic Literature" (1818; excerpts). Trans. Alfred and Eva Jospe. In *Studies in Jewish Thought.* Detroit: Wayne State University Press, 1981.

Zweig, Stefan. *The World of Yesterday.* London: Cassell, 1943.

Acknowledgments

Tracking down the life story of a man who died in 1942, I came to know many wonderful people who lived during the early half of the last century. To my sorrow, some of them have since passed away, as they were in their late eighties or nineties at the time we met. I am particularly sorry that Miriam Ashurbekov, in Baku, and Zuleika Assadulayeva-Weber, of Baku and Virginia, did not live to read about the adventures and fate of Lev Nussimbaum, whom they knew as a boy. I have similar regrets about Jenia Graman, née Almuth Gittermann, who spent the early part of her life as a dancer in musicals in Nazi Germany, and emigrated to England in the 1950s, carrying in her bag a copy of *Ali and Nino,* which she had found in a Berlin bookstall; becoming obsessed with the novel, she translated it into English and devoted years of her life to getting it published. (When I met Jenia, in a hospital in England, she was apparently speechless after two severe strokes, until we discovered she could still communicate with me in her native language, German, and a lifetime of hidden memories came pouring out.)

Two deaths during the course of my research were entirely unexpected: Robert Jones, my first editor at HarperCollins, offered unbridled excitement and good humor during our early conversations about the book, though he soon grew too ill for us to continue them; I remain deeply grateful. And Professor Gerhard Höpp, of the Zentrum Moderner Orient, in Berlin, who was perhaps the single other person in the world who knew about Lev's unique career in Germany, as a result of his comprehensive study of Muslims in the Third Reich: Over the years, we became friends and traded stories and information over heavy Prussian meals in the dark haunts of his native city. Dr. Höpp was himself a man of secrets and a quiet sadness, and I believe his interest in Lev-Essad-Kurban was one of his few pleasures outside of his beloved collection of polar expeditionary stamps. He always asked with great interest when I would finish this book, and I am sorry that I was too slow for him to see it.

Countless people, from Baku to Vienna, helped me track down my elusive subject; it feels like a small lifetime of friendships and encounters has passed during the writing of it, and I thank everyone for their hospitality, their generosity, their company. I owe particular gratitude to Alessandro Andreae, Fuad Akhundov, Norma Brailow, Leela von Ehrenfels, Baroness Mireille von Ehrenfels Abeille, Amir Farman-Farma, Countess Raimonda Gaetani-Pattison, Noam Hermont, Peter Mayer, and Peter Viereck.

On the writing and publishing side of this project, Daniel Menaker gave me brilliant editorial guidance from start to finish. Tina Bennett offered her unwavering focus, insight, and enthusiasm. Noah Strote helped sift thousands of documents, and John Glassie gave advice and inspiration on matters large and small.

Warm thanks to the following people: Fabrizio Andreae, Leni & Mario Attanasio, Franzie Baumfeld, Anna Baldinetti, Dan Bora, Jean Bower, Martijn Ernst Buijs, Rich Conaty, Romolo Ercolino, Giorgio Fabre, David Fairman, Nicoletta Flatow-Rispoli, Leon Friedman, Ingrid Fülöp-Miller, Deborah Garrison, Klara Glowczewska, Basia Grocholski, Murray Hall, Stephanie Higgs, Therese Kirschner-Mögle, Reingard Klingler, Felix Koch, Walter Loewendahl, Jr., David Mabbott, Richard Murphy, Ertugrul Osman, Peter Reiss, David Remnick, Steven Sanders, Count Franco Sersale, David Sheen, Captain Brian Sheppard, John Spalek, Melanie Thernstrom, Daniel Thiesen, Adam Watson, Dorothy Wickenden, and Janet Wygal.

Thanks also to my family, but especially to my wife, Julie, for her infinite patience and good judgment while I was writing, and to Lucy and Diana, for their impatience for me to finish.

Permissions Acknowledgments

TEXT PERMISSION CREDITS

NORMA BRAILOW: Excerpts from the unpublished manuscript entitled *Survivor's Tale* by Alex Brailow, and the introduction by Alex Brailow to the unpublished manuscript entitled *The Oriental Tales of Essad Bey*. All materials reprinted by permission of Norma Brailow.

THE NEW YORK TIMES: Excerpts from "He Has Lived His Stories" by William Leon Smyser (*New York Herald Tribune*, December 16, 1934), copyright © 1934 by The New York Times Co. Reprinted with permission.

THE NEW YORKER: Excerpt from The Talk of the Town: "Viereck" by M. Anderson Maloney (*The New Yorker*, June 15, 1940). Courtesy of *The New Yorker*/The Condé Nast Publications, Inc.

PENGUIN GROUP (USA) INC.: Excerpt from "Positano" from *America and American and Selected Nonfiction* by John Steinbeck, edited by Susan Shillinglaw and J. Benson, copyright © 2002 by Elaine Steinbeck and Thomas Steinbeck. Used by permission of Viking Penguin, a division of Penguin Group (USA) Inc.

SIMON & SCHUSTER, INC., AND DEUTSCHE VERLAGS-ANSTALT GMBH: Excerpts from *Blood and Oil in the Orient* by Essad Bey, translated by Elsa Talmy, copyright © 1930 by Deutsche Verlags-Anstalt, Stuttgart and English translation copyright © 1932 and copyright renewed 1959 by Simon & Schuster, Inc. Rights outside of the United States, Canada, and the Philippine Republic are controlled by Deutsche Verlags-Anstalt GmbH. Reprinted by permission of Simon & Schuster, Inc., and Deutsche Verlags-Anstalt GmbH.

PETER VIERECK: Excerpts from "The Red Menace in the United States" (*German Outlook*, January 27, 1934), speech by George Sylvester Viereck at Madison Square Garden, May 17, 1934, and quotes from *Glimpses of the Great* by George Sylvester Viereck, 1930. All materials used by permission of Peter Viereck.

PHOTO SECTION

Baku Christmas party photo courtesy of Miriam Ashurbekov. Photos of young Lev and his Berlin companions courtesy of Norma Brailow. Photo of book jacket from *Blood and Oil in the Orient* courtesy of Simon & Schuster. Photo of Erika Loewendahl courtesy of Die Deutsche Bibliothek, Exilarchiv, Frankfurt. Photo of "Vienna gang" courtesy of Franzie Baumfeld. Photo of Lev in Caucasian costume from the *New York Herald Tribune* courtesy of The New York Times Company. *Sunday Mirror Magazine* page courtesy of the Hearst Corporation. Nightclub photo of Lev and Erika (New York *Daily News*) courtesy of the Associated Press. Photos of Lev as a boy, in fur hat; of Baron Omar-Rolf von Ehrenfels; of Baroness Elfriede Ehrenfels; the 1920s movie still; and of Lev and Giamil Vacca-Mazzara, all courtesy of Baroness Mireille von Ehrenfels-Abeille. Lev's gravestone photo by Tom Reiss.

Section-opener photos: Part One: Courtesy Azerbaijan National Photo Archives; Part Two: Author's Collection; Part Three: Courtesy Corbis

Index

About the Author

TOM REISS has written about politics and culture for *The New York Times, The Wall Street Journal, The New Yorker,* and elsewhere. He lives with his wife and daughters in New York City.

About the Type

This book was set in Garamond, a typeface designed by the French printer Jean Jannon. It is styled after Garamond's original models. The face is dignified, and is light but without fragile lines. The italic is modeled after a font of Granjon, which was probably out in the middle of the sixteenth century.